Practical HOME GARDENING

Practical HOME GARDENING

EDITED BY

ROY HAY MBE, VMH, Consultant Editor

AND

JANET BROWNE Editor and Contributor

This edition produced exclusively for

WHSMITH

© Ward Lock Ltd 1983

Produced especially for W.H. Smith & Sons by Ward
Lock Limited, 82 Gower Street, London WC1E 6EQ,
a Pentos Company.

House Editor Denis Ingram
Layout by Heather Sherratt

Text filmset in Plantin
by Text Filmsetters Limited, Orpington, Kent

Printed and bound in Spain by Graficromo, S.A.,
Cordoba

ISBN 0 7063 4262 3

Contents

Acknowledgements

The publishers gratefully acknowledge the following for granting permission to reproduce the colour photographs: Harry Smith Horticultural Photographic Collection (pp. 17 & 35), David Squire (p. 148), and BLV Verlagsgesellschaft mbH, Munich (the remainder).

The publishers also gratefully acknowledge BLV Verlagsgesellschaft mbH, Munich for granting permission to reproduce all the line drawings, except for those mentioned as follows. The drawings on pp. 9, 22 (lower), 28, 29, 33, 37, 39, 46, 51, 55, 109 (top), 113 (lower), 124, 184, 186, 189, 192, 193, 196 (right), 197, 204 (a-d), 207, 208, 210 (left), 213, 216, 217, 224, 236, 241 & 243 are by Nils Solberg and are after drawings which appeared in *Complete Home Gardening* by Margot Schubert, published by Ward Lock, 1977, the copyright of the original drawings belonging to BLV Verlagsgesellschaft, Munich. The drawings on pp. 50, 57, 58, 59, 65 (top), 190, 191, 198, 204 (e-g), 234 & 238 are by Nils Solberg. The drawings on pp. 74, 75, 76, 77, 78 (left), 79, 80, 85 (left), 86 (right), 88, 97, 98, 99, 103 (left), 104, 105 (right), 106, 114, 115, 119, 121 (right), 140 142, 143 (top), 144, 146, 151, 152, 153, 154, 155, 156, 161, 162, 166, 167, 168, 171, 173, 175 & 200 are by Rosemary Wise.

PART I:

PLANNING AND CONSTRUCTION

1
Designing your garden

There are as many garden plans as there are gardens, for however many similarities there may be, no one garden is exactly like any other. One gardener may be lucky enough to own a large plot of land in attractive surroundings where he can easily integrate house and garden as one; another may have only a small, narrow plot, the shape of a pocket handkerchief, behind a terraced house, or a garden fitted into an awkward corner or crammed between neighbouring buildings.

No one can say this book (or any other book) has the right design for your garden, so go and lay it out accordingly. You can plan a garden of your own to your personal taste; in fact, you have even more freedom than if you were getting your own house built, when your wishes cannot always be carried out to the last detail. Of course the design of your garden will be limited by expediency and the depth of your purse – and here a well-thought-out plan is really essential; random laying out of a garden can affect your pleasure, as well as the utility of your property, just as much as the building of an unplanned house would do. So if you are going to design your garden yourself, first make a list of requirements, then draw them roughly to scale on graph paper.

Some pre-requisites, ideal and practical

The first principle in designing a garden is to preserve a sense of proportion, not just in the garden itself, but in its relation to its surroundings. It ought to fit naturally into the atmosphere of its setting, though by no means should you be unadventurous and avoid all innovations. It can be taken for granted that you know the aspect of your garden regarding sun and shade, its exposure to cold north or east winds, the composition of its soil, and – except on recently developed building sites – the means of artificial watering available. Then there is the presence (or absence) of paths giving access to be considered, as well as your legal relationship with any neighbours; all these play a part in the planning of your garden. On the outer edges of the garden, at least, your neighbours are bound to have some influence on your plants and their environment. So let us start by thinking of every garden as a living community of plant life, constantly growing upwards and outwards. This is something you should always bear in mind, or you will find that one set of plants is depriving another of air and nourishment.

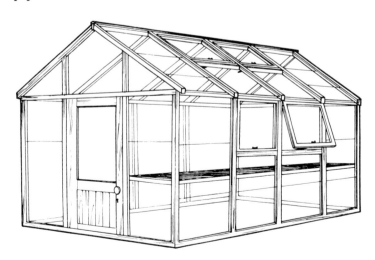

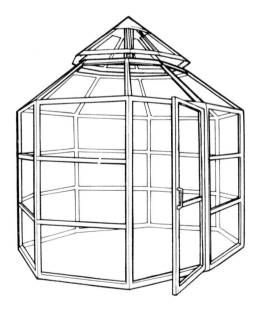

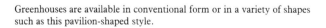
Greenhouses are available in conventional form or in a variety of shapes such as this pavilion-shaped style.

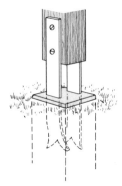

Two suggested types of pergola in a sitting area: *left*, one made of squared posts; *right*, one of round posts.

Pergola posts should be set in concrete, to avoid the wood rotting.

Any groups of large trees already in existence have a considerable effect on the look of your garden, and if you possess such trees you should regard them as a valuable bit of capital to start with, and include them in the new design. They will be linked by new plantations of small shrubs, integrated with flower beds and sitting areas near the main path; sometimes you may need a space where guests can park their cars. Bear in mind that you might want to make additions later on in the shape of large installations like a swimming pool and/or a water garden, or a summerhouse or arbour, and pick a good sunny position near the kitchen for the greenhouse. Garden designs seldom give much guidance on such matters: and it is necessary to take particular notice of the necessity for planning underground installations such as water taps, fountain leads and mains electricity – often needed for the greenhouse.

Even these few pointers show that it is not so easy to draw up a good garden design which leaves room for possible future developments. Moreover, these days more and more garden owners are departing from the old, conventional categories of separate flower and vegetable gardens. They dream of having beauty and utility combined, and expect to be able to manage their gardens with the minimum of effort. From the first moment of planning all this demands the sure hand of an experienced garden designer, with a breadth of vision and a wealth of practical knowledge which even the most gifted amateur gardener cannot possess.

Wherever financially possible, then, get the advice of a good landscape architect. The garden designs reproduced on the following pages prove my point. Not only do they show a whole range of different kinds of typical gardens, but they have all passed their practical test, since they are genuine designs drawn up for actual clients.

One more comment: plans such as these are not, of course, drawn up only for the interest of people with new garden plots. The owners of matured older gardens like to look at such plans now and then, and may find suggestions they can put to good use in small alterations. Gardens are like houses: you sometimes feel like having a good turn-out, making changes and moving things around. You may, for example, start with an outgrown sandpit and end up with a swimming pool.

And one final point: not everyone finds plans easy to read, so a perspective drawing should accompany the ground plan of each of the areas, to show you how the design should look in practice some day: 'some day' means after the first, always rather difficult preliminary stages, when the new garden is maturing. I need hardly add that local circumstances and your own personal wishes allow all kinds of alterations to the plans suggested.

Large garden adjoining a house on a level site

Size of plot: 1555 sq yd (1300 sq m). The first of our garden designs is a good example of some of the points just mentioned. There were some large spruce trees growing along the western side of the property, and in spite of the shade they cast it was best to keep them. So shrubs suitable for shady positions were planted in this part of the garden. Where no such shade exists, different shrubs could be planted. Similarly, if you wanted to keep a good view out over open country beyond the garden, you could plant a

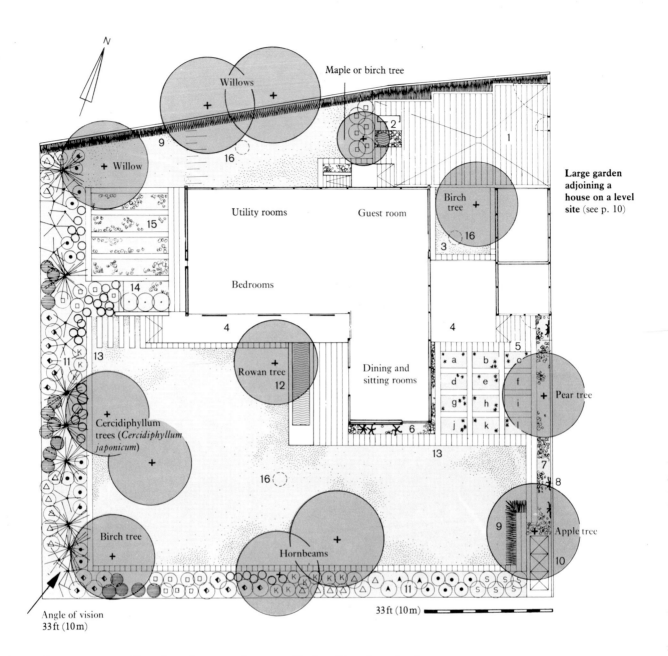

Large garden adjoining a house on a level site (see p. 10)

Labels within plan:
Willows · Maple or birch tree · Willow · Birch tree · Utility rooms · Guest room · Bedrooms · Birch tree · Rowan tree · Dining and sitting rooms · Cercidiphyllum trees (*Cercidiphyllum japonicum*) · Pear tree · Birch tree · Hornbeams · Apple tree

Angle of vision 33 ft (10 m)

33 ft (10 m)

1 Paved approach area
2 Gravel bed and water basin
3 Lawn
4 Terrace
5 Beds divided by paved paths, containing roses, sub-shrubs and ornamental grasses
6 Gravel bed with ornamental grasses
7 Herb bed
8 Virginia creeper
9 Deciduous hedge (maple, hornbeam)
10 Compost heaps
11 Flowering shrubs
12 Garden pool with water plants
13 Paved edging
14 Soft fruit bushes
15 Beds for herbs and salad vegetables
16 Seepage pits for overflow from gutters and pools, covered with 12 in (30 cm) soil

Flowering and ornamental shrubs planted:

Maple, *Acer ginnala*

Cotoneaster

Dogwood, *Cornus alba*

Cobnut, *Corylus avellana*

Bachelor's buttons, *Kerria japonica* 'Pleniflora'

Lonicera pileata

Perpetual-flowering red shrub roses

Lilac, *Syringa vulgaris*

Viburnum lantana

Planting of formal paved garden to right of the house:

a) Lavender, *Lavandula spica*

b) Stonecrop, *Sedum*

c) Ornamental grass, *Festuca scoparia*

d) Floribunda roses

e) Ornamental grass, *Festuca cinerea*

f) Thyme, *Thymus serpyllum* 'Coccineus'

g) Ornamental grasses, *Festuca scoparia* and *Pennisetum orientale*

h) Floribunda roses

j) Stonecrop, *Sedum*

k) Pansy, *Viola cornuta*

l) Candytuft, *Iberis sempervirens*

11

Size of plot 1555 sq yd (1300 sq m)

herbaceous border at that end of the lawn instead of the screening shrubs.

The plot is divided into an approach area to the house, and the garden proper, with its informal borders of flowering shrubs. One very practical detail is the narrow paved path running round the lawn to form an edging, which facilitates neat cutting without the boring job of clipping the edges. A very pleasant feature is the formal little 'Paradise Garden' to the right of the house, with its rows of small rectangular beds. They contain ground cover flowering plants chosen to bloom in succession over a long period, but they could also be used as garden beds for children, integrated with the adults' garden. The two cercidiphyllum trees on the left of the lawn are another eye-catching feature: for more information about these interesting exotic trees, see the chapter DECIDUOUS GARDEN TREES. The small kitchen garden on the west side of the house will supply the family with herbs and a few salad vegetables like radish and lettuce. There are a few soft fruit bushes, to give the children something to nibble at. See plant pp. 11–12.

Narrow garden behind a house

Size of plot 981 sq yd (820 sq m). The owner of this property specified that managing the garden was not to entail too much work. Local building regulations meant that the two garages had to be one each side of the house. The actual garden area behind the house is too small to allow for informality in the design; in cases like this geometrical shapes look more attractive, and though the contours of the paved strips around the small square beds may look rather severe at first, the growth of the plants will have softened this impression by the second year. These beds of ground cover and low-growing flowering plants are laid out so that you get a good view of them from the house, without having to go out into the garden, while the paved paths between them (15½ in (40 cm wide)) make it easy to walk between the beds and inspect the plants close to. You can smell the flowers and do any necessary little jobs without actually setting foot on the beds. See plan p. 13.

In the front garden, the space between the paved path and the road could simply be sown with grass, since it would be

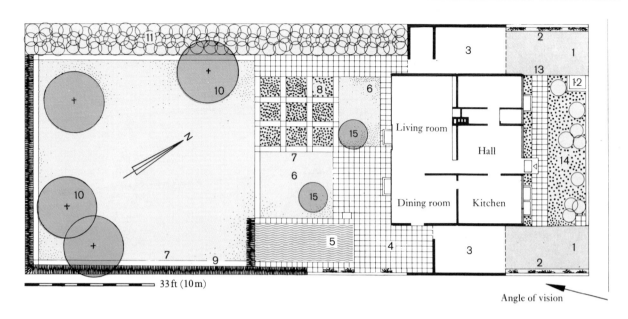

— 33 ft (10 m)

Angle of vision

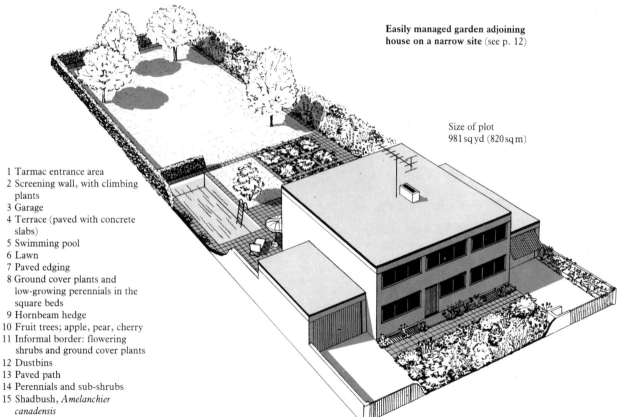

Easily managed garden adjoining house on a narrow site (see p. 12)

Size of plot
981 sq yd (820 sq m)

1 Tarmac entrance area
2 Screening wall, with climbing plants
3 Garage
4 Terrace (paved with concrete slabs)
5 Swimming pool
6 Lawn
7 Paved edging
8 Ground cover plants and low-growing perennials in the square beds
9 Hornbeam hedge
10 Fruit trees; apple, pear, cherry
11 Informal border: flowering shrubs and ground cover plants
12 Dustbins
13 Paved path
14 Perennials and sub-shrubs
15 Shadbush, *Amelanchier canadensis*

easy to bring a lawn mower from one of the garages, or you could have a large bed of perennials and sub-shrubs, along with a few annuals to provide cut flowers. Or again, some evergreens interspersed with shrub roses would make a stylish effect, and be easy to tend. An interesting alternative is to cover the area with shingle and plant a few specimen architectural subjects as 'dot' plants.

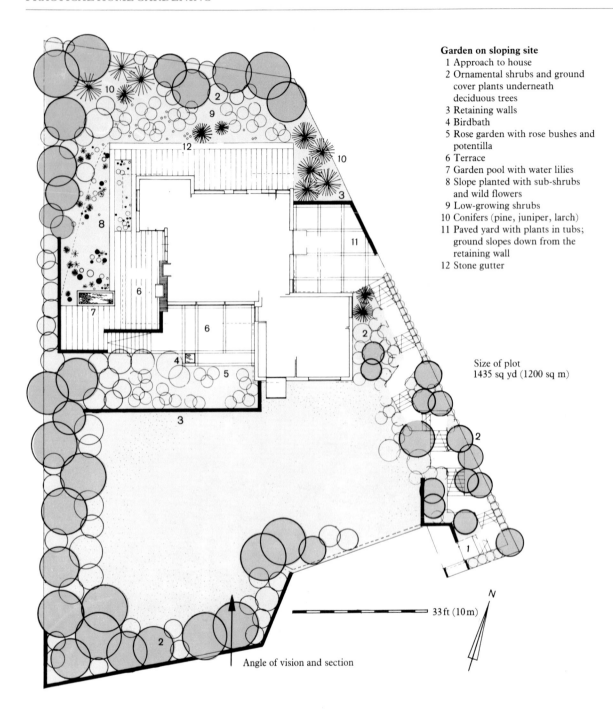

Garden on sloping site
1 Approach to house
2 Ornamental shrubs and ground
  cover plants underneath
  deciduous trees
3 Retaining walls
4 Birdbath
5 Rose garden with rose bushes and
  potentilla
6 Terrace
7 Garden pool with water lilies
8 Slope planted with sub-shrubs
  and wild flowers
9 Low-growing shrubs
10 Conifers (pine, juniper, larch)
11 Paved yard with plants in tubs;
   ground slopes down from the
   retaining wall
12 Stone gutter

Size of plot
1435 sq yd (1200 sq m)

33 ft (10 m)

N

Angle of vision and section

Garden adjoining a house on a sloping site

Size of plot 1435 sq yd (1200 sq m). The problem of this plot lies in a gradient of 13 yd (12 m), which means the area has to be divided into several levels or terraces. Retaining walls are essential, and so is a flight of steps, broken by several landing stages to avoid any impression that you are walking along a straight corridor, as well as making the climb easier for elderly people. Plants put in with an eye to effect on either side of the steps give a pleasing view of the house and garden, whether you are going up or down.

There is plenty of variety in the other garden plants too; they are deliberately concentrated more formally close to the house itself, giving way to a more informal effect on the southern side of the slope. On the north side of the house, the slope is planted with ground covering sub-shrubs which will need almost no attention within 2-3 years. The different levels of the terraced areas around the house itself mean they can be used at the same time, but for different purposes, by all the members of a fairly large family. See plan pp. 14–15.

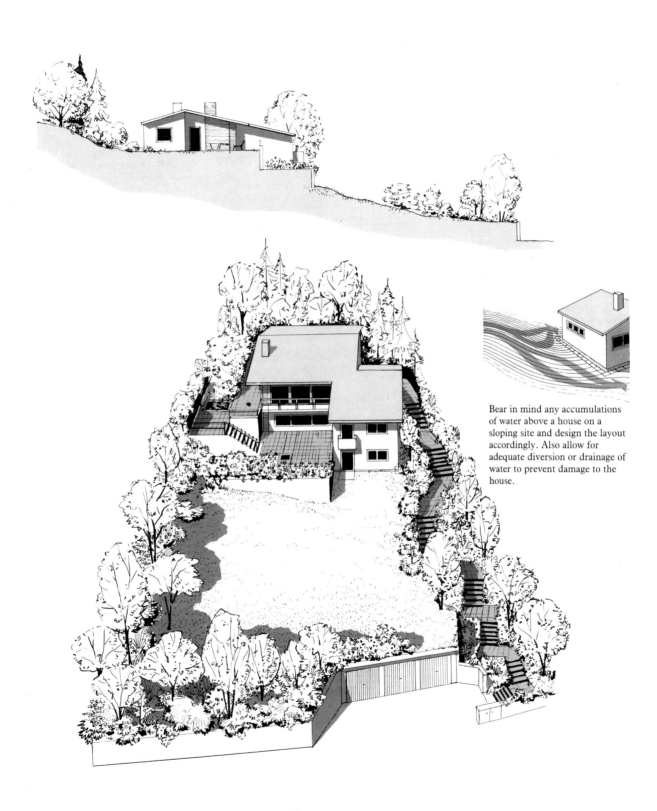

Bear in mind any accumulations of water above a house on a sloping site and design the layout accordingly. Also allow for adequate diversion or drainage of water to prevent damage to the house.

Section: for angle, see the plan opposite.

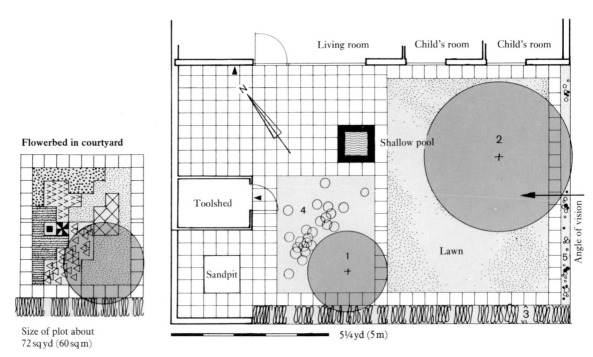

Flowerbed in courtyard

Size of plot about
72 sq yd (60 sq m)

5¼ yd (5 m)

Living room   Child's room   Child's room

Shallow pool

Toolshed

Lawn

Sandpit

Angle of vision

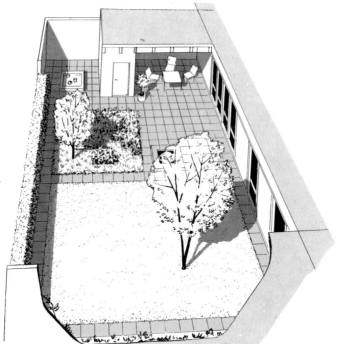

Small courtyard garden
1 Small deciduous tree: Japanese
  maple, common pear, cercidiphyllum
  tree
2 Medium-sized deciduous tree
  (ornamental cherry, rowan, birch)
3 Clipped hedge (hedge maple,
  hornbeam)
4 Flower bed (see key to plants)
5 Climbing plants (clematis,
  Virginia creeper, trumpet vine)

Key to plants in flower bed (4)
 1 Japanese maple, *Acer palmatum*
20 *Primula bullesiana* hybrids
20 blue dwarf irises
20 pansies, *Viola cornuta*, yellow
 1 leopard's bane, *Doronicum
   cordatum*
 1 ornamental grass, *Pennisetum
   orientale*
30 stonecrops, *Sedum* varieties
 7 veronicas, *Veronica longifolia*
40 ornamental grasses, *Festuca
   scoparia*

Small courtyard garden

Size of plot about 72 sq yd (60 sq m). You could have this
enchanting little 'outdoor room' as a little garden within a
garden, as well as an independent unit. The built-in tool
shed makes a room-divider, marking off the play area with
its sandpit for children. The bed in front of the play area,
containing a wide variety of plants, is in proportion to the
size of the garden as a whole, and the rest of the garden is
taken up by lawn, with a medium-sized ornamental tree to
break up the lawn area with decorative effects of light and
shade. The small pool in the paved area should hold
enough water to supply the flower bed.

An attractive and colourful effect can be achieved in the garden by using dry stone walls to raise a mixed planting area of permanent and bedding plants.

Four garden features. *Top left:* eye-level flowers. *Top right:* a rustic fence. *Bottom left:* electricity in the garden. *Bottom right:* a screen for privacy and shelter.

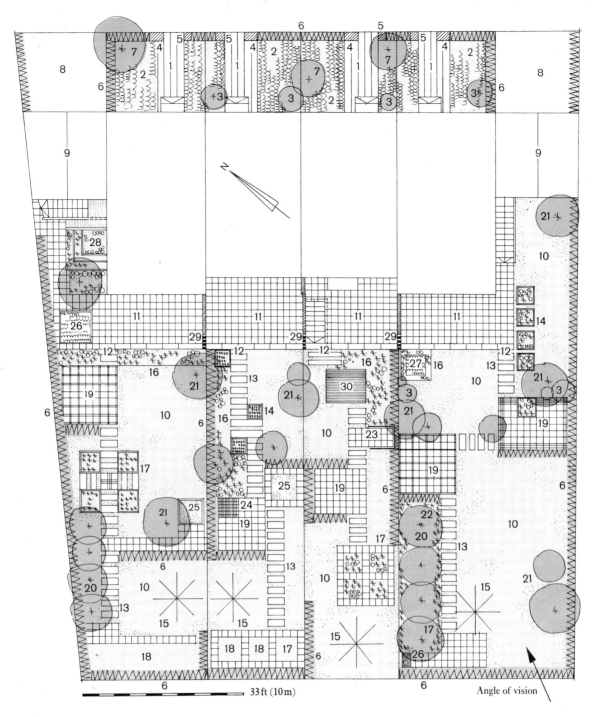

33ft (10m)

Angle of vision

Four gardens of terraced houses

(see p. 20)

1 Front gardens and approach to houses
2 Dwarf shrubs and small perennials
3 Ornamental shrubs
4 Dustbins
5 Posts
6 Clipped hedge
7 Rowan tree
8 Entrance area
9 Garage
10 Lawn
11 Terrace
12 Stone steps
13 Stepping stones
14 Flower trough
15 Space for clothes dryer
16 Perennials
17 Herbs and annuals

18 Vegetables
19 Sitting area
20 Fruit trees
21 Ornamental trees
22 Strawberries
23 Shower installation
24 Barbecue
25 Sandpit
26 Shallow pool
27 Water garden
28 Gravel bed with ornamental grasses
29 Slatted wooden screening fence
30 Sitting area paved with granite stones 6 × 6 in (15 × 15) cm; obtained second hand, with a joint ¾ in (2 cm) wide between the paved area and the lawn

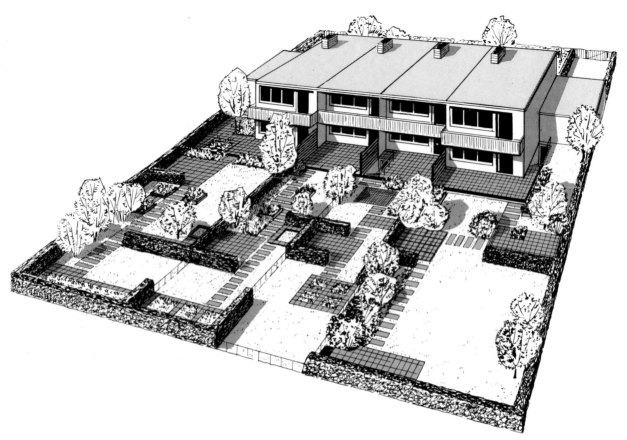

Four gardens of terraced houses (see also plan on p. 19)

Four gardens of identical terrace houses

We all know the problems of gardens belonging to terrace houses: they nearly always give an impression of monotony, because the plots are badly proportioned. They may be only 6½-9 yd (6-8 m) wide, but a length of 27 yd (25 m) is quite common. However, where people have to live so close together, dividing fences are essential, and in this case an attempt was made to get round the problem by using very light fencing, only 32 in (80 cm) high, so as to open up the whole area visually, and the designer aimed for an illusion of unity by planting hedges, though in actual fact each of the four properties remains quite separate. The effect is maintained by the design of the paths, and the way the garden areas are divided up to suit the requirements and habits of different kinds of family. For instance, a family with small children needs a play corner with a sandpit; the family whose children are nearly grown up prefers square flower beds and a herb garden; one of the householders wanted a separate quiet sitting area as well as a family terrace; a young couple fancied a paved concrete area for a barbecue, and so on and so forth. The general design is illustrated by the plans on pp. 19–20.

The hedges, which also act as windbreaks, are the usual height of 5½ ft (1.70 m), and are sight screens as well.

Hedges in front gardens, however, should not exceed the usual fencing height. And the frontage of terraced houses should really contain ground cover plants; lawns are ruled out because mowers would have to be brought through the houses, and obviously cutting such a small area, negotiating all the corners and fences, is a particularly tricky job – not to mention the fact that a lawn right beside the road is apt to suffer from other nuisances! From the visual point of view, in fact, it is more attractive if the entire frontage of the terrace can be a single green area, not even broken up by hedges between the houses, but with just the one low hedge, with or without a fence, running parallel to the road.

Two patio gardens with different layouts

Size of each plot 92 sq yd (77 sq m). Small patio gardens, like their close relatives, courtyard gardens, can also be a delightful extra within the garden proper. However, the patio gardens shown on pp. 21–22 as plans and perspective drawings belong to a new estate of houses with such small gardens sold ready for occupation. The plans, therefore, stick to things suitable for this type of garden, to preserve future owners from the grosser errors of planning and bad taste.

1 Medium-height deciduous tree
  (birch, rowan, hornbeam, sumach)
2 Flower bed (St John's wort,
  coneflower, iris, ornamental
  grasses, roses, potentilla; see also
  planting plans)
3 Climbing plants (clematis, Virginia
  creeper, Russian vine)

**Key for plants in bed in sunny
position**
55 ornamental grasses, *Festuca
   scoparia*
 1 leopard's bane, *Doronicum
   cordatum*
20 coral flowers, *Heuchera*
20 medium-height Michaelmas
   daisies, *Aster*
 9 coneflowers, *Rudbeckia*
 1 ornamental grass, *Miscanthus
   sacchariflorus*

**Key for plants in bed in shady
position**
30 Bergenia varieties
 5 leopard's banes, *Doronicum
   cordatum*
 1 bugbane, *Cimicifuga racemosa*
50 ground cover bugle plants,
   Ajuga reptans 'Purpureus'
 9 astilbe varieties

Two patio gardens (see also next page). The
plan of the site as developed shows a
typical layout for such gardens.
Suggestions are given for plants
suitable for the bed in the plan
below according to whether it is in a
sunny or a shady position; the two
garden designs could be reversed.
Size of each garden, not including
the house, about 92 sq yd (77 sq m).

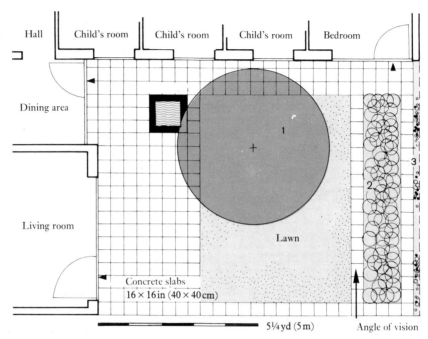

Hall   Child's room   Child's room   Child's room   Bedroom

Dining area

Living room

1

Lawn

3

2

Concrete slabs
16 × 16 in (40 × 40 cm)

5¼ yd (5 m)   Angle of vision

Plans for planting in
Sunny position   Shady position

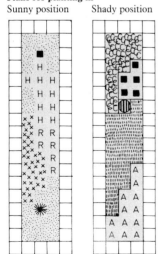

Plan of site as developed

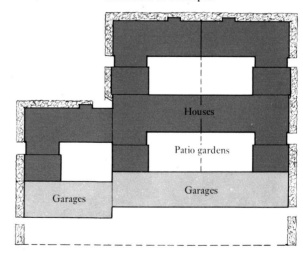

Houses

Patio gardens

Garages   Garages

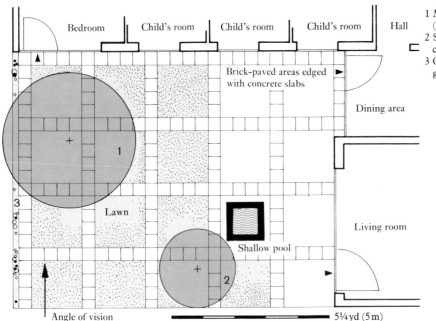

Bedroom Child's room Child's room Child's room Hall

Brick-paved areas edged with concrete slabs

Dining area

1

Lawn

3

Shallow pool

Living room

2

Angle of vision

5¼ yd (5 m)

1 Medium-height deciduous tree (rowan, locust tree, laburnum)
2 Small flowering tree (magnolia, crab apple, tamarisk)
3 Climbing plants (roses, morning glory, cup-and-saucer plant)

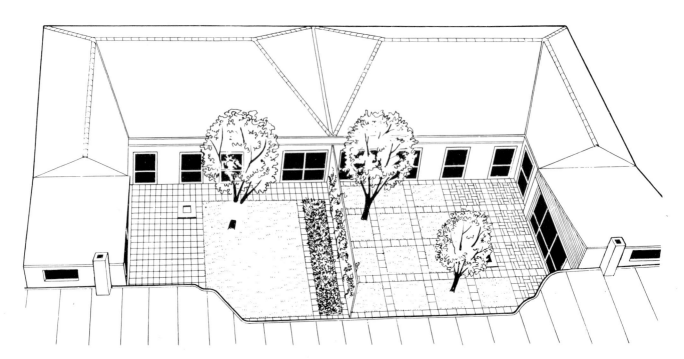

The left-hand patio contains a bed which can be planted with either shade- or sun-loving plants, according to the aspect of the garden. The little lawn has the effect of a carpet laid outside the living rooms, and again is surrounded by a paved edging. The slatted fence between the two gardens should be covered with climbing plants to provide ornamental greenery – here the two neighbours must come to an agreement.

The basic feature of the right-hand patio garden is a paved area containing square beds which can be sown either with grass or flowering perennials. Other parts of the garden, used by the family as a sitting area, can be paved with concrete or gravel, and one of the square beds might be kept for use as a sandpit. The shallow pools to provide a water supply are the same as the one in the courtyard garden on p. 16. The two patio designs can be reversed according to the situation and aspect of the houses.

Putting a plan into practice

So we have our garden design – and now what? If a house has just been built on this site the garden plot will very likely look far from inviting. A big clearing-up operation is essential to remove rubble, stones, and unwanted plants. Normally the next step is to erect a fence around your garden, but there are exceptions to this rule: if large quantities of soil are going to be moved, or stone walls and steps built, a fence sometimes gets in the way, and it is better to postpone putting it up.

The diagrams of stone walls on p. 25 show a number of typical garden walls and other constructions, including the paved lawn edging already mentioned which facilitates the care of your lawn. The retaining walls themselves are built either to contain extra soil brought in on a level site, or to act as support to terracing on a natural slope.

On sloping ground, steps are built at the same time as any walls, because they help to make the whole plot more accessible. On level sites, too, the making of paths is always one of the first jobs to be done; after that you can start dividing up the plot, bit by bit, and making preparations for putting in the first plants. The garden designs in this book show the importance of good garden paths from both the visual and the practical point of view.

Just a reminder: the width of paths depends partly on the standard sizes of paving stones available, but you should also think how many people will want to walk comfortably side by side. The amount of space needed per person is 24-28 in (60-75 cm) – that is to say, young lovers can manage with less than a metre for the two, while old married couples should have at least 4 ft (1.20 m). With stepping stones set in a lawn, one usually reckons on using slabs 20 in (50 cm) wide, leaving a distance of 26 in (65 cm) between the middle of one slab and the middle of the next. Paths to facilitate working between flower and vegetable beds need be only 12 in (30 cm) wide.

You can see from the diagram on p. 26 the importance of a proper foundation for a path. These days everyone knows that gravel paths are no cheaper, do not look so good, and are less pleasant for walking on than paved paths. Paved paths, in fact, are becoming more and more of a popular ornamental feature: they point the way to the garden of the future. In any case, walls, steps and paths are the framework of your garden, and you must deal with them, and complete the proper cultivation of the soil, before you start thinking about plants. Here again, the biggest plants come first: trees, shrubs and hedges. Modern gardening techniques, and the growing of container plants, help to bridge the seasons and mean that plants can now be put in the ground at times which used to be impossible.

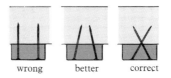

wrong   better   correct

Correct angling of the nails when making your own fences. Correct bevelling of posts and laths helps water to flow off, increasing the durability of your fence.

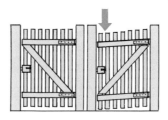

Right and wrong ways to fasten Z-shaped struts to a garden gate. The gate should not sag downwards as indicated by the arrow.

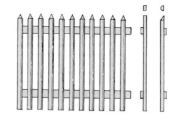

Simple fence of flat or semi-cylindrical wooden or plastic palings.

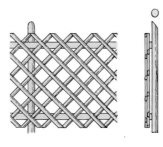

Lattice wooden fencing.

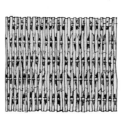

Wattle fencing of split rods or twigs; alternatively, the woven effect can be horizontal.

Garden steps

Section

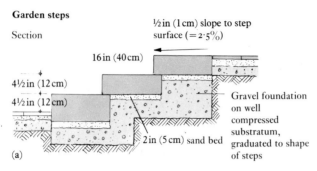

½ in (1 cm) slope to step surface (= 2·5%)

16 in (40 cm)

4½ in (12 cm)

4½ in (12 cm)

2 in (5 cm) sand bed

Gravel foundation on well compressed substratum, graduated to shape of steps

(a)

A formula for well-made steps: 2 × height of riser + 1 × width of tread = 25 in (64 cm)

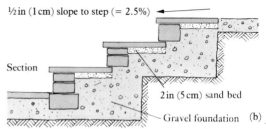

½ in (1 cm) slope to step (= 2.5%)

Section

2 in (5 cm) sand bed

Gravel foundation (b)

Solid steps, consisting of solid blocks of stone with faced surfaces. The height of the step = the height of the stone itself. Measurements given are only an example. Cost of material relatively high, but the steps are attractive, durable and easy to lay. They fit well into the gradient of the slope (see below).

Stones of thinner slabs, consisting of one slab for the tread and smaller pieces as risers. Laid on a foundation of binding gravel topped by a 2 in (5 cm) sand bed. The substratum of the ground is graduated to the shape of steps so that it will integrate better with the construction. Cheaper than solid stone steps, since the risers consist of smaller stones or broken pieces.

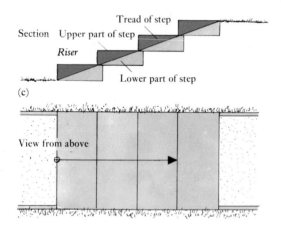

Section   Upper part of step

Tread of step

Riser

Lower part of step

(c)

View from above

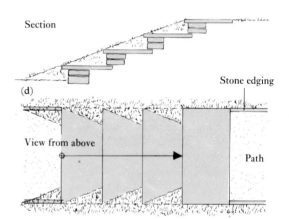

Section

Stone edging

View from above

Path

(d)

Solid steps: the gradient of the slope runs level with the line of the back of the steps, since the whole upper part of each step is faced, and thus is on view. Rather more expensive than steps made of thinner slabs and risers.

Stones of thinner slabs: the gradient of the slope runs level with line of the front edge of the steps, since the edges of the risers are not faced and so should be sunk in the ground. This means the steps get dirty more easily, and it is difficult to mow the surrounding slope.

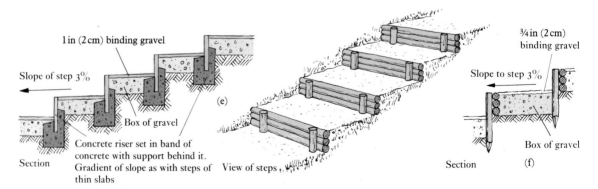

1 in (2 cm) binding gravel

Slope of step 3%

Box of gravel

Concrete riser set in band of concrete with support behind it. Gradient of slope as with steps of thin slabs

Section   View of steps

(e)

¾ in (2 cm) binding gravel

Slope to step 3%

Box of gravel

Section   (f)

Stone or wooden steps set straight into the ground. Economical, but there is a risk of erosion.

Steps made of wooden posts held by pegs: cheapest of all. Variable in their setting into the slope.

Natural stone soil-retaining walls

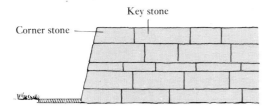

Laying stones in a regular pattern of layers. Keep (a)
plant life to a minimum by using mortar.

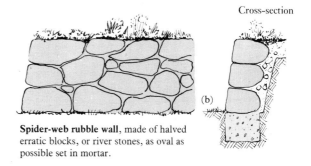

Cross-section

(b)

Spider-web rubble wall, made of halved
erratic blocks, or river stones, as oval as
possible set in mortar.

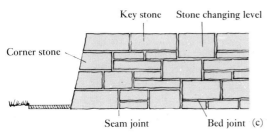

Irregular masonry: greater choice of materials than with
a regular pattern of layers. Mortar, as above. (c)

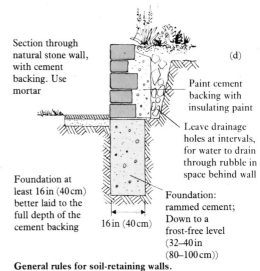

Section through
natural stone wall,
with cement
backing. Use
mortar

Paint cement
backing with
insulating paint

Leave drainage
holes at intervals,
for water to drain
through rubble in
space behind wall

Foundation at
least 16 in (40 cm)
better laid to the
full depth of the
cement backing

16 in (40 cm)

Foundation:
rammed cement;
Down to a
frost-free level
(32–40 in
(80–100 cm))

(d)

General rules for soil-retaining walls.
Choose stones longer than they are wide. Use the
strongest stones for the bottom layers, tapering off
towards the top, but have well-laid keystones and
corner stones. Vertical joints alone should be used only
throughout two layers at the most. Width of wall at
foot = ⅓ height of the wall.

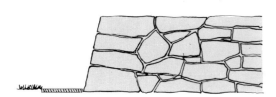

Rubble wall: joints filled in. Foundation the same as for (e)
walls of regular stones.

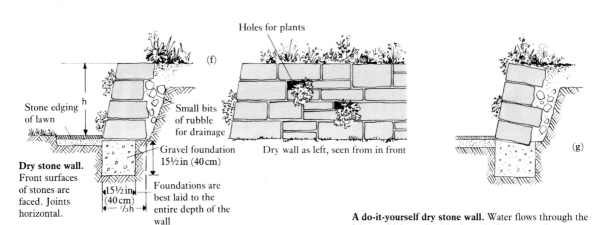

Dry stone wall.
Front surfaces
of stones are
faced. Joints
horizontal.

Stone edging
of lawn

Small bits
of rubble
for drainage

Gravel foundation
15½ in (40 cm)

15½ in
(40 cm)
⅓h

Foundations are
best laid to the
entire depth of the
wall

Holes for plants

(f)

Dry wall as left, seen from in front

(g)

A do-it-yourself dry stone wall. Water flows through the
joints, which are tilted backwards. Plants growing on top,
up to the edge of the wall and in the crevices.

Gravel path on level ground. Section through a path with a top level bound with water on a water-absorbent foundation; if the foundation is not water-absorbent, drainage must be laid under coarse gravel.

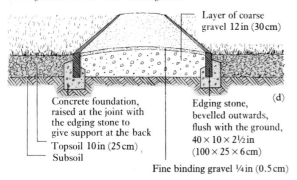

Layer of coarse gravel 12 in (30 cm)

Concrete foundation, raised at the joint with the edging stone to give support at the back

Topsoil 10 in (25 cm)

Subsoil

Edging stone, bevelled outwards, flush with the ground, 40 × 10 × 2½ in (100 × 25 × 6 cm)

(d)

Fine binding gravel ¼ in (0.5 cm)

Gravel path on sloping land

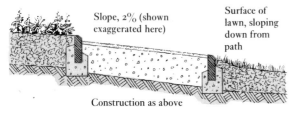

Slope, 2% (shown exaggerated here)

Surface of lawn, sloping down from path

Construction as above

Paved path

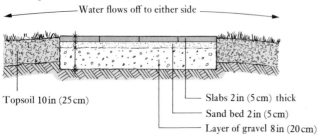

Water flows off to either side

Topsoil 10 in (25 cm)

Slabs 2 in (5 cm) thick

Sand bed 2 in (5 cm)

Layer of gravel 8 in (20 cm)

Path paved with small stones

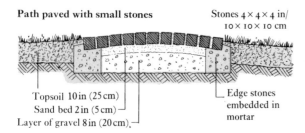

Stones 4 × 4 × 4 in/ 10 × 10 × 10 cm

Topsoil 10 in (25 cm)

Sand bed 2 in (5 cm)

Layer of gravel 8 in (20 cm)

Edge stones embedded in mortar

Path border of large granite stones

Stones 6½ × 6½ × 6 in (17 × 17 × 15 cm)

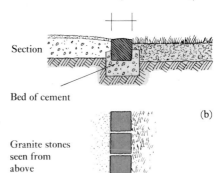

Section

Bed of cement

(b)

Granite stones seen from above

Concrete and mortar mixes

For smallish quantities of concrete or mortar, the dry ingredients may be bought ready mixed in sacks. For larger amounts, ask your local builder's merchant for advice on quantities of cement, sand and gravel required and how best to mix them.

Path border of bricks

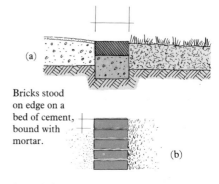

(a)

Bricks stood on edge on a bed of cement, bound with mortar.

(b)

Instead of bricks stood on edge, stone slabs laid flat on a bed of cement are an alternative

Wooden paving: round sections of tree-trunks, minimum diameter 8 in (20 cm). Laid on a 4 in (10 cm) bed of sand over firm gravel. Fill the interstices with sand.

(a)

Concrete slabs 16 × 16, 16 × 24, 16 × 32 in (40 × 40, 40 × 60, 40 × 80 cm), or 20 × 20, 20 × 30, 20 × 40 in (50 × 50, 50 × 75, 50 × 100 cm), laid in rows on a 2 in (5 cm) bed of sand. Joints up to 1½ in (4 cm) wide are filled with sand. Edges of paths run into lawns or flower beds. Top: stones of equal size; bottom, stones of different size.

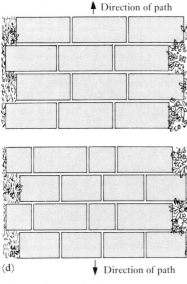

↑ Direction of path

(d)

↓ Direction of path

Hexagonal slabs of various sizes, laid as for rectangular concrete slabs. Useful for curving paths.

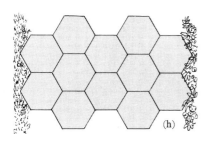

(h)

Four examples of brick paths laid on a 2 in (5 cm) bed of sand. Interstices filled with sand. Bricks laid lengthwise across the path to give an illusion of depth.

↑ Direction of path

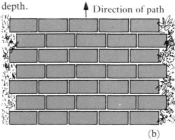

(b)

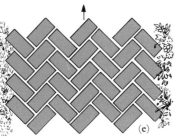

(e)

Second example of use of bricks. A choice of different shades enlivens the effect.

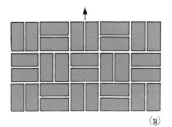

(g)

Squares, each formed of two bricks laid in opposite directions.

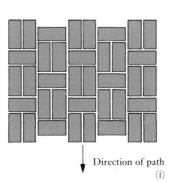

Direction of path
(i)

Squares, each formed of two bricks, laid lengthwise, with intervening single bricks.

Polygonal slabs. Minimum length 16 in (40 cm). Do not lay joints crosswise.

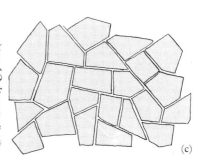

(c)

Concrete slabs, interspersed by rows of granite paving stones. Direction of path optional.

(f)

Path of interlocking concrete slabs
Size of complete slabs, 8 × 6 × 2½ in (20 × 16 × 6 cm). Half slabs for the outer edges are obtainable.

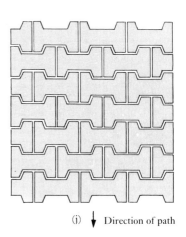

(j) ↓ Direction of path

27

2
Tools

You need garden tools to work your garden: spades, hoes and rakes have been our companions down the centuries. During the last few decades, we have found that a number of tools considered indispensable by previous generations have become just so much old iron, instead of the traditional equipment for proper garden care they used to be. Of course, horticultural technology has made enormous progress; much-improved tools for gardening work have been developed, and most recently particular emphasis has been laid on the many possibilities of mechanical aids.

It is always better to pay more for first-class equipment, since garden tools, though they are bound to come in for a lot of wear and tear, should still last a long time. This is just as true of modern mechanized garden aids as it is for ordinary hand tools.

Basic tools

Whatever your particular type of garden may be, everyone needs a certain number of basic tools. Get this equipment first, and then you can add to it gradually, according to your personal requirements. For a start, you will need something like the following:

Spade: familiar model with D-shaped handle. The slightly curved steel blade and the shank should be forged in one piece, for greater durability.

Fork: basic construction the same as the spade; many uses in digging, preparation of seedbeds, loosening the soil between shallow-rooting plants, collecting fallen leaves and rubbish.

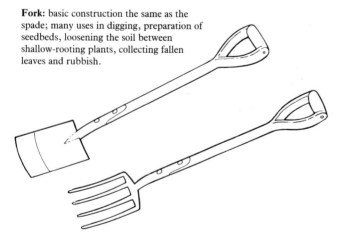

1) garden spade and fork;
2) a shovel, or a spade with a shovel-shaped blade;
3) a hoe for working of the soil;
4) a wire rake with springy steel tines;
5) a 12-toothed rigid steel rake.

In addition, a few small tools, such as a trowel for putting in small plants, a hand fork for weeding, a small claw-shaped cultivator for cleaning up thickly planted flower-beds, a dibber, garden line, a knife, secateurs/pruning shears and pruning saw.

Watering, feeding, and the protection of plants from pests and disease will entail some further purchases: one or two watering cans and buckets; a garden hose with a sprinkler attachment, a sprayer, a fertilizer spreader; also fertilizers, insecticides, fungicides and weedkillers.

Specialized tools

Over the last few years, as the structure of our work- and life-styles has changed, gardens too have undergone something of a fundamental change. When the space available was conventionally divided into flower garden and vegetable garden, gardens adjoining dwelling houses actually grew little in the way of fruit and vegetables, and in such gardens there was no need for many of those tools still required in well cultivated allotment gardens given over mainly to growing food.

Now, even in small gardens some areas are usually devoted to fruit or vegetables, and these can usually be cultivated with tools already mentioned. However, where there is plenty of room for food growing, the following tools are really essential:

A rotary hoe or cultivator, for preparing large areas of vegetable bed – there are several models of semi-automatic cultivators on the market which can be used even by handicapped people, women and children.

You will also need a claw cultivator or the familiar old deep-working swan-necked draw hoe, only if you are growing early potatoes or hoeing turnips, though even here you will find you work less efficiently with these tools, because of the strain caused by bending, than with modern tools which you use with a push-pull motion, standing upright.

Growing and harvesting fruit trees calls for some more tools. You need several good cutting implements, like long-handled pruning shears, lopping shears or a 'parrot bill' shear and a pruning saw, and a fruit picker.

If your garden contains any tall trees, you can't do without a ladder and a pair of steps; modern multi-purpose combinations of steps and ladder are available, and so are other items which may be required.

Most garden-lovers like to have a well-kept lawn. But lawns make work, and they too demand several more tools. The immense variety of novelties which keep on appearing proves that there must be a demand for them. Those recommended are discussed in the chapter on THE LAWN and its upkeep.

The type and size of your garden, and your own personal approach to gardening, will determine any other accessories you might like to have, or might find essential.

Modern wheelbarrows with a single rubber-tyred wheel are very useful; you can wheel them over even the narrowest paths, and they take all kinds of garden rubbish. Two-wheeled trucks are rapidly gaining in popularity because the weight of the load is carried on two wheels. Some two-wheeled trucks have a detachable body which can be lifted off the chassis for emptying rubbish and so on.

A small pair of steps and a long ladder are needed for many other purposes besides growing fruit, so they should get a brief mention here.

And please don't forget a toolbox, containing hammer and pincers, drills, screwdrivers, chisel, a hatchet and an assortment of spanners. Also, nails and hooks in standard sizes, screws and staples, thin and thick wire, and perhaps a few spare espalier or vine eyes.

If you want to be on the safe side, you will also keep spare parts for your garden hose fittings and for your sprayer. These are just suggestions; every gardener has to discover for himself what he or she personally finds useful and what is essential.

Care of your tools and tidiness

Even the best, and most expensive, garden tools will corrode if you don't keep them in good condition. You should never leave anything lying about the garden when you finish work, or fling it into the tool shed without cleaning it. Every item should be cleaned each time it is used, and put away in its proper place. Strong hooks fixed to a piece of wood will serve the purpose almost as well as one of those handsome tool racks of which there are several good models on the market. In fact, the ingenious folding clips often seen, really work better than hooks in the wall or in a wooden bar, because they need no special hanger on the tool itself, but will grip any handle, however smooth.

Things need not always be hung up or stood in racks; you can lean them tidily against a wall as well. So here is a piece

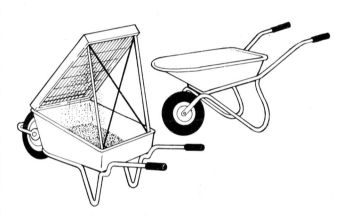

Left: Wheelbarrow and garden sieve combined. *Right:* A light, handy wheelbarrow, holding 15–17 gal (70–80 litres).

Three-pronged cultivator   Draw hoe   Dutch hoe   Pronged weeding tool and rake combined   Rake   Rake with curved teeth   Wire lawn rake

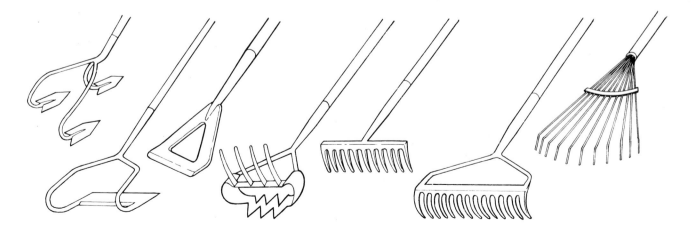

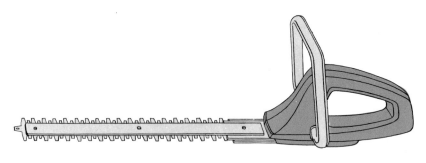

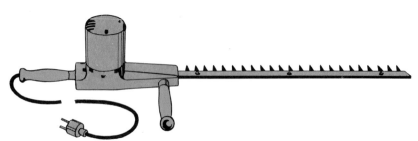

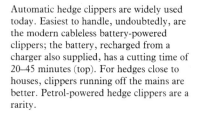

Automatic hedge clippers are widely used today. Easiest to handle, undoubtedly, are the modern cableless battery-powered clippers; the battery, recharged from a charger also supplied, has a cutting time of 20–45 minutes (top). For hedges close to houses, clippers running off the mains are better. Petrol-powered hedge clippers are a rarity.

of good advice: from the start, get into the habit of placing rakes with their tines pointing to the wall and, if possible, their handles on the ground. Anyone who has ever stood on the teeth of a rake turned towards him and received a smart blow on the head from the handle is unlikely to forget this lesson in the malevolence of inanimate objects.

A session of autumn cleaning before the slack winter season sets in is most important in caring for your stock of garden tools. In autumn every good gardener should find time to repair small bits of damage, and clean and dry everything thoroughly. If rust has set in, it can be removed with oil, or with a special solution. It is a good idea to protect metal parts which are not stainless steel by rubbing them with vaseline.

Automation

The question of whether or not automation in the garden is desirable can lead you into the realms of philosophical argument. A certain amount of garden work done correctly and by hand is a healthy, relaxing form of exercise, and so some other people are against mechanized aids, and have a certain amount of right on their side. Then again,

mechanization, as in the house, depends on which tasks *must* be done within a certain time, so that acquiring mechanical aids is worth while. Occasionally, if you know your neighbours well, you can club together and so make the best use of tools, but this does call for a lot of mutual trust.

Given an answer in the positive to the first question, the second point to consider is the engine unit. A petrol-driven motor does allow a certain amount of freedom of movement, but you usually still have to start it with a cable pull, though there are some with electric starters, and the noise and smell may annoy your neighbours. Wherever possible, electricity is infinitely preferable as a source of energy, because it keeps things much more peaceful. At all events, you should not reject out of hand the idea of an electric motor, which purrs quietly as a cat and makes no smell at all while it works, just because of the cable running between the tool itself and the power supply.

It is now possible to have electric cultivators, lawn mowers, hedge trimmers and chain saws which work efficiently and safely, especially if you have a device for rolling up the cable and a cut-out attachment at the mains plug.

PART II:

CARING FOR AND GROWING PLANTS

3
The soil, climate and situation

Many readers will probably already own a garden whose soil shows the signs of long, careful and correct cultivation over the years. We call soil like this 'well cultivated', meaning that the plants growing there have a good environment for their roots, one rich in the humus they need if they are to do well. Owners of new gardens are in a different position. They may find that their plot is in no fit state for gardening and, if a house has just been built on the site, the building operations will have entailed a lot of disturbance of the original soil structure, so that measures must be taken to prepare it for future horticultural use. Thus a new plot, or part of what was recently a building site, starts out as an equation with many unknown factors. It will certainly not be in any condition for the owner just to put in plants without more ado, however modest his expectations. You would never get a lawn, a colourful display of flowers, even a radish or a lettuce, to do well. We might all just stop and think for a while, and then we shall realize how important thorough care of the soil is.

The most important types of soil can be recognized by a manual test when the ground is rather moist.
1 'Light sand' runs through the fingers.
2 'Loamy sand' crumbles.
3 Medium 'sandy loam' can be shaped but breaks into medium-sized crumbs.
4 'Typical loam' can be moulded.
5 'Clay' can be formed into a sausage shape.

Topsoil, where the plants grow

The covering of soil in which the plants actually grow has come into being over millions of years, through all kinds of environmental factors, such as the weathering and breaking up of rocks, accumulations of silt, and the gradual onset of decomposition of the first primitive plants.

As you weigh up your first soil sample in your hand, you will be able to recognize certain broad features, but you should not stop there. You need to buy yourself a soil testing kit; there are quite a number available from garden centres. All these kits will enable you to determine your own soil pH (see later); some will also enable you to determine what nutrients are in the soil. All the kits carry full instructions for use.

To analyse your soil you take samples of equal size from about a spade's depth deep (6-9 in (15-23 cm)), from some 10-12 places, distributed as evenly as possible over your garden. A couple of tablespoonfuls of earth is enough for each sample. You then mix them thoroughly together in a clean bowl or small bucket, so that you have a genuine cross-section of your garden soil. About a pound weight (2.20 kg) of this mixture is enough for analysis.

The pH factor

The concept of the pH factor is particularly important for the understanding of all subsequent cultivation of the soil.

1

2

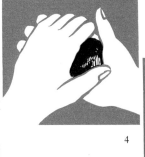

3

4

5

What this means is the reaction of the soil according to acidity (lack or deficiency of lime) and alkalinity. There are 14 points on the pH scale. The most acid point on the scale, represented by the value pH 0, is hydrochloric acid; the most alkaline, given the value pH 14, is potash. In between these two extremes, at pH 7, is the so-called neutral point. The most acid condition which plants like, or can tolerate, is pH 4·1-4·5 (good for definite lime-haters like rhododendrons, camellias and so on). On the alkaline side, plant toleration reaches only about pH 7·5. Most garden plants prefer a soil which is slightly acid to very slightly alkaline – between pH 6 and pH 7·2.

The correct balance of acidity and alkalinity is obtained on the one hand by adding lime, which keeps the soil from over-acidity and acts as a kind of buffer substance, giving a certain leeway to the combination of very diverse biological and chemical processes in the soil, and thus protecting plant growth, and on the other hand by increasing the humus content of the soil, to mitigate any excess of lime or similar alkaline influences. Since farmyard manure is almost unobtainable (though it is now beginning to become available at garden centres, processed, packed in large plastic bags and often de-odorized), other organic fertilizers are used, especially well-rotted garden compost, peat compost, all forms of peat-based fertilizers and shredded bark.

Layers of topsoil and subsoil

The diagram shows that the earth consists of 3 main horizontal layers – A, B and C. For most garden plants, the top layer is especially important, providing a good supply of topsoil rich in humus. We do not find this warming, nutritious, living layer of topsoil everywhere, and the subsoil underneath does not always correspond to the ideal either. Garden soil should warm up easily, be porous, well able to absorb nourishment, and ideally it should be sandy loam or loamy sand. This kind of soil is composed of particles about 0·03–0·07 in (1-3 mm) large, permeated by cavities and capillary or hair tubes. Topsoil, with loose granules just below it, going down some 8-12 in (20-30 cm) into the ground, and the transitional layer immediately below that, going down another 8-12 in (20-30 cm), form the environment where the roots of most of our garden plants live out their lives, and this soil is inhabited by all kinds of living things. Fungi, soil bacteria, algae, primitive animal life, worms, and so on, form an army of billions of tiny organisms. They need humus to live, and at the same time they are creating it themselves; thus they are of vital importance for the growth and health of our plants.

As distinct from the mineral components of soil, humus consists of organic material formed from the decayed remains of animal and vegetable matter, albumen, and other wholesome decomposition products. We draw a distinction, too, between incompletely decomposed 'raw' humus and acid humus as found in bogs where air has been excluded, and 'matured' humus found, say, as leaf-mould on woodland floors. For garden use, matured humus is the only suitable kind, but it can be created on a large scale from raw humus or acid humus (peat). Matured humus, in its turn, undergoes chemical changes to become 'unstable' humus, forming and giving off nutritional material in the process; it can also be present as the relatively 'stable' humus which has already undergone such changes, and creates the best possible conditions for friability and fertility of the soil.

Left: **Soil section:** the main layers.
Right: **Moisture loss by capillary action.** Diagram shows that hoed soil reduces the capillary action of soil water; uncultivated soil leads to maximum moisture loss.

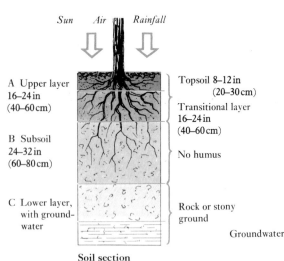

Soil section

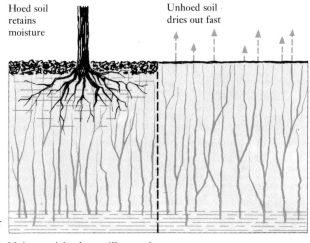

Moisture rising by capillary action

Trees, shrubs and border flowers surrounding a lawn make a pleasant and colourful spring scene in this well-planned and established garden.

Top left: bearded iris *(Iris)*. *Top right:* foxtail lily *(Eremurus)*. *Bottom left:* red hot poker *(Kniphofia)*. *Bottom right:* bedding dahlia *(Dahlia)*.

Conserving and increasing the humus content of the soil is among the most fundamental tasks of cultivation. Practical advice on the formation and care of your topsoil, as well as its humus requirements, will be found in the section on organic fertilizers, in the next chapter.

Moisture, aeration, warmth and friability of the soil

Many factors have to work together to make the soil fertile. Moisture is an absolute essential. What is needed is an active passing of water from above to below and back again. According to its individual composition, the soil itself possesses a greater or lesser capacity to retain water, so that you can achieve the degree of moisture required simply by rainfall or artificial watering from above. Sandy soils are the quickest to dry out; their water retention capacity is only 20%. Loamy soils have a good average capacity of 30-40%, while the ability of pure clay to retain water is 60-80%. Here, again, you can see that lack of balance in the composition of your soil is bound to be a bad thing.

When water fills up all the cavities in the soil there is no room for anything else, such as air, which is as essential for plant roots which need to breathe as it is for those tiny living organisms which help to regulate the formation of humus. Soil atmosphere, moreover, is rather different from the atmosphere we breathe ourselves, containing less oxygen and more carbon dioxide, and this in its turn results in a constant exchange between soil atmosphere and the air above ground, which is known as 'soil respiration'. We can make use of these phenomena for the good of our gardens by correct watering and constant aeration of the soil (or maintenance of aeration). The hoe itself, much prized formerly as a symbol of good husbandry, is really only important in the cultivation of vegetables today; it is rarely used in modern gardens with their permanent ground covering features such as lawns, or beds of shallow-rooting plants, or among shrubs and trees. The same applies to the seasonal task of digging – the spade now being little used except in the vegetable garden or for creating or re-making borders. But the value of spade and hoe in allotments or home gardens where vegetables are systematically cultivated is still largely uncontested. Here too, however, modern research has shown the value of the mulching process.

The healthy relationship between moisture retention and soil atmosphere, which depends on the actual quality of the soil itself, decides how easily it will warm up. Sunlight is the great source of energy and light, porous, very crumbly soils warm up more easily than heavy, sticky soils. Once again we want to aim for a golden mean between a soil that is too warm, because it dries out easily, and one that is too cold, because it is close-textured and thus inclined to get

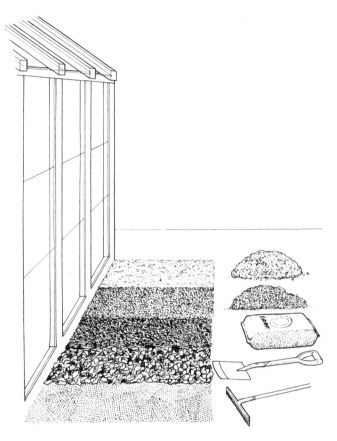

Diagrammatic representation of the various stages in improving the soil of a new garden or a plot not previously used for gardening.

water-logged. Peat, shredded bark, well-rotted compost and sometimes sand are our main allies in correcting the balance.

One more factor that helps the fertility of the soil must be mentioned: this is what is called friability. A good friable soil is not so much an end in itself, as a condition which has to be kept up, as far as possible, by constant care of the soil through the combined effects of the various factors already described. A general friability of this kind, most easily attained in rich, loamy soils, is not to be confused with the kind of friability you can create by covering the soil – an extremely useful process known as mulching. There are two methods of mulching: first you can cover the soil to about a hand's depth with organic material such as grass cuttings (though these should be used well rotted or they will generate enough heat to damage the plants), leaves or peat, and this should really be part of every gardener's programme. Mulching will be recommended again and again in this book, in all sorts of different contexts. Then there is mulching by the use of polythene specially developed for the purpose, usually strong, black plastic sheeting only 0·05 mm thick. You can buy this black

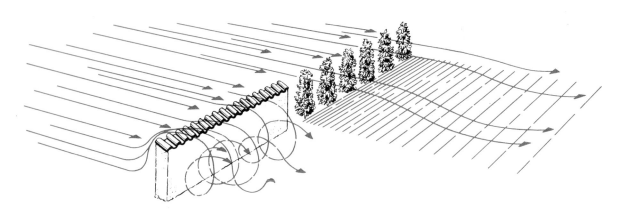

Left: A solid wall or fence creates eddies of air below it to the detriment of plants. *Right:* A hedge of plants allows a freer more gentle movement of air.

polythene sheeting in quite small quantities for use in the garden. It helps protect the soil from weeds as well as keeping it friable. In fact, constant mulching can produce such a good condition of friability in the soil, giving it a well-aerated structure inhabited by tiny micro-organisms, that hoeing and digging may be a positive disadvantage.

Altogether, soil care is a practically inexhaustible subject, and one can only lay down a few guide-lines here. Its practical application will be shown broadly in the chapter HOW PLANTS FEED.

4
How plants feed and their foods

We must distinguish between the two main aims of feeding plants. The first is general improvement of the state of the soil, which goes hand in hand with routine cultivation methods, as described in the chapter THE SOIL. It consists of providing suitable material to turn poor or unsuitable ground into good garden soil – by means of aerating it and breaking up the surface, and maintaining or increasing the humus content. The second main aim of feeding arises from the fact that different plants have different needs, and we need a certain amount of basic knowledge to understand these correctly.

Assimilation and osmosis

In our schooldays we all became acquainted with the ideas of assimilation and osmosis. The former, broadly speaking, is the process whereby plants support life by changing the materials they absorb into the specific substances they can digest: or more precisely, it is the transformation of carbon dioxide – taken in through the stomata of the leaves, with the assistance of water, chlorophyll and light – into sugar and starch, which is then further converted into substances that the plant can use. This process, incidentally, is one of the great marvels of life, in that it involves a conversion by green plants (not, however, fungi or other growths containing no chlorophyll) of lifeless, inorganic compounds into living organic matter. The second process, osmosis, consists of the interchange or ascent of liquids through the fine-pored, skin-like cell walls – it is this process which determines the capillary system whereby water rises in the soil, according to the physical rules of osmotic pressure, but it is of particular importance in the provision of nourishment for plants.

There is a third factor, related to these two basic processes of assimilation and osmosis: plants can absorb all the raw materials which are contained in the soil and prepared for them by the micro-organisms of soil bacteria only in liquid form. To put it metaphorically, plants 'drink' nourishing soup in order to live. Obviously there must be plenty of water available to provide it. Plants themselves are about 60-95% water. However, if a plant takes in a whole pint (½l) of water from the soil it can only retain a tiny fraction of that amount for itself; the rest, nearly 100%, evaporates into the air. The evaporation process, like the absorption of carbon dioxide from the air, takes place through the stomata of the leaves. It happens faster the more sunlight and warmth are available, and stops entirely only when cold weather and frosts cause the leaves to drop, and perennial plants enter their dormant season. We should think of water, then, as the essential element of plant life. Without it, plants could neither absorb nourishment from the soil, nor create the flow of sap which carries the substances absorbed by the roots in their still undigested form upwards from cell to cell. This liquid solution of nutrients from the soil comes together with the material assimilated by photosynthesis in the leaves and all the other green parts of the plant, and the combination gives rise to many complex organic compounds. The flow of sap carries them to the places where they are needed, and where they will cause the plant to grow taller and broader, develop leaves, flowers and fruits, and go through all the other processes of its life-cycle.

Nodular bacteria on pea root: symbiosis between root and nodule.

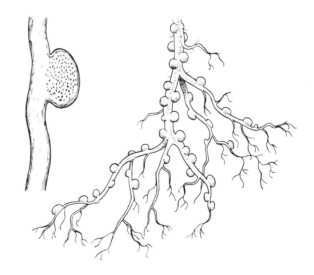

Foliar feeding

When the roots of plants are not functioning properly for any reason, applying plant foods to the leaves in liquid form will help the plants to live more healthily and encourage new root growth. This is particularly useful with newly planted trees and shrubs, and bulbous plants after flowering. It is beneficial to foliar feed healthy plants also as a supplement to soil-applied fertilizers.

Some mistaken ideas about feeding

There is no doubt at all that inexpert feeding can do a lot of harm to this marvellous cycle of plant life. Too much feeding may well do more harm than too little, upsetting the balance of the nutrient 'soup' drawn from the soil. Plants may be over-fed with nitrogen, given too much salt in the form of potash, or too many phosphates – they have to absorb it all, and can do nothing by way of protest except die. Or if wrong feeding causes them to make a lot of woody growth and produce too much foliage and few or poor fruits, people tend to blame the use of 'artificial fertilizers'!

In fact, what the plant wants is a correctly mixed diet, and it will not do well if given the wrong sorts of fertilizer. If its particular need is for a mixture of all the basic nutrients, or for some of them in certain proportions, it will not be pleased to get just nitrogen or potash, phosphates or magnesium or lime on their own. There are a number of other things that plants require, mostly in very small quantities, and these are known as trace elements or micro-nutrients; a lack of these in the soil can give rise to typical plant troubles just as easily as the lack of one or more of the basic or macro-nutrients.

A confirmation of the important principle is that all feeding processes must be harmoniously combined. However, one cannot express this equilibrium as a set of hard-and-fast rules. It has as many aspects as there are differences in the soil, situation and climate of our gardens in various different parts of the country. One can only state the general principle, and every gardener must work out the detailed application for himself.

Other organic matters

Before there were any vast chemical factories, laboratories or scientific research stations around the country, farmers and gardeners generally used muck as a fertilizer; by which they meant organic waste of every kind, especially farm manure of animal origin. It is very difficult to get hold of farmyard manure like this today and, in any case, owners of private gardens will generally prefer peat or shredded bark to 'muck' in any shape or form; they are at least as effective, hygienic and more aesthetic and, used in sensible combination with artificial fertilizers, there is a great deal to be said for them.

The main function of organic manure, and one which cannot be performed by any inorganic fertilizer, is to form and increase humus content in the soil. Soil in which good cultivated plants are grown should contain 1-3% humus. Let us just sum up the good qualities of humus once again:

1) Humus is the stuff of life to the soil bacteria, and the agent of the friability they produce. It keeps nutrients near the surface and prevents application of fertilizer from trickling away.

2) Humus controls the provision of water for the fertile layer of topsoil.

3) Humus helps to keep the soil properly aerated and makes it easier for root tips to grow.

4) Together with the soil bacteria, humus develops carbon dioxide which contributes to the conversion of nutrients for absorption by the plants.

5) Together with correct rotation of crops, humus can often prevent soil from becoming exhausted.

6) In general, humus maintains the equilibrium of the soil. It makes light, sandy soils stickier and better able to hold water and nutrients. It loosens heavy loam and clay and makes them warmer and more porous. It can turn almost any soil, however unpromising, into good garden loam, if the site is properly worked and lime added at the right time. It can act as a humus or peat bed in itself and, with proper care, drainage and the addition of lime will produce excellent plants.

However, how do we come by this miracle-working, crumbly, dark substance, which is the result of decomposition of vegetable and animal matter? The following sections give you some idea, and they will also show you how you can achieve your ends relatively quickly by the use of modern devices.

The compost heap

In theory, anyway, the compost heap is the favourite of all horticultural experts. It is considered the most valuable means of improving the soil; an ideal independent creator of humus. You can create it from nothing, at no expense at all (on paper, at least), and you can apply as much as you like to all plants – except those hating lime if Nitro-chalk is used. In practice, however, a properly composted bin, which can take two or three years to reach the right stage of maturity, is a considerable test of patience, particularly for the beginner.

Many of the things that used to go to enrich the compost heap are no longer present in modern households. Again, the gardens of today do not produce nearly so much waste matter suitable for the compost heap as large and self-sufficient vegetable gardens used to do – with the exception of grass clippings and autumn leaves. In fact it has to be

Three compost containers

Both of the above kinds can be taken apart.

Diagrammatic representation of a container made from wooden slats; the dividing slats allow the heap to be turned. In practice one of the long sides of the container would be made removable for easy access to the compost.

admitted that more and more amateur gardeners are giving up making their own compost, because of lack of space and time. They are doing their gardens no favour, as there is really no replacement for good compost. And you do not absolutely have to go back to the old three-year rotation method of building a compost heap, which was certainly rather complicated; there are various kinds of useful, space-saving compost bins which speed up decomposition to about 3 months in the summer, though rather longer in winter.

The basic processes whereby compost is created are the same as in all transformations of organic material to humus. You build three heaps at half-yearly intervals, close to each other in a shady, sheltered corner of the garden; the area of each should be about 4 x 5 ft (1·20-1·50 m); start with a layer of peat or fibrous vegetable matter, then add 6 in (15 cm) layers of all healthy, not too woody, garden waste which will decay easily, interspersed with good garden soil and peat; add a sprinkling of Nitro-chalk or proprietary compost maker to each 6 in (15 cm) layer every time you turn and move the heap, which should be done every six months, the lower layers of the three heaps being put together according to how ripe they are. If you keep the process going like this you will achieve a proper rotation which keeps you provided with compost continuously once you have got over the long initial period. It is important for air to get into the heap, as you can see from the perforated walls of the specially constructed compost bins; the bins should not be built any higher than

4 ft (1·20 m), and the composting matter not pressed down too hard. They also need moisture, so a small channel can be made in the middle of each heap, and you can add a few buckets of water occasionally. A light covering of soil mixed with a little peat tops the whole thing off.

Well-rotted compost does not have to reach a state where it is indistinguishable from soil: it is quite all right for it to contain a few coarser components.

If you are going to make compost you need to know what material should be used and what should not. Never put the parts of plants that contain seeds, invasive roots, or those that are affected by disease or pests on the compost heap; all these could be dangerous, and should be put aside, dried out, burnt and added only in the form of ashes from a bonfire. Bits of stone, wire and other hard objects have no place on the compost heap, neither does soot from any oil-heated stove, or washing-up water containing detergent (plants dislike it), or anything oily.

Things you *can* use include anything that can be turned back into soil without risk of passing on any poison or disease. Among them are healthy autumn leaves and grass clippings; also harmless annual weeds containing no seeds, fruit and vegetable waste from the kitchen, and wood ash.

Peat

Peat is a particularly pleasant, clean and versatile substance to use in the garden. You can grow fruit, tomatoes and many other plants in it, put it in window boxes or tubs on balconies and use it in or on the soil. It comes in useful anywhere you want to do away with a bad smell or sop up moisture. Peat contains humus-forming substances, and is partly pure humus formed in peat bogs where it lay compressed, away from the air, storing up all its beneficial qualities. For garden use, this peat is subjected to various processes of preparation, and sold, with or without additions, compressed into bales. Moss peat, frequently used, consists mainly of the remains of sphagnum moss; it has a great capacity to swell, which is responsible for its high moisture retention. Sedge peats, the remains of reeds and sedges, is generally darker in colour and more thoroughly decayed.

This ability to hold water means that peat has a direct and purely physical effect on the soil, enriching it in much the same way as described for humus. Of course it is important for the peat to be given enough moisture; using it dry during the growing season is quite wrong, though in autumn and winter it can be crumbled up small and scattered in dry form on soil that has been dug; the moisturizing influence of the winter frosts will make it mellow by springtime, when it should be worked into the soil, and will deploy all its beneficial qualities there.

Pure peat of this kind contains no plant nutrients in itself, but has a good effect on the ground because of its humus content and its slightly acid reaction. It is excellent as an addition to the soil at planting time, for covering depressions in the ground where water can collect around a plant, and in general as a mulch. Where it needs to be well moistened, as in the two last-named cases – you must be careful to prevent it drying out, since once it *has* dried out it is difficult to moisten it thoroughly again, and it will have difficulty in carrying out its function of maintaining the friability of the soil.

Useful organic fertilizers

Dried blood (water-soluble, 12% nitrogen and 1·5% phosphates) For plants raised under glass, and delicate specimens; takes effect very quickly in warm, moist conditions.

Hoof and horn meal (10-14% nitrogen, 5% phosphates) Like horn shavings, which are coarser in texture, assists aeration of the soil and takes effect slowly over a long period. Add about 9 oz (250 g) of bonemeal and 9 oz (250 g) potassium sulphate to 2 lb (1 kg) hoof and horn meal for a complete fertilizer.

Bone meal (moistened) A valuable but slow-working phosphate fertilizer (about 13-22% phosphoric acid, 4% nitrogen, fat content 4% at the most); particularly suitable for light soils and long-lived plants.

Other organic matters

Shredded bark This is pulverized composted bark from forest trees and is easy to handle for use as a mulch or soil conditioner in the same way as peat.

Leaf mould Dead leaves collected in autumn and 'composted' in a wire mesh bin will rot down to form a useful source of humus when added to the soil; oak and birch leaves are best.

Spent hops These are clean and easy to handle and are useful for conditioning the soil while they decompose.

Mushroom compost This is usually a farmyard manure containing plenty of straw. Unfortunately it contains lime, so must not be used on lime-hating plants or chalky soils.

Commercial fertilizers

Commercial fertilizers comprise those nutrients which come from inorganic sources, i.e. minerals. They are not synthesized from chemicals which have nothing to do with the garden, but are just as 'natural' as peat and other organic matter. The widespread suspicion of 'artificial fertilizers' is pure nonsense. Not a trace of 'artificial' origin can be found in any of the five main components applied to cultivated plants, from nitrogen compounds extracted from water and the atmosphere, to phosphates contained in certain iron ores, potash mined from huge prehistoric deposits, and lime, found naturally in great quantities as gypsum, marl and limestone, or dolomitic lime containing magnesium.

Inorganic or mineral fertilizers cannot, admittedly, form humus. All they can do is stimulate the micro-organisms of the soil where the plants take root to increase and multiply. They can, therefore, be of use to the plants only where there is enough humus present, to arouse the necessary physical and bacteriological effects which will enrich the soil and promote plant growth. This is an underlying cause of the widespread distrust of artificial fertilizers.

Things can, indeed, go wrong if minerals are applied to topsoil lacking in humus. And if you scatter mineral salts about the place at random without referring to the instructions things can go just as wrong. And if you use one nutrient instead of another, just because you have the end of a packet left, you may well get all those unfortunate results which are commonly ascribed to the ill effects of 'chemicals', i.e. artificial fertilizers.

However, though incorrect use of mineral fertilizers can be dangerous, certain of the most essential nutrients can be given only in this way, and it allows precise control of application to the needs of individual plants. The basic composition of all such fertilizers is similar; you cannot alter the content of nitrogen or potash, phosphates, magnesium or lime to your own taste, nor can you hurry up or slow down the effect they will have on the soil. This has been the case ever since the 'suspect' chemical industries first brought out their very precisely constituted products. They also offer, in the form of 'compound' or 'complete' fertilizers, mixtures of the basic nutrients which almost all plants need.

In fact there is only one group of plants which has particular needs, and must accordingly have beds of its own with suitable fertilizers: these are the lime-hating plants, formerly known as peat-bed plants. Among their most important members are rhododendrons and azaleas, and some conifers are lime-haters too. Elsewhere in the following chapters more information is given about which of the more popular plants are lime-haters and how they can be grown to give of their best in gardens.

By now, in fact, special fertilizers for different plants have made a lot of headway, and prices have shot up to correspond. If you feel like it, you can collect a whole battery of special fertilizers for tomatoes, roses, and other plants, with nutrients individually selected for each type of plant. Whether the gardener who goes in for this kind of thing will do any better than one who uses an ordinary general fertilizer is questionable – but there is no doubt that he will have to stretch his budget.

Uses of mineral fertilizers: worked into the soil and as a top dressing

We have to distinguish between two main types of use. One is the scattering of minerals on the topsoil and hoeing them in as a preliminary application of nutrients to the soil. Potash and phosphates and compound fertilizers containing them should be applied 3-4 weeks before the area is sown or planted, but nitrogen fertilizers are best applied only just before planting time. You have to work out the connection between the constitution of the soil, the chemical effects of the individual nutrients, the rotation of crops and the general cultivation of your garden. Mineral fertilizers used at this point are scattered broadcast, on windless days.

Top dressings are those easily absorbed applications of fertilizer given at certain defined intervals, and paying particular attention to the correct amount, either dry or in liquid form; they are intended to stimulate the growth of plants at the height of their vegetative period. It is better to give a little top dressing often than too much all at once. Top dressings are always applied on dull days, and if possible after rain. Dry fertilizer salts should not be allowed to lie on leaves, since they can almost all cause brown spots when they dissolve in the dew. If you do scatter the dressing dry, you should follow it up with a good sprinkling of water. Applying the fertilizer in liquid form is safer, and more quickly effective.

If you are going to mix your own mineral fertilizers, you must make sure that the crystals or powders are thoroughly mingled just before you apply them. If you are giving them in liquid form, make sure there are no lumps in the solution, and no sediment is left behind. The section later in this chapter on compatible and incompatible substances will indicate which mineral fertilizers can be mixed together.

There are three main groups of mineral fertilizers corresponding to the three most important plant nutrients: nitrogen (N), phosphates (P) and potash (K). Lime and magnesium also count as basic nutrients, but in a different way, and will be discussed in a later section of this chapter. Finally, we shall look at the trace elements of micronutrients.

Nitrogen fertilizers

Nitrogen stimulates plant growth, encourages the development of foliage and gives the leaves a good deep green colour. Hence it is specially recommended for plants which may look a little hungry, if not actually ill. Nitrogen fertilizers should not be applied to woody plants, fruit trees in particular, beyond the end of July at the latest, since if they are the production of new shoots may go on too long, and the young wood will not have matured properly before the first frosts. Other kinds of plant – for instance, lamb's lettuce and winter spinach sown in mid-August – can have applications of nitrogen, carefully measured, until September if the ground is moist enough.

Sulphate of ammonia (20-21% nitrogen in the form of ammonia) Most suitable as a fertilizer of topsoil on soils with a high lime content. Apply in spring, and it will supply all the nitrogen necessary throughout the summer.

Nitrate of soda (15-16% nitrogen) **Nitro-chalk** (20-25% nitrogen) Two excellent fertilizers, especially suitable as top dressings because the nitrogen is in nitrate form. The difference between them is only that Nitro-chalk contains a high percentage of lime (CaO).

Phosphate fertilizers

On average phosphates are used in smaller quantities than nitrogen and potash. They are, however, absolutely essential to the nourishment of plants. Every seed contains a reserve of phosphoric acid which is necessary for germination. And without phosphates and potash in the right quantity the amazing process of photosynthesis whereby the plant builds up its strength with the help of energy from the sun could not take place. In general, phosphates have a stimulating effect on root activity and help plants to grow the right colour.

Superphosphate (16-18% phosphorus, easily soluble) A good fertilizer to apply to topsoil before sowing and planting. It helps young plants to develop quickly and form strong growth. Also suitable for a top dressing.

Potash fertilizers

Potash is generally required to help the plants produce firm, sturdy growth but is sometimes also needed to offset the too lush growth induced by an excess of nitrogen. As well as being necessary for general plant health, it stimulates flowering and the ripening of fruit. One should not over-apply potash fertilizers as this can lead to magnesium deficiency.

Sulphate of potash (48-50% potash, readily soluble) Usually best applied as a top dressing during the growing season to help plants mature well.

Compound fertilizers

These are specialized chemical products containing three, four or sometimes only two of the basic nutrients, in proportions adjusted to the average needs of plants, with or without lime, in a stable combination, so that incorrect manuring can occur only if you disregard the instructions and apply too much. They usually dissolve easily and take effect quickly, so that they are especially suitable for use just before sowing and as top dressings. There are many of these compound fertilizers or 'mineral multi-nutrient fertilizers', as their official description runs.

The percentages of nutrients given in the analysis of a fertilizer always occur in the following order: 1) Nitrogen (N); 2) Phosphorus (P_2O_5); 3) Potash (K_2O); 4) Magnesium (MgO). Lime content is not specifically given; according to the particular chemical composition of the product it will usually be 8-10%, which is enough for normal lime requirements. Addition of trace elements is mentioned separately.

Compatible and incompatible substances

The chemical action of some of these commercial fertilizers means that they cannot be used at the same time as organic manures, or in combination with each other. The basic rule is that organic manures must not be mixed with inorganic nitrogen fertilizers before use. Mixing them with potash and phosphate fertilizers is not exactly harmful, but it is better to be on the safe side and apply organic and inorganic fertilizers separately. Lime should never be applied at the same time as organic matter either; scatter it over the soil one month before or three months after the addition of such humus-forming materials as compost or farmyard manure.

Lime and magnesium in the fertilizer programme

Lime has a place of its own in the garden fertilizer programme. It is not a fertilizer itself, in the same way as other mineral fertilizers, even if liming is generally considered a fertilizing method. One of its functions is to promote warmth and aeration of the soil. Lime in the topsoil helps to produce a fine, crumbly texture. It also attracts water and neutralizes or kills harmful germs; to complete this rough outline of its use in improving the soil it makes heavy, wet soil drier and less sticky, prevents panning of the surface, promotes friability, and checks the development of those acids harmful to almost all plants, which can develop even in light soils.

Lime also contributes to the inner formation of the plants, stabilizes their tissues, and has certain nutritive functions to perform in the formation of starch and sugar. Leaves contain the largest amount of lime, and it gets into the diet of humans and animals by the way of them.

The vast majority of flowers and vegetables need soil with a medium lime content. It is required to restrain harmful acids and ensure a neutral soil reaction. There is also a relatively small group of particularly lime-loving plants; their rather higher need for lime is mentioned in the plant lists. A dressing of lime every three years should be enough for them on good garden soil, so long as they are also getting regular applications of those compound fertilizers which generally contain some lime in any case. A third and equally small group comprises lime-hating plants, which will do well only in lime-free, acid, humus-rich soil. These are mentioned in the chapter EVERGREEN, SHRUBS, TREES AND CONIFERS.

The action of lime lasts longer the finer it is ground. Powdered lime is scattered thinly and evenly in autumn or early spring, and then hoed lightly into the topsoil. The soil must be dry at the time; lime becomes sticky in wet soil. As already mentioned: lime must never be applied at the same time as nitrogen fertilizers, but at least three weeks before or after them.

Ground limestone, carbonate of lime, ground chalk (80-95% $CaCO_3$, corresponding to about 45-53% CaO) Natural limestone, ground to a powder. It is not water-soluble. These are the most widely available forms of lime. They also usually contain small amounts of magnesium. Best used in accordance with the analysis of your own soil; average amounts are about 5 lb (2·5 kg) per 12 sq yd (10 sq m). Keeps well.

Hydrated lime, slaked lime (73% CaO) Derived from heating carbonate of lime; it attracts water, and is water-soluble. Suitable for heavy clay or loamy soils; not on turf. Use according to your own soil analysis; average amounts: 2-3 lb (1-1·5 kg) per 12 sq yd (10 sq m) – half the amount of ground limestone. Does not keep well.

Since the serious effects of lack of magnesium in the soil were discovered, this metallic element, chemically designated as Mg, has come close to be classed with the traditional basic nutrients of nitrogen (N), phosphorus (P), potassium (K) and calcium (C). Fertilizers with high or low magnesium content are now being produced, so that all soils can be sure of having enough of this substance, so essential to the growth of plants and the formation of chlorophyll. Many of the mineral fertilizers already mentioned contain an average 2% of magnesium, as you can see from the analyses. Magnesium is also an important component of some lime fertilizers. In general it helps phosphates to dissolve in the soil. Too much potash fertilizer, or very alkaline soil, can cause magnesium deficiency in plants.

Magnesium deficiency is manifested in leaves which appear to be suffering from chlorosis, with light green to brownish spots among veins which remain dark green; it also shows in early leaf fall, beginning with the lower leaves and fruit, which drops prematurely, is small and poorly coloured. If this happens, stop giving potash fertilizer at once and apply a proprietary fertilizer containing sequestrated (chelated) magnesium; such a product will usually have iron in it as well, as this is another essential element that can get 'locked-up' in alkaline soils.

Trace elements or trace nutrients

Trace elements are not mysterious powers in the soil, but plant nutrients which simply happen to be present in very small quantities, as compared to the basic nutrients, and are therefore also called 'micro-nutrients'. The present state of research into the subject shows that of the very numerous trace elements in the soil, boron, manganese, copper, zinc, molybdenum and iron are necessary for plant nutrition. Cobalt and iodine are not used by the plants themselves, but plants pass them on to the animal kingdom. Nearly all amateur gardeners use fertilizers containing trace elements these days, though they are not always necessary. If you discover any abnormal phenomena in your garden, such as failure of green plants to form chlorophyll properly, and the only possible explanation is some deficiency in plant nutrition, you should get a scientific analysis of your soil or the leaves affected. Increasing the supply of boron, manganese and copper by adding them in the form of fertilizer should be an emergency measure only; since some trace elements can be harmful given in excess.

5
Watering

Water has three very different functions in the garden. First, it enables us to install garden pools, where we can create enchanting worlds of plant life in a small compass and add fish and other creatures to complete the life-cycle of a pond and its environment. A long chapter in PART THREE: ORNAMENTAL PLANTS will give more information about WATER GARDENS. Second, water offers us opportunities for sport, recreation and refreshment; we probably think first of swimming pools and paddling pools, but there is quite a range of other installations and pieces of equipment in existence which can be incorporated in the garden. Third, however, used carefully and correctly, water is the great source of life for the plant growth in our gardens – which, being artificial man-made creations, could not manage on natural rainfall alone. Good gardening and the proper use of water are very closely connected, as we shall see in the following pages.

Taps should be at least 2 ft (60 cm) above ground level. A layer of gravel will prevent puddles forming.

Plants and watering

If we are to regulate the use of water in the garden to our own particular needs, we must start by looking at the composition of the soil. If your soil is heavy and sticky, it will not absorb water easily, and thus must be watered sparingly, in small amounts each time. Again, a clayey subsoil or one of heavy loam, with only a thin covering of topsoil above it, needs careful watering, because it is not porous and will incline to waterlogging. So really lavish watering to encourage plant growth is apparently called for only where you have good soil which has been well cultivated over a long period. Its fine crumbly structure and friability ensure that the plants will get the right amount of moisture for their needs and absorb only what they require. Light, shady soils, especially, often have too little capacity to retain water, but you can even out this tendency by taking the correct measures: for example, adding peat or other organic matter.

In fact it is in well-tended gardens, even without the many new means of watering available nowadays, that we see how properly manured soil, well aerated in autumn and spring, and kept friable by good mulching at the right time in summer, can get by with very little artificial watering or

Trolley to carry a hose; a multi-purpose tool. Remove the hose and its holder and the sturdy trolley will carry all kinds of loads, from dustbins to beer barrels. Hang a disposable plastic sack on it and use it for collecting rubbish. Store the hose during winter by hanging its circular holder on the wall.

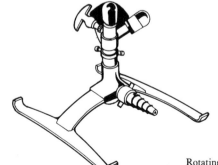

Rotating sprinkler. Note the skids which allow the sprinkler to be dragged easily over the lawn.

even none at all. However, an unusually dry, hot summer which dries and hardens the ground despite all precautions does call for different measures; adequate watering is essential if the plants are not to suffer damage. And it is not only sappy, herbaceous plants which fall victim to droughts; shrubs and trees are affected too, though the worst of the harm may not be obvious until a year later.

However, owners of new gardens should note that too much watering and spraying of previously uncultivated plots where the soil is not naturally porous will only make it worse: stickier and heavier. When proper soil cultivation is not adopted in time, the surface may cake and take grotesque forms: see previous chapter, THE SOIL.

6
Sowing and planting out

Long before we can think of actually sowing seeds, the question of what to order comes up, usually while we are planning our gardening programme for the coming year. This is certainly one of the most important annual events for every keen gardener, and means as much for you personally as your household; these days we are almost sure to be ordering vegetable and herb as well as flower seeds.

Seeds, from ordering to sowing

In our own gardens, nothing but the best seeds and plants will do. Cheap offers which fail to fulfil their promise almost always mean losing a year's crop. Moreover, we can make a lot of trouble for ourselves by economizing in the wrong way. Using up last year's left-over seeds, or seeds from an even earlier date, is one such mistake; you may try testing their ability to germinate, but this is not a foolproof guide. It is equally risky to use seeds saved from last year yourself; you can never be sure they will run true to variety, or be as healthy and productive as was the parent plant. Some golden rules for every sensible amateur gardener: work out the area to be cultivated correctly, buy only fresh seeds, and only the best, and be brave enough to throw away any left over.

You should also give certain vegetable and flower seeds a preliminary dressing with a fungicide. This is most easily done by adding a small quantity of fungicide powder to the seed packet and shaking the packet till the seeds are coated in the powder. Many vegetable seeds come ready treated. It is particularly important to treat peas and beans of all kinds, and early sowings of radish, cucumbers and spinach.

You should take the greatest care with the chemicals themselves, which are often poisonous: keep children out of the way while you are doing the job, do not keep any left-over seed, and certainly do not feed it to pets.

Pelleted seed: here every individual seed is given a protective coating, which also makes it bigger and easier to sow singly. Pelleted seed was first intended for use in machines for sowing large areas, but small packets for home gardeners are becoming increasingly popular: you can get pelleted onion, lettuce and carrot seed, among others.

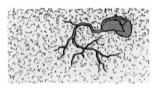

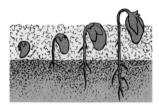

Seed and germination: if the subsoil is too loose, the earth will fail to give the seedling any firm structure to grip, and it will become deformed (top). Seeds should be sown on a fairly firm layer of soil, but covered with a fine tilth (bottom).

Sowing in the open – right and wrong ways

Though it seems so easy, sowing is not as simple as it looks. We have seeds of all kinds and all different sizes, from those almost as fine as dust to large beans, so you don't want to sow them all the same depth in the ground or the same distance apart. Here, of course, the composition of your soil comes into it; germination will proceed unhindered in light soils even if the seed is sown rather deep, while a heavy, sticky soil can offer the seed so much resistance that it will just lie buried there and rot. In addition, dampness and dryness can affect germination. And we must not forget that many failures are due to the impatience of the beginner, who cannot wait until the weather and the soil are ready.

The biggest mistake of all is sowing too thickly. You cannot always put this right later by thinning out the seedlings, not to mention the waste of good seed. The directions given in the chapter GROWING VEGETABLES FOR PLEASURE about the distance between rows and the spacing of seeds should be followed to the letter; similarly when you are calculating the amount. As a rough rule of thumb: large seeds, like those of peas, beans, beetroot or sweetcorn should be covered by about three times as much soil as their own breadth. Fine and very fine seeds, like carrots, parsley, lettuce and many herbs, are sown in shallow drills, and sometimes mixed with sand to make for thinner sowing. They are not pressed down and covered with soil, but have a mixture of damp peat and fine sowing compost scattered over them.

Seeds of fast-germinating vegetables like radish or lettuce are sometimes mixed with those of slow-germinating ones like carrots or onions; the fast-germinating vegetables, known as 'indicator crops', showing where the rows are, making it easier to cope with weeds, which will often come up earlier than the slow germinators. You can often harvest the radishes just as the first leaves of the carrot seedlings are forming.

Vegetables are usually sown in rows, though some people include extra clumps of lettuce, carrots or radishes at the ends of rows of other vegetables, or even between the rows. When flowers are sown in the open the seeds are more often sown broadcast, or in groups.

Sowing flowers and vegetables under glass

Many seeds are so sensitive to cold that they cannot be sown in the open until after the middle of May, which would be too late for the crop to grow to maturity before the autumn frosts. Early germination of the seed of such plants, in places that can be kept warm, a greenhouse, heated propagating unit or frame, lengthens their period of vegetation by weeks or even months, and brings forward the flowering of plants and the harvesting of vegetable crops. Fine seeds are best sown in pots, seedboxes or trays. The holes or slats at the bottom of the box are covered with crocks. A proprietary seed sowing compost of loam mixed with other constituents is added up to ½ in (1·5 cm) below the top of the box. If you prefer, use a peat-based soilless growing mix, but be sure to follow the instructions given.

When sowing in a soil-based compost, sow the seeds in rows or broadcast, according to size, sprinkle sand over them, cover the box with a sheet of glass or plastic and put a small piece of wood underneath, to let in air. As soon as the first seedling leaves show, remove the covering, at first for short periods and then entirely. The compost must be kept moist for further growth. When the seedlings are standing thickly together they must be individually 'pricked out'. For this operation, you use a ready-made compost in other containers, i.e. clean trays or pots.

Pricking out is an essential but fiddly job, leading to the production of stronger, healthier seedlings. Roots that have already grown too long can be nipped off with the fingernail except in the case of lettuces. Each plant needs enough space to form its own little ball of soil around its roots. Sowing under glass is a kind of arithmetical exercise: you begin on a small scale and find things have suddenly shot up.

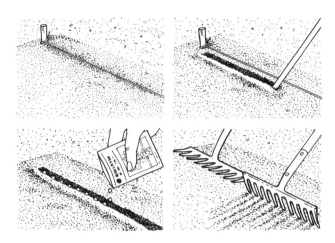

Break up and smooth the soil, use a garden line, draw out a drill, sow evenly, press the seed very gently down and cover the drill.

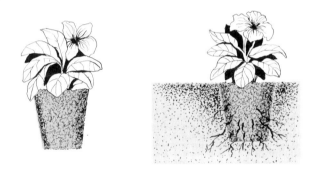

Peat pots, before and after planting out.

Larger seeds, like beans, cucumbers, marrows, squashes, sweetcorn, sunflower or ricinus (castor oil plant) seeds can also be sown directly into peat pots, made of compressed peat rich in nourishment. These peat pots, also available in double strips joined together, are later planted out complete with the seedlings, and disperse into the soil. This is the most labour-saving way of putting out young plants, and has no drawbacks. Usually, three seeds are planted in a triangle in each small pot. If all three germinate, you then remove the two weaker seedlings and let the strongest carry on growing. Pricking out in the old sense is unnecessary with these methods. However, some plants which grow very vigorously, like marrows or squashes, sunflowers or ricinus (castor oil plant), may need transferring to bigger pots before they can be planted out.

Pre-sown packs of seeds are now available, which just need water added to the growing medium, the lid put over the top to form a mini-propagator, and the seeds then left to germinate. Once germination has taken place, the lid is removed and used to form a drip tray until the seedlings are pricked out.

Sowing and pricking out seedlings in plastic seedtrays using a soil-based compost.

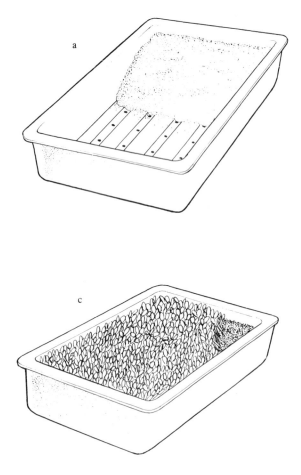

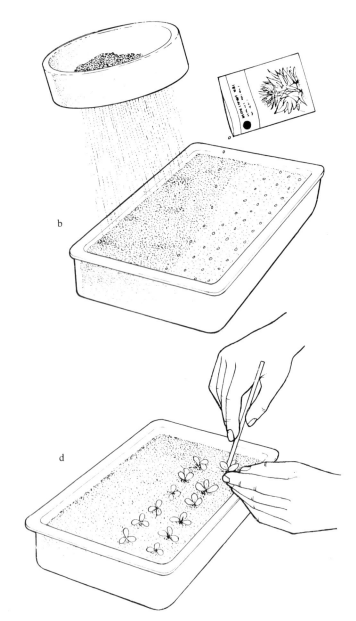

Any plants raised in heated conditions must be properly hardened off before they are set out in the garden. This means gradually acclimatizing them to the colder conditions of the outside world.

The use of plastic to outwit the seasons

These days sowing under glass and raising plants that can be protected from sudden cold spells and consequent damage present hardly any problems and for this we also have to thank the practically inexhaustible potentialities of plastic. Naturally, a keen gardener who is also a do-it-yourself man can erect an old-style heated glass frame near his house, with a wooden framework and glass panels, but

a modern plastic or fibreglass frame is more practical, and considerably easier to handle. If possible, it should have electrical heating and soil warming cable regulated by a thermostat, but this is not an absolute essential. For instance, double-glazing by means of panels of strong clear polythene can trap warmth successfully enough to compensate for quite considerable changes in temperature. Quick assembly frames are very useful; the standard size of 40 × 60 in (100 × 150 cm) can be extended by additional parts until it is 6½ yd (6 m wide), or again it can be reduced in size when necessary. It may be mentioned in passing that plastic propagator covers to be placed over seedboxes instead of glass panes have long been obtainable.

These days greenhouses are expensive to purchase, heat

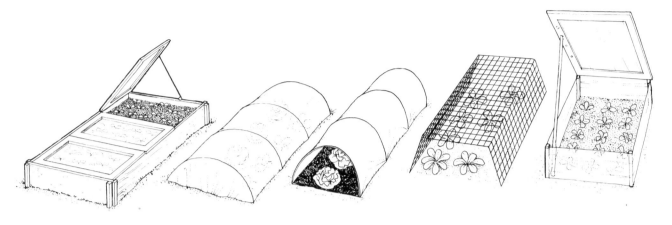

Garden frame. Usual measurements:	Large tunnel cloche: 52 × 20 × 98 in (130 × 50 × 250 cm)	Ordinary tunnel cloche: 26 × 18 × 98 in (65 × 45 × 250 cm)	Plastic-covered steel framing: width 60 in (150 cm); can run to 16–33 ft (5–10 m) long	Plastic-covered frame: 40 × 60 in (100 × 150 cm)

and maintain, and most gardeners find that frames are more than adequate for raising the plants they wish. It is certainly most sensible to think in terms of heated and cold frames first, and then possibly invest in a greenhouse at a later date if you really decide it is necessary.

There is an endless variety of polythene cloches, with or without top ventilation; you can use wire hoops driven into the ground to stabilize them. Another practical idea is plastic-covered steel framing, which you can buy in a roll, cut to size, and bend to the shape needed in your garden. All these portable protective devices, as well as individual plastic cloches or rows of cloches fitting together, have one great advantage in that you can put them anywhere in the garden (just as people used to do with old boxes, though of course this was a cruder method), whenever some particular plant needs to be brought on faster or have its season extended.

Naturally, many gardeners get by without any of these aids and prefer to buy their seedlings direct from garden shops or centres. There are some quite good reasons for this: professional gardeners, with their expert knowledge and superior technical equipment, may well deliver stronger and healthier plants than those you grow from seed, but the drawback is that they may not raise exactly the varieties you want.

Planting out

Planting out young plants is a job that has to be done in all kinds of different conditions, not always the most favourable ones. If you take seedlings from a thickly sown area, the little roots, suddenly removed from the soil, may be damaged in the process, and then you have a wilting plant which may droop for several days, whatever you do. If it does recover it may do so with difficulty and suffer considerable setbacks to its further growth. The seedlings of sappy, herbaceous plants plucked up like this will suffer

more than, say, strawberry plants, which are transplanted when the vegetation is already dying down. The strawberry is used in the pictures here as an example of the typical method of transplanting plants with roots fairly free of soil.

Before they are removed from their old quarters, it is important for seedlings to be given a good watering at the right time in the seedbed where they were raised, so that their roots and the surrounding soil will cling together. Then prepare holes for planting at the new site, having previously marked out rows and the spacing of the plants with a string and a garden measuring line. It is best not to

Planting strawberries. (a) Planting hole prepared with trowel. (b) Plant placed in hole. (c) Soil firmed around roots. (d) Surface soil firmed by hand.

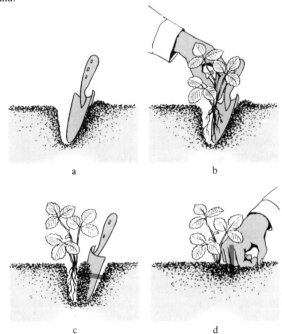

51

use a dibber, because it makes rather sharp-pointed holes in the ground which are nearly always too narrow, and tends to compress the soil around the sides of the hole. Instead use a hand trowel, which will dig broad, roomy holes some 6 in (15 cm) deep. Put the seedling into the hole, without bending or crumpling its roots, so that the crown of the plant is just level with the surface of the soil and not covered by it. Then gently replace the soil in the hole with the blade of the trowel, and firm it with your hands, making sure the entire hole is filled and at the same time forming a little trough or depression around the plant for watering. Water lightly and then surround the plant with a mulch such as damp peat.

The faithful old flowerpot still has its uses in sheltering the roots of a plant and the surrounding ball of soil before it is transplanted into the open or into a larger container. The pre-requisite is that the plant should have taken root properly, so that the ball does not fall apart as you remove it. If you want to be very cautious, or you are using a plastic pot instead of an earthenware flowerpot, you could run a sharp knife around the inner edge before knocking the pot against the side of a bench, as always recommended. With larger plants, it is best to break the pot in order to free the roots and the ball of soil.

Removing the roots of a conifer from their wrappings.

Removing a plant from its pot: give the flowerpot a sharp tap on the edge of a bench.

Trees, especially conifers, are usually offered for sale with roots and ball of soil sewn or tied up in a piece of coarse sacking reinforced with synthetic fibres, specially designed for this form of packing. You put the plant into the hole prepared for it, which will be the right size for the wrapped roots, then undo the wrappings and pull them carefully away from below. Now fill up the hole, taking care that the tree is planted at the right depth, and make a small depression around it for watering. Again, after watering cover the soil with damp peat.

The most significant development of all in methods of planting is undoubtedly the advent of 'containers', which

means you can set out plants at any time of the year when the soil conditions are suitable. These containers, usually made of soft plastic and obtainable in many sizes, from the smallest flowerpot to preserving-pan size, are very durable, and so cheap that, among their other uses, you can sink them into the ground to protect valuable flowering bulbs from attacks by vermin. Lattice-work containers are best for this purpose, as well as for raising vegetables and smaller flowering plants. For larger plants, especially all kinds of ornamental trees, the tree nurseries prefer perforated containers with slits only along the sides. However, the advantages of modern container growing go far beyond the protection of bulbs from vermin. You can simply remove flowers in their useful containers from the ground after the end of their flowering season and put them somewhere else, out of sight, while you brighten up your garden with new plants coming into bloom. The fading foliage of flowering bulbs is often, and rightly, thought unattractive, but if they are in containers they can be moved out of sight without disturbing the later growth of the plant. The greatest advance, however, is that we can now feel free from the old, hallowed planting dates, which used to depend inexorably on the time of germination, in later summer and autumn, on the temperature of the soil and the falling of a plant's leaves. Now, whether your plant is a rhododendron or a rose bush, a lily or a dahlia, if it is in a container you can move it from place to place as you like, even in full bloom.

Basic planting rules

Supports of all kinds, from beanpoles to stakes for trees, should always go into the ground at the same time as you prepare the planting site itself. Wooden stakes must be well sharpened at the bottom and either singed or painted with a protective solution to make them rot-proof. Plants

Everlasting flowers *(Helichrysum bracteatum)*.

Four annuals. *Top:* centaury *(Centaurea moschata)* and salpiglossis *(Salpiglossis sinuata)*. *Bottom:* Gazania *(Gazania splendens)* and Indian pink *Dianthus chinensis)*.

should be set in the ground at the same level as they were growing in the nursery or in the pot. With vegetables and summer annuals the upper part of the crown, right below the germinating leaves, is the limit. Any special rules for other plants will be found in the relevant chapters. No plant should be set in the ground so low that the central point of growth is covered with soil and thus damaged.

With the exception of edible bulbs, flowering bulbs and tubers, every plant should be carefully watered after transplanting it – not by having water just sloshed over it, or through a rose, but from the spout of a watering can; do not wet the leaves. Covering the depression for watering you have made around the plant with damp peat or other mulching matter will protect the soil from panning and drying out on the surface too fast.

All planting jobs should be done, if possible, on dull, damp days, or at least during the evening. Sunny weather and sharp, drying spring winds often make it advisable to provide some kind of shelter. With vegetable beds, you can simply lay pieces of rush matting over low stakes driven into the ground, with crosspieces holding the framework together; they can easily be removed again later. The same

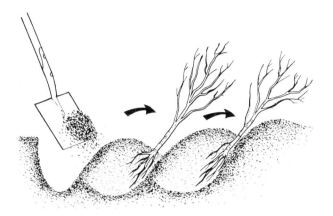

Heeling in woody plants for a waiting period. Do not forget to keep the roots straight.

form of protection comes in useful when you are sowing seeds in high summer.

Roses and other shrubs which cannot be planted out at once should be 'heeled in' in a shady, sheltered place. Woody shrubs like these can be left like this all winter.

7
Increasing plants

At some time or other, you are almost certainly going to find it necessary to increase your garden plants. This may be because they have become old and are not performing as well as they should; you might wish to increase the number of a particular type of plant; or you may just want to give some away to friends and neighbours.

I have already covered one way of raising new plants – from seed – in the chapter SOWING AND PLANTING OUT. The other type of propagation is by vegetative means; that is, by division, layering, cuttings, grafting and budding. Raising plants by these methods means that the youngsters will be identical to the parent plant.

Division of plants

This is the simplest method of increasing plants and is mainly used for herbaceous perennials and quite a few shrubs. It means exactly what it says: you divide up large plants which have many growths at the base into smaller pieces, each with their own roots and buds.

Simple plant division Dig up the plant when it has finished flowering or is in a dormant state, and pull and tease the roots apart with your fingers if you can. If the clump is too tough, either get two garden forks and insert them into the centre of the crown and lever them backwards and forwards to break up the clump, or use a sharp knife or sharp spade and cut the crown into sections. It is often advisable to discard the central and oldest part of the crown and only replant the younger outside pieces, which should be roughly the size of your fist.

It is important to get the new pieces of the plant back into the ground, or a pot of soil, as quickly as possible as they tend to wilt. They will soon recover, though, if they are well watered in and an eye is kept on them to see that they do not dry out or are not disturbed until they have started making new growth.

Tubers Potatoes and Jerusalem artichokes can be propagated by simply cutting the tuber into pieces, making sure each piece has at least one 'eye' (growth bud). Dahlia tubers need rather different treatment. When they have

been started into growth in the spring, by moistening the sand or peat and putting them in a warm place, the tubers will swell up and after a few days it is then easy to see how to cut the stem vertically, in such a way that each cut results in a piece of dahlia which has at least one growth bud at the base of the piece of stem, as well as one or more tubers.

Rhizomes After flowering, dig up the plants and cut the rhizomes into sections 2–4 in (5–10 cm) long, making sure each piece has a growth bud and some roots. Throw away the oldest pieces and replant the new sections horizontally to the same depth as the old plants. When dividing irises by this method, cut the leaves back to half their length to reduce water loss.

Suckers Some plants, such as lilacs, some barberries, and fruits, such as raspberries, produce new stems from below ground level, which are called suckers. At the normal planting time (usually in the autumn), the soil above the suckers can be removed and they can be severed or pulled off from their parent and then be planted elsewhere.

Layering stems

This is a method which is very useful for increasing woody plants and climbers. What one does is to split the stem slightly and place the wounded section into soil or growing compost to induce it to produce roots, and so form a new plant. The great advantage of this method is that the young plant is not finally removed from its parent until it already has its own roots and can look after itself.

Ordinary layering Choose a branch or twig that can be bent easily to reach the ground. At a point about 12 in (30 cm) from the tip, with a sharp knife make an angled slit on the underside which goes only about one-third of the way through the branch or twig. Open up the slit slightly by bending it gently upwards. Make a hollow in the ground and put some coarse sand in the bottom, then gently push the slit piece into the sand, hold it in position with a piece of wire shaped like an inverted U, and cover it over with soil. Insert a cane beside the layer, and tie the tip to it with soft string. Water as necessary and leave for a year before cutting the new plant from the old with secateurs.

For plants that dislike root disturbance, such as clematis and certain climbers, the same general layering method can be used, but a pot of growing compost is sunk into the soil for the layered piece to be pegged into. In this way, the new plant can be moved with the minimum of root disturbance.

Some plants, such as strawberries, layer themselves naturally by runners, and it is no problem to obtain new plants from them, though it is sensible, in order to get healthy young plants, to restrict the number to no more than five runners and cut off the others. Other soft fruits with long arching stems, such as blackberries and loganberries, also *Forsythia suspensa*, often root themselves naturally where the shoot tips touch the soil. If these new youngsters are required, cut them from their parents, leave them for a week or so to recover from the shock, then move them to their new homes. Although currants and gooseberries do not tip layer themselves naturally in this matter, nevertheless they can be induced to do so by pegging 4 in (10 cm) of young shoot tips into the soil. The best time for this type of layering is during the summer, so the new plants can be moved in the autumn.

Air layering This is essentially the same as ordinary layering but is used to increase trees and shrubs that do not have low-growing shoots, or any that are pliable enough to be pegged into the soil. You make the same sort of slit 12 in (30 cm) from the tip of the selected shoot, which should be young and growing vigorously, bend it open very gently and put in a tiny stone or some strands of sphagnum moss to keep it slightly open. Slip a transparent or opaque length of plastic tubing (or a plastic food bag with the bottom opened up) – about 6–10 in (15–25 cm) long – over the shoot and place it so that the cut is about in the middle. Secure the bottom of the tubing to the shoot with insulating tape, then fill it with equal parts of moist sphagnum moss or perlite mixed with potting compost, and secure the top as you did the bottom. It usually takes about six months for roots to form, and when these are seen through the plastic the new plant can be cut with secateurs from the old, put in a pot of compost and kept in a shaded position until well established. Do not forget to water it when necessary.

Increasing your plants from cuttings

Cuttings are pieces of plants that are taken from their parents and treated in such a way as to encourage them to form their own roots and shoots. With the exception of hardwood stem cuttings and root cuttings, others need a humid atmosphere, shade and generally some warmth, which means at the very least using pots, compost and polythene bags in the home. If you have an electrically heated frame or propagating case, it certainly makes the job much easier. For the sophisticated gardener who has a greenhouse, and who can afford it, mist propagating units are available for rooting cuttings; these incorporate thermostatically controlled soil warming cables and automatic electronically controlled mist-watering devices.

Hardwood cuttings These are taken from deciduous trees, shrubs and climbers just after leaf-fall, and from conifers and other evergreens at the same time of year, and can be rooted in the open ground. Production of roots may take as long as 12 months, and in severe winters protection with cloches is often helpful. With a sharp knife, cut off the top 6–12 in (15–30 cm) of the chosen stems just below a node (stem joint), and place the cuttings in a well-prepared V-shaped soil trench in a sheltered corner of the garden. A layer of sharp sand or peat at the base of the trench helps rooting, and the cuttings should be set half their length deep and 3–6 in (8–15 cm) apart. After frosty weather tread the soil to prevent air pockets, and in summer water to keep the soil nicely moist.

Semi-hardwood cuttings These can be taken in just the same way as described previously but are cut from shoots of the new season's growth when it has just started to get woody, normally mid-summer to early autumn. Some gardeners, however, find that they can root semi-hardwood heel cuttings better than nodal ones. To get a heel cutting, hold the shoot firmly at the base, between finger and thumb, and carefully pull it downwards, so that it comes away with a 'tail' of bark. Trim the 'tail' with a sharp knife.

Semi-hardwood cuttings should be rather shorter than hardwood ones, say 4–6 in (10–15 cm) long, or even less for conifers and heathers – and the lower leaves, and the growing tips, should be removed. The basal ends should

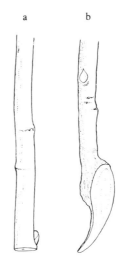

Types of cuttings. (a) Nodal cutting, with a clean cut just below a node (stem joint). (b) Heel cutting, obtained by pulling off a young side shoot with a piece of old main stem wood attached.

be dipped into a hormone-rooting powder or liquid to encourage root formation, and then the lower third of the prepared cuttings put round the edges of pots or in boxes of special rooting compost, or a 50:50 mixture of coarse sand and peat or perlite. As the cuttings needs a humid atmosphere, cover the pots or boxes with polythene tied round to form a tent, or put the containers in a frame with the light (lid) kept tightly closed. Soil warming cables in the frame are a great aid to quicker rooting. Watering the cuttings from time to time will help control water loss through the leaves (transpiration), and shading on hot sunny days is essential to prevent wilting. Once the cuttings have rooted, as will be seen by their sturdiness and the appearance of new top growth, they are ready to be hardened off, in the usual manner as for seedlings. Planting out into the open ground is best delayed until the following spring.

Softwood cuttings Softwood cuttings are taken in spring and summer when the stems are immature. They are taken in exactly the same way as for other cuttings, but are shorter still, only 2–5 in (5–13 cm) long. The tips and lower leaves are removed, the cuttings treated with hormone powder or liquid, and then inserted in a suitable rooting medium, all as mentioned previously. The only real difference is that softwood cuttings require higher temperatures than other cuttings, but still the same closed humid conditions. In return, they will probably have rooted in 10 days or so. It is important to watch for wilting and attacks of disease, and spraying with a suitable fungicide is helpful. Once rooted, harden off the cuttings as you would any other plants raised in warmth but which then have to go back outside. One useful tip – when gathering a number of shoots to make softwood cuttings, place them in a polythene bag and keep the neck closed, which will prevent them from wilting and give them a healthier start in life.

One group of plants that has its cuttings prepared in a slightly different way is the *Dianthus* family (carnations and pinks). Instead of cutting non-flowering side shoots, you simply pull them out from between a pair of leaves – and they are immediately ready for putting in pots or boxes.

Pipings of carnations and pinks. (a) Non-flowering side shoot pulled out from the main stem by hand. (b) The pipings set around the edge of a pot containing a sandy peaty compost.

Root cuttings Many plants with fleshy roots, such as phlox and anchusa, can be increased by root cuttings. Unearth one side of the plant and remove some of the roots. Cut those of a pencil thickness or more into 3–4 in (7·5–10 cm) lengths, with an oblique cut at the end furthest from the plant, and insert vertically in pots of cuttings compost, oblique cut downwards. The thinner roots are best cut into slightly longer pieces and laid horizontally on the compost. Both sorts should be covered with ⅜ (1 cm) of the compost.

Root cuttings. (a) Cut fleshy roots into 3–4 in (7.5–10 cm) lengths, the lower end with a sloping cut; insert in a pot of compost, sloping end down. (b) Fibrous root cuttings are laid horizontally on compost in boxes and covered with a layer of the same compost.

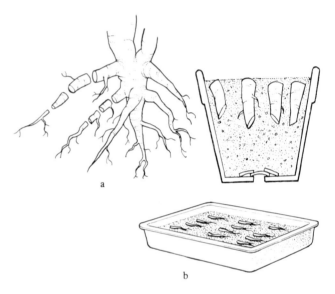

Grafting is tricky

The term grafting means the joining together of the roots and main stem of one plant (stock or rootstock) with a stem of another plant (scion) so that the two grow together to form one plant. You need to be a rather dedicated gardener to carry out this operation in its various forms, but grafting does have the advantages of being reliable when other methods of propagation fail; it can be used to make shrubs grow like small trees; and, above all, by careful selection of the stock it can influence the behaviour of the scion – something that is of great importance in the growing of top fruits where, perhaps, a certain variety of apple is wanted and by using the right rootstock that tree is kept dwarf (and so suitable for a small garden) whereas otherwise it might be too large.

When grafting it is absolutely essential that the stocks and scions to be grafted are compatible: this means they must be very closely related to each other in the same plant family. Before embarking on this method of propagation, one should seek expert advice or refer to a well-illustrated book on the subject, as there are several ways in which it can be done.

New plants by budding

Budding is somewhat similar to grafting in that a growth bud from a scion plant is inserted on the stem of a chosen rootstock plant. It is used mainly for propagating fruit trees and roses.

Shield budding As roses are deservedly so popular, it is quite possible that some of you might wish to have a try at doing some rose budding yourselves. You will probably need to buy in the necessary rose rootstocks, usually *Rosa laxa* or *R. multiflora*, though the dog rose of hedgerows, *R. canina*, is equally suitable, but you can almost certainly get the necessary buds from your own or your friends' roses.

Budding usually takes place in mid-summer and the selected rose buds should be those taken from halfway up a strong stem. With a sharp knife, preferably a budding one, make a shallow upward cut from below the bud, going behind it and coming out well above it. Carefully remove the woody piece behind the bud (the heartwood), but leave the leaf stalk for easier handling. Then make a T-shaped cut in the bark of the rootstock (just below ground level for bush roses), lift the corners of the bark with your fingers or the blunt end of the budding knife, trim the bud shield to shape, and slip it into the T and carefully tie it in position with adhesive tape, or raffia covered with grafting wax, or use a budding tie. Once it is obvious the bud is growing away strongly, remove the tie and cut back the rootstock to just above the bud. With good fortune, you should end up with a healthy bush of the rose variety you have chosen. One important point to watch for is the appearance of rootstock suckers. These must be removed by pulling them off from their source by hand.

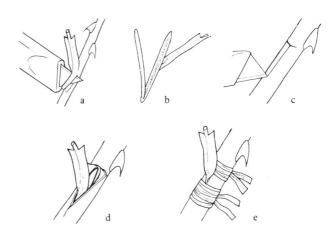

Budding roses. (*a*) Cut a bud and its leaf stalk from halfway up the chosen stem, cutting upwards with just a sliver of bark and wood. (*b*) Remove the woody piece, leaving only bark, bud and leaf stalk. (*c*) Make a T-shaped cut in the bark of the stock. (*d*) Ease back the bark flaps and slide in the bud. (*e*) Cut away any of the shield above the T-cut, replace the stock bark, and bind with raffia or proprietary tie above and below the cut surfaces.

Cautionary note!

If you are increasing plants for your own use or as gifts, this is quite in order. If you are thinking of selling them you must take care not to infringe the British Plant Varieties and Seeds Act, 1964. This Act allows nurserymen and seedsmen to patent any newly raised plant which is different from any other already in commerce and which maintains its stability of character. The rights are granted for 15 years, and during that period it is an offence for anyone to sell such plants without a licence from the raiser and the payment of a fixed royalty per plant to him or her. Most catalogues indicate which are patented plants but, if in doubt and you wish to sell, check the position before you do. It is better to be safe than sorry in a court of law!

PART III:
ORNAMENTAL PLANTS

8
The lawn

The lawn really does deserve to be called the heart of the garden these days. It *is* a fact that a thick carpet of bright green is an essential part of the furnishings of that pleasant 'outdoor room', which I suppose is the dream of every gardener.

Moreover, the dream and its realization do not lie so far apart as they did a few years ago. Today, a good lawn is no longer just the essence of a miraculously luxurious garden created with endless work, and considerable expense of money and trouble. The basic principles of lawn care have changed to a considerable extent. We have known for some time a lot more than we used to about the nature and habits of those hundreds of grasses which go to make up a lawn. New and improved specialized fertilizers have been developed, which can also act as weedkillers, and the array of tools available for lawn care has been improved and extended in hitherto undreamt-of ways. In fact, if we didn't have to put in a little work preparing the lawn site properly, and later on giving it a bit of care and treatment, we might almost say the modern lawn grows of itself.

New strains of grasses have been developed by horticultural breeding institutes, especially in England and the USA. These grasses have outstanding qualities. One is happy to accept that a new lawn may take a little longer to establish, because later on these high-quality grasses will grow sideways rather than upwards, and thus will need less mowing than lawns of the old type.

However, we must face a few problems of design. What about the actual shape of the 'heart' of the garden? Do we stick to the old gardening principle that a lawn looks larger the less you divide it up with paths and flower beds? And have you stopped to think that all these extras in a lawn mean more work when you are cutting it? You are increasing the number of lawn edges, which usually need clipping with a special tool, or some laborious work with the edging shears once you have mown the lawn. You can avoid this job by laying a paved edging round your lawn, as shown in several of the garden designs in the chapter DESIGNING YOUR GARDEN. However, if you absolutely must have

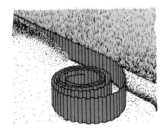

Left: Plastic edging strip sunk in the ground preserves a neat edge and prevents the grass from growing down into beds and borders.

Below: Rose-beds in a lawn: left, the wrong way, right, the correct way to place them.

flower beds round your lawn, they should be flush with the very edge of the lawn.

If, having taken into account the fact that it may make your lawn look smaller, you do decide to plant large but useful specimens such as fruit trees in it, there is no need these days to spoil the look of the lawn by leaving a circular bed around the tree. In any case, you will need to aerate your lawn from time to time with a spiked roller, and you should do this particularly thoroughly in the area over-shadowed by the foliage of the tree; it will do the roots a lot of good. This is the best way to replace the unattractive circular bed round a tree.

Good lawns need good soil

If your lawn is to do well, good nourishing soil is an essential; where nothing else will grow, grass won't grow either, only weeds. As all grasses are shallow-rooting plants, you need only dig the site a spit deep. On the other hand, a really useful, close piece of turf will develop only on a layer of topsoil at least 5–6 in (12–15 cm) deep with good subsoil below it. A lawn will never thrive on builder's rubble, and thorough preparation of the soil on a new site is essential. If you intend to sow in spring (at the earliest in the second half of April, at the latest in the first half of May) this should be done the previous autumn. The soil, dug over and with peat added, as well as sand and compost (with no weed seeds capable of germination in it!) all worked in, can then be left lying in large clods over the winter to get the benefit of the frost, and should then be given a general fertilizer in early spring.

And now to sow the lawn

Shortly before sowing, which should take place on a dry, still day, break up and rake the soil. If you only have a small area to deal with, treading over it on boards fastened to your feet while you sow broadcast by hand will be suf-ficient. It is important to sow the seed evenly to prevent a patchy result. If you have a larger area, you will need to use a roller and a seed distributor, or you could use a fertilizer spreader to distribute the seed instead. This will enable you to do the job faster, and economize on seed. However, the actual amount of grass seed you need depends very much on what mixture you choose. Recommended amounts vary between $\frac{1}{2}$–$1\frac{3}{4}$ oz per square yard (15–50 g per square metre). To ensure that grass grows thickly at the edges of the lawn, draw out a drill and sow some extra seed in it. Then rake the area to cover the seed with a thin layer of soil, roll or tread the surface, and finally give the whole area a light sprinkling with water. Time of germination: 8–14 days.

If the summer has not been too dry, the weeks between mid-August and mid-September are a good time to sow lawns as well. In warm soil, the grass seed often germinates within a few days, and if there is some fine autumn weather with heavy dews at night it will grow so fast that you can cut it twice before winter sets in. Whether the site can be prepared as thoroughly in later summer as it can for a spring sowing is another matter.

Apart from sowing, easily the most important method for amateur gardeners, there is another way to start a lawn. Turves cut to standard size can be delivered ready for laying; they are more expensive than seed, and because of transport costs are worth it only for large areas.

What mower to choose?

A hand machine is really adequate for small surfaces, less than 60 sq yd (50 sq m). But a small, modern electric mower does the job more easily. For medium-sized lawns, the choice between an electric mower running off the mains or a petrol-driven machine depends on the circum-stances; this has already been discussed in the section on automation in the chapter TOOLS. I would always go for the electric machine.

Whether or not you need a mower with a wider cutting surface than average (which is about 16 in (40 cm)) is dependent on the lie of the land quite as much as the actual size of the lawn area. Wide cutting surfaces of over 20 in (50 cm) will save you work only on level land. Small, easily manoeuvred mowers with a cutting surface only 10–12 in (26–32 cm) are infinitely preferable on sloping ground, and where the lawn is not a single unbroken unit.

Cutting the grass

Once the young grass is $1\frac{1}{2}$–2 in (4–5 cm) tall, you should give it a light rolling. However, not everyone owns a roller or can borrow one. To be perfectly honest there are many quite respectable lawns which have never seen a roller in their lives, and are none the worse for it. Most lawns are too compacted anyway and the weight of a powered mower does all the rolling that is needed.

The first cutting should be given when the young grass is 3–4 in (8–10 cm) tall. Once there used to be a hard-and-fast rule that this 'maiden cutting' had to be done with a scythe or sickle, to spare the tender young roots. But the gardener of today can simply get out his modern lawn mower and feel how gently it glides along, cutting so well that there is no danger of uprooting the seedlings. The blades should be set high for this first cutting: 2 in (5 cm). When the lawn is going to take a lot of wear and tear, but you still want to treat the grass well, I should recommend you to stick to this setting of the blades later on too. A lawn's powers are not inexhaustible, and the shorter you keep the grass, the more energy it has to put into replacing the leaf area you have cut – and the more it suffers from periods of drought or other setbacks. You can lower the blades to a height of 1 in (2·5 cm) only for what are called luxury grade lawns, which

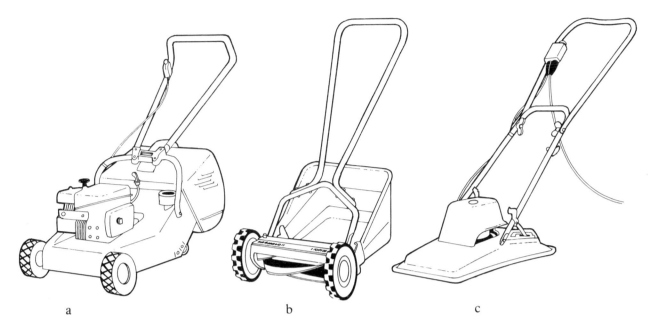

a   b   c

Lawnmowers. (*a*) Rotary, petrol-engined mower, able to cope quickly and efficiently with large areas of lawn. (*b*) Hand mower with cylindrical cutting blades. (*c*) Electric, hover or 'air-cushion' mower.

take hardly any traffic on them and are very carefully tended.

Frequency of cutting has nothing to do with this; it depends on the seed mixture used, the weather, fertilizer, and how fast the grass grows. Even a lawn always cut with blades set at 2 in (5 cm) will have its individual rhythm of growth, and can sometimes, especially if it is an old lawn, with plenty of nourishment available, be ready to cut again in less than a week in damp summer weather. Apart from the fact that you don't want the grass to get too long, cutting is good for it.

However, if on occasion your beautiful lawn seems to be looking like a meadow just before haymaking time (after you come back from holiday, for instance), do not cut it right down all at once. Lawn grass should only have a third of its entire length removed at a time. So you will be helping to keep it in good condition by cutting in two operations, with a brief interval between them, until you get it back to the right length.

As summer passes into autumn, the rate of growth slows down and you can increase the interval between cuttings. Mow for the last time at the end of October or the beginning of November, according to weather conditions. The later the better, because the grass should be short during the winter, to prevent it from starting to rot if it is covered by snow for any length of time.

Grass clippings and neatening-up work

Every time the lawn is mown you will end up with a lot of grass clippings to be dealt with somehow. You can rake them up, or use a lawn sweeper; there are also lawn mowers with grass boxes or bags to save you the work of collecting

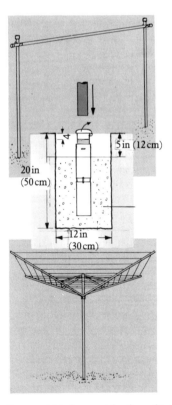

Posts for washing lines, uprights for carpet-beating poles and revolving clothes driers are placed in prepared sockets before use. This concrete socket, lined with metal and with a plastic inset and cover (do-it-yourself) is flush with the lawn, and will not get in the way of the mower.

65

A lawn sweeper will collect grass clippings and fallen leaves.

them. Or, you may keep the grass clippings so small and short that they can be left lying on the lawn as a kind of green manure.

However, ordinary grass clippings ought not to be left on the lawn. You can use them on the compost heap, or as a mulch on flower beds. Like other methods of mulching, the use of grass clippings is most effective in promoting friability, but the clippings do not look very attractive as they turn yellow. So people who are very keen on the look of the thing cover the mulch of grass clippings with a layer of damp peat, and later work both into the ground. The ignorant simply throw their valuable grass clippings away.

Next comes a neatening-up operation: trimming edges, clipping back grass encroaching on stepping stones or anywhere else it ought not to be. This is the finishing touch that makes the lawn look really well cared for. It can be a tiring job if you have to work bending down with ordinary shears, which may not be too sharp (cutting grass close to the ground can quite easily blunt them) and they fail to cut properly at every second snip of the blades. Owing to their special construction, edging irons and electric edging shears are less trouble. There are also long-handled tools which save you from having to bend; to give a satisfactory 'clean' cut, they should be lightly sharpened each time of use and reset from time to time. Motorized edging shears mounted on a single wheel are excellent, but expensive.

Give the lawn enough to drink

Unless rain falls immediately you should water the lawn after every mowing, though not so lavishly as to cause puddles or boggy patches on it. A lawn sprinkler should never be left in the same place for hours, but should be moved around quite often (each according to its mode of operation). Mobile sprinklers covering square or circular areas or segments of areas will see to a gentle and even distribution of water by themselves. Stationary sprinklers should be moved every 20–30 minutes. As with all artificial watering, it is better to do the job once, thoroughly, than little and often. As applied to lawns, this means not giving a surface sprinkling every day, but spraying them once or twice a week in dry periods so thoroughly that the water gets down to the lowest parts of the root structure. However, exactly when you need to do this depends on your soil; you have to find out by trial and error. Light soils absorb water faster and better than heavy ones. In fact, you can tell if your lawn is suffering from drought before distinct brown patches appear. It is at risk as soon as the grass does not spring back into place easily, and begins to look slightly blue, instead of bright green.

Aerating and feeding your lawn

Lawns need more than just water. Turf that is rather too dense, together with subsoil that does not drain well, can present problems because there is not enough aeration. For small areas, an ordinary spiked roller will aerate the lawn well enough; its tines penetrate the turf without much difficulty, and aerate the soil without removing any of it.

Most important of all, however, is the provision of nourishment. If you starve your lawn you need not be surprised if it looks thin and is in poor condition generally. Like all other cultivated plants, lawns need regular feeding every year. This first compound fertilizer is given in late autumn (November/December) after the last mowing. The usual amount is reckoned as 33–44 lb (15–20 lb) of peat compound fertilizer per 120 sq yd (100 sq m). It is crumbled up finely, spread evenly, and dry, over the entire surface, worked gently into the grass with a broom and left there during the winter. At the end of winter (the end of February to the beginning of March) the second application of compound fertilizer with peat and humus should be given. The best way to apply it this time is to scatter it (again, in a dry state). If fed in this way, the lawn will show strong growth, and form a good, close turf, particularly in half-shade, where summer growth is not always all that could be desired.

The lawn needs feeding in summer too, to help it make up for the constant loss of material it suffers from mowing. It used to be customary to give a top dressing of fast-acting nitrogen fertilizer about every four weeks from the end of April to the end of September. If you didn't go about this job very carefully you were almost bound to end up with some ugly scorched patches. Such problems have all been overcome now we have the new specialized lawn fertilizers. If they are used according to the instructions nothing can go wrong. These fertilizers are all top dressings, and so are used only during the growing season. They are first applied in April/May. The effect of them is often immediate, and usually lasts so well that no further summer fertilizer is necessary. However, in some cases a second application in August/September is advisable to make sure the grass will go on growing strongly right up to the start of winter.

These summer fertilizers contain a large amount of nitrogen, which is most important in lawn care. They also contain the two other basic nutrients, phosphates and potash, in carefully calculated amounts, and magnesium and trace elements. Even if you have given your lawn a second top dressing in summer, you should still apply a compound peat humus fertilizer at the end of winter if you have any. Enriching the lawn with material including humus in this way is particularly good for it, since otherwise it is getting only inorganic fertilizers.

Spring and late summer fertilizer can be applied in liquid form with a watering can to very small areas, like lawns in front gardens. It is quite easy to apply fertilizer by hand to rather larger areas, up to 60 sq yd (50 sq m). If you have to deal with an area over 60 sq yd (50 sq m), it is worth getting a fertilizer spreader. It will soon pay for itself, because it enables you to spread fertilizer evenly and economically. A fertilizer spreader can also be used for various other jobs in the course of the year. It makes spreading sand or salt in winter on icy drives and paths an easy job. A top dressing should never be applied immediately after mowing, but a few days later; never in bright sunlight, but if possible in cloudy weather or in the evening. And if you are not sure of having some rain soon, you should finish the fertilizing operation by giving the lawn a good watering.

Moss, weeds, and other threats to the lawn

If moss appears in a lawn it is nearly always one's own fault. It usually has nothing to do with the unhealthy 'souring' that can attack the lawn (and which will not be banished from it along with the moss by indiscriminate doses of lime), but is caused by quite different matters, connected with basic neglect of the lawn as a whole.

1) Poor cultivation of the soil when the site was first prepared. Usually you can cure this only by the costly business of digging up and re-sowing your lawn, avoiding the original mistake. In some cases, however, 'repairs' can be carried out.

2) An unsuitable seed mixture may have been used (for instance, grass which does not tolerate shade may have been sown under trees). Usually you can put this right only by re-sowing the mossy parts.

3) Lack of nourishment. See previous remarks on fertilizers.

4) Shaving the lawn too close. See remarks on correct mowing.

5) Water-logging, often as a result of the formation of hollows where puddles can collect. Remove the moss-infested turf, fill in the hollows with a mixture of sand and peat and make sure the surface is level, re-sow the affected patches or lay turves. Some people grow a special supply of turf for the purpose.

6) Compression of the soil as a result of heavy rolling or too much wear and tear allows moss to invade the weakened grasses. Aerate the turf thoroughly again, fill the holes left by the aerator with a mixture of sand and peat, add fertilizer, water the lawn, and keep the lawn in good health by proper care in future.

7) Genuine lack of lime and 'souring' of the soil. Get an exact soil analysis made or buy a simple soil-testing kit and do it yourself, so that you know the pH value and precisely how much lime is lacking, and ask the institute which gives you the analysis to recommend a fertilizer. See also the chapter THE SOIL.

From all this, you can see that it is not a matter of getting rid of moss, something that can easily enough be done with a chemical weedkiller. What we have to do, and it is the same with weeds, is find out the mistake that has been made in tending the lawn, avoid it in future, and achieve a stretch of turf which is so healthy, dense, and resistant to attack that no unwanted guests can find their way in again. Overcoming the after-effects of an attack on weeds is much the same as with moss. These days, actually getting rid of moss or weeds is much easier than it used to be, thanks to the top quality chemical weedkillers available.

These days, we tend not to deal with lawn weeds by digging or pulling them out by hand; we try to keep them down naturally by regular mowing and other methods of lawn care. Where a bit of weeding *is* necessary it can be done by means of a compound fertilizer containing a chemical weedkiller, or you can use an aerosol or watering can, taking care to aim the weedkiller at the right spot and stick to the instructions; you only want to kill the weeds, and not harm the grass itself by an overdose of hormone weedkiller.

Perhaps the fact that toadstools in a lawn are an almost fashionable affliction now may have something to do with good lawn care. An expert is quite glad to see the brown caps of this lawn fungus (*Ophiobolus graminis*) appear; they show that the soil is slightly acid and suitable for a lawn. Frequent cutting and destruction of the caps will keep them from spreading unchecked. You can also treat a lawn infested by toadstools by watering it with a fungicide.

Worms are generally welcome in the garden, as voluntary soil aerators and a guarantee that the soil is in good condition. However, they are 'Enemy Number One' in a lawn. Their slimy worm casts clog up the young grass, their extensive tunnelling systems impair the growth of good thick turf, and make the surface of the lawn soggy after a heavy shower. Collecting these unappetizing little casts will only stop them getting spread about the lawn; it will not prevent the worms themselves increasing and multiplying. The usual pest-killers applied to plants do not work because they are only for use against insects, but there are proprietary wormkillers which can be used effectively. While it is highly desirable to get rid of the worm casts – which can easily be done with a broom – it is, in fact, questionable whether one really wants to kill the worms. While they may be undesirable in a lawn, they are

Flattening small bumps and raising hollows in your lawn: make a crosswise incision, level out or add to the soil below the turf, lay the edges of the cut turf back together.

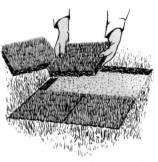

Improve the look of the lawn by laying healthy turves in bare patches.

essential for healthy soil and healthy plant growth throughout the rest of the garden.

Other enemies of the lawn from the animal kingdom, such as moles, can be controlled according to the general rules in the chapter PLANTS NEED PEST AND DISEASE PROTECTION. Specialized ant powders are effective against ants, which are often a considerable nuisance. Pouring boiling water over them works too, but may also scald the surrounding grass.

If you need to inspect a young lawn, and don't want to leave footsteps on it, it is a good idea to put down a long plank and walk over it.

Ground cover plants for use as a 'lawn substitute' or to prevent weed growth

Botanical name	English name	Habit of growth	Height	Flowering season	Colour of flowers	Remarks
For very dry, sunny situations; also on slopes and banks						
Armeria maritima	Thrift, sea pink	Forms tufts or hummocks; herbaceous perennial	2 in (5 cm)	Apr.–May	Pink	Does well even on poor, dry soils
Artemisia glacialis	Wormwood	Creeping; herbaceous perennial	4 in (10 cm)	June–July	Yellow	Silver-grey, feathery leaves; likes lime
Cerastium tomentosum, etc.	Snow-in-summer	Creeping; herbaceous perennials	4–8 in (10–20 cm)	May–June	White	Grey leaves; several varieties grow very strongly
Chamaemelum nobile 'Treneague'	Chamomile	Creeping; herbaceous perennial	2 in (5 cm)	No flowers	–	Mid-green leaves
Hypericum × *moserianum* 'Tricolor'	St John's wort	Sub-shrub, forming clusters	6 in (15 cm)	June–Aug.	Lemon-yellow	Yellow-green foliage; very undemanding
Juniperus horizontalis etc.	Creeping or prostrate juniper	Creeping; evergreen coniferous shrub	6–8 in (15–20 cm)	Insignificant	–	Green and blue-green forms
Nepeta × *faassenii*	Catmint	Creeping; herbaceous perennial	10–12 in (25–30 cm)	June–Oct.	Mauve	Undemanding
Phlox subulata	Moss phlox	Creeping; herbaceous perennial	2–4 in (5–10 cm)	May	White, pink, mauve	For small areas and slopes
Potentilla alba, *P. verna*, etc.	Cinquefoil	Creeping; herbaceous perennial	2–8 in (5–20 cm)	Apr.–Aug.	Yellow or white	Grow creeping varieties only

Botanical name	English name	Habit of growth	Height	Flowering season	Colour of flowers	Remarks
Sedum album, S. kamtschaticum, S. spurium, etc.	Stonecrop	Creeping; herbaceous perennials; forming clusters or a dense mat	2–8 in (5–20 cm)	June–Aug.	Pink, red, yellow	Various leaf forms and colours
Thymus serpyllum, etc.	Wild thyme	Evergreen creeping herbaceous perennial	2–3 in (5–8 cm)	July–Sept.	White, pink, carmine	Will grow on the poorest soil; aromatic
Veronica gentianoides etc.	Speedwell	Creeping herbaceous perennial	2–4 in (5–10 cm)	Apr.–July	Bright blue	Grow creeping varieties

For sun to half-shade

Botanical name	English name	Habit of growth	Height	Flowering season	Colour of flowers	Remarks
Ajuga reptans, and its varieties	Bugle	Creeping; herbaceous perennial	6 in (15 cm)	Apr.–May	Violet-blue	Spreads well
Cotoneaster dammeri, etc.	Dwarf cotoneaster	Evergreen creeping shrub	6–8 in (15–20 cm)	May–June	White	Grow creeping varieties only
Cotula squalida		Creeping; herbaceous perennial	1–2 in (3–5 cm)	July–Aug.	Insignificant	Bronze-green leaves
Hypericum calycinum	Rose of Sharon	Sub-shrub	10–16 in (25–40 cm)	July–Sept.	Yellow	Large flowers with attractive stamens
Lamium galeobdolon	Yellow archangel	Creeping: herbaceous perennial	12 in (30 cm)	May–June	Yellow	Variegated leaves
Lysimachia nummularia	Moneywort, creeping Jenny	Creeping; herbaceous perennial	2–4 in (5–10 cm)	May–Aug.	Golden yellow	Likes damp places; grows strongly
Polygonum affine	Knotweed	Creeping; herbaceous perennial	8–12 in (20-30 cm)	May–Sept.	Pink, red	Undemanding
Prunella grandiflora	Self-heal	Creeping: herbaceous perennial	6 in (15 cm)	June–Sept.	Pink, purple	'Little Red Riding Hood' good small variety
Stachys lanata 'Silver Carpet'	Lamb's ear	Herbaceous perennial	2–4 in (5–10 cm)	No flowers	–	Silvery, feathery leaves
Trifolium repens	Wild white clover	Creeping; herbaceous perennial	2 in (5 cm)	June–Sept.	White	Kentish strain particularly effective

For half to full shade

Botanical name	English name	Habit of growth	Height	Flowering season	Colour of flowers	Remarks
Asarum europaeum	Asarabacca	Creeping: herbaceous perennial	4 in (10 cm)	Mar.–Apr.	Purple-brown	Insignificant flowers; otherwise very useful

Botanical name	English name	Habit of growth	Height	Flowering season	Colour of flowers	Remarks
Duchesnia indica	Duchesnia	Creeping; herbaceous perennial	3 in (8 cm)	May	Yellow	Flowers followed by inedible red fruits
Epimedium perralderianum	Barrenwort	Creeping; herbaceous perennial	10 in (25 cm)	Apr.–May	Yellow	Other attractive cultivated species
Gaultheria procumbens	Partridge berry, wintergreen	Spreading; evergreen shrub	Up to 8 in (20 cm)	July–Aug.	Pale pink	Pretty bright red berries
Hedera helix, H. canariensis, H. colchica	Ivy	Creeping; evergreen shrub	2–4 in (3-10 cm)	–	–	Many variegated leaf forms available
Oxalis oregana, O. magellanica	Oxalis	Creeping; herbaceous perennial	2–6 in (5–15 cm)	May–June	Pink, white	Avoid invasive bulbous species
Pachysandra terminalis	Japanese spurge	Creeping; evergreen sub-shrub	Up to 12 in (30 cm)	Apr.–May	White	Leathery leaves; roots put out runners
Sagina subulata	Pearlwort	Creeping; herbaceous perennial	1–2 in (3–5 cm)	June–Aug.	White	Grows less thickly in shade
Tiarella cordifolia	Foam flower	Spreading herbaceous perennial	4–6 in (10–15 cm)	May–June	White	Forms a dense carpet of maple-leaf like leaves which turn red in winter
Vinca minor	Lesser periwinkle	Evergreen sub-shrub	4 in (10 cm)	Apr.–May	Pale mauve	Flourishes in shade
Waldsteinia ternata	Barren strawberry	Creeping; herbaceous perennial	4 in (10 cm)	Apr.–May	Yellow	Gives thick cover even in shade

Chinese Lantern *(Physalis alkekengii)*.

Garden view with ground-level birdbath. *From front to back:* lavender, roses, stonecrop, evening primrose, gypsophila, lychnis, delphinium.

9
Annuals and biennials

Annuals may not lead the orchestra in the great symphony concert of the garden, but with all the harmony of their shapes and colours that accompanies us from spring until well into autumn they are an essential part of it. Indeed, without these delightful flowers, which are inexpensive, easy to manage, and live out their short lives with a minimum of attention, our gardens would lose many of their prettiest visual effects, especially as there are gaps in the succession of flowering that you cannot achieve with other kinds of plant, and it would not be so easy to fill them without a bit of magic from a seed packet. And how would owners of new gardens manage to enjoy their gardening if they had to wait until perennials, shrubs and trees had grown enough to look good, and their lawns were a fine green carpet of turf?

By long-established convention, annuals are divided into two groups:

1) Hardy annuals, sown out of doors where they are to flower. However, if you want to bring on their flowering season early it is sometimes advisable to raise them under glass, in pots or seed trays.

2) Half-hardy annuals, which are always sown initially in heat in trays, boxes, pots or in a frame, pricked out and moved to other containers one or more times, and only planted out in the open in late May or early June when the danger of frost is over. Since raising annuals under glass calls for more expertise, as well as a lot of room and time, if you are to end up with strong, healthy seedlings many people prefer to buy young plants ready to be put out from a nursery gardener. However, if you would like to try your hand, see the hints in the chapter SOWING AND PLANTING OUT.

But, in the nature of things, garden-lovers are particularly fond of hardy annuals. There may be many much-loved and beautiful flowers among the half-hardy annuals, but from the point of view of sheer quantity there is nothing to beat the 'pleasure from a packet' you can get, at relatively low cost, from hardy annuals. A few years ago we used to complain of a certain monotony among the usual assortment on offer, but there have been many advances in the field of annuals, and now even medium-sized businesses stock hundreds of different varieties of flower seeds.

Preparation of the soil and cultivation

The soil of the flower beds should be prepared in good time, using a cultivator or small rotary hoe, and enriched with humus. If necessary, sterilize the soil with bromophos or HCH (BHC) dust (wait three weeks!) or with a combined seed dressing. Water the site if necessary, with a rose on the watering can, the day before you sow. Sowing itself differs according to the species and size of the seeds. Most very small flower seeds are mixed with sand first. They should have a very fine layer of soil containing humus sifted over them. One can cover the new sown area with damp sacking or with stout paper until the seeds germinate, to protect them against too much sunlight, drying out, and being scratched up by birds. Diseases and pests (such as aphids), which are covered later, are dealt with according to the general rules of plant protection. For the rest, annuals should be given the same basic care as all other garden plants. You need to keep them free of weeds, water them thoroughly, either early in the morning or in the evening during periods of drought, and give fertilizer from time to time.

Removing flower heads

Given this amount of loving care, annuals will flourish either in beds on their own, or in among your perennials, and will soon be in full bloom; their flowering season will last longer if you are careful to control the formation of seeds by cutting off all dead flowers. Of course, removing the flower heads is not suitable for all annuals; it depends on their habit of growth. For instance, it is easy to dead head cosmos, and the operation is visibly beneficial; it would take far too much time and patience to treat clarkias, candytuft and similar small-flowered plants in the same way. Many annuals seed themselves readily, so that you will find whole colonies of 'foundlings' appearing next spring in all kinds of places, begging to be given a good place in your garden. It is not a bad idea to have a bed planted with the left-overs, if possible, so that you will have replacements in case of accident.

Transplanting, complete with roots and ball of soil, from one part of the garden to another is sometimes tolerated even by plants which are usually supposed to be impossible, or difficult, to transplant. I have even moved sunflowers in bud, standing a yard (metre) high, in the middle of summer, and they scarcely seemed to notice. I must admit that we had cool, rainy weather at the time – I don't think I should have dared to do it in a dry, hot period.

About the plant lists

I shall set out my summary of annuals (and similarly of perennials later on) first according to their height, since, along with their flowering season and the colour of their blooms, this is their most outstanding horticultural characteristic. Accordingly, those general rules which the gardener should observe in relation to the visual harmony of shape and colour and other characteristics apply: do not put tall plants like cosmeas or garden poppies or the handsome salpiglossis in a rockery among clumps of alpines and dwarf plants; avoid jarring dissonances of colour, such as mixing bright red salvias with vivid pink and purple clarkias and crimson amaranthus; make sure each plant fits into its setting. Also bear its flowering time in mind. Within my division of groups according to height, the plants are arranged alphabetically according to their invariable botanical names, printed in italics, and not according to the various native names which come after.

Hardy annuals: up to 10 ft (3 m)

Helianthus annuus, **Sunflower.** Height up to 10 ft (3 m); flowering time summer/autumn: cream to deep purple. Sow three seeds at a time and remove the two weaker seedlings later. Distance between plants should be at least 20–24 in (50–60 cm). Among the most interesting sunflowers are varieties of *Helianthus annuus*, growing to about 4 ft (2 m+), which have flowers in combinations of copper or bronze, red and yellow. For perennial sunflower see chapter HARDY PERENNIALS.

Hardy annuals: 2–5 ft (60–150 cm)

Amaranthus, **Love-lies-bleeding, Joseph's coat.** Height, according to species and varieties, 24–31 in (60-80 cm); flowering time July till first frosts; colour of flowers: purplish brown, crimson, also whitish green. The species *A. tricolor* (Joseph's coat), which comes from India, has strikingly patterned reddish green leaves; the flowers themselves are greenish, and the familiar drooping form, *A. caudatus* (love-lies-bleeding), grows 2–4 ft (60–120 cm) high, has green leaves and crimson flowers. Half-hardy in some areas.

Centaurea, **Cornflower, sweet sultan.** Height 2–2½ ft (60–80 cm); flowering time July to September; colour of flowers: white, pink, mauve, blue. Sow in the open in April, thin out later to a distance of 12–20 in (30–50 cm) between plants: any soil, prefers sun. Varieties of *Centaurea cyanus*, cornflower-blue, shades of red, white, single or double, height 35 in (90 cm) and *C. moschata* (sweet sultan), flowers of various colours, height 31 in (80 cm), all look attractive.

Coreopsis, **Coreopsis, tickweed.** Height 2–3 ft (60–100 cm); flowering time summer/autumn; golden-yellow, maroon or crimson star-shaped flowers with brown centres. Sow in rows in the open from the end of March to the beginning of April, thin out to 12–16 in (30–40 cm); young plants will take root easily. Generally sold as mixtures of varieties of *Coreopsis tinctoria* and *C. drummondii*. The dwarf varieties, only 8–12 in (20–30 cm) high, are good for bedding.

Delphinium ajacis, **Annual larkspur, rocket larkspur.** Height, up to 40 in (100 cm); flowering time June to September; flowers borne in racemes: white, pink, ultramarine to dark blue. Sow in the open where it is to flower in early summer, or sow the previous autumn; for late summer flowering sow in March/April; sow thinly in rows, or else sow broadcast, and thin the seedlings to 16–20 in (40–50 cm) round each. A good selection: *Delphinium ajacis* vr. 'Dwarf Hyacinth-flowered'. Equally beautiful in their own way are *D. consolida* 'Giant Imperial' varieties, with many flowering stems branching out from the base, white or mixed colours, usually pure violet, growing up to 50 in (125 cm) tall.

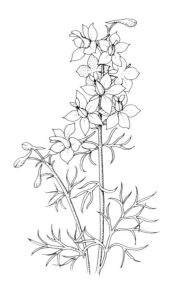

Delphinium ajacis, Larkspur

Gaillardia, **Gaillardia, blanket flower.** Height 12–40 in (30–100 cm); flowering time August/October; colour of flowers: bright yellow to blood-red. Sow in the open from the end of March to the beginning of April. Later thin out to 12 in (30 cm) round each plant. Sun and good soil. Choose annual varieties and hybrids of *G. aristata*. Perennial gaillardias: see chapter HARDY PERENNIALS.

Helichrysum bracteatum, **Everlasting flower, straw flower.** Height 1–3 ft (30–100 cm); flowering time July/October; flowers red, pink, white; the calyx of the flower is stiff and straw-like. Sow thinly where the plants are to flower at the end of April, and thin out to 12–16 in (30–40 cm). Good soil and sun. To dry the flowers as a charming winter decoration, cut the buds just before they open and hang them up in bunches tied by the stems.

Kochia, **Summer cypress, burning bush.** Height 24–31 in (60–80 cm); small, insignificant flowers. There are two varieties cultivated: 1) *Kochia scoparia trichophylla*, whose fine, narrow leaves turn deep red; 2) *Kochia* 'Childsii', with even more delicate foliage which keeps its light green colour. These charming light green little foliage plants seed themselves readily, and live almost unaided from one summer to the next, but must be treated as half-hardy in some areas.

Lupinus hartwegii, **Annual lupin.** Height 24–28 in (60–70 cm); flowering time June/October; colour: blue flushed with white or pink. Sow in the open where the plants are to flower, very thinly, in April, and thin out to 4 in (10 cm). Needs sandy, lime-free soil, and does not like being transplanted. Varieties of *L. hartwegii* include those with flowers of yellow, pink and lavender. Cutting back the stems after flowering is recommended.

Malope trifida, **Malope.** Height 2–3 ft (60–100 cm); flowering time June/July to October; colour of flowers:

Malope

white, pink, purple. Sow at the beginning of April, later thin to 16–20 in (40–50 cm) round each plant. The large, handsome, cup-shaped flowers grow on short stems from the axils, as is usual with the mallow family. To prevent mallow rust, spray with a copper preparation or with propiconazole.

Tagetes **African, French and Afro-French marigolds.** Height 24–30 in (60–75 cm); flowering time July/autumn; colours: golden-yellow, orange, red, velvety brown. Sow thinly in rows where the plants are to flower from the middle of May and thin to 16–20 in (40–50 cm), or buy plants ready to put out. Likes rich soil that absorbs water and sun. Extremely robust as cut flowers, remaining fresh for three weeks or more. For small varieties and hybrids see **Hardy annuals under 12 in (30 cm).** Often treated as half-hardy.

Xeranthemum annuum, **Paper flower.** Height up to 40 in (100 cm); flowering time July/October; colours: white, pink, violet. Useful for bunches of dried flowers. The narrow, downy grey leaves grow on tall, straight stems which bear colourful flower heads. They keep even better if cut in dry weather just before they open. Sow thinly in rows in May, at a distance of 8–10 in (20–25 cm); give them a sunny position and water now and then.

Hardy annuals: 12–28 in (30–70 cm)

Calendula, **Pot marigold.** Height 12–28 in (30–70 cm); flowering time June/September; colour of flowers: canary yellow to deep orange. Sow in the open from the end of March to the beginning of April. Thin out young plants to 10–12 in (25–30 cm). For later flowerings make sowings in succession until the beginning of June. The plant seeds itself freely. Strains such as 'Pacific Beauty Mixed' and 'Radio' have flowers borne on long stems and are good for cutting.

Cheiranthus cheiri, **Annual wallflower.** Height 12–20 in (30–50 cm); flowering time August/October; colours: shades of red, yellow, bronze; fragrant. Most of the biennial cultivated plants can be raised on occasion as annuals, both double and single forms, with the object of getting them to flower over a long period in the autumn, instead of at their usual early summer flowering season. Sow in the open in April, thin out to 8 in (20 cm).

Chrysanthemum, **Annual chrysanthemum.** Height 12–24 in (30–60 cm); flowering time July/September; colour of flowers: all colours except blue. Excellent for cutting. Varieties of *C. carinatum*, *C. spectabile* and *C. coronarium* are most usually grown, in single or double-flowered forms. Sow in the open in April and thin to 12 in (30 cm). See chapter HARDY PERENNIALS for perennial types.

Clarkia, **Clarkia.** Height 16–24 in (40–60 cm); flowering time summer/autumn; colours: mauve, salmon-pink, deep red. Clarkia is closely related to the godetia. Varieties of *C. elegans* and *C. pulchella* are usually available. Raising under glass is necessary if you want early flowers. Otherwise sow in April where the plants are to flower, thin out to 10 in (25 cm); likes a sunny position. Cutting the plant back when it is mature does it good.

Eschscholzia californica, **Californian poppy.** Height 12–24 in (30–60 cm)); flowering time summer/autumn; colour of flowers: yellow, orange, carmine. Leave 8–12 in (20–30 cm) space all round the plant. Sown where the plants are to flower, in spring, it will flower until October, and seeds itself freely. Several lovely varieties, including double forms.

Eschscholzia californica, Californian poppy

Godetia, **Godetia.** Height 16–24 in (40–60 cm); flowering time summer/autumn; colour of flowers: white, yellow, red, mauve. The flowers may be single, semi-double or double, the last two generally prettily frilled. Sow thinly in rows at the end of March and transplant the seedlings to a distance of 6 in (15 cm) later.

Gypsophila elegans, **Gypsophila.** Height 12–20 in (30–50 cm); flowering time spring and autumn; colour of flowers: white, pink. Like all gypsophilas, this, the only cultivated garden species of the annual form, is a graceful plant. The long stems are suitable for bunches of cut flowers. Sow in September for a spring flowering, and make successional sowings from March to the end of July for summer flowers. Thin seedlings to 6–8 in (15–20 cm). For other gypsophilas, see chapter HARDY PERENNIALS.

Helipterum, **Helipterum.** Height 12–24 in (30–60 cm); flowering time June/September; colour of flowers: white, yellow, pink. The helipterum is one of those flowers that can be dried and used for flower arrangements. Sow in April, where the plants are to flower in rows, thinly, and thin out later to 6–8 ins (15–20 cm) apart. Flowers appear eight to twelve weeks after sowing. There are various cultivated forms, with single and double blooms.

Lathyrus odoratus, **Dwarf sweet pea.** Height 12–28 in (30–70 cm); flowering time early summer to autumn; colour of flowers: all shades of white, pink, red, blue, purple, lavender, yellow. Sow in the open where the plants are to flower in April, and space the seeds 4–6 in (10–15 cm) apart and 3 in (8 cm) deep. These dwarf varieties need no support and are best pinched to encourage bushiness and a mass of flowers. For tall climbing varieties see chapter CLIMBING PLANTS.

Linum grandiflorum, **Flax.** Height 12–16 in (30–40 cm); flowering time June/October; colour: blood-red. Sow in the open when the plants are to flower from April onwards, thin out to 8 in (20 cm). Very undemanding; likes sun. The variety 'Rubrum' has brilliant red flowers.

Nigella damascena, **Love-in-a-mist.** Height 8–24 in (20–60 cm); flowering time summer; colour: blue or white with green. Sow in the open in spring or autumn, thin out to 4–6 in (10–15 cm). The most handsome variety is the double 'Miss Jekyll', with sky-blue flowers on long stems. 'Persian Jewels' has rose, pink and white tints in addition to light and dark blue. All are good for cutting.

Papaver, **Poppy.** Height 20–24 in (50–60 cm); flowers from early summer to early autumn, many colours: does not like being transplanted. The most important species here is *Papaver somniferum*, the opium poppy. Sow in autumn for an early flowering, and for later flowerings sow thinly in the open in March, where it is to flower, and thin out to 8–12 in (20–30 cm). Poppies like sunny positions. The plant seeds itself freely, so break off the seed capsules just before they ripen. *Papaver rhoeas*, the field poppy or Shirley poppy, is obtainable in delightful pastel shades. There are double and single varieties, growing to 24–28 in (60–70 cm) in height.

Phacelia tanacetifolia, **Phacelia.** Height 16–24 in (40–60 cm); flowering time June/September; colour of flowers: white, sky-blue. Make successive sowings from the end of March to June, thin out to 4–6 in (10–15 cm), or transplant in clumps. Another attractive species I should mention is *Phacelia campanularia*, with bell-shaped, gentian-blue flowers, only 6–12 in (15–30 cm) in height.

Scabiosa atropurpurea, **Sweet scabious.** Height 16–24 in (40–60 cm); flowering season summer/autumn; colour of flowers: white, blue, red, deep purple. Sow in the open at the beginning of May for summer flowering through till September. The taller, large-flowered strain 'Monarch Cockade Mixed' is probably better known than the basic species and is very good for cutting, as the flowers will last a long time. Likes a sunny situation. Keep dead-heading. Packets of mixed strains are also available. For *Scabiosa caucasica*, see chapter HARDY PERENNIALS.

Tropaeolum majus nanum, **Nasturtium.** Height 8–12 in (20–30 cm); flowering time June/September; colours: all shades of yellow and orange through to scarlet. The non-climbing dwarf forms of *Tropaeolum* are among the most rewarding and delightful annuals to grow. Either single or double, they are jacks of all trades and will create a blaze of glorious colour on the poorest of soils. Do not sow until well into May, sowing two to three seeds at once, at a planting distance of 6–8 in (15–20 cm). For the large climbing species see the chapter CLIMBING PLANTS.

Hardy annuals: under 12 in (30 cm)

Dimorphotheca, **Star of the Veldt.** Height 12 in (30 cm); flowering time end of June/October; colour of flowers: white, orange, salmon; petals edged with bright orange, shading to reddish brown. *D. aurantiaca* and its hybrids are most usually grown. Do not sow in the open until the middle of May to the beginning of June. Cultivate as for *Calendula* (p.75).

Iberis amara, **Candytuft.** Height 4–12 in (10–30 cm); flowering time May/August; colour of flowers: pink, lilac, maroon, red; borne in clusters. Sow where you want the plants to flower and thin out to 8 in (20 cm). Cultivation and cutting back as for *Lobularia*. The best to grow are 'Improved White Spiral', 'Red Flash', and 'Dwarf Fairy Mixed'. As distinct from this annual form, *Iberis sempervirens*, the evergreen candytuft, is a perennial sub-shrub of broad, bushy habit, which is described in the chapter ROCK GARDENS.

Lobularia maritima, **Alyssum.** Height 3–6 in (8–15 cm); flowering time summer, depending on the time of sowing; colours: white, pink, purple, mauve. Often known as *Alyssum maritimum*. Favourite cultivated varieties are 'Little Dorrit' (white), 'Royal Carpet' (deep violet), and 'Wonderland' (red). Sow in succession from March to June. Continues in flower for a month. If you cut the plants hard back after flowering a lavish second flowering will appear within a few weeks.

Mesembryanthemum criniflorum (Dorotheanthus bellidiformis), **Livingstone daisy.** Height 6–8 in/15–20 cm; flowering time June/September; colour of flowers: white, pink, purple, mixed seeds; needs a warm, sunny situation and dry, light to sandy soil. Sow in the open in April and give protection from late frosts. The flowers open fully only at midday in bright sunshine.

Nemophila menziesii (N. insignis), **Baby blue eyes.** Height 6–8 in (15–20 cm); flowering time summer to autumn; colour of flowers: blue; white and pink varieties also available. *Nemophila* requires light shade at the edge of groups of trees under ornamental shrubs. Sow in the open from March to April, with successive sowings until June according to when you want the flowers. The flowering season will last only 4–6 weeks.

Nemophila, Baby blue eyes

Portulaca grandiflora, **Sun plant.** Height 4–6 in (10–15 cm); flowering season, summer; all colours apart from blue, both single and double. Sow in the open in May where the plants are to flower. The seeds, which are very small, should only be pressed lightly into the ground. Will do well in any sandy, dry sunny position.

Reseda odorata, **Mignonette.** Height 8–12 in (20–30 cm); flowering time June/October; insignificant greenish or reddish petals with yellow or red stamens, very fragrant. Best sown in the open where it is to flower in the middle of April and thinned out to 5–6 in (12–15 cm) apart. Successive sowings can be made until June. Undemanding.

Silene armeria, **Campion catchfly.** Height 12 in (30 cm); flowering time July/September; colour of flowers: carmine. A colourful annual which will often bloom as early as May if sown in autumn. Spring sowings present no problems. For perennial varieties, see the chapter HARDY PERENNIALS.

Tagetes patula, **Dwarf French marigold.** Height up to 8 in (20 cm); flowering season according to the time of sowing; colours: yellow, bronze, red; double and single varieties. Do not sow in the open before the middle of May, you will then get flowers in August. For earlier flowerings raise in trays indoors, or in a nursery bed. Plant out 6–8 in (15–20 cm) apart. Grows in thick clumps covered with little flowers. Not hardy in all districts.

Half-hardy annuals: over 3 ft (100 cm)

Althaea rosea (chinensis) hybrids, **Annual hollyhock.** Height 6½–8 ft (2–2·5 m) (stake the plants!); flowering time August/September; all colours except blue, many varieties. Sow in trays indoors or raise under glass in March; plant out in April at a distance of 20–32 in (50–80 cm); likes deep, fresh soil. Half-shade. *Malva crispa*, the frilled hollyhock, is another annual, growing to 3–6½ ft (1–2 m), and useful at the back of a herbaceous border to fill any gaps. For perennial hollyhocks see chapter HARDY PERENNIALS; for biennial hollyhocks, see BIENNIALS. It is not always easy to draw a sharp distinction between annual and biennial forms. In mild areas annual hollyhocks can be treated as hardy annuals.

Cleome spinosa, **Spider flower.** This tall plant, usually growing to over 3 ft (1 m) high, bearing many branches all the way up the stem, looks rather like a narrow bush, with curiously formed flowers borne in panicles at the ends of the shoots. Planted in groups, *Cleome* is an eye-catching plant anywhere. The best varieties for planting in groups are 'Pink Queen', the pure white 'Helen Campbell' and 'Colour Fountain Mixed'. Young plants are put out in the open in the latter part of May, and spaced 20 in (50 cm) apart. Flowering from July to the end of September.

Cosmos, **Cosmea.** Height up to 4 ft (1·30 m); flowering time June/late autumn; colour of flowers: pure white,

Cosmos, Cosmea

pink, scarlet, dark violet, yellow. Most important species: *Cosmos bipinnatus* and its hybrids, with feathery, fine-cut leaves; *C. sulphureus* with its beautiful hybrids in shades of orange to gold. Set out young plants about the middle of May and put them out 16 in (40 cm) apart. Keep them fairly short of nourishment, for if they have rich soil or a lot of fertilizer they will simply run to foliage without forming many flowers. As mentioned already in this chapter in the section on removing flower heads, dead-heading withered cosmea flowers has a particularly good effect.

Ricinus communis, **Castor oil plant.** Height 6½–10 ft (2–3 m); flowering time autumn; flowers white and insignificant. Plant the speckled beans in good compost in small flower-pots in the middle of March, and keep them at room temperature. After the roots show through the bottom of the pots transfer to larger pots. Transplant the ricinus plants, which will be a good size by now, to a sunny, warm, sheltered site in the garden after the last May frosts, or in more exposed places not till the beginning of June. Its majestic appearance, and handsome palmate leaves, has given it the name of 'Palma Christi'. I would select the forms 'Zanzibarensis' with enormous leaves up to 10 in (25 cm) across; and 'Sanguineus', about 6½ ft (2 m), with very large leaves, greenish red to blood-red. The seeds, which ripen in a spiny case, are poisonous so it is best to break them off in good time.

Ricinus, Castor oil plant

Half-hardy annuals: 2–3 ft (60–100 cm)

Antirrhinum majus, **Snapdragon.** Height up to over 40 in (100 cm); flowering time June/October; many colours. Raise young plants to put out in late May 10–12 in (25–30 cm) apart. It will be happy with almost any garden soil, likes sun or half-shade. It keeps on and on producing flowers until the first frost, and often seeds itself so freely that you will find a number of seedlings next spring which have over-wintered and can be transplanted. (See also dwarf varieties on p.85.)

Callistephus chinensis, **China aster.** Height up to 24 in (60 cm); flowering time summer/autumn, all colours, single or double blooms. Put out in May. The China aster is one of the favourite and most important annuals. You can have countless different varieties blooming in your garden in succession, from the end of July to the first frosts. It makes few demands, likes a sunny position and well-drained soil which has been manured some time before. Grow only 'wilt-resistant' varieties.

Mirabilis jalapa, **Marvel of Peru, four-o-clock flower.** Height up to 40 in (100 cm); flowering time July/September; colour of flowers: white, yellow, red, and also striped mixtures of these colours. Plant out from the end of May, 20 in (50 cm) apart, in deep, loamy soil containing some lime. Needs a sunny position; water in dry weather. Like dahlia tubers, should be lifted in autumn and stored during the winter.

Nicotiana, **Tobacco plant.** Height 24–32 in (60–80 cm); flowering time summer/autumn; colour of flowers: all shades of red, yellow, white. The hybrid forms of the tobacco plant embrace a number of beautiful and decorative flowers, very easy to grow. Best known are forms of *Nicotiana affinis*. Plant out after the middle of May in good soil, water in dry weather, and give occasional applications of fertilizer.

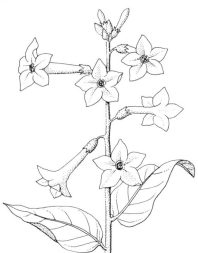

Nicotiana, Tobacco plant

Penstemon hartwegii, **Annual penstemon.** Height 28 in (70 cm); flowering time summer/autumn; colour of flowers: white, pink, red, carmine, blue, often striped or flushed, with a white throat. Especially handsome are 'Large Flowered Mixed' and 'Bouquet Mixed'. Plant out after the middle of May.

Rudbeckia hirta, **Annual coneflower, black-eyed Susan.** Height 32 in (80 cm); flowering time August/September; colour of flowers: golden yellow, orange, sometimes bicoloured, often with a dark centre. The annual rudbeckia very much resembles the perennial species, described in the chapter HARDY PERENNIALS. It comes from North America, and forms handsome, strong, bushy plants. An outstanding new strain is called simply 'Giant Tetraploid Hybrids' and has beautiful daisy-shaped flowers up to 7 in (18 cm) across. Another favourite is *Rudbeckia hirta* 'Marmalade'. Annual rudbeckias are fairly undemanding; plant them after the middle of May. They usually seed themselves.

Salpiglossis sinuata, **Salpiglossis.** Height 24–32 in (60–80 cm); flowering time summer; colour of flowers: white, yellow, pink to dark red, blue, with coloured veins and a velvety texture. This is the only species worth cultivating, along with F_1 and F_2 hybrids bred from it. Sow in heat in March and plant out in late May. Of course so magnificent a plant needs good, nourishing soil. It does not require a lot of water. Cultivate more or less as for *Nicotiana*.

Zinnia elegans, **Zinnia.** Height 24–40 in (60–100 cm); flowering time summer; all colours except blue. Outstanding as a long-lasting cut flower. Sow in a warm nursery bed from March to the beginning of April, plant out in the middle of May 12 in (30 cm) apart; protect from cold. Zinnias are easy to transplant so long as the ball of soil round their roots remains intact and the job is not done in bright sunlight. You can even buy plants in flower. Fertilizer and plenty of water will increase their willingness to go on blooming for some months. There are countless species, varieties and hybrids, including dwarf forms growing only 6 in (15 cm) high.

Zinnia elegans, Zinnia

Half-hardy annuals: 8–36 in (20–60 cm)

Calceolaria gracilis, **Slipper flower.** Height 12–16 in (30–40 cm); flowering time July until the first frosts; colour: yellow. All the work really necessary is putting it in in June and taking it out after the first frosts – and in return you get flowers for a good quarter of the year.

Coleus blumei, **Flame nettle.** Height 8–24 in (20–60 cm); flowers insignificant but leaves of many colours and usually variegated. Plants can be bought in mid-May ready to put out in borders or as an edging plant. Likes a very sunny situation and damp soil with plenty of peat and as little lime as possible. Removing flower heads will increase the beauty of the foliage. Many varieties available.

Gazania, **Gazania.** Height 8–20 in (20–50 cm); flowering time June/October; the new hybrid varieties range from many shades of gold and orange to carmine. They will do well where there is plenty of sun and good, dry soil containing little nitrogen. Put out in the latter part of May.

Heliotropium, **Heliotrope, cherry pie.** Height up to 24 in (60 cm); flowering time July/September; colour of flowers dark violet. Set out plants, complete with ball of soil, after the middle of May and give them a sunny, sheltered position.

Impatiens, **Balsam, busy Lizzie.** Height 12–24 in (30–60 cm); flowering time June/September; all colours apart from yellow and blue, many bicoloured; many varieties and hybrids. Buy young plants from a garden centre and plant 6–8 in (15–20 cm) apart. It requires nourishing, damp soil and does not mind shade. It also does well in boxes on balconies, and as a pot plant.

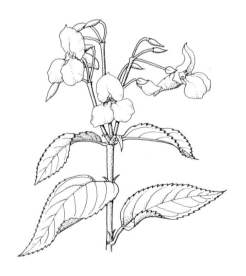

Impatiens, Balsam

Matthiola incana, **Stock.** Height 20–24 in (50–60 cm); flowering time June to autumn; all colours. There is an extensive range of classes and special strains. Plant close together (no more than 4 in (10 cm) apart) from the last third of May onwards. Where single-flowering plants appear among the double ones pull them out. There are also dwarf stocks, only 8–10 in (20–25 cm) high.

Mimulus, **Monkey flower.** Height 8–20 in (20–50 cm); flowering time June/September; colours: yellow, flecked, also crimson. The monkey flower is a marvellously vivid plant, whose charm lies in the frequent changes of colour of the flowers. There are many fine cultivated forms. In mild areas *M. luteus* in particular lasts so well that it is grown as a perennial. All monkey flowers require damp soil with plenty of humus and nourishment. Light shade beside a garden pool (not with its feet in stagnant water, though) is exactly right for it.

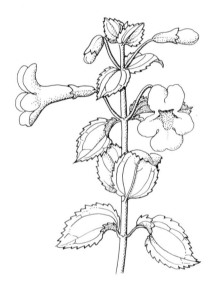

Mimulus, Monkey flower

Pelargonium, **Geranium.** Height 8–24 in (20–60 cm); flowering time summer until autumn; colour of flowers: shades of white, pink, red. The many new hybrids are easy to raise from seed in warm conditions and are best transplanted to 4 in (10 cm) pots before setting out in June. Plants can also be bought when in flower. Can be lifted and used for cuttings in late autumn.

Petunia hybrids, **Petunia.** Height 12 in (30 cm); flowering time June to autumn; colours include cream, pink, red, mauve, blue, primrose and bicolours. New strains and classes are being bred all the time. F_1 hybrids are considered particularly resistant to rain. Every catalogue will give you details. Set out well-grown plants already in flower from the middle of May onwards; they take root

Four popular summer flowers. *Top left:* snapdragon *(Antirrhinum). Top right:* scabious *(Scabiosa). Bottom left:* spider flower *(Cleome spinosa). Bottom right:* Canterbury bell *(Campanula medium).*

Top left: white garden daisy. *Top right: Coreopsis. Bottom left: Rudbeckia. Bottom right: Erigeron.*

Top left: Anemone. Top right: stonecrop *(Sedum). Bottom left: Aubrieta. Bottom right:* house leek *(Sempervivum).*

The winter aconite *(Eranthis hyemalis)* is the first spring flower to blossom after the snow.

easily when planted with the ball of soil intact, and will carry on growing. For the rest, give them enough water in dry periods and keep dead-heading the withered flowers.

Phlox drummondii, **Annual phlox.** Height 12–20 in (30–50 cm); flowering time summer/autumn; colour of flowers: all colours, sometimes with an eye. A distinction is drawn between tall and short annual phloxes; there are many varieties of both. The tall annual phlox, *Phlox drummondii grandiflora*, has been known in our gardens for over fifty years, but new strains and improvements are still being produced. The dwarf forms of *P. d. nana compacta* grow only 8–10 in (20–25 cm) tall, and are cultivated in the same way. You can safely plant out seedlings about the middle of May.

Salvia splendens, **Salvia.** Height 14–16 in (35–40); flowering time summer; colour of flowers: purple, shades of red. The bright red of salvia is seen anywhere where loud colours are called for. Plant small groups in a border of perennials, or mix salvias and ageratums. 'Tom Thumb Scarlet' is a charming dwarf variety, height 7–8 in (18–20 cm).

Salvia

Verbena × hybrida, **Garden verbena, vervain.** Height 7–8 in (15–40 cm); flowering time June/October; many colours. Young plants with a good ball of soil can be put out any time after the middle of May, either before or during flowering. Catalogues always name many individual varieties and mixtures of the various tall or short types. A particularly popular addition is the 'Rainbow Mixture'.

Half-hardy annuals: under 12 in (30 cm)

Ageratum, **Ageratum.** Height 6–8 in (15–20 cm); flowering time summer to autumn; colour of flowers: blue, pink,

white. The ageratum is so common a garden plant that I need not say much about its cultivation. The tall ageratum – height of stem up to 24 in (60 cm) – is good for cut flowers.

Antirrhinum majus dwarf hybrids, **Dwarf snapdragon.** Height 8 in (20 cm); flowering time June/October; all colours. The delightful dwarf forms of the tall snapdragon, described earlier (p.78), are cultivated in the same way. Suitable for planting in the joints of dry walls.

Begonia semperflorens group, **Begonia.** Height 3–8 in (8–20 cm); flowering time June/October; colour of flowers: white, pink, red. Leaves green or purple. Many varieties. Sun and half-shade. Set out young plants in May. *Begonia semperflorens* is more often planted in tubs on balconies than in the open. For tuberous begonias, see chapter BULBOUS PLANTS.

Celosia, **Cockscomb.** Height 10–14 in (25–35 cm); flowering time summer; colour of flowers: red or yellow. You can get some remarkable effects from the cockscomb *C. argentea* 'Cristata' with its grotesque appearance and *C.a.* 'Plumosa' varieties with their pyramidal flowers. It needs very nourishing soil, frequent applications of compound fertilizer in liquid form, and a sunny position.

Dianthus, **Annual pink.** Height 4–12 in (10–30 cm); flowering time mid-summer to autumn; colours: red, pink, white, variegated, also double forms. Set out young plants 10 in (25 cm) apart. Cultivation as for perennial pinks (p. 104). The most important varieties and hybrids: 'Persian Carpet', 'Queen of Hearts', 'Magic Charms' and 'Telstar'. The *D. heddewigii* 'Dwarf Baby Doll Mixed' strain has large flowers on short, erect stems.

Dianthus, Pink

Lobelia erinus, **Lobelia.** Height 4–6 in (10–15 cm); flowering time June/September; colours: blue, red and white. Lobelias can be transplanted at any time, even in flower. They like poor soil and will go on blooming tirelessly until the first frosts if you keep cutting back the withered flowers. Favourite varieties: the azure 'Cambridge Blue'; the deep blue, white-eyed 'Mrs Clibran Improved'; the carmine 'Rosamond', which has a white eye; the large-flowered white 'White Lady'. For the popular old trailing lobelia *L. erinus* 'Pendula', see the chapter CLIMBING PLANTS.

Nemesia strumosa, **Nemesia.** Height 6–12 in (15–30 cm); flowering time summer to autumn; colours: shades of blue, red, white. Plant out 6 in (15 cm) apart in May. Grows easily and flowers quickly. Popular varieties include 'Blue Gem' and 'Carnival Mixed'.

Biennials

Between the annuals and the long-lasting perennials is a small but horticulturally important group of biennial flowering plants. They are sown between early summer and autumn of the first year, germinate and put out leaves, and are usually transplanted to their eventual site some time from late summer onwards. Here they spend the winter, sometimes with some kind of protection over them. The flowers and seed-bearing organs develop during the next vegetative season. Finally, biennials seed themselves freely, and then die. However, not all of them die down completely at the end of their second summer; given the right conditions some of them will keep going for several years, and in fact are so persistent that the precise classification of such in-between species is somewhat dubious. My list of biennials, again, is alphabetically arranged according to their botanical names.

Since one wants the development of biennials to proceed slowly during the first summer and autumn it is best to raise pansies or forget-me-nots, sweet Williams or biennial wallflowers, in a seedbed under some kind of protective covering which will give shade and retain humidity. For summer-time seedbeds of this kind see the chapter SOWING AND PLANTING OUT. You can also use empty frames whose glass panels can easily be shaded with

Love-in-a-mist

Poppy

matting. There is no need for any special feeding, especially not for the young plants. Keeping them short of nourishment suits them better, and restrains their growth.

Most biennials need to be pricked out after the formation of the third leaf, when they should be given 2–4 in (5–10 cm) between the seedlings, before they are put out to their final site in autumn. One more thing: it is always a good idea to give some form of light protection against cold from the end of November onwards. Raising biennials in one's own garden can be tricky, and some gardeners prefer to buy young plants at planting time.

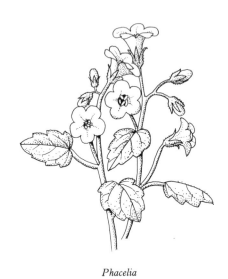

Phacelia

Summary of garden biennials

Althaea rosea (A. chinensis), **Hollyhock.** Height up to 10 ft (3 m) (stake the plants!); flowering time July/September; colours: white, red, pink, mauve and subtle shades of yellow. Sow in the open in June/July; it is not necessary to prick the plants out. The best time to plant out is October, since the hollyhock grows very long tap roots, and it is often difficult to transplant the next spring. Take care that the roots do not get bent or twisted. Needs good, well-manured soil, plenty of space – plant out 24 in (60 cm) apart – and sun. If the soil is too dry, or the plants are too close together, the hollyhock is prone to hollyhock rust. Several hybrid varieties are grown as annuals; see under **Annuals.** For perennial hollyhocks, see the chapter HARDY PERENNIALS.

Bellis perennis, **Daisy.** Height, up to 6 in (15 cm); diameter of plants 4–6 in (10–15 cm); flowering time March/October; colours: white, pink, red. Sow in the open in August, mixing the very fine seeds with sand; no need to prick out. Plant out in autumn 4–6 in (10–15 cm) apart.

Sows itself very freely. Both these self-sown young plants and those raised from seed bear mostly single blooms, so it is better to propagate the plant by division every year, choosing only specimens with good double flowers. Countless varieties, including F_1 hybrids, in many colours ranging from white, through carmine, to dark red.

Campanula medium, **Canterbury bell.** Height 20–35 in (50–90 cm); flowering time June/August; colours: white, blue, pink; bears clusters of large, hanging flowers. Sow in a cold frame or a sheltered seedbed in the open in May/June, prick out, and plant out in autumn 12–16 in (30–40 cm) apart. Will do well in any sunny part of the garden.

Cheiranthus cheiri, **Wallflower.** Height 12–28 in (30–70 cm); flowering time April/July; colours: shades of yellow, red, bronze, purple. Fragrant. There are two forms of growth: 1) The rather round, many-branched 'bush wallflower', with single or double flowers, and a wonderful scent – there are also dwarf bush wallflowers, only up to 12 in (30 cm) high. 2) The single-stemmed, large-flowered 'erect wallflower', which reaches its full height and beauty only in the best soils. Sow in a cold frame or sheltered seedbed in the open in May, pricking out advisable, plant out August/September at a distance of 10 in (25 cm). Wallflowers love nourishing, loamy soil and sunlight, and will sometimes last three or four years. *Cheiranthus allioni,* Siberian wallflower, and its varieties are also popular and tend to flower for a longer period. See section on **Annuals** for the cultivation of the same species as an annual.

Dianthus barbatus, **Sweet William.** Height 12–24 in (30–60 cm); flowering time June/August; colours: purple, red, white. Sow in June in a cold frame or sheltered seedbed in the open. Prick out the seedlings, plant out in autumn. Sweet Williams love full sun and nourishing soil. The clove pink, carnation or gilly flower, *Dianthus caryophyllus,* is sometimes cultivated as a biennial too. Its beautiful double varieties nearly always produce a certain percentage of single flowers. For annual species of *Dianthus* see the preceding section; for perennial pinks see chapters HARDY PERENNIALS and ROCK GARDENS.

Digitalis purpurea, **Foxglove.** Height up to 60 in (150 cm); flowering time June/July; colours: many shades from white to crimson, also blotched and striped forms. Sow in a seedbed in the open in June; it is not necessary to prick out. Plant out in August at a distance of 12–16 in (30–40 cm). Foxgloves like light shade and soil with plenty of humus, not too much lime, and rather dry soil. Small species like *Digitalis lutea* are perennials. The largest and most attractive flowers are produced by the 'Excelsior Hybrids'.

Digitalis purpurea, Foxglove

Euphorbia lathyrus, **Caper spurge.** Height 16–40 in (40–100 cm); flowering time July/August; flowers yellow but insignificant, surrounded by broad, tall leaves. Sow in June/July, for preference in groups scattered throughout the garden, or plant out in the same way in the autumn. These are undemanding plants, and sow themselves so freely that their offspring can become as much of a nuisance as weeds. The roots are said to excrete a substance disliked by moles.

Myosotis, **Garden forget-me-not.** Height 3–8 in (7–20 cm); flowering time April/June; colours: azure-blue, deep blue, also pink and white. The original species are *Myosotis alpestris,* the alpine forget-me-not, and *Myosotis sylvatica,* the woodland forget-me-not, from which are descended the varieties preferred for growing in the garden and the large-flowered hybrid forms more often used in pots. Sow in a seedbed in the open in June/July, prick out, and plant out in September 6 in (15 cm) apart. It seeds itself so freely that you will have more young plants than you know what to do with in succeeding autumns. All forget-me-nots like a good, rather damp soil, and sun to half-shade. Tall varieties are suitable for cut flowers. For perennial forget-me-nots see chapter HARDY PERENNIALS.

Senecio cineraria, **Senecio.** This attractive plant, with its many-lobed, downy grey leaves, is on the very border of the biennial group. However that may be, *Senecio,* still known commercially by its old botanical name *Cineraria maritima,* is so remarkably a handsome a plant that one would not want to do without it. It fills gaps in closely carpeted beds and in borders of perennials. It can grow to 8–16 in (20–40 cm). Even prettier, because the leaves are more feathery and it is more compact in growth, is the strain 'Silver Dust'. Cutting back in spring will prolong the life of the plant. If treated as a biennial, sow in summer and give winter protection. In exposed areas, it is better raised and treated as a half-hardy annual.

Verbascum, **Mullein.** Height 60–80 in (150–200 cm); flowering time June/August; colour: yellow. Sow in a seedbed in the open in June/July; it germinates in 6–10

Verbascum, Mullein

days. Plant out in August/September. Very undemanding, but likes sun. Seeds itself freely, and often lasts more than two years, like a perennial. The old, original species (*V. bombyciferum, V. nigrum, V. olympicum*), which really are only biennial, are often replaced these days by hybrids such as the 'Phoeniceum Hybrids', with yellow, apricot, creamy white, rose or mauve flowers, 'Arctic Summer', or 'Suttons Silver Spire'. Since the seeds of these hybrids do not breed true, the plants must be propagated vegetatively, by dividing or taking root cuttings.

Viola × *wittrockiana* hybrids, **Pansy.** Height 8–12 in (20–30 cm); flowering time spring and autumn; all colours, mostly with markings. Sow in a sheltered seedbed in the open in July, prick out once, plant out in the open from September onwards at a distance of 6–8 in (15–20 cm). In exposed areas it is better to keep the young plants in their sheltered bed during the winter and not plant out until spring. Sun and nourishing soil are desirable for the flowering site. There are countless strains of pansy; you will find details in any catalogue. The hardiest are the so-called 'Winter Flowering Mixed' strains, which, if sown early, will begin to flower the same winter, and start flowering again as soon as the snow has melted. The word 'giant' indicates the size of the flowers, which can be really enormous, up to 4 in (10 cm) across. Thus we have the famous 'Roggli Giant Strain' and a number of more modern hybrids.

10
Hardy perennials

Perennials are the backbone of the flower garden. Living in the same spot for years, as they often do, they establish a decorative scheme of their own; they make all kinds of gardening pleasures available with their many different possible uses, from borders and informal groups to rock gardens and dry walls. There are a good many things to be borne in mind if you are a beginner and do not want to pay too highly for your apprenticeship. Some people will choose any sort of bed, stick a few plants in the ground because they liked the look of them, and think they have done all that is necessary. Not so: it takes proper knowledge to grow really beautiful, free-flowering perennials. We have to take into consideration the conditions in which various plants like to live, their height, their size, their flowering times and the colour of their flowers if we are to choose the right perennials and put them in at the right places. And they are joined by all the other ornamental plants – annuals and biennials, flowering bulbs and tubers, ornamental grasses and ferns, roses and ornamental shrubs, evergreens and conifers – to make up the kind of garden which really looks like a work of art.

Beauty through harmony

The first flower of all is the Christmas rose, at the turn of the year. It is followed by smaller plants such as the snowdrop, aconite, crocus, scilla, grape hyacinth, hepatica and saxifrage, and larger ones such as the tulip, hyacinth, narcissus, arabis, the whole colourful tribe of primulas and many others, until in May we have buds and flowers in profusion to see us through the summer months. We pass into autumn with dahlias, and Michaelmas daisies provide a last blaze of colour at the end of the gardening year. All of these flowers, however, need to be carefully used, kept within bounds, and grown in harmony with each other.

Tall perennials must grow behind, not in front of, smaller kinds. Cottage garden flowers like hollyhocks or golden rod look out of place among the exotic dwarf conifers of the modern rock garden. You can plant miniature roses or pinks in a cheerful, homely bed containing columbines, gypsophila and dicentra or bleeding heart. On the other hand, the harmonious blend of colour of red climbing roses, delphiniums and madonna lilies always seems to express the glory of the garden at its most beautiful, and the bright yellow of broom, with the deeper gold of the trollius or globe flower, stands out particularly well in contrast to the blue of bell-flowers and the taller species of speedwell. Even more than in a short-lived flower arrangement, the colours, flower shapes and whole arrangement of the plants according to certain basic rules give a herbaceous border an artistic harmony, which for the most part is deeply rooted, for biological reasons, in the needs of various plants which either go well together or are mutually exclusive.

For the rest, everything we plant in our beds or borders should be rewarding and undemanding to grow, and should stay in the same place for several years if possible without any deterioration in the plant's willingness to flower, and without spoiling the general impression. Of course, one could easily extend the lists which follow later by adding dozens of delightful flowers, and many gardeners may find some of their favourites missing from my selection. However, that is inevitable, within the limits of a book such as this, and so I will fall back on the old saying that a true master shows his art in restraint.

Composition of the soil and general rules for planting

All perennials, unless anything to the contrary is expressly indicated, need soil which has been deeply dug, if possible

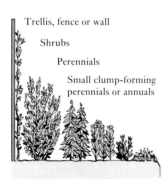

Trellis, fence or wall

Shrubs

Perennials

Small clump-forming perennials or annuals

Remember differences in height when planting a border, putting the tallest plants at the back. When planting a bed, the tallest subjects are placed in the middle.

to a depth of two spits, and has had the subsoil beneath it turned or loosened with spade or hoe. Altogether, the soil should be cultivated to a depth of about 20 in (50 cm). In doing this, one must take care that the layer of topsoil remains on top. If you have good garden soil, well cultivated over a long period, feed it by working in as much good compost as possible, or if compost is not available, a mild peat-based compound fertilizer in the correct quantity. If the soil is heavy and sticky, one should also add equal quantities of peat and sand, to lighten and aerate it. For light soils peat only is sufficient; it should be moistened and crumbled up fine the day before application. A bale of peat will be enough to supply about 12 sq yd (10 sq m); one must take care that the peat is worked only into the topsoil layer. Naturally, this general rule does not apply to all perennials. Where particular demands are going to be made on the composition of the soil in certain individual cases – for instance, if a plant dislikes lime, needs an exceptionally rich soil, or a particularly poor one – you will find this indicated in the individual descriptions. One should always bear in mind that planting perennials is a long-term measure, and needs to be done with all the appropriate attention to detail.

If plants have been out of the ground for some time when they reach you and look rather limp, they should be allowed to recover before planting: store them in a cool place, give them a good drenching with water, or heel them in a shady, very damp spot in the garden. Only fresh, firm plants are ready to go into the ground, and in a fit state to take root successfully – a considerable task for them to perform. When planting, prune all fibrous roots that are too long; a circle of roots a hand's breadth long around the stock is enough. Fleshy or woody roots can be slightly pruned too; take care that each cut is made cleanly, and the cut surface slopes diagonally outwards. It is a great mistake to force roots into the ground bent and twisted, against their natural direction of growth. You should also be careful, when firming the soil, not just to compress the plant; apply pressure to the whole surrounding area. Perennials dislike air pockets in their roots, and loose soil round them, as much as they hate to be planted either too deep or too shallow. Some apparently inexplicable losses are the result of such mistakes made through ignorance. If you plant delphiniums, columbines or lupins above the

Be careful to plant at the correct depth. Growth buds of the paeony should be just visible. If you plant too deep the paeony will not flower.

crown of the plant, or put paeonies into the ground too deep, you will not get their glorious blue, mauve and red flowers. They will simply go on strike, and may even die.

The best tool for planting perennials is the human hand, because of the sensitivity with which it can work. When the ground is so heavy or the roots so large that something more is needed, use a hand trowel to help you put the plants in. Always make a little trough or depression round the plant, for good moist conditions are the best way to ensure that it will take root well. It is also helpful to cover the soil around the plant with damp peat, compost, shredded bark or a light covering of leaves, to prevent the ground from drying out around the young, sparsely leaved plants, especially in the spring planting season. Other planting requirements are mentioned under the descriptions of individual plants.

Differences in the intensity of colour of the flowers are usually related to climate and situation. The higher our gardens, the deeper and brighter are the colours of our flowers. The same species of delphinium may be pale blue in a valley or on low ground, but deep gentian-blue in the purer air of higher altitudes. Conversely, alpine flowers, which have still not received enough attention from plant breeders to be sure of retaining their true colour, may well lose some of their depth of colour when transplanted to a lower level, however well they are acclimatized.

When and how much to plant

A basic rule is to plant all perennials during their dormant season, and so it is possible to plant many of them at the time when there is a pause in their growth in mid-summer, as well as the usual seasons: the autumn months, from early September to early November, and the springtime, when the ground is open but before the first young shoots come up. Of course, plants supplied in pots or containers can be planted even during their period of growth. However, we should always be on our guard against planting too much, too confusedly, in beds that are too wide; 6½ ft (2 m) should be the maximum width. A border that can look very sparsely filled, in fact almost empty, during its first summer can grow to be a positive jungle within the next two years, and the back of it will soon become quite impenetrable. You can get a pretty effect from planting several perennials of the same species in groups in such a way that there is a kind of natural rhythm in the transition from one variety to another. You should always leave a few spaces for annuals in your herbaceous border too. They help to create the most artistic effect, with the widest range of colours, especially in small borders, and as most summer-flowering perennials are rather tall the interpolation of annuals is a good way to make a transition to the lower, edging plants. A labour-saving modern idea is to keep the soil of the border practically free of weeds by planting decorative ground cover species, making a special eye-catching effect

Goat's beard	Monkshood		Sweet-scented raspberry	Bugbane VIII–IX		Monks-hood VII–VIII, X
VI–VII	Japanese anemone (pink) VIII–X	VII–VIII, X	VI–VIII	Japanese anemone (pink)	July-flowering cimicifuga VII–VIII	Monks-hood VII–VIII, X · Colum-bine V–VII
Japanese anemone (white) · Monks-hood VII–VIII, X	Columbine (yellow and red)		Japanese anemone (white) VIII–X	VIII–X	Colum-bine (yellow) V–VII	Fern
Fern · Barrenwort		V–VII	Fern	Geum V, IX	Balloon flower VII–VIII	
IV–V	Candelabra primula		Christmas rose (red) (white) I–III		Barrenwort	
Dwarf cotoneaster	Creeping jenny V–VII	V–VII		Pachysandra	IV–V	

Two planting plans for herbaceous borders, for half-shade and for sun. Squared-off planting areas 20 × 20 in (50 × 50 cm), one or several plants to each square according to size; width of bed 9 ft (2.80 m). Height of plants rising towards the back, but the heights should be well integrated. There will always be something in flower.
Ornamental shrubs create a pleasing effect even in winter.

The beds should look something like our pictures at the height of the summer flowering season in June to August. There are innumerable different possibilities, depending on the depth of your border and your choice of plants. The border can be extended on either side, by repetition of the plan shown in the same or a slightly different arrangement, just as you like. This gives large borders in particular a welcome 'rhythm' of recurrent combinations of plants. Since the individual species will spread at different rates, any impression of a severely geometrical plan will soon disappear. The front of the border, containing ground cover plants or low tufts or clumps, is only 12 in (30 cm) deep in each case. The Roman numerals indicate the months of flowering time. It would be easy to bring forward the start of the border's flowering period by putting in bulbs (snowdrops, aconites, scillas, crown imperial, etc). Or you could equally well make a beautiful additional effect by planting some lilies in the border for half-shade. The minimum number of stone slabs to facilitate working is placed in the border. As the plants will soon grow very close together the work you need to do, especially weeding and hoeing, will become much less. The planting plans shown here are first

Lysi-machia	Delphinium		Shrub rose (red or pink) VI–X		Rudbeckia VIII–IX		Michael-mas daisy IX–X	Lysi-machia VI–VIII	Hollyhock		Delphin-ium VI–VII, IX
		Madonna lilies VI–VII		Lavender VII–VIII	Medium-height Michaelmas daisy IX–X		Lysi-machia VI–VIII	Delphinium		VII–X	Red rose VI–X
VI–VIII	VI–VII, IX										
Red rose VI–X	Poten-tilla V–IX	Tall variety of veronica	Dwarf aster IX–X	Medium-height Michael-mas daisy	Dwarf aster IX–X	Madonna lily VI–VII	Oriental poppy VI	VI–VII, IX	Medium-height Michaelmas daisy IX–X		Lavender VII–VIII
Tall variety of veronica VII–IX	Gypso-phila VI–VIII	VI–IX	Helianthemums (yellow)		Medium-height campanula VI–VII	Gypso-phila VI–VIII		Poten-tilla V–IX	Dwarf aster X–XI		
Gypso-phila VI–VIII	Evening primrose and blue flax VI–IX		Campa-nula VI–VII	VI–VII	Gypso-phila	Evening primrose and blue flax VI–IX		Medium-height campanula VI–VII	Helianthemums (yellow) V–VII		Gyso-phila VI–VIII
Aubrieta IV–V	Alyssum IV–V	Candytuft IV–V	Dwarf iris (yellow) V	Aubrieta IV–V	VI–VIII	Dwarf iris (blue) V	Alyssum IV–V	Aubrieta IV–V	Candytuft IV–V	Aubrieta IV–V	

and foremost for people really interested in plants who like to keep adding to their collection, making changes and trying out something new. Of course a large border laid out with ground cover plants and a few taller single specimens or shrubs to catch the eye is simpler to manage, and can be a very effective sight.

by the use of a few well-chosen and carefully placed taller specimens.

The old idea was that a border of hardy flowers had to have a background – a hedge, a wall, or a fence. Nowadays we lean more towards free-standing beds not more than 4–5 ft (1–1·5 cm) across. You can reach into them from both sides for hoeing and dead-heading without having to tread on the ground. Also, the plants do not become 'drawn', reaching for the light as they do in a bed with a solid background. Hence many plants will not need staking.

After the plants have taken root, further maintenance does not stop short at the removal of dead leaves, faded

Early, single, paeony *(Paeonia officinalis)*, one of the most handsome perennials.

Top left: Adam's needle *(Yucca filamentosa)*. *Top right:* sea holly *(Eryngium)*. *Bottom left:* goat's beard *(Aruncus)*. *Bottom right: Liatris.*

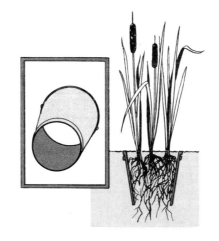

An old bucket without a bottom is the best way to control invasive plants.

flowers and dry stems. Many perennials grow so freely as to be a nuisance. Certain ornamental grasses such as *Carex* and *Typha* are notorious in this respect. You may also have a good deal of trouble with rudbeckias, Chinese lanterns (*Physalis*), Michaelmas daisies, and particularly with perennial knot-weed (*Polygonum*). Sometimes the method of containing the roots in an old bucket without a bottom, does the trick. Other plants will even grow through the sides of the bucket and keep presenting their owners with new offspring. All you can do is cut the roots as deep as possible. It is also necessary to keep the border free of weeds and watch out for pests and diseases. All advice given elsewhere in this book about sterilizing the soil, spraying, picking off insects, keeping down voles, moles and other miscreants, is equally applicable to the herbaceous border.

Basic rules for mulching, feeding and winter care

Plenty of organic matter and fertilizers are essential if the beds are to keep healthy. Since the plants will soon be standing very close together, they will be taking a great deal of nourishment from the soil, and this will need constant replacement during the summer growing period. It is best to use compound fertilizer in soluble form. Applications of soluble fertilizer every two or three weeks from the time buds appear to the end of the flowering season are very welcome. With plants which are cut down to the ground in late autumn, or are no longer visible above ground, because they have lost their foliage, we can cover the beds with a good layer of peat or shredded bark, mixed with a general-purpose fertilizer such as Growmore. It can lie through the winter, and be carefully hoed into the ground, avoiding shallow-lying roots, in spring. Mention of any winter protection required is in the individual descriptions.

But perennials are not by any means all alike, and the kind of cover provided must be adjusted to the character of the individual plant. Plants such as delphiniums and monkshood, whose shoots die down very early, are cut right down to the ground in late autumn; the dying basal leaves are removed as well as the tall, dead stems, and a nourishing protective layer of peat and humus fertilizer can be spread evenly over the plants.

However, different treatment is necessary for perennials which form young shoots or basal leaves ready for spring in the summer of the preceding year, like Michaelmas daisies, rudbeckias, heleniums and a number of others. We cut only the old flower-stems of these plants down, and they spend the winter with a thick shock or a kind of small cushion of leaves above ground.

Finally, there is a large group of perennials which can almost be described as evergreen, and consequently should not be cut down. This group includes various species of iris, euphorbia, and several sturdy ornamental grasses. In such cases mulch is applied close to the plants, but not right over them, and any further protective covering necessary must be able to let the air in.

In dry summers thorough watering which will sink in at least 20 in (50 cm) is necessary every four to six weeks, as well as mulching and feeding. Some perennials, especially phlox, have such a dense network of roots that nests full of dust can form in their interiors, and it takes a great deal of water to get rid of these accumulations. Sometimes this can only be done if you raise a little embankment of earth round the entire bed or the group of plants concerned.

Moving perennials

However well you care for them, the time will come when the soil gets tired, and many of your perennials begin to lose their looks. They flower less freely, grow new shoots only round the edges and leave ugly bare patches inside the plants, raise themselves half out of the ground, and show other signs of deterioration. In general, this happens after five to six years in the same place, and then it is high time to move them, rejuvenating the plants by division. Old-established perennials which are *not* divided when they are moved hardly ever do well. In most gardens the space available for flower beds is decided by a planned lay-out of the whole area which takes into account buildings and any large trees present; however, it is possible to move plants in such a way that one does not put the same, or closely related, varieties back into their old places. All remains of roots should be carefully removed from the ground when the plants are taken out, the soil should be well dug and have plenty of humus fertilizer worked in. Fast-acting peat-based fertilizer is good too. The soil can be completely regenerated if you dig out the old topsoil and replace it with a new layer.

In all cases this rejuvenating job is done in autumn, and it is particularly successful if the beds can be left empty all winter. If you can do this, the plants must be stored somewhere away from frost, under a good layer of soil. They can spend the winter out in the garden, too, if you have enough nourishing compost or similar material, leaf mould and twigs to keep them heeled in so that frost will not affect them. Plant out again in spring according to the usual rules. For heeling in, see also the chapter SOWING AND PLANTING OUT.

Raising perennials from seed

Perennials are usually bought from a nursery as young plants, or are obtained by the division of mature rootstocks or other methods of vegetative propagation. They will give you flowering plants sooner than those you try to raise from seed, a process which is usually beyond the amateur's horticultural knowledge and technical equipment.

However, there are some perennials which are relatively easily raised from seed sown out of doors, just as Nature herself propagates by seeding and needs no greenhouse or spatula for pricking out plants. There are two possible sowing times: June and September. Any deviations from this rule will be found in the descriptions of individual plants. Those species which require a long dormant period between the ripening and germination of the seed are sown in September. Among others, this group includes *Centaurea, Corydalis, Cyclamen, Delphinium, Helleborus, Iris, Paeonia, Primula vulgaris* and *P. elatior*, as well as most other outdoor primulas; also *Trollius*.

Suitable for late sowing also, which can only be done when the ground is open and there is no frost, are *Aconitum, Aguilegia, Eryngium*, various species of *Gentiana, Phlox, Viola odorata*. These belong to the group known as 'frost-germinating' plants. Like winter wheat, their seeds need cold to bring about the inner change necessary for germination, and the later development of flowers and fruits is affected too. This is one of the most interesting areas of modern plant biology, although we cannot go into it in more detail here.

Outdoor seedbeds for perennials sown in autumn should be kept at a constant level of moisture and free of weeds

until the cold weather sets in, and then lightly covered with dead leaves held in place by twigs for the winter. When the seedlings have grown big enough they should be transplanted either to a nursery bed or put out in their final positions directly. If possible seedlings should be pricked out to a distance of 2–4 in (5–10 cm), which helps them to form a better ball of soil round their roots and develop into strong, compact plants. However, the job must be done in good time: as soon as you can handle the seedlings. Similarly, putting them out in the border should not be put off until the roots of the seedlings have become intertwined with each other and the leaves are crowded together. As I said earlier: raising perennials from seed is a labour of love, and if you are going to go in for it you must expect to have some failures now and then.

Tall perennials about 5 ft (150 cm) high and over

Althaea rosea, **Hollyhock.** Height up to 6½ ft (200 cm); diameter 12–20 in (30–50 cm); flowering time July/October; colours: white, pink, red, also mauve and yellow. Planting time autumn or spring; can be grown from seed. Likes a sunny sheltered position. Planting distance at least 20 in (50 cm). They all like good, deep-dug soil, plenty of manuring, and sun. They can be propagated by division of the rootstock. For annual and biennial hollyhocks, see chapter ANNUALS AND BIENNIALS.

Aruncus sylvester, **Goat's beard.** Height 3–6½ ft (100–200 cm); diameter (24–32 cm); flowering time June/July; colour of flowers: ivory. Plant in March; it is easy to divide the woody root. Needs moist, nourishing soil, does best in half-shade but will also grow in full shade. One of the most handsome of the cultivated spiraeas, with plumy white panicles of flowers. Male and female flowers are borne on separate plants. Only male flowers reach the full size; the female flower panicles are rather smaller.

Cephalaria gigantea (tatarica), **Giant scabious.** Height up to 6½ ft (200 cm); flowering time June/August; colour: yellow. Plant in spring or autumn. Ideal back of border plant in a sheltered position, and it is advisable to support the plants. Likes any soil but needs full sun.

Cimicifuga, **Bugbane.** Height 32–78 in (80–200 cm); flowering time July/August, September/October; colour of flowers: white. It is a late flowerer, so plant in spring. Likes half-shade to shade. The tall spikes of creamy flowers last into November. Needs good, rich soil, and only requires full sun in areas which do not get much rain. All-the-year-round mulching with damp peat, compost or grass cuttings is also to be recommended. There are several species, including *C. cordifolia* and the imposing *C. race-*

mosa. C. foetida 'White Pearl' is a particularly fine white-plumed variety.

Crambe cordifolia, **Ornamental seakale.** Height up to 7 ft (210 cm); flowering time May/July; colour of flowers: white. Will grow in any soil, in sun or shade, and the tall branching stems of white flowers look effective against an evergreen background.

Delphinium, **Delphinium.** Height up to 6½ ft (200 cm); flowering time June/ July and September; colour of flowers: innumerable shades of blue to violet, also white and yellow, and varieties with a dark eye. Plant in March, or directly after its second flowering. Choose a sunny, sheltered position enriched with plenty of nourishing material. If the beauty of the flowers decreases after a few years, the first place to look for the cause of the trouble – more so than with any other garden plant – is in dryness under the roots. See if this is the trouble before you move the plant.

Supporting delphiniums.

Stems which have just finished flowering should be cut down to 4 in (10 cm) above the ground; stems whose inflorescence is already showing the formation of seed organs should be left 10–12 in (25–30 cm) above the ground, as this is said to bring on the shoots for autumn flowering faster. Make sure the roots and the soil around them get plenty of water during the season of growth. The tall plants need regular applications of fertilizer. Do not use a fertilizer containing a lot of nitrogen; this will encourage the formation of too much foliage and make the plant more susceptible to aphids and liable to snap in the wind. It is advisable to support the plants carefully to prevent the flower spikes from breaking. Especially tall stalks with a thick, heavy head of flowers can be individually staked with bamboo canes or the familiar steel wire supports used for tomatoes and beans. Keep the stake as well hidden as possible. The soil should not be worked too deeply when preparing and manuring it for the winter, to avoid any damage to the roots. Do not use a spade, just hoe lightly.

Delphiniums are now divided into three main groups: the *D. elatum* varieties, the large flowered 'Pacific' hybrids, and lower growing modern 'Belladonna' varieties which make bushy plants and are the most suitable for small gardens.

Eremurus, **Foxtail lily.** Height of the flower stem 5–8 ft (150–250 cm); flowering time June/July; colour of flowers: golden yellow, whitish, red, orange. Planting time only between August and the beginning of October; planting site only in full sun. The foxtail lily is among the most handsome of perennials for use as a single specimen or in groups. It needs very nourishing, but well-drained soil, which must not be too wet. Spread the roots out like asparagus crowns at a depth of 6–8 in (15–20 cm) and fill in the hole with good soil-based compost. Do not cover with leaves or similar material in winter but, if you can get it, with very well-rotted animal manure. Best known species: *E. stenophyllus bungei*, and *E. olgae*. The fragrant pink 'spears' of *E. robustus* grow tallest (about 10 ft (over 3 m)). The very beautiful 'Shelford' Hybrids only 40 in (100 cm) tall, in all the *Eremurus* colours, are also available.

Macleaya cordata, **Plume poppy.** Height 3–6½ ft (100–200 cm); flowering time July/August; colour: yellowish

Macleaya cordata, Plume poppy

white; planting time spring; situation, sun to half-shade. Best used as a tall plant at the back of a border. A handsome, strange and mysterious-looking plant; but unfortunately very invasive. Likes loamy soil. Propagate by root suckers.

Rheum emodi, **Ornamental rhubarb.** Height up to 6½ ft (200 cm); broad, spreading, bushy habit. Flowering time June/August; colour of flowers: greenish white or red; planting time autumn; situation, sun to half-shade *R. palmatum*, the 'Tibetan rhubarb', which bears yellowish white flowers in June/July, has deeply cut leaves; *R. palmatum* 'Rubrum' has reddish flowers, but here again the foliage is the main attraction. All of them, like their edible cousin, are gross feeders, and will display their full beauty only if they get plenty of nourishment.

Rudbeckia, **Coneflower, rudbeckia.** Height 1½–6½ ft (50–200 cm); broad, bushy plants; flowering time July/September; colour of flowers: golden yellow; planting time October or March; propagation by division of roots. It will grow in any garden soil, needs sun to half-shade. Most rudbeckias in cultivation are the much improved, low-growing hybrids, such as 'Goldsturm' and 'Goldquelle'.

Rudbeckia, Coneflower

Verbascum olympicum, **Mullein.** Height up to 8 ft (24 m); flowering time June/August; colour: yellow; planting time autumn; situation: any soil in full sun and particularly good for dry, stony gardens. Produces rosettes of hairy, silvery leaves in first year, but throws up spikes of flowers in second and subsequent years. Several varieties available which produce yellow, pink or white flowers.

Yucca filamentosa, **Yucca, Adam's needle.** Height 5 ft (150 cm); flowering time July/August; colour of flowers: creamy white or yellowish; planting time April; situation, sunny and dry. This magnificent tropical plant cannot be unreservedly recommended for growing out of doors, as it is not hardy in exposed areas. The stemless varieties are most suitable for garden use, especially *Y. filamentosa* and its variety *Y.f.* 'Variegata' with green, yellow and pink leaves. It is easy to grow; likes good well-drained soil with a certain amount of lime. Occasional applications of fertilizer encourage the growth of the stiff, sword-shaped leaves, usually tipped with brown and ending in a spine. The inflorescence, which will not appear for some years, grows 4–8 ft (120–240 cm) high. But once the yucca does begin to flower, it should go on doing so every year, if properly cared for.

Perennials of medium height, 20–60 in (50–150 cm)

Achillea, **Milfoil, yarrow.** Height up to 36 in (90 cm); flowering time June/September; colour of flowers: white, golden yellow, purplish red; planting time March. Situation, sunny and dry. Otherwise the various different yarrows are very undemanding. For small forms see the chapter ROCK GARDENS. Among the best is the exceptionally tall *A. filipendulina* 'Gold Plate', with large, golden yellow umbels of flowers and finely cut, grey-green leaves 48–55 in (120–140 cm). I should also mention 'Coronation Gold', 28 in (70 cm) tall, and the deep red *A. millefolium* 'Cerise Queen', which is 32 in (80 cm) tall.

Agapanthus, **African lily.** Height up to 36 in (90 cm); flowering time July/September; colour of flowers: blue; planting time April; situation, rich soil, sun sheltered from cold winds. Hardiest form is 'Headbourne Hybrids'. Give winter protection by covering with peat.

Alstroemaria, **Peruvian lily.** Height up to 36 in (90 cm); flowering time June/July; colour of flowers: pink, yellow, orange; planting time March/April; situation, sunny and sheltered. Best forms are *Alstroemaria aurantiaca* 'Dover Orange', *A.a.* 'Lutea', yellow, and *A. pulchella*, red. In cold areas it is advisable to protect the plants during the winter.

Aconitum, **Monkshood.** Height, according to variety, 40–60 in (100–150 cm); flowering time June/July, July/August, September/October; colour of flowers: yellowish white to dark blue; planting time autumn; likes a very sunny position. The beautiful monkshood has the drawback of being poisonous. But if you have no need to worry about this, this erect, decorative, mountain plant with its deeply cut, finger-shaped leaves and beautiful hooded flowers looks very well in the garden. It likes a cool position, sunny or not according to the amount of rainfall in the area. After flowering it is cut down to the ground, like a delphinium. Transplant as little as possible. Aphids are a sign that it is in too dry and sunny a place. Best-known species: *A. napellus*, bright violet-blue with several cultivated forms: *A.n.* 'Carneum', pink, and *A.n.* 'Bicolor' with white and blue flowers.

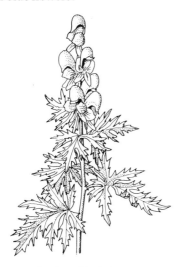

Aconitum, Monkshood

Anchusa azurea (A. italica), **Anchusa, Alkanet.** Height up to 60 in (150 cm); flowering time June/August; colour of flowers: gentian-blue. Planting time spring. Planting site, sun to half-shade. If you are raising plants from seed, sow in April; it is better to buy young plants with a good ball of soil. Needs good, well-dug soil. For the rest, cultivate like the perennial hollyhock, *Althaea. anchusa azurea* 'Loddon Royalist' is a good variety.

Anemone × *hybrida (A. japonica)*, **Japanese anemone.** Height up to 4 ft (120 cm); flowering time August/October; colours: white, pink, red, mauve. Very beautiful. Several semi-double varieties. Planting time, March only; situation, half-shade. Be sure to plant out with a good ball of soil. Propagate later from root suckers. To develop its root system, which usually spreads horizontally, the anemone needs nourishing soil containing humus, a certain amount of space, and a good protective covering of peat and leaves in winter. Otherwise it is undemanding and one of the best autumn-flowering plants.

Aquilegia hybrids, **Columbine, aquilegia.** Height 20–32 in (50–80 cm); diameter 8 in (20 cm); flowering time April/July; colours: white, yellow, red, blue, violet; planting time autumn or spring; situation, sun to half-shade. Easily raised from seed; sow where the plants are to flower in autumn, winter or very early spring (this needs frost to germinate) and the plants will flower next summer. It also

seeds itself freely. Root division is rarely successful. Likes well-manured soil with plenty of humus. An essential component of the middle area of a herbaceous border, even though the leaf rosette, which often turns red later, is all that is left after the beautifully coloured flowers on their long, slender stems have faded. The 'McKana' hybrids are good and there are several new varieties.

Aster, **Aster, Michaelmas daisy.** Height 12–48 in (30–120 cm); flowering time autumn; colour of flowers: all shades. Planting time autumn or spring. Must have a sunny, airy situation. Asters are stars in the flowery sky. There are innumerable differences of flowering time, colour, height and character of foliage. *A. amellus, A. novae–angliae* and *A. novi-belgii* are those most often grown, in many different varieties. For dwarf Michaelmas daisies see also ROCK GARDENS. Bees and butterflies love them. Not all varieties offered in glowing terms come up to expectation. However, problems are often due to mistakes in cultivation rather than the variety itself. The best way to prevent such typical troubles as mildew and aster wilt is to plant with the ball of soil intact, in a good, airy, sunny position. It is better, too, to mix asters with other perennials and not grow them in large beds on their own. Water during the flowering season.

Astilbe, **Astilbe.** Height 36–60 in (90–150 cm); flowering time July/August; colour of flowers: white, pink, salmon, mauve, carmine. Like the spiraea, with which it is often confused, the astilbe, with its finely cut foliage and feathery-looking flower panicles, likes nourishing, rather moist soil, and light shade. The plants look best in the vicinity of shrubs and close to water, where they can be left undisturbed for years. Propagation by division after flowering. If used as a cut flower, put in water immediately.

Campanula, **Bellflower.** Height 40 in (100 cm); flowering time June/August; colours: white, pink, blue, violet;

Campanula, Bellflower

planting time March or August; situation, sun to half-shade, not dry. Can be raised from seed sown where the plants are to flower in March. It makes few demands on the soil. Among the best-known perennials is *C. persicifolia*, the peach-leaved bellflower, with several beautiful varieties; all it needs is to have the ugly withered heads removed. Cutting back hard after flowering does wonders for the plant. Popular species include *C. glomerata*, *C. lactiflora*, and *C. latifolia* and their varieties. For dwarf forms see the chapter ROCK GARDENS; for biennials, see chapter ANNUALS AND BIENNIALS

Chrysanthemum indicum, **Garden chrysanthemum.** Height up to 60 in (150 cm); flowering time August/November; colours: white, yellow, pink, red, bronze. Plant out only in spring; propagate by cuttings or raise from seed. Chrysanthemums like good, nourishing, loamy to sandy soil and manuring in spring; they need sun and some kind of winter protection. There is no more beautiful and rewarding autumn flower for the garden than the chrysanthemum, available in countless varieties of inexhaustible richness of colour. It will survive slight night frost in late autumn. There are large and small-flowered double varieties, pompon varieties, single-flowered varieties; they are all excellent as cut flowers. They are about the latest of autumn-flowering plants.

Chrysanthemum maximum, **Shasta daisy.** Height 32–40 in (80–100 cm); flowering time June/August; colour of flowers: white; planting time autumn or spring; likes sun to half-shade. Careful selection and breeding over the years has produced large-flowering single cultivated forms, also 'semi-double' varieties, such as 'Esther Read', 'H. Seibert' and 'Wirral Supreme'. Since the bushy plants spread very readily they should have plenty of room; leave a distance of 28–32 in (70–80 cm) all round them when planting.

Coreopsis verticillata, **Coreopsis.** Height 20–32 in (50–80 cm); flowering time June/September; colour: bright yellow; planting time autumn or spring; sun or half-shade. A very easy and rewarding perennial for the border, 'Grandiflora' is especially handsome, with many branches, hardy and undemanding to grow. Another species, *C. grandiflora*, and its varieties, is also deservedly popular. See also chapter ANNUALS AND BIENNIALS for other forms of this flower.

Dicentra spectabilis, **Dicentra, bleeding heart.** Height up to 32 in (80 cm); diameter 32–40 in (80–100 cm); flowering time April/July; colour: red and white. Plant out divisions of the fleshy, swollen roots in autumn, or in spring just before the first shoots appear. Careful: they are very brittle. Makes no great demands on the soil, but because of the danger of rotting it should not be too heavy or too wet. The plant does not like very bright sunlight. *D.*

Dicentra spectabilis, Bleeding heart

spectabilis has received most attention from breeders; less well known, *D. eximia*, pink, and *D.e.* 'Alba', white.

Dictamnus albus (*D. fraxinella*), **Burning bush.** Height 24–40 in (60–100 cm); flowering time June/August; colour of flowers: red and pink, and pure white. Planting time, autumn or spring. Likes sun. Its common name is derived from the fact that on a warm evening it is sometimes possible to ignite the aromatic oil given off by the flowers.

Doronicum, **Leopard's bane.** Height up to 40 in (80 cm); flowering time April/June; colour of flowers: yellow; better planted in autumn than in spring; propagate by division of roots after flowering. Sun to half-shade. A particularly pretty and undemanding member of the daisy family. The tallest is *D. plantagineum* 'Harpur Crewe'. Very well known, too, is the smallest variety, 'Goldzwerg' only 10 in (25 cm) high. *D. cordatum* is a rather later-flowering species.

Doronicum, Leopard's bane

Echinops, **Globe thistle.** Height 40–50 in (80–150 cm); flowering time June/September; colour of flowers: pale blue, dark blue, silver-grey. Planting time autumn or early spring. Situation: sunny and dry. *Echinops* means 'hedgehog-headed', a very apt description of this picturesque plant. Undemanding if the soil contains a certain amount of lime. Propagate by division of the rootstock or by removing suckers. *E. humilis* and *E. ritro* are the two species most commonly grown.

Erigeron, **Fleabane.** The hybrid varieties, including 'Adria' and 'Foerster's Liebling' grow to between 16 and 32 in (40 and 80 cm), flowering from June to August; colours: rose-pink to dark violet. Otherwise, treat as for the species *E. speciosus*; see chapter ROCK GARDENS.

Eryngium, **Sea holly.** Height up to 48 in (120 cm); flowering time June/August; colour of flowers: steel-blue, reddish purple; planting time, spring only; needs sun. Best kinds to grow: *E. alpinum*, the tall *E. giganteum* which is only a biennial, but seeds itself every other year, *E. planum, E. tripartitum,* and *E. bourgatii.* Eryngiums, with their oddly blue-tinged and deeply cut foliage belong in any herbaceous border. It likes full sun, a dry, sandy soil, very little watering and feeding.

Gaillardia hybrids, **Gaillardia, blanket flower.** Height up to 36 in (90 cm); flowering time June/September; colour of flowers: red, yellow, copper. Planting time autumn or early spring; situation: sunny. The perennial varieties, which have been developed into very showy ornamental plants, are nearly all hybrids of *C. aristata.* Easy to raise from seed. Division of roots is best done in autumn.

Gypsophila paniculata, **Baby's breath.** Height up to 36 in (90 cm); diameter 8–20 in (20–50 cm); flowering time July/September; colours: white and pink; situation: sunny. The double pink 'Flamingo' goes on flowering longest – often into November. The white 'Bristol Fairy' and 'Compacta Plena' are large-flowered and very rewarding to grow. See also chapters ROCK GARDENS and ANNUALS AND BIENNIALS.

Gypsophila paniculata, Baby's breath

Helenium, **Helenium.** Height up to 60 in (150 cm); broad bushy plants; flowering time August/October; colours: bright yellow with brown centre, copper-red or pure

mahogany-red, as in 'Bruno'. Planting time April; likes a sunny position. Prefers damp, nourishing soil and sun. Many colourful varieties and hybrids. Easily propagated by division.

Helianthus, **Perennial sunflower.** Height about 60 in (150 cm) or more; flowering time September/October; colour of flowers bright to deep yellow. Planting time autumn or spring. Situation: sunny, open. It is worth trying one or other of the garden forms of this showy autumn-flowering plant; they are mostly varieties of *H.* × *multiflorus.* I must also mention the elegant willow-leaved sunflower, *H. salicifolius*, remarkable chiefly for its attractive narrow leaves and good as a single specimen, for instance planted beside a garden pool.

Helianthus salicifolius, Willow-leaved sunflower

Heliopsis, **Heliopsis.** Height 36–48 in (90–120 cm); flowering time July/September; colour of flowers: golden yellow, orange. Planting time autumn or spring. Situation: sunny. The heliopsis is closely related to the perennial sunflower. The bright, ray-shaped flowers of the new varieties such as 'Golden Plume' or 'Gigantea' can reach a diameter of 4½ in (11 cm).

Hemerocallis hybrids, **Day lily.** Height 24–32 in (60–80 cm); flowering time, according to variety, the end of May to September; colour of flowers: lemon-yellow, light

Hemerocallis hybrid, Day lily

and dark orange, pink, blood-red; also double flowers. Planting time spring, autumn, and also during flowering. Prefers a sunny position. They must be left undisturbed if possible so that the clumps of roots can extend, putting out more and more flower stalks with more and larger flowers on them. Divide every 6–7 years.

Iris, **Iris.** Height 12–40 in (30–100 cm); flowering time May/June; colour of flowers: all colours except bright red; planting time, according to the flowering period, autumn or spring; situation: dry, sunny, open, half-shade at most. The irises described here grow from rhizomes, swollen roots divided after flowering to produce new plants. The rhizomatous iris, like the bulbous iris described later (p. 115), is a member of an ancient aristocracy of flowers, but it has taken modern breeding to bring out its true distinction. Dry, good soil and sun are enough to get it to display all its richness of colour.

The following classifications of the genus *Iris* are now generally accepted:

1) Standard varieties: distinguished within their various different colour classes by general reliability of flowering, stability of stems, and good health.

2) Fancy varieties: with curious markings or other special features.

3) Tall bearded irises: with several sub-divisions, such as varieties suitable for naturalizing (needing no transplanting, and little or no care in an informal part of the garden); shorter varieties for the fronts of borders; and the tall bearded iris itself, which rejoices in an almost unlimited range of colours, shapes and flower sizes. Also good for cut flowers and other decorative purposes.

Tall bearded iris

4) Dwarf or miniature irises: those charming small forms which grow no taller than 12 in (30 cm), and bear only one flower on each stem. *I. pumila*, flowering in April (and mentioned also in the chapter ROCK GARDENS), belongs to this group.

The small-flowering pale blue or purplish blue varieties of the Siberian iris, *I. sibirica*, are also suitable for banks by water. The Japanese irises, *I. kaempferi* and *I. laevigata*, with their beautiful varieties, are true waterside plants, which like lime-free soil beside or actually in water. More about them in the chapter WATER GARDENS.

Kniphofia, **Torch lily, red hot poker.** Height 20–48 in (50–120 cm); diameter 10–12 in (25–30 cm); flowering time according to variety June/September; colours: orange to coral-red, yellow. Many excellent varieties. Planting time in April; propagate by division. Situation: sunny.

Liatris, **Blazing star, gayfeather.** Height about 40 in/ 100 cm; flowering time July/August; colour of flowers: purple-pink. Planting time autumn or spring; its planting site should suit the character of this impressive North American from the prairies. The almost club-shaped inflorescences are borne on strong stalks rising from grass-like, overhanging shocks of leaves. Their crowded florets open from top to bottom, departing from the usual practice of plants similarly formed. Propagation by division in autumn, or it can be raised from seed. The variety 'Kobold' is an elegant small form, only 16 in (40 cm) high.

Ligularia, **Ligularia.** Height 32–40 in (80–100 cm); flowering time July/September; colour of flowers: golden yellow, orange: planting time autumn or spring; situation: moist soil, sunny. The best garden form is *L. clivorum* 'Desdemona', with dark red foliage. *L. × hessei* grows to 6½ ft (2 m).

Lupinus polyphyllus, **Lupin.** Height up to 40 in (100 cm); flowering time, according to variety, June/ September; many colours. Situation: acid soil, sun to half-shade. The arrival on the scene of the Russell hybrids has solved many problems. It is best to raise lupins from seed, since divided plants, especially when they are fairly large, have some difficulty taking root. For annual lupins, see ANNUALS AND BIENNIALS. As leguminous plants, lupins are often attacked by leaf beetles or weevils; treat them as for peas. Weevils, which cannot fly, can be controlled by putting lime round the plants.

Lychnis chalcedonica, **Campion.** Height 32–40 in (80–100 cm); flowering time June/August, colour of flowers: scarlet. Planting time March/April. Situation: sunny. *L. chalcedonica* comes from a region from Southern Russia to Central Asia. Its bright colour makes it an essential part of a herbaceous border. Cut back immediately after flowering. Likes an open, sunny position. Propagation by division; when planting in large groups space 20 in (50 cm) apart. The dark red double variety *L. viscaria* (now properly *Viscaria viscosa*) 'Splendens Plena' forms a kind of transition to the lower-growing viscaria; see the next section, on **Small perennials**.

Lysimachia punctata, **Yellow loosestrife.** Height 24–40 in (60–100 cm); flowering time June/August; colour: golden yellow. Flowers are borne in whorls one above another. Any situation other than one in sandy soil will do, including half-shade. Spreads itself by suckers.

Monarda, **Bergamot, Oswego tea, monarda.** Height up to 40 in (100 cm); diameter 12–20 in (30–50 cm); flowering time July/September; colours: scarlet and violet, also white and salmon-pink; planting time March, propagation by division. Situation: sun to half-shade. The scarlet *M. didyma* 'Cambridge Scarlet', flowering in July/August, is outstanding but has a tendency to be invasive.

Monarda, Bergamot

Paeonia, **Peony, paeony.** Height 24–40 in (60–100 cm); diameter 28–32 in (70–80 cm); flowering time May/July; colours: white, pink, red, yellow; best planting time August/November. The crowns must be placed just below the surface of the ground, in such a way that the buds for next year are just visible. Plants put in the ground too deep will not flower. Even properly planted paeonies take two or three years to get going properly. They like warm, sheltered places, good deeply-dug soil, plenty of manure and plenty of sun. The familiar old *P. officinalis* has been more or less ousted by the handsome hybrids of *P. lactiflora* but we can still find attractive varieties of *P. officinalis*, both single and double, flowering from May onwards. For *P. suffruticosa*, the tree paeony, see the chapter HEDGES AND FLOWERING DECIDUOUS SHRUBS.

Papaver orientale, **Oriental poppy.** Height, according to variety, 20–40 in (50–100 cm); flowering time June/July; colour of flowers: ranging from satiny white through salmon-pink to fiery red, scarlet, carmine and bronze. Planting time spring or autumn. Situation: very sunny,

dry. It is an undemanding plant and likes to stay in the same place as long as possible. When the flowers are over cut down the fading leaves, and it will start shooting again until late summer.

Penstemon, **Penstemon.** Height 20–28 in (50–70 cm); broad, erect bushes; flowering time June/September; colour of flowers: scarlet, orange, mauve; planting time autumn or spring; situation: sunny. The perennial penstemon is very attractive with its spikes of bell-shaped flowers and will go on flowering for a long time if you keep cutting it back. Soil containing sand and humus, not too dry, is best for it. Give some winter protection in exposed areas.

Phormium, **New Zealand flax.** Height 24–60 in (60–150 cm), though some varieties grow taller; flowering time July/September, but plants grown mainly for their superb variegated sword-shaped leaves striped in many colours. Planting time, spring. Situation: deep, moist soil in sunny situation. This plant is becoming more popular, as hardy varieties of *P. tenax* and *P. cookianum* are introduced, and winter protection is needed in only the coldest of areas.

Phlox paniculata, **Phlox.** Height 28–40 in (70–100 cm); diameter 24–40 in (50–100 cm); flowering time, according to variety, from May/June to September/October; colours: all shades from white to dark red and violet-blue, with the exception of yellow. Planting time April. Propagate by division. Situation: sunny and open. Countless well-known old and new varieties. Problems and diseases of the roots are usually the result of wrong feeding and a poor choice of varieties. If the stem and bulb eelworm (*Ditylenchus dipsaci*) attacks the roots, causing the shoots to be short and brittle and the leaves to turn first pale and then limp and brown, all you can do is have a good clear-out, add plenty of lime to the spot, and avoid growing phloxes there for the next 4–5 years. Well-tended plants will keep their looks for ten years or more.

Phlox

Physalis, **Chinese lantern.** Height 16–24 in (40–60 cm); whitish, insignificant flowers; but when the fruits ripen the large, red, lantern-shaped calyx is striking, and *Physalis* at this stage is used for decorative purposes; it will last a long time in a vase. Situation: sun to half-shade; plenty of lime in the soil is desirable. The species *P. alkekengii* and the larger *P. francheti* 'Gigantea' are obtainable. Some winter protection is a good idea in exposed places.

Polygonatum, **Solomon's seal.** Height up to 36 in (90 cm); flowering time May/July; colour of flowers: green, white; planting time autumn or spring; situation: any soil in partial shade. Several species and varieties; *P.* × *hybridum* (often called *P. multiflorum*) 'Variegatum' has white striped leaves. Propagate by division of roots.

Pyrethrum, **Painted daisy.** Height 30 in (70 cm); flowering time May/July; colour of flowers: shades of pink, white, red; planting time autumn or spring; situation: any soil, sun or shade. A number of single and double flowered varieties are available of these attractive plants. Propagation by root division.

Salvia, **Flowering sage.** Height about 32 in (80 cm); flowering time July/September; colour of flowers: bright blue, violet-mauve; planting time autumn or better still spring; situation: half-shade, dry soil. Several species and varieties. Cut back hard after flowering. Propagation is by root division in spring. For other forms in cultivation, see the chapter ANNUALS AND BIENNIALS.

Salvia, Flowering sage

Sidalcea, **Mallow.** Height up to 36 in (90 cm); flowering time June/September; colour of flowers: white, also rose-red and purplish red; planting time autumn or spring; situation: sunny, likes light soil without much lime. Several species and varieties. Propagation by root division or from seed.

Solidago, **Golden rod.** Height up to 36 in (90 cm); flowering time July/September; colour of flowers: yellow; planting time autumn or spring; situation: ordinary soil, sun or half-shade. Several good modern varieties such as 'Crown of Rays', 'Goldenmosa' and 'Lemore'. Propagation is by root division.

Small perennials for the front of borders, up to 24 in (60 cm)

Brunnera macrophylla, **Caucasian forget-me-not, brunnera.** Height 20 in (50 cm); flowering time April/June; colour of flowers: blue; planting time autumn or spring; situation: sun to half-shade, not too dry. A little gem of a plant, flowering indefatigably in its unpretentious way, and with attractive dark green, bushy foliage.

Convallaria majalis, **Lily of the valley.** Height 6–8 in (15–20 cm); planting time autumn, until November; flowering time May; colour of flowers: white. Fragrant. Lilies of the valley like shade to half-shade and fresh sandy loam. Lift the crowns and propagate by division in autumn every 3–4 years. Poisonous in all its parts. *C. majalis* 'Rosea' is a form with pink flowers.

Dianthus, **Pink.** Height up to 12 in (30 cm); colour of flowers: white, pink, dark red; planting time autumn or spring; situation: good soil in full sun. Pinks are so easy to grow that their many small forms are extremely suitable for the rock garden. For annual pinks, see chapter ANNUALS AND BIENNIALS. There is a considerable range of modern pinks on the market, mainly forms of *D.* × *allwoodii*. Perennial pinks can last for many years. Propagation by division, layering or cuttings. For small perennial species see chapter ROCK GARDENS.

Geranium, **Crane's bill.** Height 16–24 in (40–60 cm); spread 16–20 in (40–50 cm); flowering time June/September; colour: white, pink, red, violet; divide and plant after flowering is over, and also in spring. Situation: sun to half-shade. Several beautiful species, varieties and hybrids, among which can be recommended are *G. grandiflorum*, *G. ibericum*, *G. endressii*, and the hybrid 'Johnson's Blue', with light blue, 2 in (5 cm) wide, cup-shaped flowers. For dwarf geranium, see chapter ROCK GARDENS.

Geum, **Avens.** Height 16–20 in (40–50 cm); flowering time May/September; colour of flowers: yellow, orange, red to dark red; planting time early spring; situation: sun to half-shade. The geum is one of those stalwarts that give no trouble for years on end. The pretty, spreading, rosette-shaped foliage appears in the spring, and innumerable long flower stalks spring from its centre in the course of the summer. Propagation by root division in early spring; otherwise leave the plants undisturbed as far as possible. Particularly fine are some of the large-flowered hybrids such as 'Georgenberg' (deep yellow) and 'Mrs Bradshaw' (scarlet).

Helleborus, **Christmas rose, Lenten rose, helle-bore.** Height 6–24 in (15–60 cm); flowering time December/April; colours: white to pink, green; root division and planting are done in autumn; likes half-shade. The best-known species are *H. niger*, the Christmas rose, and *H. orientalis*, the Lenten rose. When you are planting, prepare a rather large hole, and work some humus and loam into the site. These handsome evergreen perennials will do well in well-drained soil containing plenty of lime; frequent applications of fertilizer will encourage growth. They take some time to mature into thick, bushy plants flowering around Christmas and in February/March. *Helleborus* does best in half-shade in front of groups of conifers. It is advisable to give some protection, in the form of twigs, against hard frosts. Rather taller than the large-leaved white form are the *Helleborus* hybrids, which have white, pink and carmine flowers and do not bloom until February/April. They too have evergreen foliage, borne on long stems. The green hellebore, *H. viridis*, which has greenish flowers in rather sparse panicles, is interesting rather than beautiful, but can be grown even in the rock garden if its situation is not too dry; flowering time March/April, height 12–16 in (30–40 cm).

Heuchera, **Coral flower.** Height 16 in (40 cm); flowering time May/August; colour of flowers: shades of red, pink; planting time autumn or spring; situation: good soil, sun or light shade. Propagation by root division. The modern hybrids and varieties of *H. sanguinea* make good front-of-border plants.

Hosta, **Plantain lily.** Height 8–24 in (20–60 cm); flowering time June/August; colour of flowers; pink, white,

Hosta, Plantain lily

mauve; foliage variegated green, white or gold according to variety, and the leaves are wavy-edged; division of root-stocks and planting done in spring; situation: sun to half-shade. A favourite border and edging plant, with handsome foliage and long-stemmed spikes of flowers. The more shady its general position the less freely it will flower. There are a number of species and varieties.

Limonium, **Sea lavender.** Height 20–24 in (50–60 cm); flowering time May/July and July/September; colour of flowers: pale mauve, violet-blue; planting time autumn or spring; situation: sun. All varieties are easy to grow and flower profusely. A good taller species is *L. latifolium*.

Linum narbonense, **Blue flax.** Height 20–24 in (50–60 cm); flowering time June/August; colour of flowers: bright sky-blue; planting time autumn or spring; situation: sun to half-shade. Otherwise undemanding. Besides this very lovely, dainty perennial, of medium height, there are several charming small forms suitable for the rock garden, and the annual flax mentioned in the chapter ANNUALS AND BIENNIALS. It tends to die back in exposed areas in winter but seeds itself.

Linum, Flax

Oenothera, **Evening primrose.** See chapter ROCK GARDENS

Platycodon grandiflorum, **Balloon flower.** Height 20 in (50 cm); flowering time July/September; colour of flowers: blue, pink, white; planting time autumn or spring. Situation: sun to half-shade. The varieties 'Mother of Pearl' and 'Snowflake' are attractive. Dead-head daily to

Platycodon grandiflorum, Balloon flower

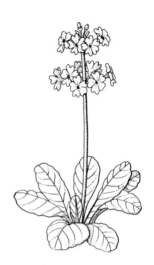

Candelabra primula

prolong the flowering season. Slow to start into growth in spring.

Primula, **Primula.** Height 4–20 in (10–50 cm); flowering time: spring to early summer; colour of flowers: all shades ranging from white to yellow, red and blue, some with an eye. There are many species of primula, and new varieties keep appearing. Perennial primulas are among the most worthwhile of spring-flowering plants. I will mention only a few of them briefly here. *P. rosea*, 6–8 in (15–20 cm) high and large-flowered, is usually in bloom in March. Its flowers appear before the leaves. It likes a damp site, and so is very suitable for planting near water. The leaves die down in autumn. Most primulas flower in April/May. The primrose, *P. vulgaris*, only 4 in (10 cm) high, is also known to most gardeners as *P. acaulis*, with many brightly coloured varieties: good in borders or colourful corners. The *P. elatior* hybrids (usually simply called polyanthus), 10–14 in (25–35 cm) high, come in a very wide range of colours. Several beautiful varieties, such as the large-flowering 'Pacific Giant', and the F$_1$ hybrid 'Regal Supreme'. The drumstick primrose, *P. denticulata*, is another old favourite: 12 in (30 cm) high, a robust plant with strong roots. Its hybrids come in shades of white, pink to lilac and dark violet. The candelabra primulas, up to 20 in (50 cm) and more high, are later flowerers, blooming in June/July. They comprise several different species, all recognizable by their whorls of flowers ranged one above another. The *P. bulleyana* hybrids are the finest of this group, which is very rich in shapes and colours. They run the whole gamut of colour, from yellow to orange, carmine, vermilion, to light blue and so on down: so many melting pastel shades that you can hardly see enough of them. One much-prized candelabra primula is the carmine *P. pulverulenta*, whose flower stalks and calyxes look as if they had been dusted with flour. All primulas are easy to grow, sensitive only to very bright sunlight and dryness, including dryness in winter. They like cool, rather loamy soil. Most primulas can be transplanted shortly before and even during flowering. It is important to water them well. Propagation by division after flowering, or sowing seed in the summer or autumn.

Pulmonaria, **Lungwort.** Height up to 12 in (30 cm); spread 10 in (25 cm); flowering time March/May; colour: bright blue, red, pink; planting time early autumn; situation half-shade to shade, or combat the effect of the sun by mulching the planting site with damp peat. Best-cultivated forms: *P. angustifolia* 'Azurea', with bright azure or gentian-blue flowers. *P. saccharata* 'Pink Dawn' has leaves splotched silvery white, as if castor sugar had been shaken over them, and reddish pink flowers. When dividing roots in August, plant them rather deeper than the original plant stood. Lungwort needs moisture and humus if it is to do well.

Saponaria officinalis, **Soapwort.** Height 16–24 in (40–60 cm); spread 10–12 in (25–30 cm); flowering time July/October; colour: pink; planting time spring; situation: sun to half-shade. Divide the roots in April. This erect, bushy plant likes nourishing but rather dry soil and has a fragrant soap-like smell. See also chapter on ROCK GARDENS.

Scabiosa caucasica, **Scabious, pincushion flower.** Height 24 in (60 cm) or more; spread 16–20 in (40–50 cm); flowering time June/October; colours: mauve, blue, dark violet, also white. Planting time spring; situation: sunny. Raising from seed sown on the flowering site in March is better than dividing and transplanting. Scabious will grow in any good garden soil; young plants should have some form of winter protection. For annual scabious, see chapter ANNUALS AND BIENNIALS.

Trollius, **Trollius, globe flower.** Height up to 24 in (60 cm) or more; flowering time May/June; colour: sulphur-yellow to dark orange; planting time autumn; situation: sun to half-shade. Cutting back the stems immediately after flowering is good for the growth and appearance of the plant. Propagate by division in July or by sowing seed in autumn/winter; however, it seeds itself easily. Likes good garden soil, some moisture, and occasional applications of fertilizer. There are several species and hybrids, including 'Bressingham Mixed Hybrids'.

Trollius, Globe flower

Veronica longifolia, **Speedwell.** Height up to 24 in (60 cm); spread 12–18 in (30–45 cm); flowering time May/September; colours: blue, white; planting time March/April; situation: sunny. Fow low-growing varieties see chapter ROCK GARDENS. It forms good firm plants on nourishing garden soil and is also good for cutting. Among the established taller varieties, which are of upright habit, is the sturdy 'Foerster's Blue', 24 in (60 cm) tall. Other good species include *V. gentianoides*, *V. spicata* and *V. teucrium* and their varieties.

Viola, **Viola, violet.** The viola genus, naturally, is headed by the sweet violet, *V. odorata*, 2–4 in (5–10 cm) high; flowering time March/April; colours: violet, also white, yellow and red; planting time autumn; situation: half-shade. If you want to raise them from seed, sow in autumn as they are among the frost-germinators. There are a handful of attractive varieties. Less well known is *Viola cornuta*, which closely resembles the pansy; height up to 12 in (30 cm); fragrant flowers borne right through from April to October. It is rather sensitive to heat and needs a moist, light position. *V. cucculata* and *V. labradorica* are two more useful perennial species.

For other low-growing plants which are often entirely suitable for edging perennial flower beds or borders, see the section on **Ground cover plants for use as a lawn substitute** in the chapter THE LAWN.

11
Bulbous plants

Bulbous, tuberous and corm producing flowering plants are an important part of our colourful garden flora, which would be much the poorer without tulips and lilies, dahlias and gladioli, or the charming smaller flowers, from snow-flake to autumn crocus. On the other hand, though the basic form of bulbous plants is so simple, they call for almost as much care and understanding as other flowers, although the hardy ones can remain undisturbed in the ground for years on end. The half-hardy kinds have to be lifted at the right time of year, stored correctly, and replanted annually, which, like other recurrent garden jobs, means a certain amount of extra work.

Soil requirements, preparation of the soil

To assess the soil requirements of bulbous plants correctly, we must ask: what actually is a bulb? These fleshy structures of concentric layers arranged around a disc-shaped base-plate on the underside are not roots in the normal sense, but consist of stem and leaf parts. Like tubers and tuberous rhizomes, they act as storage organs, using their hoarded treasure to promote the development of strong roots below ground as well as the growth above ground of leaves and flowers which have been lying, as it were, 'prefabricated' inside the bulbs. The function of the parent bulb, corm or tuber is over only when successful growth and provision of further nourishment, or the formation of daughter bulbs or cormlets, have been assured by the plant's regular absorption of its supplies.

The dry, brown outer skin is the only protection bulbs have against pests living in the soil, and it does not offer much defence against their nibbling, or against dampness in the soil and soil infections. Tubers are more at risk from rotting and infectious diseases, including viruses, than from pests. The breeding of 'mouse-proof' tulips some-times claimed by gardeners is, unfortunately, just a castle in the air so far. However, we do now have the useful method of container planting, especially of larger bulbs, which was described in more detail earlier.

Bulbous, and tuberous plants and corms do not like heavy, sticky soil, but prefer soil that is light, sandy, and well drained. They hate water-logging as much as they hate fresh animal manure, not that that is very often found in a garden. It is nearly always advisable to give them some fertilizer. The best to use is one of the well-known peat humus fertilizers, making your choice according to the requirements of individual plants as regards lime. Mineral fertilizers are not so good when you are preparing the planting site, since they are supposed to have a rather bad effect on the first delicate little roots that the bulb puts out, and we must also take into account that if we keep the ground well drained they will be relatively quickly dispersed. Used three weeks before planting, according to the directions, at least a part of mineral fertilizer will no longer be present in the topsoil to be absorbed without risk by the first, gradually forming roots; it will have sunk further down. Regular applications of lime are important for many bulbous and tuberous plants. The particular lime requirements of various plants will therefore be mentioned in the individual descriptions.

Prepare thoroughly for planting

The larger species, such as almost all lilies, tulips and narcissi – also dahlias and gladioli – are always planted between 6 and 12 in (5 and 30 cm) deep. The layer above the bulb should consist of a nourishing soil made up of equal parts of loam, sand and humus or compost. Press it down lightly so that no air pockets remain. If you are planting in autumn do not water, but add a covering of peat. When planting in spring fill the hole only two-thirds up, and keep it very moist. Where the cultivation of bulbous and tuberous plants differs from these general rules, you will find it mentioned in the individual descriptions.

Depth of planting, winter protection, planting time

In general, hardy and half-hardy bulbs and tubers should have two to three times as much soil as their own thickness

Modern bulb planters do the job properly, at the right depth, and without compressing the soil. *Upper left:* the planting tool. *Right:* planting a bulb. *Lower left:* Planting holes with plugs of turf/soil

How to recognize bulbs by their shape.

over them. However, if the soil is light you can go a little deeper – or in heavy soil, which needs lightening with sand, you can plant a little higher. The growth of the plant above ground is relevant to planting depth; gladioli often topple over because the tubers were not planted deep enough; plant them 5–6 in (13–15 cm) deep. Shallow planting also increases the risk of frost damage to bulbs which are claimed to be hardy, but often are not. So some kind of winter protection in the way of peat compost or similar material is advisable in general, essential in some cases, and you will find these mentioned in the individual descriptions. Newly planted bulbs and tubers sometimes need to be given protection against frost.

The usual planting time for hardy bulbous plants is autumn, not too late, between the beginning of September and the end of October (for departures from this rule see the individual descriptions). Early planting is always an advantage, because bulbs and tubers will take root better in warm soil, before the first frosts. Many of the smaller, hardy species are excellent in the rock garden, where they will live in harmony with its other inhabitants for years, if not disturbed by over-zealous hoeing and weeding or eaten by mice or other pests. They come up faithfully every spring, or you find their children and grandchildren suddenly appearing in unexpected places – many bulbs and tubers are known to have an impulse to wander and to self-seed.

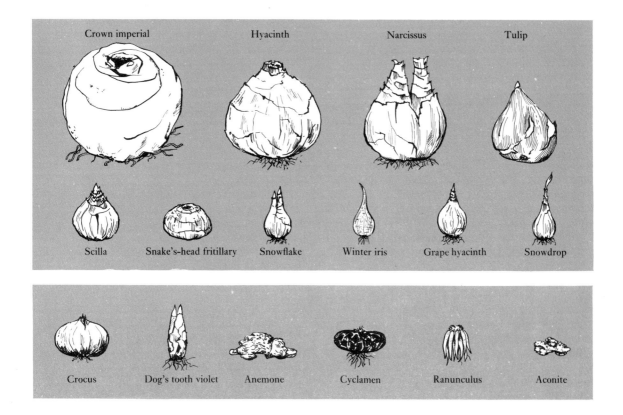

Crown imperial   Hyacinth   Narcissus   Tulip

Scilla   Snake's-head fritillary   Snowflake   Winter iris   Grape hyacinth   Snowdrop

Crocus   Dog's tooth violet   Anemone   Cyclamen   Ranunculus   Aconite

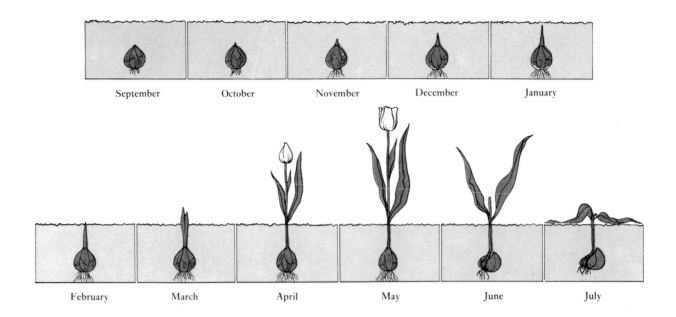

September   October   November   December   January

February   March   April   May   June   July

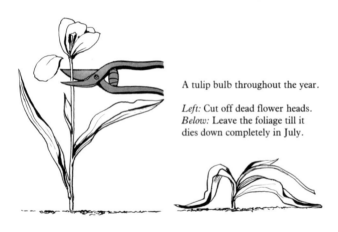

A tulip bulb throughout the year.

Left: Cut off dead flower heads.
Below: Leave the foliage till it dies down completely in July.

The assortment of bulbous plants available has increased a great deal over the last few years. Spring and late summer catalogues full of enticing pictures can make decisions difficult for the gardener. But no one should be tempted to fall for cheap, give-away offers. The quality of bulbs and tubers is so important that it is better to pay a little more and ensure that they are of impeccable origin.

Routine care: feeding, treatment of leaves and flowers

Good development over the years depends to a great extent on the provision of constant and adequate nourishment. It really is necessary to emphasize this; so many otherwise quite reasonable gardeners labour under the delusion that bulbs and tubers can replenish themselves out of nothing,

and need no feeding. However, if your tulips, lilies, dahlias or gladioli fade before their time, or your daffodils fail to flower properly, it is often because they are hungry. So always give enough food. This means working a peat-based fertilizer into the soil, either early in spring or late in autumn according to the growth cycle of the particular plant (use about 8 oz per square yard (250 g per square metre), and applying fertilizer, preferably in liquid form, during the main growing season. As it is particularly important for bulbs and tubers to go through their full cycle of growth, coming to complete maturity before winter sets in, they, like trees, need applications of fertilizer in good time. Without it, they will be sluggish to start growth, and the passage of the plant into its dormant state, a process bound up with the natural withering of the foliage, will be affected. The unfortunate results will be increased susceptibility to frost damage of bulbs left in the ground, and impaired keeping qualities in those lifted for winter storage.

Once the flowering season is over, no more fertilizer should be given. The only exceptions are the autumn-flowering *Crocus speciosus* forms, and *Colchicum* (meadow saffron) species and hybrids. These should be fed from the time the leaves come up in spring until the tips of the foliage begin to turn yellow.

It is a general rule for all bulbs and tubers, large and small, that we let them keep their leaves, but cut off the flower heads when the seed-cases begin to form at the latest. The development of seeds means an expense of energy which drains the reserves of the bulb or tuber. The foliage, however, is important to the entire nutritional organization of the plant. If it is cut down, the material which goes back into the storage organ in the course of its natural withering will be lost.

Bulbs for the garden. *Top left:* lilies *(Lilium candidum)*. *Top right:* fritillaries (*Fritillaria meleagris* 'Purple King' and *F. meleagris* 'Alba'). *Bottom left:* snowflakes (*Leucojum vernum*). *Bottom right: Narcissus* 'Cragford'.

111

Crown imperial *(Fritillaria imperialis)*.

Hardy bulbous and tuberous plants

All those marked with the Letter **R** are also suitable for rock gardens. The arrangement is again in alphabetical order of the botanical names.

Allium, **Allium, flowering onion.** Height 6–36 in (15–90 cm); planting time October; flowering time May/August; colours: white, yellow, red, also blue. Pretty spring and summer-flowering plants, all equally undemanding. There are several species which are particular favourites: *Allium moly*, with bright yellow flowers in umbels, star-shaped, planting distance between bulbs about 5 in (12 cm), some winter protection desirable; *A. neapolitanum*: snow-white, bell-shaped flowers with dark stamens, delightful for rock gardens and small nosegays; *A. ostrowskianum*, carmine-red flowers, height not above 6 in (15 cm), for rock gardens; also *A. sphaerocephalon*, 28–36 in (70–90 cm) tall, flowering reddish violet in July/August, and useful for cutting and dried flowers: one of the largest alliums. **R**

Anemone, **Anemone, windflower.** Height 4–10 in (10–25 cm); planting time autumn or spring; flowering time March/May, or in autumn if planted in the spring; colour of flowers: white, pink, red, blue, violet. Popular species and varieties include *A. blanda*, *A. coronaria*, especially the 'St. Brigid' and 'De Caen' forms, and *A. fulgens*. Give extra lime. The dark tubers or 'claws' of the anemone, like those of its close relative the ranunculus, are planted only 1½–2 in (4–6 cm) deep and 3–4 in (8–10 cm) apart. Half-shade and rich soil are desirable, and some form of winter protection in severe cold; you can cover with twigs or dead leaves. There are countless cultivated forms, in single and double varieties, which can be planted in succession to prolong the flowering season. When planting in spring, soak the tubers in water for 24 hours first. Very pretty and long-lasting as cut flowers. You get a more profuse flowering from tubers planted in autumn.

Camassia, **Quamash.** Height up to 30 in (70 cm); flowering time May/June; colour of flowers: blue or cream. The early, light blue *C. cusickii* is on the market, as are rather later *C. leichtlinii* (cream) and *C. esculenta* (deep blue). Plant bulbs in groups of three or five, 3–4 in (8–10 cm) deep, between August and October. Best site: a sunny, undisturbed, but not dry place in a herbaceous border. Avoid heavy soil and water-logging.

Chionodoxa, **Glory of the snow.** Height 5–6 in (12–15 cm); planting time autumn; flowering time March/April; colour of flowers: mostly sky-blue, shading to white inside, also white, pink and lilac flowered varieties. Plant the little bulbs, 2–3 in (5–8 cm) deep and quite close together, and they will spread year after year to form bigger

Chionodoxa, Glory of the snow

clumps. Recommended species: *C. luciliae*, *C. sardensis*, *C. gigantea*.

Colchicum autumnale, **Meadow saffron, naked ladies.** Height 6–12 in (15–30 cm); leaves up to 16 in (40 cm); planting time August; flowering time autumn; colour of flowers: pinkish mauve to purple, white. Give extra lime. Plant the egg-shaped bulbs down to 8 in (20 cm) deep. The beautiful flowers will soon appear. More important than the original species are the far more magnificent, large-flowered garden hybrids. As the best of a good dozen or so I will just mention the double 'Waterlily'.

Colchicum autumnale, Meadow saffron

Colchicum bulbocodium, previously *Bulbocodium vernum*, **Spring meadow saffron.** Bears its delicate mauve flowers in February/March. **R**

Crocosmia, **Montbretia.** Height up to 30 in (70 cm); flowering time June/August; colour of flowers: yellow, orange, pink. Plant bulbs 2–3 in (5–8 cm) deep and 4–6 in (10–15 cm) apart in clumps in early spring in sandy, free-draining soil. The newer varieties and hybrids, such as 'Emily MacKenzie' and 'Solfataire', are an improvement on the species. (Crocosmias are often listed among hardy perennial plants in catalogues.)

Crocus, **Crocus.** Height 3–4 in (8–10 cm); planting time, if possible, August; flowering time spring or autumn; colour of flowers: all except true red. Besides the familiar spring flowers, usually hybrids of *C. vernus*, we also have the equally large species *Crocus speciosus*, which flowers in the winter, with broad-tipped petals, usually light purple, on the outside, and smaller white to pale lilac petals in the interior. The corms of both species are planted in groups, 3–4 in (8–10 cm) deep. Keep to the correct planting time, especially for *Crocus speciosus*. Both species will do as well in the rock garden as in other good sunny situations with well-drained soil; they prefer a poorish soil to one too rich in nourishment. The delicate and very early species of wild crocus, such as *C. ancyrensis*, *C. chrysanthus*, *C. susianus*, *C. imperati*, are gaining favour these days. **R**

Cyclamen, **Cyclamen.** Height 4–6 in (10–15 cm); planting time August or spring; flowering time autumn, winter or spring; colour of flowers: deep pink, also white. Give extra lime. Over the last few years the hardy, fragrant cyclamen has become a distinct favourite among all those gardeners who like to grow something a bit special. The tubers are offered in most catalogues, and there are also some less common species of this enchanting plant. The rock garden is not always the best site, since the cyclamen likes half-shade and a light soil containing humus, which can be supplemented by the addition of some leaf mould. The tubers must lie firm once planted, and be covered with about 1 in (2–3 cm) of soil. The luxuriant foliage is a pretty sight, as well as the flowers themselves. A favourite late summer-flowering cyclamen is *C. europaeum*; *C. neapolitanum* does not flower until September; the very hardy *C. coum*, and its varieties and hybrids, is a winter-flowering plant, and thus is planted only in autumn. *C. persicum* is a delightful spring-flowering species for sheltered gardens.

Eranthis, **Aconite.** Height 2–4 in (5–10 cm); planting time August/October; flowering time, January onwards; colour of flowers: bright yellow. The earliest to flower is *E. hyemalis*, followed in March by *E. cilicica*. Later still the fragrant, large-flowered hybrid *E. × tubergenii* 'Guinea Gold' appears. This charming plant is not a bulb, being a close relative of the anemone and the ranunculus. Plant the little tubers in groups, 1½–2 in (4–5 cm) deep. **R**

Erythronium dens-canis, **Dog's tooth violet, trout lily.** Height 4–8 in (10–20 cm); planting time September/October; flowering time March/May; colour of flowers: white, deep pink to purple. Its bulb, which really does look like a dog's tooth, is planted as fresh as possible, about 2 in (5 cm) deep, in half-shade, and in rich, fairly damp soil, where it will develop grey-green leaves flecked with purple, and will flower profusely. Increase by offsets. **R**

Fritillaria imperialis, **Crown imperial.** Height 24–40 in (60–100 cm); planting time August/September; flowering

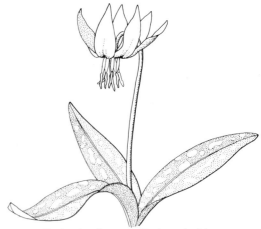
Erythronium dens-canis, Dog's tooth violet

time April/May; colour of flowers: yellow or orange, black with a white heart at the base of the flower. Unfortunately, the crown imperial, with its striking flowers hanging under a shock of green leaves, has an unpleasant smell. Plant 8–12 in (20–30 cm) deep. Always leave it strictly alone. Best varieties: the yellow 'Lutea' and the orange-brown 'Orange Perfection' and 'Aurora'.

Fritillaria meleagris, **Snake's-head fritillary.** Height 8–10 in (20–25 cm); planting time autumn; flowering time April/May; colour of flowers: pale violet, white, or with a dark chequered pattern. At first the stems, bearing buds resembling a lizard's head, are half-lying on the ground, and you think that nothing much will come of them. Then, one morning, you suddenly find them standing bolt upright and proudly displaying their curious chequered flowers. Plant the bulbs, which are the size of plovers' eggs, in groups of 10–20, about 2–3 in (6–8 cm) deep. Propagate by offsets. **R**

Galanthus, **Snowdrop.** Height 6–8 in (15–20 cm); planting time autumn; flowering time February/March; colour of flowers: white with a green half-moon on the tips of the inner petals; fragrant. Give extra lime. Plant bulbs in groups in September, putting them in 4 in (10 cm) deep and 3–4 in (8–10 cm) apart; otherwise, leave them alone. To increase, divide old clumps when in flower.

Hyacinthus orientalis, **Hyacinth.** Height 10–12 in (25–30 cm), planting time August until November; flowering time April/May; all colours. Give extra lime. For the garden buy the smaller forms specially meant for this purpose, and do not just use superannuated forced bulbs from bowls indoors. Plant between August and November, the best time being the end of September till the beginning of October, 4–6 in (10–15 cm) deep, according to size, and with the same amount of space between them. The site should be warm and sunny and not too moist. If you like to see a bed full of handsome hyacinths standing erect and you want to protect the bulbs, which are often imported and thus relatively expensive, from being nibbled by mice, it is a good idea to lift them annually after they have flowered and the foliage has died down – however, if you prefer less showy flowers, with a more informal and natural look about them, you can leave them in the ground to take their luck as it comes, and you may find that they survive half a dozen years or more. Since growing individual hyacinths in containers is rather complicated, I would recommend a bed containing wire netting over a 12 in (30 cm) layer of gravel when you are planting large areas, to keep mice away. Many catalogues offer 'miniature hyacinths' for rock gardens, where they look extremely pretty.

Ipheion uniflorum, **Spring star flower.** Height 4 in (10 cm); flowering time May; colour of flowers: pale blue. Previously known as *Triteleia* or *Brodiaea*. The plant grows in large groups with grassy foliage. Only the species named, and its variety 'Wisley Blue', are completely hardy.

Ipheion uniflorum, Spring star flower

Iris xiphioides and *I. xiphium*, **English, Spanish and Dutch iris.** Height 16–20 in (40–50 cm); planting time October/November; flowering time, according to variety, May to July; colour of flowers: white, mauve, blue, purple, yellow, brown; beardless. These 'orchid-flowered' bulbous irises come out just about the time tulips are finished, at a season which is relatively short of flowers. There are many hybrids and varieties to surprise and delight us, and they are excellent as cut flowers too. The

Dutch irises are the first to appear. About two weeks later they are followed by the Spanish forms, and after another two weeks by the English. They should all be planted 3–4 in (8–10 cm) deep, at a distance of 3–4 in (8–10 cm). They do well in any kind of soil.

Iris reticulata, **Winter iris.** Height 6 in (15 cm); planting time August/October; flowering time: March, colour of flowers: blue, purple. To avoid any confusion, these beautiful irises, flowering early in the year, should be grown separately from other kinds. *Iris reticulata*, like the yellow *I. danfordiae* and the less well-known *I. bucharica* and *I. histrioides*, is among the most important dwarf species. It is a dwarf form particularly suitable for the rock garden as well. Plant 2–3 in (5–8 cm) deep, in well-drained sandy loam. Completely hardy. **R**

Ixia, **Corn lily.** Height 18 in (45 cm); planting time, late autumn to November; flowering time June/July; colour of flowers: white, pink, red, orange, mauve. Plant the little bulbs 3–4 in (8–10 cm) deep, as late in the year as possible, in groups. They need some form of winter protection, which should be removed in good time in spring. Propagate by offsets.

Leucojum, **Snowflake.** Height 8–24 in (20–60 cm); planting time autumn; flowering time spring, summer or autumn; colour: white with petal tips of green or yellow. In error, people sometimes call the winter snowflake *L. vernum*, a snowdrop, but it is much larger, the flowers are rounder, and have petals all the same length. The summer snowflake is *L. aestivum*, and the autumn ones are *L. autumnale* and *L. roseum*. Plant 4–6 in (10–15 cm) apart. Likes moist soil containing humus.

Lilium, **Lily.** Height 16–70 in (40–180 cm); planting time autumn, except for the Madonna lily, *L. candidum*, late August, and spring for *L. auratum* and *L. speciosum* and their hybrids; flowering time June/September; colour of flowers: white, pink, yellow, orange, red, spotted and bicoloured. Hitherto the lily has demanded a lot of attention and been rather a difficult plant for gardeners to cultivate, not least because of its great diversity of origin. The great event of our time has been the change this fine plant has undergone through breeding, especially by the Oregon Bulb Farm, which has given quite a new look to its present and future prospects. The lily can now be robust as well as beautiful, and may live for years even in quite unpretentious gardens. These days the more vulnerable wild and original species of lily have increasingly made way for many hybrids and varieties with an incredible profusion of flowers, and good resistance to changes in climate and to disease.

Be careful when you are buying lily bulbs. The plump freshness of their fleshy scales indicates good quality. If you cannot plant your bulbs at once, keep them, still in their packing, in a cool place. If the scales do begin to look slightly shrivelled, bed the bulbs in damp sand until they recover. Planting sites must be carefully chosen. Morning or evening sun is better than a south-facing position with full sun, for the old rule of thumb that lilies like to have their heads warm but their feet cool still holds good. It is easy to achieve this desirable state of affairs by planting ground cover plants around them. The soil must be well cultivated to a good depth, be well drained, and have no tendency to waterlogging. On level sites it is possible to build up small mounds in which to plant lilies. They go well in groups, but must be planted some distance apart, because they will live in the same spot for years and need a considerable amount of room in which to spread themselves. They like protection from wind, but cannot stand water dripping on them, so they should never be planted underneath trees or tall shrubs. Most lilies prefer soil with a pH value of 5·5–6·5 (slightly acid to neutral). However, some lilies are definitely lime-haters, and so will not do well in normal garden soil. Some examples of lilies which *do* like lime: *L. bulbiferum, L. candidum, L. chalcedonicum, L. henryi, L. longiflorum, L. martagon, L. × testaceum* and all martagon types. Some examples of lilies which do *not* like lime: *L. auratum, L. japonicum, L. pardalinum, L. speciosum, L. superbum,* all lilies originating in the USA, all the Bellingham hybrids, all *L. auratum* and *L. speciosum* hybrids.

The majority of garden lilies belong to the so-called stem-rooting group: besides their real roots, beneath the bulb, they also put out roots from the main stem above the bulb. These roots absorb nourishment from the humus in the topsoil during summer and grow anew every year. Hence stem-rooting lilies need to be planted deep. Measured from the tip of the bulb, these should be covered with earth to a depth of three times the length of the bulb. Deep planting of this kind also acts as winter protection and gives the plants a good firm anchorage in the soil. The most important exception to the deep-planting rule is the madonna lily, *L. candidum*, which should be covered with 1–2 in (3–5 cm) of soil at the most, and does not need protection; in winter it puts out no roots from the stem.

The soil should be given a general purpose fertilizer several weeks before planting. When you have dug a hole in the prepared soil, re-fill it with soil to a few inches (centimetres) below planting depth and add a layer of about 2 in (5 cm) sharp sand. Place the bulbs directly on the sand, settling the fresh roots carefully. Then place a little sand around them, pressing it down gently, and put back the rest of the soil in the planting hole. You end up with a slight mound which will level out later of its own accord. Unlike all other flowering bulbous and tuberous plants, lilies should be generously watered at planting time. As winter protection, a covering of 4 in (10 cm) dead leaves or twigs is enough. To prevent the bulb beginning to shoot too early, and thus risking frost damage, remove this covering early in spring. Several species of lily need con-

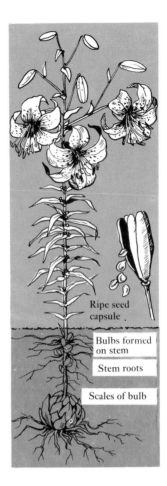

Ripe seed capsule

Bulbs formed on stem

Stem roots

Scales of bulb

Diagrammatic representation of typical stem-rooting lily, showing how small bulbs are formed both beneath the soil surface on the main stem and above the surface in the leaf axils.

stant winter protection, such as the rather vulnerable golden-rayed lily, *Lilium auratum*, also *L. speciosum* and its hybrids.

Subsequent care presents no problems. All lilies grow better the less you disturb them. At the end of winter give them some compound fertilizer, not too rich in nitrogen, and apply liquid fertilizer every few weeks from the appearance of the first shoots to the end of flowering (on no account go on later!). Again, a greater potash than nitrogen content is best. When flowering is over the bulbs will mature better if you do not water, even in dry weather. Always remove faded blooms to discourage the formation of seeds. Only a few lilies, such as *Lilium regale*, a particularly rewarding garden plant, will seed themselves. It is not necessary to move the plants for some years; wait until you see that lilies which used to grow strongly are coming up with shorter stems and producing smaller flowers. Of course they should be moved only during their dormant season, in accordance with the procedure described for planting new bulbs. You can remove poor-looking scales at the same time and dust the bulbs with charcoal powder to protect against infections. The lily's chief enemies are voles and field-mice, snails, and the stem and bulb eelworm, lily beetles and lily thrips, as well as aphids, dangerous as carriers of lily viruses. Top of the list of fungus diseases is lily disease (*Botrytis*) and basal rot (*Fusarium*). For controlling these see the chapter PLANTS NEED PEST AND DISEASE PROTECTION.

Montbretia, see **Crocosmia**

Muscari, **Grape hyacinth.** Height 8–10 in (20–25 cm); planting time September/October; flowering time April/May; colours: light to violet-blue. The little bulbs of these delightful plants with their aromatic scent should be planted about 2–3 in (5–8 cm) deep in autumn. They will do best in a sunny position. They increase freely by seeding themselves. Particularly interesting is the 'Oxford and Cambridge' *M. tubergenianum*, with the top half of the flowers sky-blue and the lower half dark blue. **R**

Narcissus, **Narcissus and daffodil.** Height up to 16 in (40 cm); planting time September/November; flowering time March/May; colour of flowers: white, yellow, orange, pink, bicoloured or with red eye, single and double blooms. There are forms with both long and short trumpets and cups. New varieties are constantly appearing. Give extra lime. Narcissus bulbs are planted 6–8 in (15–20 cm) deep, but not too close together, to give them room to spread over the years. The soil should be rich in humus, but not too dry, and never sandy. They tolerate sun as well as half-shade – the poet's narcissus (*N. poeticus*) prefers a rather moist site. A pre-requisite of regular flowering is to leave narcissi strictly alone until the leaves die down of themselves. They will do happily in many places, from rock gardens to shrubberies. Flowering begins in March, with the *N. cyclamineus* type, followed by large-cupped double narcissi and trumpet narcissi, or daffodils, in shades of white, yellow, or bicoloured. The tall, small-cupped narcissi also bloom in March/April. Rather later come the poetaz narcissi, bearing several rather smaller, very fragrant flowers on each stem, and finally the *N. poeticus*, pheasant's eye, varieties. The dainty dwarf narcissi, flowering in April and May, are particularly good as companions of botanical tulips in sunny rock gardens. Narcissi can be grown in containers outdoors and brought into the home for a splendid show of spring colour.

Nerine, **Nerine.** Height 6–24 in (15–60 cm); flowering time September/October; colour: pink. Plant the bulbs 4 in (10 cm) deep, preferably in well-drained soil in a sheltered south-facing position. Give some protection in winter in exposed positions. Divide the plants every five years or so, but otherwise they prefer to be undisturbed. *N. bowdenii* and *N.b.* 'Fenwick's Variety' are the hardiest nerines for outdoor growing.

Ornithogalum umbellatum, **Star of Bethlehem.** Height 4–12 in (10–30 cm); planting time autumn; flowering time March/May; colour of flowers: white. A charming little flowering bulb, tolerates dry conditions, and so is particularly good planted in drifts on a sunny slope. The small, white, pear-shaped bulbs are planted 3–4 in (8–10 cm) deep, at a distance of 6–8 in (15–20 cm). Propagation by offsets. I should also mention the silvery grey and pale green flowering *O. nutans*. **R**

Oxalis adenophylla, **Wood sorrel.** Height 4 in (10 cm); flowering time April; colour: mauve-pink. Plant between September and November; the planting site should contain humus, be well drained, and free of lime (mix the soil with sharp sand). Given some winter protection it will last for years. Charming in the rock garden. **R**

Puschkinia libanotica, (*P. scilloides*), **Puschkinia, striped squill.** Height 4–6 in (10–15 cm); flowering time March/April; colour of flowers: light blue with darker stripes, or pure white. Plant 2 to 3 little bulbs at a time in August/September, 4–5 in (10–12 cm) deep. Good neighbours for *Eranthis*, *Muscari* and *Scilla*. **R**

Ranunculus asiaticus, **Garden ranunculus.** Height 8–12 in (20–30 cm); planting time spring; flowering time April and later; colour of flowers: red, yellow, white and pastel shades. Give extra lime. The most handsome variety is the paeony-flowered ranunculus, with double, almost rose-like blooms, which are very good as cut flowers and last a long time. The more of them you pick the more they grow. Cultivate like the anemone; give protection in winter.

Scilla, **Scilla.** Height 4–12 in (10–40 cm); planting time August/October; flowering time, according to variety, March/April or the end of May; colour of flowers: blue, also white, pink, and reddish purple. The bulbs of the various species of scilla are best planted in drifts, 2–3 in (5–8 cm) deep. They prefer good soil which is dry in summer. Self-sown seedlings grow as thick as grass. The best known is *Scilla sibirica*, used in alternation with

Scilla

snowdrops as an edging to garden paths, or naturalized in the lawn, or planted in the rock garden. The bluebell, *Scilla nutans* now properly *Endymion hispanicus*, a large, bell-flowered species with many varieties, has spikes of flowers almost like the hyacinth on stems about 12 in (30 cm) tall; the colours are light blue, also white and pink, and the plant flowers from the middle to the end of May.

Sternbergia lutea, **Sternbergia.** Height 4–6 in (10–15 cm). Plant as early as June/July, about 4 in (10 cm) deep, for crocus-like, yellow blooms appearing with the leaves from September to October. Will only do well on very sunny, sheltered sites, for example, the south-facing slope of a rock garden. The leaves stand through the winter. **R**

Trillium, **Trillium.** Height 8–12 in (20–30 cm); flowering time April/May; colour: white, yellow, pink, red. Likes a deep peaty soil in a shady position. Plant in autumn 3–4 in (8–10 cm) deep. *T. erectum* and *T. grandiflora* 'Plena' are two fine forms.

Tulipa, **Tulip.** Height 4–32 in (10–80 cm); planting time September/December; flowering time February/May; colour of flowers: all colours, including green, except blue. The garden tulip is produced in new forms and colours every year in varieties ranging from extremely tall, giant-flowered tulips to extremely small, multi-flowered ones. Normal planting depth is 4–6 in (10–15 cm), with 6–8 in (15–20 cm) between the bulbs. Plant in autumn where they are to flower. When the flowers are over and the leaves have died down, lift the bulbs and store them in a dry, cool place, until it is time to plant them again. If the leaves of the tulips have not died by the time you want to lift the bulbs, they can still be dug up but planted elsewhere temporarily to finish growth.

However, if you want tulips to be naturalized in an informal corner of the garden, they not only can, but should, stay in the ground. They will not develop into good, strong, bushy plants, like the small wild tulip, unless they do so. To this group, along with many others, and with a good dozen varieties of its own, belongs *Tulipa kaufmanniana*, which flowers in April. It is followed by the scarlet *Tulipa fosteriana* and the redder *Tulipa greigii*, again with many fine varieties. However, the most charming of all are the 'lady tulips', *Tulipa clusiana*, in shades of white and pale pink, and *Tulipa praestans*, bearing 2–5 flowers on each stem. Other popular species tulips include *T. eichleri*, *T. kolpakowskiana*, *T. saxatilis*, *T. sylvestris* and *T. urumiensis*.

At planting time you will find a wide range of tulip bulbs on offer at any garden shop or centre; you have only to decide on your own particular needs. The approximate flowering time of the different types of tulips is first the Early Single Tulips in the middle of May (10–15 in (25–38 cm)) followed by the Early Double Tulips at the end of the month (12 in (30 cm)). Then come the Paeony-

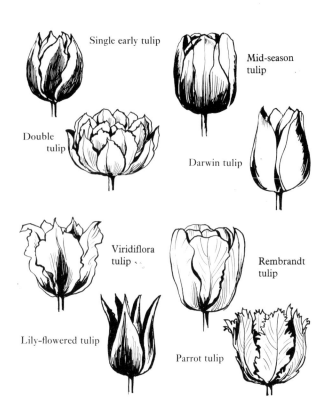

Types of tulip flowers.

flowered, Mid-season and Darwin hybrid Tulips in late April and May (15–24 in (38–60 cm)), and the Lily-flowered, Multi-flowered and May-flowering Tulips (18–30 in (45–75 cm)) in early May, with the Parrot, Rembrandt and Viridiflora Tulips (9–24 in (23–60 cm)) finally in mid-May.

Usually single tulips of medium height look better in a garden than specimens which are very long-stemmed and have complicated flowers; the latter kind easily get tousled by the wind, and the weight of the flower heads can cause them to snap or bend in rain. Finally, tulips mingle well with other kinds of plant – but not, if you can help it, as isolated specimens; use them as groups of a dozen plants at least.

Unfortunately, it is not unusual for keen gardeners to let tulip seeds ripen and try to rear their own plants. In theory there is nothing against this, but as with lily seeds it will be some years before a bulb capable of flowering develops, and thus it will not run true to variety but will be a chance product. However, if you propagate the standard varieties from offsets, they will breed true.

Apart from mice, tulips do not suffer much from pests but they are prone to a number of fungus infections, bacterial and virus diseases, which can cause heavy losses. It is difficult, and often impossible, to cure these. The best advice I can give is to be sure you always buy healthy bulbs from a reliable source. In the long run it is wisest to burn any diseased tulip bulbs – flowers, foliage and all. **R**

Half-hardy bulbous and tuberous plants

If a plant is not completely hardy it will usually be very vulnerable to late or early frosts. This is why, with a few exceptions, bulbs and tubers of this group are planted out at the beginning of May, so that new growth will not appear before the danger of frosts in mid-May is past. When such plants have been raised under glass they are not planted out until after the middle of May. For the rest, the cultivation of half-hardy bulbous plants is very much the same as for their hardy cousins.

Acidanthera murielae, **Acidanthera.** Height 24–28 in (60–70 cm); planting time, the beginning of April to the middle of May; colour of flowers: white with a purple eye; likes sun to half-shade in a place that is not too dry. Cultivate like the gladiolus. Plant the bulbs 5–6 in (12–15 cm) deep, 12 in (30 cm) apart. After the leaves die down lift, clean and store in dry peat in a frost-free place over the winter.

Begonia, tuberous group, **Tuberous begonias.** Height 12–16 in (30–40 cm); flowering time June/October; colour of flowers: ranging from white through yellow to orange and dark red. There is an enormous selection available with single or double flowers. Begonias like a shady or at least half-shady situation. Buy one-year-old plants in June, or you can get two-year-old plants capable of flowering in the middle of May. Starting the tubers yourself is not difficult: plant in pots from February onwards; the tubers should be level with the tops of the pots. They will begin to put out shoots, and can be planted, as usual, after the last May frosts.

After flowering, begonia tubers need a dormant period. Root stocks planted out are cut short after the first frosts, the tubers are lifted, and over-wintered like dahlia or gladiolus tubers, though they can be started in pots or boxes in February as described previously. Another method is to put the tubers in a shallow box of sand in autumn, soon after they have dried off, in such a way that the cut stems are just peeping out, and leave them there until it is time to plant them in their pots. Many of the newer varieties will tolerate a certain amount of bright sunlight. There are some tuberous begonias, such as the *B. multiflora* and *B. pendula* varieties, which are useful for window boxes and hanging baskets.

Canna × hybrida, **Canna lily.** Height 20–32 in (50–80 cm); flowering time June till the first frost; colour of flowers: yellow, orange, red; situation: very sunny, warm and sheltered. Well-drained, rich soil is best; the plants like to keep their feet warm. Plant out at the end of May or the beginning of June. Cut the stalks short in autumn, raise the tubers and keep them through winter in moderate warmth, so that they do not dry out completely, perhaps in a cellar where you have a boiler for central heating. Store them in slightly moistened sand. Divide the tubers at the end of February (make sure each part divided has an eye) and plant in pots with fresh compost. Grow on until May in a steady temperature of 62–65°F (18–20°C), harden off well before planting out.

Canna lily

Dahlia, **Dahlia.** Height, according to variety, 6–98 in (15–250 cm); flowering time July to autumn; all colours except blue; likes a sunny, open position, and moist, rich soil. There are special varieties for dry soils. The dahlia is extremely sensitive to frost. Its tubers, which must not be kept too dry during the winter (or they will shrivel), or too moist (or they will rot), are never planted out before the beginning of May. Distance from one plant to another on all sides is 20–40 in (50–100 cm) according to the size of the variety. When you dig the planting holes put in a stake for tying up the taller plants; putting one in at a later date only too often results in damage to the tubers. Bought tubers should usually be flowering size. When dividing large clumps of tubers yourself, make sure each piece of stem has at least one eye, or it will not be possible for it to produce a shoot. After planting, the young root-buds should be covered with about 2 in (5 cm) of soil. Water more or less generously according to the state of the weather. If there is any danger of frost affecting shoots that are already showing, cover with flowerpots or cloches. Cold weather delays growth and flowering, but the plants usually make up for lost time later.

To get strong, bushy plants and plenty of flowers keep only the three strongest shoots on each and apply a compound fertilizer in liquid form every 2–3 weeks from early

Paeony-flowered dahlia

Dwarf-bedding dahlia
(single or double)

Official division into groups of dahlia varieties: Decorative, Cactus and Semi-cactus dahlias are further sub-divided into Giant, Large, Medium, Small and Miniature groups, depending on the flower size.

summer onwards. Keep tying the plants as they grow and later on remove dead flowers. If you do this the dahlias will keep putting out new flower buds on slender stems from the leaf axils until well into late autumn.

In autumn let the tubers mature in the ground as long as possible. When the first frosts have struck down flowers and foliage, cut down the blackened stems to close above the ground, loosen the soil around the plants, and then, using a spade and going carefully, raise the whole clump of tubers without harming it. Dry off in the sun if the weather is fine and there is no frost; otherwise dry off in a moderately warm place indoors, remove any soil clinging to the tubers, label them, and spread them out side by side, but without touching each other, on dry peat or sand.

Eucomis, **Pineapple flower.** Height, according to variety, 24–40 in (60–100 cm); the most important are *E. bicolor*, *E. punctata*. Very interesting plants, with striped leaves and stems. The greenish-white flower with its pineapple-like tuft of leaves on top appears in June/July and carries on until the first frost. Plant bulbs 6–8 in (15–20 cm) deep in April/May. It is possible to leave the bulbs out all winter, with a good protective covering, but I lift and divide the clusters of bulbs in autumn and over-winter them like dahlias and gladioli. *Eucomis* is also a good plant for tubs.

Freesia, **Freesia.** Height 12–16 in (30–40 cm); planting time of prepared bulbs, April; flowering time July/Octo-

ber; colour of flowers: all pastel shades; situation, sunny and sheltered. The new outdoor freesias are already so well acclimatized that gardeners can look forward confidently to enjoying their long-lasting, fragrant flowers. Tubers are planted in groups about 3 in (8 cm) deep, 4 in (10 cm) apart in April. Lift the tubers when the first frosts come, store like gladiolus corms. They are not always sure to flower again, so it is as well to buy a few new tubers every year.

Galtonia candicans, **Californian hyacinth, summer hyacinth.** Height about 3 ft (1 m); planting time, mid-April; flowering time the end of July to September; colour: white. The erect leaves are fleshy and grey-green, sometimes with white markings, similar to those of the garden hyacinth in shape and arrangement. In July, 15–30 pure white bell-shaped flowers form a magnificent cluster, visible from some way off, around the upright flower stem. Plant the bulbs at least 10 in (25 cm) deep from the beginning to the middle of April. They flourish in any soil, like sun to half-shade, and are excellent, long-lasting cut flowers for large vases.

Gladiolus, **Sword lily, gladiolus.** Height up to nearly 5 ft (1·5 m); planting time, beginning of April to the end of May; flowering time July to the first frosts; colour of flowers: all shades. Everything said earlier about the raising, care and storage of dahlias also applies to the gladiolus. It is particularly important for the roundish corms to be well dried off when they are lifted in autumn; only then should you cut off the withered leaves. Gladiolus breeders, like dahlia and rose-growers, have developed many new shapes and colours over the years, giving their favourite flowers a good deal of resistance to rain. The modern hybrids are either large or small flowered. Gladioli must be planted deep enough to keep them from damage by wind and rain. In light soil they will need rather more covering over than in heavy soil, and small corms are not planted as deep as large ones. In any case, planting depth should be 4–6 in (10–15 cm), distance between plants 3–4 in (8–10 cm) for large corms and distance between rows 8 in (20 cm). Successive plantings of early, mid-season and later varieties will give you a flowering season of 4–5 months. If you do not want to run any risks, stick to buying fully developed corms of guaranteed size and variety, though the annual renewal of the corm, with the parent corm giving way to the new main corm, can go on for ever so long as it remains healthy and is treated properly. The large-flowering hybrids take first place among the standard varieties available today. The enormous assortment is constantly being changed and extended.

Cut off the dried foliage in autumn and remove the remains of the parent gladiolus corm.

There are also a few hardy species of gladiolus, though it is not always easy to get hold of them. The most frequently available is *Gladiolus byzantinus*. Its rather loud, dark-red colour has something of the character of a wild plant, and the flowers look very modest beside the magnificent cultivated varieties. The plant likes a very sunny position, and as it grows to only about 24 in (60 cms) is a pleasant flower even in a rock garden. Plant the small corms in April/May and let them grow and propagate themselves undisturbed over a period of years. All gladioli make excellent cut flowers.

Hymenocallis, **Hymenocallis.** Most species of this magnificent tropical plant are only suitable for a heated greenhouse. However, *H. calathina* can be grown out of doors in the summer. Plant the bulbs, which are the size of a fist, in a very sheltered, sunny place with good rich soil in the middle of May. The wonderful cream or snow-white flowers will appear at the end of June or the beginning of

July, after the formation of a number of light green, ribbon-shaped leaves. Give plenty of fertilizer during the period of growth and keep the plant moist. Lift the bulbs in good time and keep at 60°F (16°C) during the winter.

Sprekelia formosissima, **Jacobean lily.** Plant the black-skinned bulbs 3 in (8 cm) deep at the beginning of May; if they have been stored correctly (keep them warm and dry) during the winter you will get the flowers at the beginning of June, or at the same time as the foliage grows. They are borne on a tall stem, bright red, 4–5 in (10–12 cm) large, and shaped like the cross of the Order of St James. They like a warm, sheltered place, full sun, richly manured, good soil. Lift at the beginning of October.

Tigridia pavonia, **Tiger flower, peacock flower.** Height 16–20 in (40–50 cm); planting time, the end of April; flowering time July/August; colour of flowers: white, yellow, vermilion, purplish red, with corresponding splotching of the cup-shaped base. Many varieties. Situation: warm, sunny, sheltered. Very good, rich soil; not dry. Buy only top-quality bulbs and plant about 3 in (8 cm) deep, 4–5 in (10–12 cm) apart. Frequent applications of fertilizer will increase the plant's willingness to grow; if the soil is too poor it will not flower at all. In my experience lifting early – before dahlias and gladioli – and placing the bulbs in dry peat, to be stored at a temperature of not less than 50°F (10°C), is one of the secrets of getting them to flower regularly. Some catalogues include the tiger flower under the name of *Ferraria pavonia* though this is, in fact, a different, dull plant.

Tigridia pavonia, Tiger flower

12
Roses

June has been nicknamed 'the month of the rose', since time immemorial, though these days the flowering season of the rose extends weeks and months beyond such a limited span of time. The rose, in all its diversity of shape and colour, accompanies us from the first warm days of May to the very threshold of winter, where it takes its leave with the poet's 'last rose of summer'.

The rose today and its classification

Many of the ancient and noble old species of rose have disappeared in the course of the centuries, growers having turned their attentions elsewhere. It was their determined efforts that developed the scented tea rose, considered to be the very peak of perfection, and the hybrid perpetuals into the equally exquisite hybrid teas, which now stand at the head of the official classification system of roses under the modern heading for garden and exhibition purposes as large flowered roses. Hybrid teas are still the beautiful aristocrats of the rose world, but nowadays their high-bred sensitivity goes hand in hand with such robust good health that they are very resistant to frost and to typical rose diseases. The tendency over the years has been for these large flowered hybrids to be grown as bushes, instead of standards; the bush form is undoubtedly more practical, and fits better into a small garden. The large rose-growing firms' catalogues will give information on more recent and the very newest varieties, as well as the still popular older varieties, and specialist rose firms list older species and shrub roses and their new varieties. For the rest, I shall just say that the large flowered roses hold the past, present and future of the rose in perfect equilibrium.

H.T.s will undoubtedly maintain their position at the top of the popularity poll for many years as there is nothing quite to compare with an exquisite long petalled bloom with a high pointed centre, whether seen on the plant in the garden or indoors in a vase, and especially if it is fragrant.

Second place is occupied by the floribunda or cluster flowered rose, which was created by crossing hybrid teas and polyanthas. In the early days they were known as hybrid polyantha, but the interbreeding became so complex that in fact there is now little or no polyantha blood in the class and for this reason the omnibus term 'floribunda'

was later adopted. Their flowers are borne in clusters or trusses and bring a wealth of colour to the garden throughout the summer.

A more recent development in breeding is the grandiflora or floribunda-H.T. type. These varieties have the dual benefit of hybrid tea shape blooms which are produced on short stems from a cluster.

The basic type of the miniature rose is the dwarf China, dwarf Bengal or Fairy rose, *Rosa chinensis semperflorens*, 8–12 in (20–30 cm) high, and there are many most charming hybrids derived from it.

I have deliberately not recommended any names of large flowered, cluster flowered or miniature roses as new varieties are introduced in abundance each year and good rose-growers' catalogues list and describe the varieties available most admirably. From such catalogues it is possible to select those varieties that have the characteristics that appeal to you and are suitable for your garden.

Species roses include those botanical wild species which propagate by seeds and suckers, and also cultivated strains which remain true to the character of the wild rose despite

Hybrid tea or large flowered   Floribunda or cluster flowered

122

their greater intensity of colour and freer flowering habit. Many of them produce fine hips, and can be considered both decorative and useful. The main representative of this interesting class is, of course, the familiar wild briar or dog rose, *Rosa canina*, with single, pale pink blooms flowering on two-year-old wood; it grows to 6½ft (2 m). Other handsome species roses: 'Persian Yellow', *R. foetida* 'Persiana', flowers double and bright yellow, height up to 6½ft (2 m); *R. hugonis*, from China, single flowers, golden yellow and very early, with finely cut foliage and graceful drooping branches, height up to 5 ft (1·50 m); *R. nitida*, pink, beautiful colouring in autumn, height 3 ft (1 m); the Scotch rose, *R. spinosissima*, single flowers very freely borne, carmine, height 4 ft (1·5 m); *R. rugosa*, the Ramanas rose, large red cup-shaped flowers, produces the best hips for culinary use, height about 5 ft (1·50 m); *R. sericea pteracantha*, small white flowers, filigree-like foliage, vigorous bushes with translucent deep red thorns on the young growth, height up to 8 ft (2·5 m) – a favourite for the floral arranger.

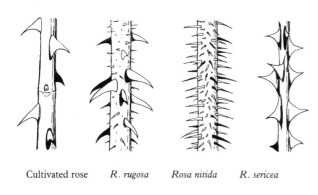

Cultivated rose   *R. rugosa*   *Rosa nitida*   *R. sericea*

The group of shrub roses includes hybrids of different origin and character. One of the most delightful is *R. × centifolia* 'Muscosa', more familiarly known as the moss rose because of the moss-like growths on the calyx and stems, very fragrant bright pink flowers, which develops to a height of about 5 ft (1·50 m). The bottle-shaped red hips of *R. moyesii*, which follow the single red flowers, bring a new dimension to the rose gardens in the autumn; height up to 10 ft (3 m). 'Canary Bird' is one of the earliest shrubs to bloom and the single bright canary-yellow flowers are produced in abundance along the branching stems. The creamy white 'Nevada' raised in 1927, which is purported to be a hybrid from *R. moyesii*, and its sport 'Pink Nevada', (correctly called 'Marguerite Hilling'), which appeared thirty years later, produces masses of bloom which cover the whole bush from a height of 8 ft (2·45 m) to ground level. 'Frühlings gold', raised in Germany in 1937, is a spectacle with its large creamy white flowers on long arching branches.

The *R. rugosa* varieties such as 'Alba' (white), 'Frau Dagmar Hartopp' (rose-pink), 'Roseraie de l'Hay' (crimson-purple), 'Scabrosa' (mauve-pink) make excellent shrubs about 6ft (1·85 m). The abundance of rich green glossy leaves which clothe the whole plant make them ideal for use as hedges. The flowers are produced from June till October and are followed by large tomato-like hips. The so-called hybrid musks which have a branching habit of up to 5 ft (1·5 m) will flower throughout the summer.

There are some really delightful modern garden shrub roses, often with the blooms followed by interesting, decorative and colourful hips.

Climbing roses adorn the garden for weeks and months on end, often growing to a great height. These days a great variety is available; they are hybrids, the offspring of unpretentious wild roses. Their shoots grow up to 20 ft (6 m) long, and they will cover arches, arbours and fences with garlands of living green.

There are two main groups of climbers: those that flower once only, with a profusion of blooms borne in the months of June and July, and those that are recurrent-flowering, with a first great burst of colour in June. Careful dead-heading encourages repeat flowering. 'Mme. Gregoire Staechelin', syn. 'Spanish Beauty', with large fragrant pink blooms produced in heavy clusters is one of the most handsome of the climbers that flower once only. Popular also are the rampant climbers such as *R. filipes* 'Kiftsgate' and *R. helenae*, which may be planted to grow into established trees and produce a wealth of 'blossom' in June. Unfortunately all are white. There are also the ramblers such as 'Excelsa' (red), 'Sander's White' and 'Dorothy Perkins' (pink) with their shiny foliage and clusters of small rosette-shaped flowers.

The hybridists have made considerable progress with climbing varieties and there are now many that flower throughout the summer. 'Handel' (1965) with its shapely but delicate cream edged pink blooms is one of the best. 'Hamburger Phoenix' (1955), a hybrid from *R. kordesii*, has dark crimson semi-double blooms followed by large orange red hips and is ideal to grow against a pillar up to 10 ft (3 m). The old favourite 'Mermaid' (1918) with its delightful single yellow blooms and foliage that is often retained well into the spring must be included in this group.

Finally there are climbing roses which are sports of existing varieties but most have now been discarded in favour of the recurrent flowering types. Still popular, however, are 'Climbing Mrs. Sam McGredy' derived from the hybrid tea, and 'Climbing Iceberg' from the floribunda.

A word to rose enthusiasts

Unless anything is expressly said to the contrary, all varieties I have mentioned here are suitable for average conditions in the garden. Many of them have proved their worth over years and decades. If you are after novelties, and many are introduced each year, you will always find them in rose catalogues; only growing a new introduction will show you if it is a good one. However, new introductions from home and abroad are also tried out in trial grounds specially set aside for the purpose; it may be several years before they are issued with a certificate of garden worthiness.

Standards are coming back into fashion these days: half-standards, or small standards only 20 in (50 cm) tall have two great advantages: 1) they are less at the mercy of the wind; 2) you can look down on them, and thus get a good view of the whole head in flower. The usual height for full standards is 36 in (90 cm). 'Weeping' standards are very tall, usually about 4 ft (1·20 m), and are basically climbers with shoots that are not too long, grown on rootstocks of *R. canina*. I cannot really see why weeping standards are not grown more often, since most gardens must probably have a place that would show up their picturesque charm and amazing profusion of flowers to advantage.

Apart from the *R. rugosa* varieties already mentioned other perpetual-flowering shrub roses which can be used for hedges are 'Sparrieshoop', white and pink, height 5 ft (1·50 m); 'Elmshorn', salmon-pink, 5 ft (1·50 m); 'Heidelburg', blood-red, 6½ ft (2 m); 'Wilhelm', dark red, 6 ft (1·80): 'Nymphenberg', yellow and red, 6½ ft (2 m). If you want a good thick hedge, planting distance should be about 36 in (90 cm). One can also grow smaller 'ornamental' hedges, using vigorous H.T. or floribunda bush roses. This is simply a modified version of planting in groups. Obviously climbing roses can almost all be trained to form hedges. Roses to be trained along walls, trellises or wires should be planted at a distance of 3–6½ ft (1–2 m), according to their habit of growth.

In brief: there is no such thing as a 'black rose', since black is not really a colour, and trying to create such a thing by various kinds of secret methods can lead to nothing. All one will end up with is a very dark, velvety red. Blue roses, on the other hand, are quite commonplace these days, and no longer tend to revert to a dingy old-rose colour like the first blue roses of the fifties. 'Lilac Charm' and 'Blue Moon', both lilac, are well established, though both do change colour as they fade.

A general gardening book cannot possibly contain all there is to be said about roses. If you do not find what you are looking for here I would suggest you buy a specialist rose book.

Preparation of the soil and planting

Roses will grow in any soil that is not too poor or too wet, and small improvements to the site will help to make them feel at home. They prefer a mild, loose, slightly acid soil. The widespread opinion that they need clayey loam is a mistake. However, where the soil is very sandy the addition of plenty of compost, humus, peat and, if possible, some loam will be an advantage. Roses also need suitable

Rose-covered arch. *Left:* How young plants are arranged. *Right:* Fully mature plants in flower.

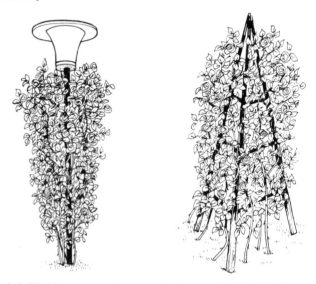

Left: Climbing roses growing up a garden lampstand. *Right:* Climbing roses growing up a triangular framework.

feeding, and this can best be given in the form of a good compound fertilizer. In addition, they can have an application of lime at intervals of a few years, when it seems necessary. If the whole rose bed cannot be treated in this way, then you can make do with preparing planting holes measuring some 20 × 20 × 20 in (50 × 50 × 50 cm). Preparation should be done at least four weeks before planting. Autumn is the best time to plant, though full standards and the less robust varieties can be planted in early spring, as soon as it is possible to work the ground once it has dried out and warmed up sufficiently. If you are going to plant at this time of year, you will need to water particularly well in dry spells.

The planting rules set out in the chapter HEDGES AND FLOWERING DECIDUOUS SHRUBS apply in general to all roses, from hybrid teas to climbers. However, there are a few small deviations which should be mentioned. All roses not delivered in containers need to have their roots well soaked, or if they have travelled a long way, the roots should be put in water at room temperature for some hours, or overnight. Next comes the necessary process of pruning the roots. Trim off all damaged or broken roots, making a clean cut, and shorten the main roots to about 12 in (30 cm), cutting so that the cut surface points diagonally downwards. Remove weak, fibrous roots. Container roses can be transplanted even in flower.

It is necessary to prune the shoots above ground only if you are planting in spring; when planting in autumn leave them alone, and do not cut back until next spring, when all weak shoots should be removed entirely, and the main shoots pruned to 3–5. Make a diagonal cut just above the top outward facing bud, and be careful not to crush or tear the shoot. Climbing roses are cut back to 20–24 in (50–60 cm). In planting all roses, a well developed network of roots is more important than the amount of shoots above ground. Newly planted roses should have sun and plenty of air, but need protection from biting north and east winds. Planting distance is 14–16 in (35–40 cm) for low-growing bush roses, 20–24 in (50–60 cm) for larger varieties. Shrub roses and climbers will need a planting distance of 3–5 ft (1–1·50 m) between them, according to the purpose for which you intend them. Similarly, standards should not be planted any closer together than the measurement of their height. This will entail a planting distance of 4½–5½ ft (1·40–1·60 cm). Miniature roses are spaced about 12 in (30 cm) apart.

Stakes for standards are driven into the ground before planting. To prevent the heads being blown over by the wind when they are heavy with flowers, and perhaps wet from rain, the stake should go well up into the head itself and be tied there. However, do not tie so tightly that the stem of the rose will be damaged by rubbing. Use a figure-of-eight knot, or a special tree tie, as when staking fruit trees.

When you are actually planting, spread the pruned roots evenly out over a slight mound raised at the bottom of the planting hole, fill up the hole with good soil mixed with loam and compost, and tread or press it well down. Take great care that roses whose point of union with the rootstock is at the neck of the plant have this point covered, as shown in the diagram. Finally, raise a little wall of earth round the newly planted rose so that you can give it a thorough watering. Afterwards you should protect the planting site from drying out by mulching it. Given this treatment, bush roses should begin to put out vigorous shoots at once. Standards that fail to produce any shoots can be laid down and have their heads buried in soil, and their stems wrapped in sacking which is kept moist, or some similar material; these emergency measures will often save the plant. Put them upright again as soon as the new growth begins; continue to keep the stems moist. In hot, dry weather give plenty of water, even to roses which

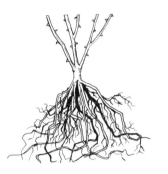

Rose roots before and after pruning.

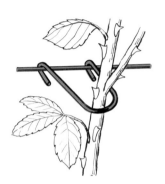

Useful wire clip for tying rambling roses and other plants which do not support themselves.

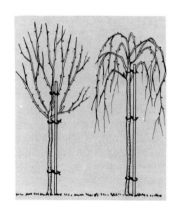

Standard and weeping standard roses, correctly staked and tied.

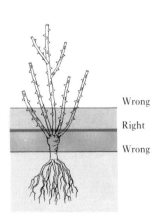

Wrong

Right

Wrong

Correct planting depth; the point of union with the stock must be only just covered.

125

have obviously taken root and are making good new growth.

Watering, feeding, hoeing

These three jobs are among the most important for the well-being of the rose throughout the year. However, it has always been held that in no circumstances should roses be drowned with water or watered with a sprinkler fitting on a hose during the heat of the day. Recent experiments suggest that dowsings with water daily throughout summer can eliminate both black spot and mildew – though this discovery goes against all that has been preached about watering roses for decades. As yet there is no sufficient evidence to prove that spraying roses with water when the sun is on them either harms or helps them unduly.

Again, the basic rules for feeding are the same as for hedges and flowering shrubs. It is a good idea to alternate organic and mineral fertilizers, but be careful to avoid giving an overdose of inorganic fertilizer. An application of compound fertilizer with a high potash content may be applied every two to three weeks from the time new growth begins in spring to the end of June. There are also a number of branded solid, liquid and foliar rose feeds available.

As well as feeding roses, it is important to keep the ground around them loose, friable and free of weeds. If you have bush roses your choice is between hoeing and weeding or mulching with peat, grass clippings and similar material. I would always advise mulching: it saves work and is good for the roses and the soil. It helps keep down weeds, but of course has no effect on suckers, of which many roses produce a super abundance; all you can do about suckers is keep removing them as they come up by tracing them back to the point from which they start and pulling them away. They should not be cut. They can be identified by their finely cut, light-coloured leaves.

It used to be the thing to grow roses in beds of bare soil, but now more and more people are growing other plants at low level in their rose beds –partly because ground occupied by plants provides a living mulch, suppressing weeds and keeping the soil moist. Early-flowering, low-growing

Always water rose bushes at the roots, never by overhead spraying on to the foliage or flowers.

plants like polyanthus and forget-me-nots are ideal, with an edging of pinks or carnations. Scented plants are supposed to enhance the scent of the roses. For this reason some people use an edging of chives or dwarf lavender, and one of the variegated forms of thyme or marjoram as ground cover.

Basic rules for pruning

Annual pruning is a springtime job which should be done soon after the severe winter conditions have passed. Vigorous roses are not pruned as hard as those that make less growth. Bushes in beds for display are always pruned hard. The first thing to do is remove all thin, over-crowded and crossing shoots. Remaining strong shoots from the previous year are cut back to their three or four lowest fully-formed buds, which can be expected to produce good growth in the coming season. Vigorous varieties can have one or two more buds left on the wood.

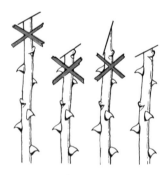

Cut just above the bud.

Naturally, these rules can be modified according to situation, climate, the general condition and the age of individual plants. But one can hardly expect a beginner, or a weekend gardener who is short of time, to observe such niceties. As a general rule of thumb, then, cutting back to three, four or five buds will produce vigorous growth and fewer but better flowers.

Climbers, shrub roses and species roses are not pruned regularly, but do need thinning out, but rambling roses in particular should have worn-out old wood removed and new shoots tied in after flowering. Since the apparent advantages of autumn pruning are much discussed these days, privately and in print, I should like to say that the uncertainty of our weather alone is a good argument against it. If we have a hard winter there will be frost damage to the cut surfaces of the wood, which inevitably will not have healed up yet; not just the top bud but the second and perhaps the third buds down on a shoot will die. However, you can do a kind of temporary pruning in autumn, cutting back to eight or ten buds which reduces wind rock – then you still have the main job to do in spring,

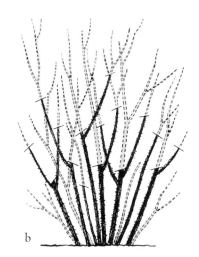

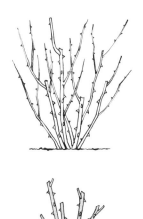

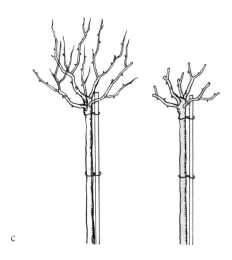

a   b   c

Above: Spring pruning (drawings show the roses before and after): (*a*) bush rose; (*b*) shrub rose (as for ornamental shrubs, but thin out rather more); (*c*) standard.

Left: How to remove dead wood.

when you have to cut back properly, and remove the frost-damaged ends of the shoots.

There are disadvantages to cutting roses with long stems during the summer; the more wood is removed, the more leaves go too – and the greater the effort the plant has to make to replace these essential parts before any more flower buds can develop. So cutting roses on long stems means waiting quite a time for a second flowering, and sometimes not getting one at all. Wilhelm Kordes once said, with some truth, 'Many roses are cut to death in summer!' Picking roses in summer, then, and dead heading the withered flowers, is a delicate job; you need green fingers to guide your secateurs/pruning shears correctly, avoiding anything too drastic. Very vigorous varieties which produce new shoots and plenty of flowers whenever you cut roses do not suffer, however long a stem you remove. However, summer pruning of less vigorous hybrid teas and floribundas should be kept within bounds; cut back some at least of the withered flowers only to the nearest healthy bud. Roses which bear clusters of flowers are usually not cut back till the whole cluster has finished flowering, though the blooms of large cluster flowering floribundas, and also of large-flowering climbers can be individually dead headed to advantage – provided you have time for this fiddly job. This applies only to perpetual

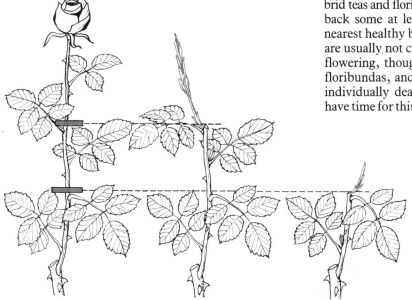

The harder you cut back, the longer before you get a second flowering.

or repeat-flowering species; wild roses which flower only once, like *Rosa hugonis*, and climbing roses which bear decorative hips, or hips for culinary use, are not, of course, dead headed.

A good way to produce large specimen blooms is to thin out the buds while they are still small and green.

Summer pruning: removing buds to obtain large blooms.

Roses need a change of scene too

How long can a rose stay in the same place without showing signs of deterioration? There are some rose beds which have been established for ten years or longer. Others will show signs of exhaustion within a shorter period and, if the plants are moved, they will not do any better; when this happens you have no choice but to make a clean sweep. The cause of this 'exhaustion' of the roses may be chemical reactions in the soil which we do not yet fully understand, or perhaps be due to separation of the roots, or damage by eelworms, and it cannot easily be put right. If you propose to replant new roses in old rose beds, it will be necessary to change the soil.

Rose diseases and pests

If the shoots, leaves, buds and even thorns of a rose look as if they were covered with white powder, it has got mildew. If the leaves turn yellow with dark blotches on them, starting with the leaves nearest the ground, the rose has got black spot. Apart from usual methods of plant hygiene, give plenty of potash and very little nitrogen, do not allow waterlogging, and make sure the soil is well aerated.

Among pests, roses may be attacked by aphids, sawflies, chafers, leafhoppers and tortrix caterpillars. Beetle larvae and mole-crickets – and even voles – may get at the roots and cause severe damage. For details of how to control pests and diseases, see the chapter PLANTS NEED PEST AND DISEASE PROTECTION.

And finally: the scent of roses

In writing of the scent of roses the first thing to be done is to correct some widespread errors. It is not true that only some hybrid tea roses are really fragrant, although most of the best-known fragrant roses are in fact hybrid teas. It is not true that old roses had a larger proportion of fragrant varieties than modern roses; the proportion of very fragrant to less fragrant roses, or roses without any scent at all, has remained about the same. Moreover, the fragrance of a rose is not a constant factor; its intensity depends on a number of circumstances, like the time of day, the weather and the condition of the rose bush, and the same applies to the way in which the fragrance spreads.

Climbing roses are always popular, and this one shows the benefits of careful treatment.

Clematis 'Nelly Moser', a large-flowered hybrid.

13 Climbing plants

Climbing plants can be very helpful in making up for any imperfections in your garden, linking things together, softening the severity of geometrical shapes, heightening the general impression of comfort, and filling up any gaps or shutting out unattractive views. They can give an impression of tropical luxuriance, and are a welcome aid to garden design for the gardener with an artist's eye. Annual climbing plants, in particular, are a godsend to new gardens, which would often look very bleak and bare without them, since perennials take longer to get going.

There are climbing plants of all kinds, for all kinds of different uses. Almost all the large groups of garden plants, from simple annuals to evergreen shrubs, have some good climbers among them; only bulbs, ornamental grasses and conifers seem to be averse to climbing, rambling and twining, scrambling or coiling (or just an artistic draping effect). The following list of plants tries to bring out the essential nature of each plant and indicate its best use, and how to care for it. The basic question of whether and where climbing plants should be grown (particularly as applied to creepers on houses) must be left for the gardener himself to decide. At any rate, planting creepers to grow up walls is only one way to use climbing plants.

Trellises should stand some 4 in (10 cm) away from the wall. These days there are plastic trellises which are much easier to put up than the old types that had to be driven into the wall and then have wires or colourless nylon fishing-line stretched between them. They are also of course, much better than expensive wooden trellises, which will not last for ever. Rust-proofed and painted steel trellises are popular too, because of their simplicity. Old gas pipes embedded in cement are still used for supporting a free-standing trellis. If you are planting against a wall which will be painted or plastered from time to time, it is best to use trellises which can be taken off the wall and laid down on the ground, plant and all, until the work is done and they can be put back. Wire pyramid-shaped frameworks offer all kinds of new possibilities in the way of decorative effects.

Annual climbing plants, hardy and half-hardy

Cobaea scandens, **Cathedral bell.** Climbs 13–16½ ft (4–5 m) high and the same distance laterally. Large, deep blue bell-shaped flowers. The variety 'Alba' has greeny white flowers. Raise under glass in pots from the beginning of March, or buy young plants in the middle of May. Sunny situation, plenty of top dressings and water. For trellises, free-standing frames, espaliers, fences. **Half-hardy.**

Cucurbita, **Ornamental gourd.** Grows upwards, clinging with simple tendrils, to a height of 20–26 ft (6–8 m). The flowers produce curious, long-lasting fruits, which can be dried and polished for indoor decorations. There are a number of varieties producing different shaped fruits. Sow in the open at the beginning of May, or raise under glass from the beginning of April onwards. It needs good support to bear the weight of its growth. Sheltered position, not too much fertilizer.

Eccremocarpus scaber, **Chilean glory flower.** Climbs to 10–13 ft (3–4 m), with clinging tendrils. Ornamental foliage, red, orange or yellow bell-shaped flowers. Sow in a warm frame from February onwards, prick out later. A beautiful but rather tender plant, needing a sheltered position. **Half-hardy.**

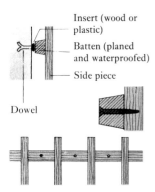

Insert (wood or plastic)

Batten (planed and waterproofed)

Side piece

Dowel

How to put up a trellis. Detachable frameworks of similar construction can be bought.

Ipomoea, **Morning glory.** Twines to a height of 6½–16½ ft (2–5 m), according to variety or species. Bears many flowers, which last only a day, from July to September; beautiful colours. Best raised under glass from March onwards for plants with a good ball of soil. Put out after the middle of May at a distance of 6 in (15 cm). For pyramidal frameworks, trellises, wires, strings. Situation, sunny and sheltered; soil containing humus, not much fertilizer, avoid nitrogen. **Half-hardy.**

Lathryus odoratus, **Sweet pea.** Climbs to 5–6½ ft (1·50–2 m), like the vegetable pea. Beautiful flowers borne from June/July until the first frosts; many colours, fragrant. Sow in the open from the beginning of April, putting in three seeds at a time, about 1 in (3 cm) deep, at a distance of 8–10 in (20–25 cm). Soak the seeds first. For pea-sticks, pea supports, wire netting, espaliers. Easy to grow. Give plenty of water and fertilizer.

Sweet peas cling with tendrils from their leaves.

Phaseolus coccineus, **Runner bean.** Habit of growth and cultivation as for all stick beans; sow in the open late May, or raise in pots under glass from the beginning to the middle of April. Flowers red, white, yellow, followed by long edible seed pods; some modern varieties produce stringless beans. All varieties are suitable for covering large areas with greenery in a hurry, also for growing up wire pyramids, poles, wires. They fall into the category of plants that are both decorative and edible.

Beans twine to the right unlike the hop which twines to the left.

Thunbergia alata, **Black-eyed Susan.** Tie up the shoots, which are 3–5 ft (1–1·50 m) long, or let them trail. Charming yellow flowers with a black eye, borne from June to autumn. Raise in the greenhouse, or in trays indoors, from March onwards, prick out twice – or, if preferred, buy young plants from a nursery after the middle of May. Delightful on small trellises or trailing over a dry wall. Needs a warm, sheltered position, sun to half-shade; will not do well in cold, rainy summers. **Half-hardy.**

Tropaeolum majus, *T. peltophorum (lobbianum)*, *T. peregrinum (canariense)*, **Nasturtium.** *T. majus* is prostrate rather than climbing, throwing out shoots up to 6½ ft (2 m) long; yellow and red flowers from June to October. *T. peltophorum* and *T. peregrinum* (canary creeper) throw out shoots up to 13 ft (4 m) long, and are both climbers. The latter has finely lobed leaves, will tolerate half-shade in among trees, and produces many bright yellow flowers. The flowers of *T. peltophorum* are like those of *T. majus*. As well as the species, there are several pretty cultivated forms, including varieties with pure scarlet, pure orange, particularly large and double flowers. The mixtures of seeds sold with the outer husk removed are faster and more certain to germinate. Sow 2 or 3 seeds in the open, at a distance of 8 in (20 cm), not before mid-May, since the plants are very sensitive to frost and cold. Raising under glass in pots from March onwards will ensure that you have plants with a good ball of soil which will flower early. Support the climbers by tying them up. Rewarding and undemanding plants for filling gaps; they dislike wind and very strong sunlight. May be attacked by aphids.

Climbing, twining and clinging shrubs

Actinidia, **Chinese gooseberry, Kolomikta vine.** Deciduous twining shrubs, shoots up to 26 ft (8 m); very vigorous; leaves fall late. The branches of *A. chinensis* have red hairs; its leaves are red-veined. Male and female flowers borne on separate plants. Flowers, white with long stamens, hanging in clusters, fragrant; flowering time June/August; edible yellow fruits resembling gooseberries in August/September. *A. kolomikta* is grown mainly for its green, pink and white leaves. These beautiful climbers need nourishing, moist soil, a sheltered situation, sun to half-shade. You can buy young plants in pots or containers; spring is the best planting time. Use to cover walls facing south, east or west. Very handsome on pergolas, poles, or grown over an old tree. If grown up a large wall surface use horizontal wires to help support the growth.

Ampelopsis, **Ampelopsis.** Deciduous climber, twining shoots up to 33 ft (10 m) long; forms coiling tendrils. Hop-like leaves, often variegated. Flowers, insignificant; ornamental pea-sized berries in autumn, first blue, then turning yellow. Plant like a vine; cool soil containing some lime. Give compound fertilizer every autumn. For fences and espaliers on walls in any position, sun or shade.

Aristolochia macrophylla (A. durior), **Dutchman's pipe.** Deciduous climbing shrub, shoots up to 26 ft (8 m) long, is slow to develop when young, but later becomes very vigorous and will cover large areas; twines to the right. Bears yellowish green and brownish flowers like little tobacco pipes in June. Bright green leaves up to 10 in (25 cm) broad and long, ornamental, overlapping one another like tiles. Keep the soil rich and moist. Otherwise, an undemanding plant. Best in shade, but will tolerate half-shade to a moderate amount of sun. For wire fences, walls of houses (support with wires), growing over arbours and pergolas. It needs strong supports because of its own considerable weight.

Campsis radicans, varieties and hybrids, **Trumpet creeper, trumpet vine.** Deciduous climbing shrub; puts out aerial roots and is self-clinging to some extent. Shoots 20–26 ft (6–8 m) long. Large trumpet-shaped flowers, orange, yellow, scarlet, in clusters of up to 12, borne from July to September. Not a beginner's plant. Only for very sheltered, sunny situations; not entirely hardy. Plants should be pruned back in early spring. Some support is desirable. *C. grandiflora* is another popular species, but needs winter protection.

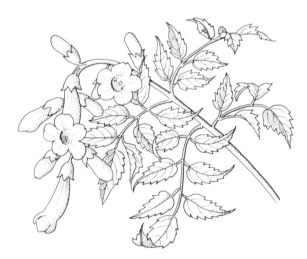

Campsis, Trumpet creeper

Celastrus orbiculatus, C. scandens, **Staff vine.** Deciduous twining stemmed shrub; length of shoots 26–40 ft (8–12 m). *C. scandens* is not quite so vigorous as *S. orbiculatus*. Long panicles of insignificant flowers; long-lasting fruits, bright yellow and red, or red with yellow, from October to January. Attractive leaves which turn yellow in autumn. Easy to grow in any situation; sun to half-shade. Male and female flowers are borne on separate plants; you

either need a suitable partner, or should plant one of the new bisexual strains. Avoid planting under live trees. Very good on areas of bare wall (use wires), tall poles, dead trees.

Clematis, **Clematis.** Deciduous twining shrub, in many species, hybrids and varieties; climbs by means of coiling tendrils and twining leaf-stems. Length of shoots varies a great deal, from 10–33 ft (3–10 m). Colour of flowers: white, yellow, pink, red, blue, violet, in many shades. Flowers in early and late summer; there are small-flowered and large-flowered forms, up to 4½ in (12 cm) across, all single. Best planting time: the end of April. At other times, plant as for all other plants grown in pots and containers. A basic principle for growing clematis: it needs cool, shady soil, but warmth and bright sun above ground. Plenty of mulching is important, or you can grow ground cover plants. Prepare planting holes as for evergreens; plant 16–20 in (40–50 cm) in front of a wall, to avoid the dry area at the foot; do not let water drip on the plant from above. It should be transplanted into its hole 1½–2 in (4–5 cm) deeper than it was growing before. Stakes should be driven into the ground before planting, to give some support in the early stages of growth. For the first three years after planting cut all shoots back hard to 4–8 in (10–20 cm), to avoid the plant becoming leggy. Later you need not prune so severely. Early summer-flowering clematis is pruned directly after flowering; the late-summer species (August to autumn) are pruned in early spring. The finest of all cultivated climbing plants. The most vigorous are the small-flowered botanical species such as *C. viticella* and *C. montana*, with its popular pink form 'Elizabeth'. Other species such as *C. alpina* or *C. tangutica* are smaller. Many species bear silvery seed-heads in autumn. The large-flowered hybrids are the most showy. Good for east and west walls (use wires) and for draping over fences, arbours and pergolas. The small-flowering forms are suitable for a wild corner of the garden.

The clematis has coiling leaf-stalks or tendrils.

Euonymus fortunei (radicans), **Climbing spindle.** Evergreen climbing shrub, self-clinging, with aerial roots, bushy habit of growth. Height 20–26 ft (6–8 m). Flowers and fruits are insignificant, but the dark green foliage of the species, and the variegated leaves of the varieties, are attractive. Easy and rewarding to grow, though sometimes inclined to mildew. Its aerial roots can get torn away in high wind, so fix some strong twigs or branches among its top growth to the wall. Is inclined to be prostrate and creep along the ground or over stones.

Hedera helix, **Ivy.** Evergreen climbing shrub with many cultivated forms, often with attractive variegated leaves. Puts out strong aerial roots and is self-clinging. Does not bear flowers or fruit until it is some years old, and then usually only in sunny positions. Likes deep-dug, humus-rich soil, otherwise undemanding. Ivy will tolerate either full sun or deep shade. Also a ground cover plant.

Ivy forms clinging roots.

Hydrangea petiolaris, **Climbing hydrangea.** Self-clinging and grows up to 13 ft (4 m) after a somewhat slow start. Dark green leaves and flat clusters of white flowers June/July. Likes rich soil and grows particularly well on north-facing walls or trees.

Jasminum nudiflorum, **Winter jasmine.** See chapters HEDGES AND DECIDUOUS FLOWERING SHRUBS and ROCK GARDENS.

Lonicera periclymenum, L × heckrottii, L. henryi and others, **Honeysuckle.** Species and their varieties are usually evergreen or semi-evergreen. Shoots twining to a length of 10–13 ft (3–4 m). Flowers yellow and red, very fragrant (they attract moths), borne from May to October; fruits borne in autumn, orange to dark purple. Nourishing soil containing humus will stimulate its growth and flowering. An easy plant to grow, but inclined to harbour aphids. To prevent its becoming leggy, cut back to 32–40 in (80–100 cm) every three or four years. For pergolas, arbours, trellises, anywhere that is suitable for its rather tangled growth. Likes sun but will tolerate half-shade.

Parthenocissus, **Virginia creeper.** Self-clinging, with sticky discs at the end of tendrils; on *P. quinquefolia* these are only weak, and some support is desirable. Deciduous;

puts out shoots up to 33 ft (10 m) long. Leaves are composed of 3, 5 or 7 leaflets. Flowers and fruits insignificant; the leaves have wonderful autumn colouring. Plant as for vines. Needs little attention; cut back occasionally, when necessary, to keep it in good condition. Undemanding; will tolerate industrial pollution. Species with strong clinging tendrils need no support and will grow up large walls, keeping them cool in summer. When grown directly on a wall, be careful about removing the autumn foliage.

Parthenocissus, Virginia creeper, has sticky discs on the ends of tendrils.

Polygonum baldschuanicum, **Russian vine, mile-a-minute vine.** Deciduous twining shrub, which spreads vigorously, will grow to a height of 40 ft (12 m). Flowers very freely, whitish pink flower panicles borne from June to September, later turning to decorative seed-heads. Not very suitable for sitting areas of a garden because of the constant showers of flowers and seeds. Easy and rewarding to grow, but so rampant that it can endanger gutters, tiles and woodwork.

Rosa, **Climbing roses.** See chapter ROSES.

Rubus henryi, **Climbing blackberry.** An evergreen climbing shrub, tending to spread like the rose; very thorny shoots up to 20 ft (6 m) long. Mauve flowers which are less striking than the deep green foliage, downy white on the underside; dark fruits in autumn. Situation: sunny

Climbing roses and blackberries splay out as they climb.

and sheltered. Stimulate a good bushy growth by frequent cutting back and removing weak shoots. Otherwise, cultivate like the edible blackberry. A handsome plant for trellises or wires on walls.

Vitis, **Grape vine.** Deciduous climbing shrubs which support themselves by stem tendrils. The flowers are inconspicuous but the superb autumn leaf colouring, often

The vine (*Vitis*) puts out shoot tendrils from the stem.

with bunches of small grapes (certain sorts of which are edible), make these effective plants for growing into trees, up house walls or against trellis. There are several species and varieties available. All like a well drained soil and plenty of sun. If space is restricted, remove old growths and shorten new stems in late summer.

Wisteria, **Wisteria.** Beautiful deciduous twining shrubs, differing from each other in shape, colour and size of their hanging flower clusters, which, in *W. sinensis,* are also fragrant. Length of shoots 26–33 ft (8–10 m). Plant in spring. Cut back shoots to 12–16 in (30–40 m); needs a warm, sheltered position and rich but well-drained soil. Keep the roots a certain distance away from walls and buildings. Some winter protection around the neck of the rootstock is desirable. Feeding with potash will stimulate the flowers. The wisteria is one of the great springtime glories of any garden. It needs strong support for the stems, which will later become woody and gnarled (be careful about gutters). After it has grown some way vertically to about 10 ft (3 m) it must be trained horizontally. Keep excessive growth of shoots and foliage down by summer pruning young stems back to 6 in (15 cm).

14
Hedges and flowering deciduous shrubs

Hedges have become attractive and practical features of garden design. Hedging plants, which put out plenty of new growth and thus are suitable for regular clipping, do all sort of jobs, from providing a formal dwarf hedge as an edging or in the front garden, to those medium-height hedges that surround a whole property, acting as boundary fence, sight-screen and windbreak.

However, nesting birds, caterpillars pupating, later to become butterflies, bees in search of honey, and a good many gardeners too, prefer the natural growth of an informal hedge composed of shrubs that harmonize well with each other, bearing flowers, decorative fruits, and often with interesting autumn colouring. There are pros and cons for both types of hedge. The selection of hardwood coniferous shrubs suitable for clipping as a formal hedge is smaller than the range of flowering shrubs available for informal hedges; a formal hedge also makes more work because it has to be clipped regularly, and if one plant in it dies you have a considerable problem. You can fill gaps in natural hedges by putting in a new plant any time you like, and you can alter and improve them more easily, but they will never be as dense as the formal kind. They also occupy a good deal more space.

What sort of plants to choose?

When you are going to plant shrubs, make a carefully-planned list of possibilities, and go to a good nursery or garden centre in search of those you want. Alternatively order by post from a reliable nursery, which will then dispatch your plants at the right time for planting. You will find the number of plants needed per yard (metre) later on in this chapter, in the descriptions of hedging shrubs. In planning an informal hedge one must bear in mind other factors as well as the average planting distance, also given in the descriptions; one needs to plan the whole arrangement of the hedge according to the shape of the shrubs, the colour of their foliage, succession and colour of flowers, and other details, all of which ensure that the hedge will look attractive for many months of the year. The same applies to shrubs for planting in groups or as single specimens. And of course the quality of the plants must be kept in mind too. Young plants, two or three years old, are

infinitely preferable to older ones which have already formed woody trunks. Shrubs are on sale in three different forms:

1) Simple deciduous and evergreen shrubs are bought, personally or by mail order, at the right planting time with roots free of soil. Before planting, you should soak them in water for several hours or over-night, and then prune the roots; this process involves removing any broken parts (make a good clean cut) and shortening roots that are too long, or have anything else the matter with them. All cut surfaces should slant diagonally downwards.

2) Shrubs more sensitive to moving, especially evergreens and conifers, need to be planted with a good ball of soil round their roots to ensure good future growth. They are sold with wrapped roots, and the wrappings must not be removed before it is time to plant. Shrubs sold with their roots wrapped also need a thorough soaking before they are planted, so that the ball of soil will hold together well. Keep to the correct planting dates as far as possible.

3) Container plants which have rooted in their containers so well that removing them, after a thorough watering, does not endanger the ball of soil at all. They have so many advantages, especially if you are planting rather large shrubs, so they are well worth the slight increase in price as compared to shrubs sold with wrapped roots. They can be planted all the year round, so you need not be too worried about keeping to the usual dates, and they can be left in

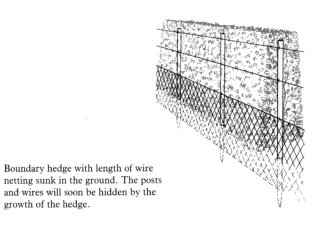

Boundary hedge with length of wire netting sunk in the ground. The posts and wires will soon be hidden by the growth of the hedge.

their containers for days or even weeks, so that you are not racing against time to get your formal hedge planted – and if you have an informal hedge in mind, you can try out the effect of your young shrubs, which may already be bearing leaves and flowers, on the planting site itself before you actually put them in. Of course the containers will need watering during this period, like flower pots or tubs.

Preparation of the soil and planting

Boundary hedges do not always have the best of soil to grow in, but they are planted very closely, especially formal hedges. For this reason the planting site should be prepared several weeks before the plants go in, and the soil worked and enriched to a depth of 20–24 in (50–60 cm). Remove stones and weeds. If you are likely to have trouble with rabbits or voles a length of strong, galvanized wire netting should be sunk vertically in the soil. If possible, it ought to go 20 in (50 cm) down into the ground and stand the same height above it. Then dig a trench close to its inner side. On average the trench should be one spit deeper and wider than the extent of the shrubs' roots or the size of their wrapped roots and ball of soil. If you have no length of wire netting or fence to act as a guideline, mark out your trench with a string first. The earth you dig out, containing its layer of topsoil, should be piled up on the edge of the trench in such a way that you can do the job of enriching it by working in compost, shredded bark or damp peat (but not fertilizers) any time you like. The bottom of the trench should be loosened too, and enriched later with compost, shredded bark or peat (but again, no fertilizers). Usually a single row of plants is enough for a formal hedge, and this gives the plants a better chance to grow well than the double row which is sometimes recommended. If you *are* planting a double row, the trenches should be dug either side of your wire netting, bearing in mind any existing boundary lines. But you can make a single row of shrubs denser, in fact almost impenetrable, by using plants that make long shoots and weaving these shoots into the lower parts of the hedge.

Preparation of the soil for informal hedges, and the planting of groups of shrubs and single specimens, is done in the same way: dig planting holes of the right size, enrich the soil waiting to be put back, break up the bottom of the holes and add peat, shredded bark or compost.

The best planting time for deciduous shrubs with bare roots is between the end of October and the middle of November. Spring planting in March/April is preferable only in very exposed situations, or for certain special cases which will be found in the individual descriptions of shrubs. Evergreen hardwood shrubs and conifers are planted either just before their new growth begins at the end of April, or after the growing season, at the end of August. See the following chapters for more about the planting dates of evergreens and conifers, and special

instructions for preparing the soil to receive lime-hating shrubs.

No matter what the planting time, all shrubs with free roots should have them pruned before planting, as I said earlier. If you are planting in spring the upper part of the shrub should be pruned too. If you are planting in autumn, however, cutting back about one third of the parts of the shrub above ground, in order to stimulate growth, should be left until the following spring. Side-shoots are shortened in the same way. Coniferous shrubs planted as single specimens or informal groups are not pruned.

Once you have made all your preparations you can start the actual planting. For a formal hedge, lay the plants in the trench at the right distance apart, and half fill it with the enriched soil. Tread the soil down lightly and then give the roots a good soaking with a steady but gentle flow of water from a hose. After this first lot of water has seeped away stand the plants upright and fill the trench right up. Tread down the surface and water again. At the end of this process, the young shrubs should be standing a little higher out of the ground than they did in the nursery. Plant single specimens, and shrubs with wrapped roots or removed containers, according to the same basic method. When the soil settles, there will be a slight depression along the side of the trench where a formal hedge is planted, and similarly in the vicinity of single specimens; this should be covered at once with damp peat, compost, shredded bark, dead leaves or similar material. This is the best way to protect the plants from frost damage in winter and drying winds in spring. You may need to shelter them with damp sacking during the day and go on doing so until they show strong new growth. Large shrubs, particularly single specimens, often need some support to keep them steady in high winds as well. You do not need as large a framework as for trees; usually a stake set in the ground beside the shrub and slanting in the direction of the prevailing wind will do the job. You can tie the shrub to its stake with special tree ties, or strong fibre loosely knotted in a figure-of-eight shape.

Clipping formal hedges

After planting and pruning in spring do no more clipping that summer. Regular formal clipping does not begin until the second year. Deciduous hedges and hedges of flowering shrubs such as forsythia are cut in June. Formal hedges are cut in August or from spring to autumn if more than one cut is necessary.

There is an old gardening rule to the effect that 'Tapering keeps a hedge green', and a hedge seen in cross-section should be broader at the bottom than the top. As a rule of thumb for deciduous hedges, they should deviate 4 in (10 cm) from the vertical for each 40 in (100 cm) height. Thus a formal hedge 10 ft (3 m) high would be 12 in (30 cm) broader at the bottom than the top. Conifers grow to this

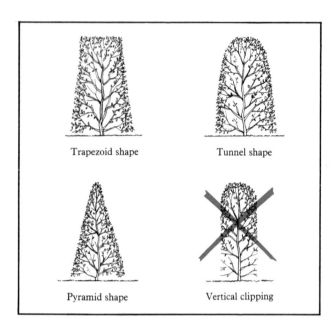

Trapezoid shape

Tunnel shape

Pyramid shape

Vertical clipping

depth, removing all remains of the old roots, and adding damp peat but no fertilizer), and put in good-sized plants, pruning lightly to slow down their growth. The old and new plants will grow together and gradually form the hedge again – but you will have to be patient.

Like the rejuvenation process, other work on the woody parts of the shrubs, such as thinning, and removing dead twigs, is done in winter, and is not part of the summer clipping programme.

Pruning natural or informal hedges and shrubs grown as single specimens

These are not clipped regularly in summer or during the period of growth; however, spring-flowering shrubs should have their faded flowers removed promptly. Winter pruning would destroy a considerable proportion of the flower-buds for the coming spring, but you do not want to let the flowers form seeds unnecessarily; it will mean a waste of the plant's energy. This applies to lilac in particular. In the same context I should mention the shortening of new growth on ornamental almonds, which is good for the general health of the plant. All you need do for summer-flowering shrubs, whose blooms appear between June and September, is to remove the dead flower heads in the course of the winter. However, there is no reason why you should not dead head immediately after the flowering season, especially if the faded flowers spoil the look of the shrub – as for instance with buddleias – or you do not want them to waste their strength on forming unnecessary seed capsules, as with hibiscus. Otherwise, all the attention you need pay informal hedges, and deciduous shrubs planted either in groups or as single specimens, is to thin them out a little now and then or do some light pruning to maintain them in good shape. Use sharp secateurs for pruning informal hedges and specimen shrubs. For special kinds of pruning for evergreen shrubs and conifers grown on their own, see chapter EVERGREEN SHRUBS, TREES AND CONIFERS.

shape naturally, and the bottom of a coniferous hedge can be even broader. Exceptions are mentioned in the individual descriptions. And formal hedges right beside a road, growing along a fence or a trellis, must also depart from the rule and be clipped to a vertical shape, at least on one side. It is not difficult to clip to the correct measurements if you use a string stretched taut, and (if you have a large hedge to cut) modern motorized tools. You can either clip the hedge flat at the top, or prune it into a tunnel-like shape, which is rather more pleasing in itself – but this is not just a matter of taste: maintaining the rounded shape means quite a lot more work.

Some hedges which have grown too high or lost their looks can be rejuvenated by cutting back hard to the old wood. A radical cure of this kind can be carried out over two to three years, to spare the plants. This is a winter job, done with a tree pruning saw. Individual plants that die in a formal hedge cannot usually be replaced simply by planting new ones. The way to get rid of bare patches is first to cut back the whole hedge as for the rejuvenation process. Then prepare planting holes carefully (working to a good

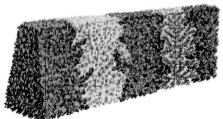

A delightful idea from Japan; a mixed formal hedge of different evergreens and conifers planted in groups and all clipped in the same way. Most attractive in summer and in winter.

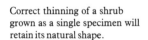

Correct thinning of a shrub grown as a single specimen will retain its natural shape.

Cutting back to a formal shape will spoil the natural habit of growth and cause a bare interior.

Shrubs for formal hedges

Berberis, **Barberry.** *B. thunbergii* and its two beautiful varieties *B.t.* 'Atropurpurea' and the even more graceful *B.t.* 'Atropurpurea Nana' are deciduous, all three bearing yellow flowers in May and quantities of red berries in autumn. *B.verruculosa*, *B.* × *stenophylla* and *B. darwinnii* are evergreen and grow very densely; golden yellow flowers in April/June, blue berries in autumn. All kinds of berberis are thorny, very undemanding in a sunny to half-shade position, and suitable for narrow hedges (10–12in (25–30cm) at the base) about 3–10ft (1–3m) high. Plant 3–4 of the larger and 5–6 of the dwarf forms per yard (metre). Trim after flowering.

Berberis, Barberry

Buxus, **Box.** The traditional box used for hedging is *B. sempervirens* 'Suffruticosa'. Evergreen. Situation, sun to half-shade, but not too dry (or the foliage may turn yellow). Can be clipped to a formal hedge shape at any height you like; allowed to grow freely, the shrubs will reach 40in (100cm). 5–6 plants per yard (metre). Trim in June.

Carpinus betulus, **Hornbeam.** Forms very dense hedges that make good nesting places for birds. The brown autumn foliage stays on the branches until spring. An open situation is desirable. 2–3 plants per yard (metre). Trim July/August.

Crataegus, **Hawthorn, May.** The species *C. monogyna* is an ideal deciduous shrub for hedging; ferocious thorns make it impenetrable, its slow growth makes it easy to keep in shape; best size: height, 6½ft (2m), breadth at base, 20–24in (50–60cm). 2–3 plants per yard (metre). *C. oxyacantha* is very similar. Trim June to August.

Escallonia, **Escallonia.** Can be used for hedging. See Chapter 16.

Fagus sylvatica, **Beech.** Many cultivated forms are available. More suitable for large gardens; it can easily look too sturdy growing around a small plot. The copper coloured beech, *F.s.* 'Dawyck', is especially attractive for a tall, slender hedge. 2–3 plants per yard (metre). Trim July/August.

Forsythia, **Forsythia.** The erect species make an unusual but suitable formal hedge, being particularly beautiful during the flowering season in April/May, but also most attractive in their green summer foliage. *F.* × *intermedia*, in the older, smaller-flowered varieties, is the best. Planting beside a few wires or a length of wire netting running along the length of the hedge is advisable. Regular clipping in spring soon after flowering is over ensures plenty of buds from year to year. 2–3 plants per yard (metre) will soon form a thick hedge.

Ilex aquifolium, **Holly.** Its prickly, dark green and shiny leaves make this an excellent, if slow-growing hedging plant. If berries are required, male and female plants should be planted together. There are many different forms, some producing variegated leaves. Can be grown in most positions. 2–3 plants per yard (metre). Trim July.

Ligustrum, **Privet.** The most widely used hedging plant of all. *L. ovalifolium*, height up to 12–15ft (3·5–4·5m), is suitable for tall hedges though can be cut lower. Evergreen. For edging: the dwarf form *L. japonicum rotundifolium*, dense and compact. 3–5 or more plants, according to species or variety, per yard (metre). Trim May/June and July/August.

Lonicera nitida, **Shrubby honeysuckle.** This species and its variety 'Ernest Wilson' makes very useful low growing, neat hedges for all soils and situations, though they can be grown up to 3ft (1m) high. 3–4 plants per yard (metre). Trim April to September.

Prunus lusitanica, **Portugal laurel.** Useful for all, including chalky soils; it is a good hedging plant, growing up to 13ft (4m) if required. It produces fragrant cream flowers in June, which are followed by dark purple fruits if left unpruned. 2–3 plants per yard (metre). Trim June/July.

Conifers for formal hedges

Those conifers which have proved their worth as hedging plants are easy to grow, and will keep putting out good new shoots if a few special features of their planting and upkeep are borne in mind.

  1) It is essential to plant with a ball of soil intact; one must get plants which are either in containers or have their roots wrapped. See also the section CONIFERS in Chapter 16.

  2) The trapezoid shape, broader at the base than the top,

is natural to conifers, and with the exception of *Thuja* (arbor-vitae) hedges, this shape should be preserved.

3) Feed with compound fertilizer which has a rather high potash content.

4) Water thoroughly several times in late autumn, to prevent damage from drying out in winter; also water during any prolonged periods of drought.

Chamaecyparis, **Cypress.** Highly recommended for tall and medium-height hedges around a garden, or for screening purposes: the species *C. lawsoniana*, Lawson cypress, and its cultivated varieties such as 'Allumii' and the slow-growing 'Ellwoodii'. 2–3 plants per yard (metre). Trim June and September.

Chamaecyparis, Cypress

× *Cupressocyparis leylandii*, **Leyland cypress.** Excellent for tall hedges and screens as it grows fast and densely. Particularly useful in coastal areas and on chalky soils. 1–2 plants per yard (metre). Trim May/June.

Taxus baccata, **Yew.** Particularly good for hedges, and like box can be used for all kinds of topiary work – growing round windows, clipping into ornamental shapes, and so on. If the soil is nourishing and contains lime, it will do well even in shady positions. 3–4 plants per yard (metre) for a hedge 5–6½ ft (150–200 cm) high. Trim June/July.

Thuja plicata, **Arbor-vitae.** It is most suitable for medium-height and tall formal hedges, and is an exception in that its slender growth does not naturally taper up from a broader base. The variety 'Fastigiata' is recommended for very tall boundary hedges, which can be grown with a base only 24–28 in (60–70 cm) broad. Should not be planted in very exposed situations. Needs good soil, but tolerates chalk, and an open, sunny position. 2 plants per yard (metre). Trim June/July.

Deciduous shrubs: for informal hedges or as specimens

H = Suitable for informal hedges.
S = Suitable for groups and single specimens.

Acer, **Maple.** Some of the most delightful and beautiful of all deciduous shrubs. Height 3–13 ft (1–4 m). Flowers, if produced, are insignificant, and these, often round shaped shrubs, are grown primarily for their attractive leaves which are of various colours of green, yellow, pink, or purple, with further magnificent colours in autumn. They grow best in fertile, moist and well-drained soil in a sheltered position. The species *A. japonicum*, and *A. palmatum* (Japanese maple), and their many varieties are the best shrubby forms. For other favourite species of maple see chapters DECIDUOUS GARDEN TREES and ROCK GARDENS. **S**

Amelanchier, **Snowy mespilus, June berry, shadbush.** A beautiful spring-flowering shrub for growing as a single specimen in sun or half-shade. Foliage on new growth is usually reddish brown; fine autumn colouring and many berries. Undemanding; likes well-drained soil containing lime. *A. canadensis* grows to 10 ft (3 m) high, with racemes of white flowers in April/May. Very dark blue berries from June onwards. Also recommended, *A. asiatica* and *A. lamarckii* which flower in May. Berries can be eaten. **S**

Berberis, **Barberry.** Two typical representatives of deciduous barberries of medium height are *B.* × *rubrostilla*, bearing yellow flowers in small clusters along the slightly arched branches, and the erect *B. thunbergii* 'Atropurpurea', with red foliage that offers a wonderful play of colour in autumn, and its attractive forms. All the deciduous barberries have red fruits, which are sometimes rather prone to rust. Height 6½–10 ft (2–3 m). Planting distance about 3 ft (1 m). For other barberries see section on formal hedges; section on evergreens in chapter 16 and the chapter ROCK GARDENS. **HS**

Buddleia, **Butterfly bush.** A beautiful ornamental shrub for sunny, sheltered positions; likes plenty of leaf

Buddleia, Butterfly bush

mould. Leaves are light-grey and downy, flowers purple, white, steel-blue or mauve, 12–16 in (30–40 cm) long; flowering time June/September according to variety. The most attractive are the many varieties of *B. alternifolia* and *B. davidii*. Planting distance 3–5 ft (1–1·50 m); height, up to 6½ ft (2 m). It will often die back in frost, but always shoots up again and flowers the same summer. Much visited by butterflies during its flowering season. **S**

Calycanthus floridus and *C. fertilis*, **Carolina allspice.** Aromatically scented shrubs with fragrant, brownish red flowers appearing in July/September. Leaves bright green and shiny. Planting distance 3–5 ft (1–1·50 m); height 5–8 ft (1·50–2·50 m). **S**

Caryopteris, **Caryopteris.** The cultivated form *C.* × *clandonensis* is the best known. Two points in its favour: the late flowering season, not till August/October, and its compact size, only 3–4 ft (1–1·20 m) high. It is generally easy to grow, given a sunny position, and can be planted at the back of a rock garden, on slopes and the edges of terraces. Cutting back hard in spring stimulates flowering. It may suffer frost damage in hard winters, but will shoot up again vigorously. A favourite of bees. **S**

Chaenomeles speciosa and *C. japonica*, **Cydonia, Maule's quince, Japonica, Japanese quince.** Spiny shrubs, with shiny green foliage and white, bright pink to deep red flowers appearing in April/May. Will do well even on very poor soil if they have plenty of sun. The new hybrids are rather more difficult to grow, but even more beautiful. Height 3–10 ft (1–10 m). Planting distance about 3 ft (1 m). **HS**

Cornus mas, **Cornelian cherry, dogwood.** One of the earliest shrubs to flower; its yellow blooms appear before the leaves and later turn to edible red berries. A rewarding and unpretentious plant to grow; likes lime. Planting distance 3–5 ft (1–1·50 m). The very beautiful flowering dogwood, *C. florida*, with its large, white, star-shaped flowers up to 2½ in (6 cm) across, and magnificent autumn colouring, is rather sensitive to frost. *C. alba* 'Spaethii' has interesting yellow-rimmed leaves and striking red stems. Height 6½–13 ft (2–4 m). **HS**

Corylus, **Hazel.** Excellent shrubs for exposed positions, they grow in any soil and produce their drooping 'catkins' each February before the leaves appear. Often grown for their edible hazel nuts. Height 6½–10 ft (2–3 m) and planting distance 4–6½ ft (1½–2 m). *C. avellana*, the common British hazel nut, *C.a.* 'Contorta', the corkscrew hazel, and *C. maxima* 'Purpurea', purple hazel nut, are popular forms. **HS**

Cotinus coggygria (Rhus cotinus), **Smoke tree.** A close relative of the sumach. Its pinkish flowers, which appear in May, become striking plumes of fruits in the course of the summer. Height 6½–10 ft (2–3 m). The cultivated variety 'Foliis Purpureis' has deep red leaves. Height up to 3 ft (1 m). **S**

Cotinus coggygria, Smoke tree

Cotoneaster, **Cotoneaster.** Like *Berberis*, the cotoneaster is found in gardens everywhere, thanks to its multiplicity of form and magnificent autumn colours of leaves or fruit. We find it among the dwarf shrubs of the rock garden (p. 174), among the evergreens (p. 154), and as a tall deciduous shrub – here are two examples of the latter form: *C. bullatus*, erect habit of growth, pink flowers, large, striking, bright red berries from August onwards, height about 6½ ft (2 m); *C. distichus* with white flowers on gently arched branches, and a great many decorative red berries which last a long time, height about 6½ ft (2 m). All cotoneasters like dry soil with a good deal of lime, and plenty of sun. Planting distance about 28 in (70 cm). **HS**

Cytisus, **Broom.** The common broom, *C. scoparius*, should be mentioned at the head of the many beautiful species and varieties of *Cytisus*. Its golden yellow flowers appear in May/June, usually on the outskirts of woodland areas with sandy soil lacking in lime. It is the ancestor of the many colourful varieties and hybrids such as 'Cornish Cream', 'Killiney Red' and 'Firefly', which all need an open, sunny situation; many are not entirely hardy. Planting season spring; put in plants with a good ball of soil. Always shorten the shoots a little immediately after flowering; never cut back to the old wood. Height 5–6½ ft (1·50–2 m). See the chapter ROCK GARDENS. **S**

Daphne mezereum, **Daphne, mezereon.** A shrub flowering in early spring, with pink-purple, fragrant blossom, appearing before the leaves. The form 'Alba' has white flowers. 'Grandiflora' is deep purple. Height about

Daphne mezereum, Daphne

3 ft (1 m). Daphnes like light shade and soil containing humus and lime. See also chapters ROCK GARDENS and EVERGREEN SHRUBS. **S**

Deutzia, **Deutzia.** The species *D. gracilis* is a charming small shrub, barely 3 ft (1 m) high, covered with countless little white flowers in May. Planting distance 28–32 in (70–80 cm). The hybrid deutzias grow to over 6½ ft (2 m) and are among the best of our flowering shrubs. *D.* × 'Mont Rose', pale pink flowers on horizontal twigs, and *D.* × *rosea*, also pink, with gracefully arching branches, are particularly lovely. *D. scabra* 'Plena' has double flowers, and grows to 6½ ft (2 m). **HS**

Elaeagnus, **Oleaster.** A good pioneer plant for slopes or poor soil, but also a fine shrub in itself, with silvery white leaves and orange-red berries. Many specimens will grow into tall trees and their shallow, spreading roots, which put up countless suckers, can become a nuisance. Main deciduous species: *E. angustifolia* and *E. commutata*. Height up to 10 ft (3 m). For evergreen forms see chapter EVERGREEN SHRUBS. **S**

Euonymus europaeus, **Spindle.** The best known of the spindles, a group comprising deciduous and evergreen, large, small and climbing hardwood shrubs. The spindle, with its narrow leaves and pink to deep red berries, is easy to grow, does not mind whether it has sun or shade, and thus is useful to fill gaps in informal hedges. Height 10–16½ ft (3–5 m). Planting distance 6–10 ft (2–3 m). For *E. fortunei radicans* see the chapter CLIMBING PLANTS, and for evergreen forms see chapter 16. **HS**

Forsythia, **Forsythia.** An unpretentious shrub with great staying power, always producing flowers very freely in the spring. Its beauty has been much improved in the large-flowering, sometimes double newer strains. The familiar old forsythia owes its present revival in particular to the *Forsythia* × *intermedia* hybrids, such as 'Lynwood', 'Spectabilis', and 'Spring Glory', this last considered to be the best bright yellow variety. The rambling variety *F. suspensa*, useful on pergolas and garden arbours, should also be mentioned. Usual planting distance 5–6½ ft (1·50–2 m); see also the section **Formal Hedges** in chapter 14. **HS**

Fuchsia, **Fuchsia.** The genuinely hardy species and varieties are popular because of their late summer to autumn flowers, usually of scarlet and purple. *F. megellanica* and its varieties are often used as informal hedges in mild districts, and other pretty forms for use as specimens include 'Mrs Popple' and 'Tom Thumb'. Height up to 3 ft (1 m) and planting distance 1½ ft (0·5 m). They grow well in most soils in a sunny position. Although often cut back to ground level by winter frosts, they should shoot vigorously from the base each spring, especially if given some winter protection. **HS**

Genista, **Broom.** True broom, as distinct from the *Cytisus* varieties, usually has simple linear leaves (not very many of them) and is often spiny. Good in very sunny, warm positions, and on stony or sandy soil. Do not give fertilizer! Apart from the dwarf forms mentioned in the chapter ROCK GARDENS, the following species is suitable for planting in groups or as a single specimen: *G. tinctoria*, the well-known European 'dyer's greenweed', with yellow flowers borne in June/September, height about 3 ft (1 m). Also its varieties, which are mostly low-growing. **HS**

Hamamelis, **Witch hazel.** A remarkable shrub whose golden yellow flowers, looking like shreds of paper, appear soon after the leaves have fallen if conditions are right. *A.*

Hamamelis, Witch hazel

japonica, the Japanese witch hazel, and *H. mollis*, the Chinese witch hazel, and their varieties, bear yellow flowers in January/March. Planting distance 3–5 ft (1–1·50 m); height up to 6 ft (2 m). **S**

Hibiscus syriacus, **Hibiscus, tree hollyhock.** A shrub with a long flowering season, from the end of July to October, and flowers resembling the hollyhock. There are single and double varieties in shades of white, pink, dark red, blue and violet. Needs a warm sunny position. Planting distance 3–5 ft (1–1·50 m); can grow to a height of 6½ ft (2 m). Not to be confused with the well-known tub plant *H. rosa-sinensis*, which may spend the summer out of doors, but is not hardy. However, *H. syriacus*, too, likes a mild climate and if conditions are right develops into a superb specimen, like a living bunch of flowers in your summer garden. **S**

Hippophäe rhamnoides, **Sea buckthorn.** Silvery leaves. A close relative of the oleaster (*Elaeagnus*) with similar characteristics and requirements, but never growing beyond its shrubby form. Its orange berries are full of vitamins. Bears fruits only if it has a male or female partner, since unlike the oleaster it is not bisexual. As a native of sea dunes it is not a difficult plant but is not suitable for dry situations with no underlying water. Its beauty is somewhat affected by its habit of spreading invasively and throwing up suckers. Height up to 15½ ft (5 m). Planting distance 2½ ft (80 cm). **HS**

Hydrangea, **Hydrangea.** It is possible to put pot plants of *H. macrophylla* which have finished flowering out in the garden, and given shade to half-shade and good soil with plenty of humus they will grow into large, free–flowering bushes over the years. Some will produce pinkish flowers on limy soils and blue ones on acid soils. But there are much more interesting and completely hardy species of garden hydrangea which like the same conditions. One of the finest is *H. paniculata* in its cultivated form 'Grandiflora', bearing white inflorescences up to 10 in (25 cm) long at the ends of all its shoots from July to September. Height up to 6½ ft (2 m). *H. sargentiana* is an attractive hydrangea for high summer, flowering in July/August. It bears large, flat, bright mauve corymbs of flowers above velvety foliage. Height, again, up to 6½ ft (2 m). For the climbing hydrangea, *H. petiolaris*, see the chapter CLIMBING PLANTS. **S**

Hypericum, **St John's wort.** Best known as a perennial sub-shrub (see the table on ground cover plants at the end of the chapter on THE LAWN); the larger shrub species are very fine, for instance *H. patulum* 'Hidcote'. Its 3 in (7 cm) wide, golden yellow, cup-shaped flowers, crowned with orange stamens, appear in July/September, at a time when not so many other flowering shrubs are in bloom. Height up to 5 ft (1·50 m). The charming *H. forrestii* is only about

3 ft (1 m) high, with similar flowers and flowering season, and sometimes bearing bright red fruits. All St John's worts are easy plants and will grow in full sun or in shade, provided they have a light, rather dry soil. Its habit of throwing out strong suckers is a drawback. **S**

Jasminum nudiflorum, **Winter jasmine.** Often covered with small yellow flowers from December onwards, long before the leaves appear. Its slender branches grow to 8 ft (2·50 m) and can easily be trained along an espalier. Looks very decorative grown against a light-weight bamboo trellis. Winter jasmine is a shrub that climbs loosely and is not very rampant. Does well in a sheltered, sunny but not too dry position. See also chapter ROCK GARDENS. **S**

Kerria japonica, **Kerria, jew's mallow.** Covered with yellow flowers, either single or double, in May. There is also a form with white variegated foliage. A pretty and undemanding shrub for sun to light shade; easy to propagate from suckers. Height up to 5 ft (1·50 m). **S**

Kerria japonica, Jew's mallow

Lonicera, **Honeysuckle.** Honeysuckle is happy to grow in any position, shady or sunny, hardy, and produces a wealth of flowers and fruits. Deciduous and evergreen shrubs of many different forms. *L. tatarica* is 10 ft (3 m) tall, deciduous and early–flowering. Red berries. *L. fragrantissima* is sometimes partially evergreen, but produces its fragrant cream flowers in January/March and red berries in May. Its height is up to 10 ft (3 m). For climbing species see chapter CLIMBING PLANTS. Warning: do not grow honeysuckle near sweet cherry trees, as the dangerous cherry blackfly may lay its eggs in the honeysuckle berries. **HS**

Lonicera, Honeysuckle

Magnolia, **Magnolia.** This vigorous shrub, suitable only for growing as a single specimen, is one of the loveliest sights in a spring-time garden with its tulip-shaped flowers appearing before the leaves. The one most often grown is *Magnolia* × *soulangeana* and its varieties, such as 'Lennei', flowers red outside, white inside, and *M. liliiflora* 'Nigra', whose superb deep wine–red flowers come out rather later. Though these forms may grow into small trees in time, the star magnolia, *M. stellata*, another favourite, with white flowers, grows hardly any higher than 3 ft (1 m), and will fit into smaller gardens. It is sometimes said that magnolias have to have a mild climate, but this is only essential for the first year or so after planting, and it is easy to give the shrub some form of protection to bridge the gap. Older plants will survive any normal winter. If magnolias are to do well they need an open position, nourishing soil with fresh humus in it, and the shallow roots must be protected from damage. Magnolias are sold only with wrapped roots or in containers. **S**

Paeonia suffruticosa, **Tree paeony.** This beautiful shrub from the most ancient East Asian aristocracy of flowers is enjoying a well-earned return to favour at the moment, with particular reference also to the double-flowered garden varieties of *P.* × *lemoinei*. And indeed, with its 8 in (20 cm) wide flowers in all the paeony colours, it is one of the most unusual of medium–sized deciduous shrubs. It does require a sheltered situation, sun to light shade, nourishing, and well drained soil. Given these conditions, this rather compact shrub, not much more than 5 ft (1·50 cm), with its sturdy branches and fern-like foliage, can last for a great many years; it is worthwhile taking trouble with it. **S**

Philadelphus, **Mock orange, syringa.** One of the most rewarding summer–flowering shrubs to grow, with many tall and shorter varieties (3–13 ft (1–4 m)). The catalogues give pride of place to *P. coronarius*, 10–13 ft (3–4 m) and its varieties, some of which are single and some double. However, there are many others as well. The flowers are always white and fragrant; many are up to 2 in (5 cm) across. Planting distance, according to size, 32–40 in (80–100 cm). Will grow in any good garden soil and any situation between sun and half-shade. Important: always cut off the dead heads, but do not shorten any other long shoots. **HS**

Poncirus trifoliata, **Japanese bitter orange, trifoliate orange.** This very decorative 'orange tree', hardy in mild areas, is not nearly well enough known. It bears a profusion of fragrant white flowers in April/May and equally numerous walnut–sized fruits resembling oranges or lemons in autumn; they are not, however, edible. Height about 5 ft (1·50 m). The branches are very spiny. Prefers soil without much lime. **S**

Potentilla, **Cinquefoil, potentilla.** Besides the dwarf potentillas discussed in the sections on ground cover plants (p. 68) and rock gardens (p.172), the shrub species are very good for small gardens and shrubberies, as most of them grow no taller than 3 ft (1 m). *P. fruticosa mandshurica* has reddish brown branches bearing white flowers from May to September, and grey-green foliage. *P.f.* 'Katherine Dykes', 3 ft (1 m) high, bears delightful yellow flowers in June/July, and *P.f.* 'Tangerine' has bright orange flowers. *P.f.* 'Red Ace', with bright orange blooms and *P.f.* 'Royal Flush' which has deep pink flowers, are two delightful colour breaks, growing lower than most. **S**

Prunus triloba, **Ornamental almond.** Among all the dozens of Japanese ornamental fruit trees offered in garden catalogues, the ornamental almond, flowering in April/May, pink blossom, is the only medium–sized specimen, never growing much beyond 6½ ft (2 m). Its double flowers, like miniature roses, make it ever–popular with gardeners, and people like to grow it in their front gardens. Important: cut back all branches immediately after flowering. This will help the little tree keep its shape, and prevent bacterial die-back which may otherwise attack the branches and their tips. *P. tenella*, with pink flowers in April, grows even lower, but is less common. For the cherry laurel, *P. laurocerasus*, see the chapter EVERGREEN SHRUBS, TREES AND CONIFERS; the other, tall species of prunus will be found in the chapter DECIDUOUS GARDEN TREES. **S**

Pyracantha, **Firethorn.** Evergreen shrubs with spiny branches that make them useful for informal hedges. See chapter on EVERGREEN SHRUBS, TREES AND CONIFERS. **HS**

Rhododendron, **Rhododendron and azalea.** See chapter EVERGREEN SHRUBS, TREES AND CONIFERS. **HS**

Rhus typhina, **Stag's horn sumach.** The name is derived from the brown clusters of fruit resembling a stag's antlers which often stay on the shrub until well into winter. The flowers are yellowish white, profusely borne in early summer. The pinnate leaves have beautiful autumn colouring. Unfortunately the shrub, which often grows into more of a tree (13–16½ft (4–5m tall)), has very brittle wood. Even if it does not get damaged by winds, it will usually not live longer than eight to ten years. However, it propagates itself freely from suckers. There are several cultivated forms. One of the most attractive is *R.t.* 'Laciniata', with deep–cut, fern–like leaves, and height up to 10ft (3m). **S**

Ribes, **Flowering currants and gooseberries.** Useful shrubs (up to 5ft (1·50m)) for producing a quick result in any soil or position. The yellow, pink or red flowers appear April/May and are often followed by fruits and good autumn leaf colour. *R. alpinum*, *R. odoratum* and *R. sanguineum* and its forms are all popular. Planting distance 18–36in (50–100cm). **HS**

Rosa, **Shrub roses, roses for hedges.** See chapter ROSES. **HS**

Rubus odoratus, **Sweet-scented raspberry.** This charming shrub, with its cinnamon scent, is one of the best of the ornamental species of *Rubus*. Height up to 6½ft (2m). Planting distance 3ft (1m). Bears carmine flowers in branched panicles in June/August. The red berries are pretty, but not very tasty. It does very well in shade and so can be planted under trees and in similar places. Two slight disadvantages: it is inclined to throw out a great many runners, and like the raspberry itself has to have the old canes cut out in late summer. There are a number of other *Rubus* species such as *R. cockburnianus* and *R. deliciosus*, with attractive stems, leaves and flowers. For *Rubus henryi*, the climbing blackberry, see the chapter CLIMBING PLANTS. **HS**

Salix, **Willow.** There are many handsome cultivated forms, about 3–6½ft (1–2m) high, such as *S. hastata* 'Wehrhahnii', with reddish brown branches, and the variegated *S. lanata*, only about 3ft (1m) high, prized for its catkins and as a source of nectar for bees. All willows can grow in a fairly damp position. Planting distance about 28–32in (70-80cm). See chapter DECIDUOUS GARDEN TREES for tree forms. **HS**

Sambucus, **Elder.** The basic species, *S. nigra*, has certain unattractive qualities: it is often thickly covered with blackfly in summer, its blue-black berries, though useful in the kitchen, are messy when they drop to the ground, and its invasiveness and habit of seeding itself make a lot of work. *S. racemosa*, 10–13ft (3–4m) high, is more attractive and behaves in a more civilized way. It has red berries. Even better is *S.r.* 'Plumosa Aurea', with finely cut, golden-yellow foliage borne on red stems. Height only 5–6ft (1·5–2m). When spraying other garden plants for aphids, include the elder, or spray it on its own; this will help keep down the blackfly. Planting distance 3ft (1m). **HS**

Sorbaria, **Sorbaria.** Bright green, rowan-like pinnate leaves with large conical panicles of small white florets at the ends of the shoots. Flowers July/August. Height up to about 10ft (3m). Sun to half–shade. **S**

Spiraea, **Spiraea.** The traditional plant in this group is the red spiraea, *S. × bumalda* 'Anthony Waterer', bearing large heads of flowers in June/September; will grow anywhere in sun or half–shade; height only 30–40in (75–100cm). *S. × vanhouttei* is one of the other interesting spiraeas, most of which grow to about 6½ft (2m) tall; it is an undemanding and attractive flowering shrub, with elegantly arched branches and snow-white flowers. *S. × arguta* 'Bridal Wreath' (or 'Foam of May'), flowering even earlier, has filigree-like branches, leaves and flowers. Planting distance about 3ft (1m). **HS**

Symphoricarpos, **Snowberry.** Has graceful, green foliage and pale pink flowers which attract bees; its white or pink fruits stay on the shrub till well into the winter. Planting distance 3–5ft (1–1·50m); height up to 6½ft (2m). The various *Symphoricarpos* hybrids are the most popular forms. Flowering time June/August. Do not grow close to sweet cherries, as it acts as a host plant for cherry blackfly. Grows well in any soil or position. **HS**

Syringa, **Lilac.** Available in handsome single or double varieties; sometimes planted as a small tree. It should not be necessary to go into the artistic and poetical charms of the lilac – but we ought not to be so dazzled by the magnificent cultivated varieties like the best of the dark reds, 'Souvenir de L. Späth', or the double, pure white

'Mme Lemoine', that we forget the charming Persian lilac *S. × persica*. Its loose, pinkish lilac panicles of flowers appear among the lanceolate leaves in May, and last a long time on their fine network of twigs. Planting distance for all lilacs is about 5 ft (1·50 m); they like lime. Height 13–16½ ft (4–5 m). Always remove the dead flower–heads and do not allow seeds to form. **HS**

Tamarix, **Tamarisk.** The vigorous spring tarmarisk, *T. tetrandra*, is the first to flower in May. *T. pentandra* flowers August/September and *T. gallica* usually flowers July to September. All tamarisks are rather sensitive to cold and easily die back in frost – but they spring up again with equal ease. They prefer a warm situation near water, perhaps by the side of a pool. If they get this they will soon grow into real exhibition plants, their rosy showers of blossom swaying above the green of the garden for weeks on end. Any twig broken off and put into water will develop roots and give you a new tamarisk. Ideal in seaside gardens: very resistant to salt gales. Height up to 8½ ft (2·5 m). Planting distance about 2 ft (60 m). **HS**

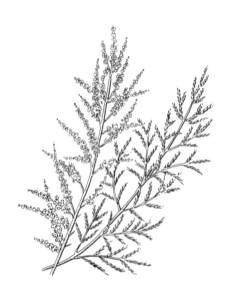

Tamarix, Tamarisk

Viburnum, **Snowball tree, guelder rose.** A group of evergreen and deciduous shrubs, single and double–flowering species, and many different habits of growth. The ordinary common snowball of our gardens, *V. opulus* 'Sterile', is deciduous, grows up to about 10 ft (3 m), and bears its balls of blossom, the size of a clenched fist, in May/June. Its wild form, which has flat-headed inflorescences, and the charming dwarf form *V.o.* 'Compactum' only 3 ft (1 m) tall, bear a profusion of red fruits in autumn. *V. farreri* (*V. fragrans*), a beautiful early spring–flowering shrub, is deciduous, grows to 10 ft (3 m), and bears pale pink clusters of flowers on all its side shoots as early as November to February, before the leaves appear. The 'woolly snowball', *V. lantana*, deciduous, up to 16½ ft (5 m) tall, has longish ovate, downy grey leaves, bears white flower clusters in May/June and pretty dark red fruits; likes lime. Several variegated garden forms have fine autumn colouring. Unfortunately viburnums, especially the deciduous species, suffer badly from aphids. Viburnums will grow in any soil and tolerate shade well. Planting distance about 2 ft (60 cm). For evergreen varieties, see chapter EVERGREEN SHRUBS, TREES AND CONIFERS. **HS**

Weigela, **Weigela.** Weigelas are among the most attractive of summer-flowering shrubs. Among many good varieties: 'Eva Rathke' (slow-growing, dark red); 'Avalanche' (pure white). Planting distance 3–5 ft (1–1·50 m); height 5–6 ft (1·50–2 m). **S**

Weigela

Which shrubs will grow where?

In full sun: most deciduous species of barberry or berberis (*Berberis*); butterfly bush (*Buddleia*); caryopteris (*Caryopteris*); japonica (*Chaenomeles*); cotoneaster (*Cotoneaster*); white and red may (*Crataegus*); broom (*Cytisus*); oleaster (*Elaeagnus angustifolia*); broom (*Genista*); hibiscus (*Hibiscus syriacus*); sea buckthorn (*Hippophae*); St John's wort (*Hypericum*); winter jasmine (*Jasminum nudiflorum*); beauty bush, Kolkwitzia (*Kolkwitzia*); medlar (*Mespilus*); cinquefoils, potentillas (*Potentilla*); stag's horn sumach (*Rhus*); various species roses and climbers or ramblers (see chapter ROSES); snowberry (*Symphoricarpos*) and snowball bush (*Viburnum*) in deciduous forms; weigela (*Weigela*).

In half-shade: snowy mespilus, service berry, (*Amelanchier*); box (*Buxus*); Carolina allspice, (*Calycanthus*); Cornelian cherry (*Cornus mas*); daphne, mezereon, (*Daphne mezereum*); deutzia (*Deutzia*); forsythia (*Forsythia*); Jew's mallow, kerria (*Kerria*); tree paeony (*Paeonia suffruticosa*); syringa, mock orange (*Philadelphus*); firethorn (*Pyracantha*); spiraea (*Spiraea*); tamarisk (*Tamarix*).

Top left: morning glory *(Ipomoea). Top right: Wisteria. Bottom left:* honeysuckle *(Lonicera). Bottom right: Cobaea scandens.*

Stag's horn sumach *(Rhus typhina)* in autumn.

In light to full shade: hydrangea (*Hydrangea*); evergreen honeysuckle (*Lonicera pileata*); ornamental raspberry (*Rubus odoratus*); most of the evergreen viburnums (*Viburnum*).

In sun and shade: spindle tree (*Euonymus*); privet (*Ligustrum*); elder (*Sambucus*); sorbaria (*Sorbaria*).

In dry, sandy soil: the maple species (*Acer*); snowy mespilus, service berry (*Amelanchier*); deciduous berberis, barberries, (*Berberis*); butterfly bush (*Buddleia*); japonica (*Chaenomeles*); broom (*Cytisus scoparius*); oleaster (*Elaeagnus angustifolia*); broom (*Genista*); sea buckthorn (*Hippophae*); laburnum (*Laburnum*); buckthorn (*Rhamnus utilis*); stag's horn sumach (*Rhus typhina*); rowan (*Sorbus aucuparia*).

In soil with a high lime content: cornelian cherry (*Cornus mas*); cotoneaster (*Cotoneaster*); mezereon, daphne (*Daphne mezereum*); snowberry (*Symphoricarpos*); lilac (*Syringa*); wayfaring tree (*Viburnum lantana*).

15
Deciduous garden trees

Over the last few years our need for ornamental trees has become greater the more we have leaned towards creating attractive gardens in which to spend our leisure time. They provide a setting for the house, and the garden itself needs them, either planted singly or in groups, to provide an element of depth. However, there is the problem of the time factor: most owners of gardens on new sites naturally want to see their trees grow fast and get some kind of return from them. It is important, however, to plant trees that are in proportion to the size of your garden. It obviously does not make sense to grow a large oak, plane, sycamore or lime, unless you have the space to allow it to reach maturity.

So far as ordinary planting and general care are concerned, there are no particular rules; the same points apply as for flowering shrubs and fruit trees.

Acer, **Maple.** Undemanding, tolerates dryness. Most maples have beautiful autumn colouring. Favourites are the Norway maple, *A. platanoides;* the sycamore, *A. pseudoplantanus; A. rufinerve,* with red leaves and white-striped bark; and also the sugar maple, *A. saccharinum,* an elegantly shaped treee. There are many good varieties listed in catalogues. Height up to 66 ft (20 m). For other species of maple see chapters HEDGES AND DECIDUOUS FLOWERING SHRUBS, and ROCK GARDENS.

Aesculus, **Horse chestnut.** Easily grown except in limy soils. Its white, yellow or red 'candles' of flowers in May, followed by round fruits ('conkers') in autumn, make these favourite family trees. *A. indica,* Indian horse chestnut, grows up to 20 ft (6 m), and others, such as *A. hippocastanum,* the common form, up to 40 ft (12 m).

Ailanthus altissima, **Tree of heaven.** Grows to 66 ft (20 m), and grows very fast, but naturally enough has lightweight wood. A handsome and decorative tree, with irregular pinnate leaves 12–14 in (30–60 cm) long, bearing white flowers in June/July. Demands a warm, sunny position. Young shoots die back easily in frost; however, new ones always spring up again. An excellent tree in towns in the UK.

Alnus, **Alder.** Ideal for damp sites with catkins in March/April lasting for much of the year. Grows fast up to 40 ft (12 m). The common alder is *A. glutinosa* and its smaller yellowed leaved form *A.g.* 'Aurea' is popular. The grey leaved form, *A. incana,* is useful for planting along street fronts. Does not like lime.

Betula, **Birch.** The silver birch, *B. pendula (verrucosa),* is one of our most popular garden trees, on account of its gracefully drooping branches, pale trunks, and beautiful colouring in spring and autumn. It is often used in picturesque groups. Height 33–50 ft (10–15 m). It is very strong, fairly resistant to industrial pollution, and will do well even in dry positions. Planting should be done only in spring. One sometimes sees the attractive weeping birch, *B. pendula* 'Youngii', in gardens. This variety needs rather moister soil. There are many other species and varieties of birch with attractive stem colours and yellow autumn leaves.

Catalpa, **Indian bean tree.** *C. bignonioides* is most commonly grown for its large heart-shaped leaves and horse chestnut-like flowers in May, followed by runner bean shaped fruits in autumn. Likes a good moist soil and sun. Height up to 34 ft (10 m).

Cercidiphyllum japonicum, **Cercidiphyllum, Katsura tree.** An interesting tree for parks and gardens, usually growing from several stems, with insignificant flowers but magnificent autumn colouring. Its fallen leaves are very fragrant; there are said to be some which have another period of fragrance when the leaves first appear, and the emergence of the leaf-buds from their rose-pink scales is considered particularly attractive. Very sensitive to cold winds. Height up to 33 ft (10 m).

Crataegus, **Hawthorn, red and white may.** Both are well-known ornamental trees, moderately vigorous in growth, their yellowish red berries at least as pretty as their blossom in late spring. They like a dry situation and soil with a good lime content. Unfortunately they harbour all kinds of insect pests but are among the hardiest and most tolerant of trees. Hard pruning (to a round shape) is good for them. See also formal hedges in the chapter HEDGES AND FLOWERING DECIDUOUS SHRUBS.

Davidia involucrata, **Ghost, handkerchief or Chinese dove tree.** Good for all fertile soils. Leaves like those of lime trees. May flowers inconspicuous but surrounded by two large, white, papery bracts. Height about 17 ft (5 m).

Fagus, **Beech.** Several cultivated forms are in particular demand because they are slow-growing. The European *F. sylvatica* has already been mentioned among those plants suitable for formal hedges; if allowed to grow as a tree it will reach a height of 30 ft (9 m) or more. The weeping beech, *F.s.* 'Pendula', is one of our finest weeping trees, along with the weeping purple beech, *F.s.* 'Purpurea Pendula'. Likes an open situation, with no shadows cast by buildings or other trees.

Fraxinus, **Ash.** Only suitable for the garden in a few cultivated varieties. The best is probably the manna ash, *F. ornus*, growing to 26 ft (8 m), and often more like a shrub. It has graceful foliage and countless panicles of white flowers in May/June. *F. excelsior* 'Jaspidea' ('Aurea') develops a pretty, rounded crown without any pruning. The weeping ash, *F.e.* 'Pendula', is decorative in large gardens too. All ashes like plenty of water in the subsoil and a good deal of lime.

Gleditsia triacanthos, **Honey locust.** Attractive feathery leaved trees. Generally spiny. Flowers insignificant but followed by long twisted seed pods. Tolerant of atmospheric pollution and grows well in fertile soil. The form *G.t.* 'Sunburst' with its yellow leaves is popular. Height up to 26 ft (8 m).

Koelreuteria paniculata, **Koelreuteria.** A very handsome tree, but suitable only for mild situations and soil with plenty of lime; flowers in upright yellow panicles in July/August, has pretty lantern-like fruits in autumn. Height up to 26 ft (8 m).

Laburnum, **Golden rain, golden chains.** One of the most graceful and attractive May/June flowering trees with long bunches of yellow blooms. The seeds in the fruits that follow are poisonous and the trees tend to seed themselves freely. Grows well on all soils. Height about 15 ft (4·5 m). The free-flowering form 'Voss' of *L. anagyroides* (common laburnum) is recommended for gardens; it produces little seed after June flowers.

Liquidambar, **Sweet gum, amber tree.** The species *L. styraciflua*, can be recommended as a very fine tree for gardens and parks. Flowers insignificant, but amazing autumn colouring of maple-like leaves, and pretty round

Laburnum, Golden rain

fruits hanging from long stems in winter; fairly young branches bear curious corky growths. As it matures the amber tree becomes very large; however, it should be about half a century before it bursts the bounds of an ordinary middle-sized garden.

Malus, **Ornamental or crab apple.** Though it has been grown in our gardens for over a hundred years now, *M. floribunda*, with its pale pink April blossom, is still the best and most popular species; height up to 16½ ft (5 m). There are also innumerable other species and cultivated varieties, some flowering in spring, some, like *M. sargentii*, only 6½ ft (2 m) tall, not until autumn. Some of them also have June decorative fruits, or magnificently coloured leaves, such as *M.* 'Echtermeyer'. Any tree nursery catalogue will list many other charming *Malus* hybrids.

Prunus, **Ornamental peaches, plums and cherries.** For ornamental almond, see chapter HEDGES AND FLOWERING DECIDUOUS SHRUBS; for cherry laurel see chapter EVERGREEN SHRUBS. We now come to real trees with an average height of about 16½ ft (5 cm). As every tree nursery's catalogue recommends dozens of species, varieties and new hybrids every year, I need mention only a few here. The cherry plum, *P. cerasifera*, is one of the best-known favourites, flowering freely in February/March. *P.c.* 'Atropurpurea' ('Pissardii'), bears pink flowers before the leaves are out; the leaves themselves are dark red, almost black. Height 13–20 ft (4–6 m). The ornamental cherries from Japan are famous: there are *Serrulata* strains such as *P. serrulata* 'Kanzan', a tree with several stems, 20–26 ft (6–8 m) high, with horizontal bow-shaped branches; flowers, deep pink semi-double. Very beautiful indeed is *P. subhirtella* 'Pendula Rosea', often wrongly called Cheal's weeping cherry, with its elegant drooping branches which almost trail on the ground in the course of time; flowers, pure pink, double; makes a good single specimen. *P.s.* 'Autumnalis' is a favourite for producing white or pink flowers from November to March, before the leaves appear. *P. serrulata* 'Erecta' ('Amanoga-wa') is narrowly columnar in shape; its double, freesia-scented pink flowers do not appear until May. All species of *Prunus* are easy to grow, happy in any reasonably well-cultivated garden soil, in sun or in shade.

Pyrus, **Ornamental pear.** Often with silvery leaves. All soils and situations. *P. calleryana* 'Chanticleer' is a pyramidal shape, reaching 20 ft (6 m), whereas *P. salicifolia* 'Pendula', the willow-leaved pear, has delightfully drooping branches. Flowers usually white in May, and some forms produce autumn colour.

Robinia, **Robinia, false acacia.** A tree grown in parks and streets and sometimes found as a shrub used in hedges. It is very undemanding, resistant to pollution; likes poor, dry soil with a fair amount of lime. Soil that is too rich and damp will lay it open to diseases of the roots within a few years, and the next high wind will bring the tree down. The creamy, fragrant clusters of flowers appear in May/June; its seed pods open and disperse the seeds later – rather too freely. In suitable places robinias will grow very fast, and can reach 33 ft (10 m). Two fine species are *R. hispida*, the rose acacia, which has drooping branches and rose-pink blossoms, and *R. pseudoacacia* 'Frisia', with a graceful habit and leaves that stay golden through summer.

Salix, **Willow.** Among the tree forms of the willow are the goat or pussy willow, *S. caprea*, broad-leaved, downy foliage, resistant to pollution, fat grey catkins; the weeping goat willow, *S.c.* 'Pendula', and the true weeping willow, *S.* × *chrysocoma*. Plenty of water in the subsoil is essential; otherwise easy to grow. See also flowering shrubs in the chapter HEDGES AND FLOWERING DECIDUOUS SHRUBS.

Sorbus, **Rowan, mountain ash.** Especially recommended as a garden tree: the pretty and useful form *S. aucuparia* 'Edulis', with edible fruits. The large scarlet berries look beautiful, and make excellent jelly. *S.a.* 'Joseph Rock' produces superb autumn leaf colours and its yellow berries do not attract birds. Flowering time May, height 13–20 ft (4–6 m). Every tree nursery stocks several varieties. Undemanding; prefers dry soils.

Sorbus, Rowan, mountain ash

16
Evergreen shrubs, trees and conifers

One of the oldest of gardening impulses is the wish to grow evergreen plants which will ensure that our gardens have a certain amount of colour and interest even in the dormant season. It is not always easy to get this wish granted, since a number of those evergreen shrubs which are also profuse in their flowering are fairly difficult to grow. With 'normal' evergreens like box, mahonia, and with conifers, we may rely on the detailed instructions for planting and care given in the chapter HEDGES AND FLOWERING DECIDUOUS SHRUBS, but we are still left with a group that used to be known as acid soil plants. The peculiarity of these, especially rhododendrons and azaleas, lies in their dislike of lime. Here, however, they are quite implacable; anyone expecting to grow the plants designated **LH** (lime-hating) in the following list on ordinary garden soil, to water them with hard water and feed them with fertilizers containing lime, is bound to be disappointed. One more word of warning: most species of rhododendron grown in the open need shelter from the wind all the year round as much as an acid soil.

Lime-hating plants require soil with a pH value of 4–5. It is hopeless trying to grow them in lime soils in specially prepared holes filled with acid soil. If you live on a limy soil and want to grow lime-hating plants, grow them in tubs and water only with rain water. No matter how well you prepare holes in the ground, the water soaking into the holes from the surrounding soil will be limy and will kill the plants after a few years. Raised peat beds are slightly better, but in general you will have a better garden if you grow plants that will thrive in it than if you try to grow plants that do not like it.

Regular mulching with peat, shredded bark, grass clippings or leaves is very important; one can also use conifer needles, or plant ground cover plants around the shrubs, to keep the soil cool and damp, but avoid hoeing and other such methods of soil care; most evergreens and conifers are shallow-rooting, and could be disturbed.

Unfortunately, there are few evergreen trees suitable for gardens, but these are included in this chapter. A number of shrubs, such as cotoneaster and bay, make very decorative small trees, especially when grown as standards with a bare main stem.

Evergreen shrubs and trees

Andromeda polifolia, **Bog rosemary.** Height 8–12 in (20–30 cm); flowering time May/June; colour of flowers: pale pink and white. A charming plant, it requires a situation which is always moist in completely lime-free peaty soil. **LH**

Arbutus, **Strawberry tree.** Sometimes grown as shrubs but more often as trees. The dark green leaves set off the white flowers and strawberry-like fruits. *A. unedo* flowers and fruits at the same time late autumn; other species flower in spring. Height up to 10 ft (3 m).

Aucuba japonica, **Aucuba.** Handsome rounded shrubs with glossy green or variegated leaves. Male and female flowers borne on different plants, so scarlet berries on females only. Height 5 ft (1.5 m).

Berberis, **Barberry.** This is such a versatile group of plants, with so many good qualities, that you can make use of it almost anywhere in the garden. Hence you will find mention of deciduous species of berberis and their cultivated varieties in the sections on formal and informal

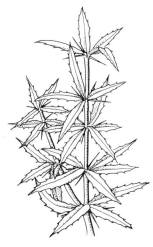

Berberis gagnepainii, Barberry

hedges and flowering shrubs in the chapter HEDGES AND DECIDUOUS FLOWERING SHRUBS and in the chapter ROCK GARDENS as well as here, but I should like to mention a few more names. The picturesque *B. gagnepainii* is a shade plant, 5–6½ ft (1·50–2 m) tall, with long, narrow leaves, golden yellow flowers in May/June and blue-black, very aromatic berries in autumn; hybrid forms bred from it, such as *B.g.* 'Wallichiana Purpurea', are very useful too. *B.* × *stenophylla*, up to 6½ ft (2 m) high and also suitable for growing in full shade, is a favourite not only for its magically fine foliage, borne on slender, slightly arching shoots, but for the profusion of golden yellow flowers it bears followed by berries.

Buxus, **Box.** The large, rather gloomy bushes of *B. sempervirens* 'Arborescens' have become as rare in today's gardens as those curious topiary figures that used to be clipped from their dense network of branches. Box is undemanding and will tolerate shade, which makes it suitable for planting underneath large groups of trees. Height if grown on its own, 10–13 ft (3–4 m). For box used as an edging plant, see the section on formal hedges in the chapter HEDGES AND FLOWERING DECIDUOUS SHRUBS.

Calluna, **Ling, heather.** Callunas can grow to a considerable height and may need regular clipping back when they have made themselves at home. As members of the *Erica* family they need plenty of sun as well as lime-free, poor soil (pH 4–5·5). Several handsome cultivated varieties of *C. vulgaris* with white and pink flowers late summer to autumn and green, gold or orange foliage. **LH**

Camellia, **Camellia.** It is often not appreciated that many camellias are as hardy as laurel. They prefer a partly shaded position, where early morning sun will not damage any frosted flowers, as these are borne in shades of white, pink or red in early spring. There are many varieties and hybrids listed in catalogues. Shelter from north and east winds. Height up to 10 ft (3 m). **LH**

Cotoneaster, **Cotoneaster.** Another extremely versatile shrub with many uses. For dwarf evergreen forms, see the table of ground cover plants (p. 68) and the section on evergreen shrubs in the chapter ROCK GARDENS. Among large, reliable evergreen forms is the willow-leaved cotoneaster, *C. salicifolius floccosus*, with particularly handsome red berries in autumn. Height up to 10 ft (3 m). There are also many variable, beautiful *watereri* hybrids, which grow into quite large bushes over the years. Their foliage will shrivel in a hard winter. *C. lacteus*, with creamy flowers in June and long-lasting red fruits, forms an attractive dense shrub; is truly evergreen. Crossing deciduous and evergreen species of cotoneaster has given rise to a number of so-called 'semi-evergreens'; some of these have become hardier than their parent forms, while others

suit themselves to the temperature and keep or lose their leaves according to whether the winter is a mild one or not. Many make decorative small trees.

Daphne, **Daphne.** Apart from the various species of daphne mentioned in the chapters HEDGES AND DECIDUOUS FLOWERING SHRUBS and ROCK GARDENS, there is also the spurge laurel, *Daphne laureola*, which grows to about 3 ft (1 m), has greenish white fragrant flowers in May, is rather particular about its position and definitely a lime-hater. Poisonous! **LH**

Eleagnus, **Eleagnus.** Important foliage shrubs with green, silver-grey or variegated leaves. Flowers inconspicuous; some forms bear small fruits. Good for shelter belts in exposed or seaside areas. *E. pungens* 'Maculata' a good foliage form. Height up to 6½ ft (2 m). **LH**

Erica carnea, **Winter-flowering heather.** Unlike many other members of the erica family grown in the garden, this heath is not lime-hating but tolerates lime well. It grows to 12 in (30 cm) with bright purple flowers which often appear before the New Year. There are many charming cultivated forms, with white, mauve or deep red flowers in January to April, according to variety, and some have attractive leaf colours. It is a good idea to cut them back immediately after flowering.

Erica tetralix, **Cross-leaved heath.** A 'true' heath with a preference for moist, peaty soils. Height 12–16 in (30–40 cm); the pink, bell-shaped flowers appear in June/September. There are white and carmine garden forms, such as 'Alba Mollis' and 'Con Underwood'. Other lime-hating summer- and autumn-flowering ericas are Cornish heath, *E. vagans*, and bell heather, *E. cinerea* and their varieties. **LH**

Erica tetralix, Cross-leaved heath

Escallonia, **Escallonia.** Although completely evergreen in warmer parts of the country, may be only semi-evergreen elsewhere. White to red flowers appear among glossy leaves in June and flowers appear thereafter inter-mittantly over a long period. Grows in any soil in sun. Tolerates salt winds. Height 6 ft (1.8 m). Hybrids, such as 'Slieve Donard' and 'Donard Radiance', grown mainly. Can be used as a hedging plant; planting distance 2½ ft (75 cm).

Eucalyptus gunnii, **Cedar gum.** Hardy, fast growing evergreen trees up to 40 ft (12 m). The rounded silver juvenile foliage is followed by greyish green sickle-shaped leaves later.

Hebe, **Hebe, New Zealand veronica.** See section on dwarf evergreens in the chapter ROCK GARDENS. Tall forms include the varieties of *H. salicifolia* and *H. speciosa*, flowering June to October.

Ilex aquifolium, **Holly.** The European holly with its coral-red berries may suffer frost damage in dry, exposed places in a very hard winter. Several cultivated varieties with variegated leaves or berries of different colours have been raised. Old holly bushes may become small trees over 16½ ft (5 m) high. Few clones are self-fertile, so you will only get berries if both male and female hollies are present. The varieties 'J. C. van Tol' and 'Pyramidalis' are sup-posed to be the most reliable for producing berries, and *I.* × *altaclarensis* 'Golden King' has beautiful variegated leaves (it is female despite its name!). In due course, hollies make attractive trees.

Kalmia, **Sheep laurel, calico bush.** The narrow-leaved sheep laurel, *K. angustifolia*, deserves mention as one of the most attractive lime-hating plants. It grows to 32–40 in (80–100 cm), bears purplish red flowers in April/June, and is completely hardy. The 8 ft (2·50 m) high calico bush, *K. latifolia*, with white or pink June flowers, is almost as attractive and useful. **LH**

Laurus nobilis, **Sweet bay, bay laurel.** Can be grown as a shrub or a tree. Its dark glossy leaves are aromatic and used for flavouring. Thrives in all soils. Trim April and August. Height up to 7 ft (2 m).

Lavandula, **Old English lavender, Dutch lavender.** The silvery grey fragrant stems and leaves are much sought after in English gardens. Flowers shades of blue July to September. Trim back after flowering to keep bushes compact. Height 2–3 ft (60–90 cm). The old English laven-ders are forms of *L. spica* and the Dutch one is *L. vera*.

Mahonia, **Mahonia.** Best known is the Oregon grape, *M. aquifolium*, easy to grow in any position. Yellow flowers in March/May, decorative blue-black berries in autumn,

as well as interesting winter colouring, with the evergreen leaves shading into red. Height up to 4 ft (1·20 m). *M. japonica* produces fragrant yellow flowers late autumn to early spring.

Pernettya, **Pernettya.** Wiry stemmed plants about 3 ft (1 m) high. White flowers May/June followed by red, pink or white berries. Most commonly grown are the *P. mucro-nata* hybrids with male and female flowers borne on separate plants, except *P.m.* 'Bell's Seedling', which is hermaphrodite. **LH**

Pieris, **Andromeda.** *P. floribunda* grows up to 6½ ft (2 m) high. White flowers are borne in erect panicles in April. *P. japonica* is said to grow up to 10 ft (3 m), and has drooping flower clusters. Both species are worth having if you prepare the soil properly for them. Beautiful planted together with rhododendrons and azaleas. The finest of the genus is *P. formosa forrestii*, with brilliant scarlet young growths and racemes of white, lily of the valley type flowers in spring. **LH**

Pittosporum tenuifolium, **Pittosporum.** The hardiest of pittosporums, growing up to 20 ft (6 m) in mild areas, its pale green leaves make it an attractive evergreen shrub or tree. Produces small fragrant purple flowers in spring.

Prunus laurocerasus, **Cherry laurel.** Suitable for grow-ing as a shade plant. The cherry laurel will bear spikes of white flowers freely in early spring. It also looks pretty in autumn, with dark berries above its deep green, glossy foliage. Height about 5 ft (1·50 m).

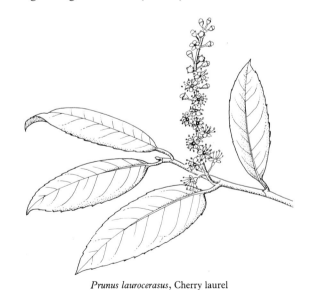

Prunus laurocerasus, Cherry laurel

Pyracantha, **Firethorn.** Similar to cotoneasters. All have white flowers in June, followed by many berries. Can

Pyracantha, Firethorn

be grown against a wall or in the open. 'Orange Glow', orange berries, and 'Flava', yellow fruits, are two attractive forms. Height up to 10 ft (3 m) or more.

Quercus ilex, **Evergreen oak, Holm oak.** A stately, broad headed evergreen form of the common oak which grows to about 20 ft (6 m). Leaves glossy above and greyish beneath. Particularly useful for chalk soils and seaside gardens.

Rhododendron, **Rhododendron, azalea.** There's nothing for it: both names, 'rhododendron' and 'azalea' must be mentioned for the sake of clarity. Botanical nomenclature now, and for some time past, has classed them both as *Rhododendron*. However, gardeners, the gardening trade and even horticultural literature still tend to keep the two groups apart. Flowering time is primarily from the beginning of April to the middle of June, the main flowering season being in May. The distinction between the mainly evergreen rhododendrons and the mainly deciduous or sometimes evergreen azaleas, which produce rich autumn colour, goes back to Linnaeus. First place among the rhododendrons is held by the original hybrids, which are hardy, have healthy foliage, and colourful, well–shaped flower clusters. However, there are also many other striking groups of hybrids, with varieties such as 'Yellow Hammer', yellow-flowering, 'Impeditum', low-growing, purple; the dwarf scarlet *R. forrestii repens*, and several other dwarf forms which are mentioned in the chapter ROCK GARDENS. Many of the newer hyrids are hardy, compact in growth and ideal for smaller gardens.

Groups of hybrids have also been raised from the original azalea species. There are the deciduous Ghent, Knap Hill, Mollis, Occidentale, Rustica and Exbury hybrid azaleas, height from 3–7 ft (1–2 m), and various groups of low–growing (up to 3 ft (1 m)) evergreen hybrids, all with flowers of many colours except true blue. These days

rhododendrons and azaleas are about the best loved of all flowering shrubs. As well as sticking to the general rules for the care of lime-hating evergreens mentioned earlier, one other point: the larger the inflorescences, the more important it is to break (not cut!) them off immediately after flowering. This stimulates the formation of next year's flowerbuds. **LH**

Skimmia, **Skimmia.** Slow growing rounded shrubs, with aromatic glossy leaves. All, apart from *S. reevesiana*, have male and female flowers on different plants, so it is necessary to plant them in groups to get bright fruits after early summer flowers. Height up to 5 ft (1·5 m).

Viburnum, **Snowball tree, guelder rose.** See chapter HEDGES AND DECIDUOUS FLOWERING SHRUBS for deciduous forms. Among the best of the evergreens are *V.* × *burkwoodii*, fragrant white flowers from January to May, *V. davidii*, turquoise berries on female plants if pollinated by male flowers from another plant, and *V. rhytidophyllum*, creamy flowers, red fruits and corrugated leaves. Height up to 10 ft (3 m).

Vinca minor, **Lesser periwinkle.** See table of ground cover plants in the chapter THE LAWN and section on dwarf shrubs in the chapter ROCK GARDENS. Particularly suitable for planting in shade under taller plants.

Periwinkle

Conifers suitable for gardens

The groups of conifers listed below include species or varieties which are dwarf or slow-growing enough to be suitable for rock gardens or growing in containers; the only exception is *Metasequoia glyptostroboides*. For a selection of these see chapter ROCK GARDENS.

Abies, **Silver fir.** I will mention just two outstanding representatives of this beautiful genus: the white fir, *A. concolor*, likes lime, has very long leaves; and the lime-hating Korean fir, *A. koreana*, a small tree (up to 10 ft (3 m))

Top left: flowering cherry *(Prunus triloba). Top right: Magnolia* × *soulangeana. Bottom left:* maple *(Acer). Bottom right: Vibernum.*

Top left: silver fir *(Abies)*. *Top right:* calico bush, sheep laurel *(Kalmia latifolia)*. *Bottom left:* yellow holly *(Ilex)*. *Bottom right:* pine *(Pinus)* with spring growth and flowers.

The two top pictures show hardy ferns; left the lady ferns *(Athyrium felix-femina)* and right the soft shield fern *(Polystichum setiferum)*. Bottom left is a decorative grass, and bottom right shows pampas grass *(Cortaderia)*.

Long-spurred columbine (*Aquilegia caerulea* hybrid).

suitable for a garden adjoining a house. The difference between fir and spruce: fir cones stand erect, fir needles are soft; spruce trees have hanging cones and their needles are usually hard and prickly.

Cedrus, **Cedar.** This is one of the classic coniferous trees. Its best-known species, the Atlas cedar, *C. atlantica*, and the blue–green form of the Atlas cedar, 'Glauca', look very attractive in large gardens. The form 'Glauca' is easier to grow and hardier than the species itself. The pendent habit of *C. deodara* is attractive.

Chamaecyparis, **Cypress.** The large, usually pyramid or pillar-shaped representatives of this beautiful genus of conifers can be recognized by their habit of growth; the leading shoot always droops slightly. For planting as a single specimen, one of the most decorative is *C. nootkatensis* 'Pendula', which, as its name indicates, has branches all of which are pendulous as well as the leading shoot, slanting diagonally downwards. Foliage, bright green: height up to over 33 ft (10 m). Connoisseurs might grow the feathery-leaved *C. pissifera* 'Plumosa Aurea', with its fine network of branches and yellow foliage; height up to 26 ft (8 m). There are a number of handsome forms of *C. lawsoniana*. Likes a rather damp soil.

Cupressus, **Cupressus.** Closely related to *Chamaecyparis* but usually more rounded branches and larger ones. Best known is *C. macrocarpa* and its forms, especially those with golden foliage such as 'Gold Crest'.

Juniperus, **Juniper.** Again, the smaller species of juniper are favourites in the rock garden. Among the best of the larger junipers are *J. communis* 'Hibernica', with bluish green needles, growing up to 13 ft (4 m) and the pencil cedar *J. virginiana* 'Glauca', up to 23 ft (7 m), with beauti-

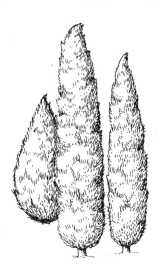

Juniperus, Juniper

ful steel-blue foliage. All junipers are hardy and undemanding, and can be grown in dry situations, though they are not always proof against industrial pollution.

Larix, **Larch.** One of our finest garden trees, though it is deciduous. The most usual species is the European larch, *L. decidua*, with bright green leaves that turn bright yellow before they fall in autumn; height, when grown in woodland areas, up to 98 ft (30 m). Equally interesting is the Japanese larch, *L. kaempferi*, which also grows very tall but forms a broader, more cone-shaped tree with branches borne horizontally. The reddish brown of its wood makes it particularly attractive.

Metasequoia glyptostroboides, **Dawn redwood.** When it was discovered in the forties, this relative of the American giant sequoias was something of a sensation. By now it has settled down in many gardens, though it is still rather expensive, and time will show how tall it can grow in Europe. It has feathery foliage, which turns bronze then yellow in autumn. A peculiarity of its own is the way it loses its short shoots along with the needles in autumn.

Picea, **Spruce.** Of the large species suitable for planting in groups or as single specimens, I would pick: the Serbian spruce, *P. omorika*, of narrow growth, needles green on top, silvery underneath; the Oriental or Caucasian spruce, *P. orientalis*, particularly attractive when bearing its large purple cones; the well-known Colorado spruce in its variety *P. pungens* 'Glauca', and last but not least the Brewer's weeping spruce, *P. breweriana*. They are all very easy to grow.

Pinus, **Pine.** My first choice from among these large, decorative trees, an ornament to any garden where they have enough room, is the Arolla pine, *P. cembra*, which grows slowly, eventually reaching a height of up to 33 ft (10 m). Another handsome pine is the Bhutan pine, *P. wallichiana*, with needles 4–8 in (10–20 cm) long which hang vertically downward; height up to 66 ft (20 m). The Austrian pine, *P. nigra austriaca*, particularly easy to grow, can be recognized by its thick, dark foliage, grows to up to 66 ft (20 m) in maturity, forms a broad, spreading crown, and seems fairly resistant to industrial pollution. All pines like an open position, and put down deep roots.

Taxus, **Yew.** One of the most important garden conifers – equally suitable as a formal hedge or a single specimen; its toleration of shade is a great advantage. The common yew, *T. baccata*, grows up to 40 ft (12 m) tall; it has some beautiful varieties such as the golden yew or the Irish yew, both 10–13 ft (3–4 m) tall. All yews are rather sensitive to industrial pollution.

Thuja, **Arbor-vitae.** Unlike the cypress, with which it is often confused, the arbor-vitae always has an upright habit of growth. It is said to be immune to industrial pollution, and is used mainly for hedges or, in its dwarf forms, in the rock garden. It is worth considering *T. orientalis* 'Conspicua' for planting as a single specimen; it has bright golden foliage arranged in flattened sprays and grows into a slender tree up to 10 ft (3 m) high.

Tsuga canadensis, **Hemlock.** One of our most elegant conifers, with its pretty, arching habit of growth, handsome foliage and profusion of cones. Rather sensitive to drying winds and soil that is too dry, but does not mind frost. Height of the species: up to 50 ft (15 m).

Tsuga canadensis, Hemlock

17
Rock gardens

When I wonder why rock gardens should have been so popular for so long – they have been a 'craze' for two or even three generations of gardeners by now – the answer is not hard to find. All other manifestations of the art of horticultural design – herbaceous borders, rose beds, groups of shrubs, the colourful flowering of annuals, bulbs, tubers – have their own rhythm of flowering and fading. However skilful you may be at planting early, mid-season and late varieties in succession, you will always have a bare patch or one without any flowers some time or other, and even the occasional evergreen does not really compensate.

The rock garden is different. It accommodates such a wealth of various kinds of plants, in such diversity that we really may say: here's richness. Within their limited space, rock gardens are so versatile that there is always something going on, something coming into leaf or flower, from early spring to late autumn and even in the middle of winter – and it all looks perfectly natural. In addition, the keen botanist has an excellent field for experiment in the rock garden. Rock gardens can look charming, playful, matter-of-fact, romantic and modern all at the same time; they unite all the various pleasures of gardening, embracing that 'sweet disorder' which means that they never freeze into a rigid system, because they are always changing.

Some mistakes, and how to avoid them

Before we consider the creation of a rock garden as it should be, let us look at it as it should *not* be. Instead of a well thought out and aesthetically pleasing design, you may find yourself with a ludicrous arrangement of symmetrically placed stones. Once your plants are growing well the stones that formed the original framework will soon be almost invisible. The basic requirement of a rock garden is that it should form a slope, and the stones are there to support plants and to break up the planting area. They should create an elegantly irregular effect, and hold the plants in place; they may well reinforce a pleasing impression, but the actual stones should not be the main consideration.

Genuine alpine plants may want very little feeding, but the lay-out as a whole will need to be tended the same as any other garden bed, and stones should never be crowded so thickly that it is impossible to work among them; besides the job of feeding, the soil will need breaking up now and then, and there will be weeds to pull out – though usually you should have the whole area almost entirely covered by your chosen plants within a few years, and that in itself will keep down the weeds.

However, when rather large stones do have to be used – for instance, in a large rock garden area – they should never look as if they have simply been dumped down. Dig a little soil out and settle the stones in the ground so that they look as if they are a natural part of it. Another point which rock garden designers have found holds good in practice is that a few large stones are always far more impressive than a lot of little ones – not, of course, that I mean you should use great blocks of stone weighing a hundredweight each. A group of three or four stones of similar composition can look well too, if it fits in as an organic part of the whole rock garden.

When you are putting the stones in place, you have to imagine they have rolled down a hillside by themselves. How would they finish up? With their heaviest – i.e. broadest – sides downwards, of course. However, there are exceptions to this rule: you might have a stone broken across and showing attractive veining, positively demanding to be set on end, even though it may be rather narrow that way up.

There is one more point to be remembered in building a rock garden; it should not form one smooth slope, with everything running in the same direction. If possible you should aim for a terraced effect so that plants themselves are growing on a horizontal plane, as shown in the picture. This way you kill two birds with one stone: in the first place the plants take root better, and find it easier to get adequate moisture, and in the second there is far less danger of the soil being washed away in heavy rain – or even when being watered – if the whole area is terraced. Finally, some of the prettiest and most popular rock garden plants, such as aubrieta, dwarf phlox and saxifrage, dwarf campanulas and many species of *Sedum* and *Sempervivum*, have a natural tendency to tumble over the stones supporting their planting sites – a very pretty visual effect of a wealth of

Horizontally arranged planting sites among supporting stones create a very natural effect, with room for all sorts of different plants.

trailing flowers is created, and is just right for the rock garden, giving the impression that it flourishes luxuriantly by itself.

These days rock gardens are often used to good effect, especially on new garden sites, to even out a difference of level between house and garden or house and street. But that is not their only function. A rock garden may be built beside water. It may act, in a modified form, as a slightly raised, wide border of stones with tufts and mats of plants growing over them beside a path which has been sunk a little way below the natural level. It can be placed in front of a shrubbery, if you take proper account of any shade caused by shrubs or trees, since rock gardens ideally face south and their plants dislike shade. Finally, the rock garden has great potential for change and development.

Dry stone walls, alpine gardens, gardening in troughs

Dry stone walls form a kind of sub-division of the rock garden proper. They have a more severely architectural quality about them, and exhibit different though related features of layout and planting. It is particularly important for a dry stone wall to have enough places where water can collect in joints and crevices after a shower. This is why such walls are always built with a slight backwards tilt, or

with intentional gaps among the stones. When building a dry stone wall one must also be careful to lay each individual stone so that it is not horizontal but slants slightly backwards; if this is done rain, or water from a can or sprinkler, will not run straight off as if running off a roof, but will be retained and trickle back into the wall and to the plants growing there.

Rock gardens and dry stone walls, having passed through years of a transitional period and overcome many childhood ailments, are now part of almost every garden, and have become independent of those considerations of landscape and climate which used to be pre-requisites. Genuine alpine gardens, however, will probably always be for connoisseurs only. There is no difficulty in growing an alpine garden if you happen to live near the mountains, but gardens at lower levels are a different matter; their very different environmental factors will soon exhaust the will to live of alpine plants not native to their climates. I do not, of course, recommend anyone to disregard conservation and go and dig up 'genuine' alpine rhododendrons or gentians, auriculas or edelweiss in the mountains and transplant them to a mis-conceived 'alpine garden'. Wrenched out of their natural environment, the plants would be subjected to such drastic biological changes that they would soon lose their original beauty and colour, and they themselves would grow poorly and then die. It is both wrong and unnecessary to dig up wild plants. And there is a considerable range of 'genuine' alpine plants and mountain flora from all over the world, along with cultivated forms which have been specially bred and well-acclimatized to lower levels; one can get a great deal of pleasure from these without any expert knowledge.

Such plants do not grow only in rock gardens and alpine gardens; they have found themselves another area, one which is appreciated by many keen gardeners – yet again, in accord with the changing conditions of our times. I am referring to those people who grow little gardens in troughs. Nowadays there are some real artists among these trough gardeners; they may possess as many as half a dozen old stone sinks, drinking or feeding troughs or their modern equivalents, usually of artificial materials, where they grow a great many charming little plants, tending each according to its needs. They do not just grow those familiar rock plants which form clumps or tufts, but a whole range of others, extending to special collections of succulents, dwarf shrubs and dwarf conifers.

All plant containers of this kind must have a drainage hole at the bottom, or two or three drainage holes if the size and shape of the container make it advisable. Waterlogging can hardly be avoided after a heavy fall of rain, or even a thorough artificial watering, and those plants grown in troughs are particularly averse to it. Raising the containers on bricks assists free drainage.

The composition of the soil is very important too. Most rock garden plants and alpines, and the succulents *Sedum* and *Sempervivum*, need soil which is very well drained if they are to take root properly. They should have a layer of broken clay pots, coarse rubble or stones 1–1½ in (3–4 cm) deep at the bottom of the container, whose sides should be at least 8 in (20 cm) high. Follow with a layer of half-rotted leaves to prevent the soil growing medium washing through. The best soil mix for most alpine plants is made up of two parts good garden soil, one part fine grade sphagnum moss peat and one part sharp sand or grit (all parts by volume). Mix together thoroughly with a gener-ous sprinkling of bonemeal. Use lime-free soil for lime-hating plants (one that is shown by a soil test kit to have a pH of less than 7). If your soil is acid, for most alpine plants that like some lime, add one part by volume to the original mix of limestone chippings or hydrated lime. If rocks are to be added to the container for extra interest, place them in position before planting.

The general outlook: choice of plants

Let us turn to the plants themselves. There are many hundreds, of great beauty and well tried suitability. Not just rock garden plants themselves, but all those which can be grown in the rock garden, according to your own particular inclinations and requirements, though they belong to other groups, from small forms of flowering shrubs to culinary herbs.

When this is the case, details of their cultivation will be found in the other plant surveys of this book, as, for instance, in the chapter BULBOUS PLANTS. Those I have added are picked for their durability and the length of their flowering season. You can look for those I have *not* mentioned in the extensive catalogues put out by large horti-cultural firms – or add to your collection by exchanging plants with like-minded friends, which, as we all know, is the most enjoyable way.

Small flowering plants for the rock garden

Achillea, **Yarrow, milfoil.** There are several dwarf species which are rewarding to grow; height between 4 and 12 in (10 and 30 cm); spread: 8–10 in (20–25 cm); flowering

A properly planted trough of alpines involves very little work and will last for years.

time: May to August, according to variety; colour of flowers: white and yellow; planting time March; situation: sunny. Will do well on any light soil; also on dry stone walls and in the joints of paved paths. Several species, such as *A. argentea* (8 in (20 cm)) and *A. aurea* 'Grandiflora, are notable for their beautiful silvery grey foliage. The familiar yellow-flowered *A. tomentosa* has rather downy leaves.

Ajuga, **Bugle.** Height 4–6 in (10–15 cm); spread, 6–10 in (15–25 cm); flowering time May/June; colour: blue; planting time: March; situation: half-shade, will grow beside pools. Prefers damp parts of the rock garden; occasional applications of fertilizer are recommended. Almost all ajugas, including the cultivated forms *A. reptans* 'Pink Elf', pink-flowered, and 'Multicolor', with variegated leaves, are invasive and must be kept under control. *A. pyramidalis,* which has erect, hairy stems and strikingly thick blue spikes of flowers, throws out runners.

Alyssum, **Alyssum.** Height 6–12 in (15–30 cm); spread, 8–10 in (20–25 cm); flowering time: April/June; colour: lemon-yellow; planting time: autumn or early spring; situation: sunny. This low-growing sub-shrub is one of those unpretentious rock garden plants which form mats or cushions, and which are also valued for their silvery evergreen foliage. Propagate by dividing the roots in autumn. The most popular is *A. saxatile,* bearing dense heads of single or double flowers in shades of yellow from sulphur to gold. *A. montanum* flowers late, from June to August. Trim back after flowering.

Androsace, **Rock jasmine.** Height 2–4 in (5–10 cm); forms mats or throws out runners; flowering time: May/June; colour of flowers: bright pink, dark red; planting time: autumn or spring; situation: must have half-shade. Androsaces can be considered only partly true rock garden plants, since the easiest species and cultivated forms to obtain prefer a position in half-shade with well-cultivated soil containing humus. However. *A. primuloides,* which likes sun and limy soil, is suitable; it bears clusters of bright pink primula-like flowers above silky-looking, hairy rosettes of leaves.

Anemone, **Anemone.** Height: 6 in (15 cm); spread, 6–12 in (15–30 cm); flowering time: April/May or July/September; colour of flowers: white, blue, also creamy yellow and carmine. One of the most pleasing of rock garden plants, from the native European anemone, is *A. nemorosa,* with its many garden forms in various colours, flowering in late summer. *A. ranunculoides* produces yellow flowers in spring. These species are all classed as wood anemones, preferring shady positions and soil containing leaf mould. However, the beautiful azure-flowered *A. blanda,* only 6 in (15 cm) tall, and its several pretty garden forms all like sun. See also *Pulsatilla,* further on in this list.

Arabis, **Arabis,** Height: 6–8 in (15–20 cm); forms large cushions; flowering time: March/May; colours: white, mauve, red. Arabis is one of the standard plants found in any rock garden, undemanding and extremely decorative. There are a number of varieties, some single, some double, headed by *A. caucasica* 'Alba Plena' and the variegated 'Variegata'. 'Rosabella' is a particularly pretty pink.

Arabis

Arenaria, **Arenaria.** Height about 2½ in (5 cm); forms grassy mats; flowering time: June/July; colours: white, pink. Grass-like leaves make these attractive plants. Most often grown is *A. balearica,* and other good species include *A. montana, A. pinifolia* and *A. purpureascens* in the form of 'Elliot's Variety'.

Armeria, **Thrift.** Height 8 in (20 cm), forms hummocks; flowering time: May/June; colours: white, mauve-pink. A small perennial of modest charm, with many pretty varieties, all of which can be used as edging plants. I use the white form, *A. maritima* 'Alba', as summer camouflage for the autumn crocus slumbering underneath it until September.

Artemisia, **Artemisia.** Height 4–6 in (10–15 cm); forms broad cushions; flowering time: July/August; colour: white. The flowers are less important than the filigree-like, silvery foliage which spreads over the ground; however, it must have light, sandy soil and an open position if it is to show off its full beauty. If they are not hemmed in by other, taller plants, artemisias like *A. lanata* or *A. schmidtiana* 'Nana' are particularly ornamental in the rock garden. Relatives of the medicinal herb wormwood.

Aster, **Dwarf asters.** Height about 6 in (15 cm); flowering time of *A. alpinus* May/June, *A. natalensis,* May/July and *A. sativus* 'Atrocaeruleus', June/September; colour of flowers: white, pink, orange, blue; planting time: only in spring, or with ball of soil intact. The whole group is so charming that one would really like to try them all in turn. The earliest and smallest look rather like over-sized daisies. All form broad, round bushes and are extremely easy to grow.

Aubrieta, **Aubrieta.** Height 4–6 in (10–15 cm); flowering time April/May; colours: blue, red, pink, white. No rock garden or alpine garden or dry wall would be complete without the enchanting melting colours of aubrieta in spring. They make almost no work, will grow well anywhere, and tumble over the stones with their downy, grey-green foliage. They go very well with *Alyssum* and *Iberis*. Finest varieties: the rose-red 'Belisha Beacon', violet-purple 'Bob Saunders', the light blue 'Dream', bright pink 'Bressingham Pink', the mauve-pink 'Riverslea'. Cut back after flowering.

Aubrieta

Campanula, **Bellflower, campanula.** Height 6–12 in (15–30 cm); spread, 6–8 in (15–20 cm); flowering time June/September; colours: blue, white; planting time: September or March; situation: sun, also half-shade. As well as those large campanulas already described in the chapter HARDY PERENNIALS, there is a whole range of charming small forms, particularly suitable for edgings and rock gardens, being very easy to grow. *Campanula carpatica*, with its erect, branching stems, is a typical example; it forms clumps, is happy in any kind of soil, and does not mind really bright sunlight. *C. portenschlagiana* spreads to form extensive mats. For other campanulas, see chapters ANNUALS AND BIENNIALS and HARDY PERENNIALS.

Cerastium, **Snow in summer.** Height 2½–4 in (6–10 cm); very rampant; flowering time: May; colour: white. Can be planted at almost any time. Situation: sunny. Cerastium, with its downy grey leaves, goes well with aubrieta, thrift, dwarf phlox or veronica. However, its

friends have to be protected from it. *C. tomentosum*, with silvery foliage, is reasonably restrained and *C. columnae* is non-rampant. Very undemanding, will even grow among rubble; good as a ground cover plant.

Dianthus, **Pink.** The low-growing perennial species of pink, which usually form mats of leaves, are favourites for rock gardens, dry walls and as edging plants. Their carpets of white, pink or carmine flowers appear in spring, or some in mid-summer. Planting time autumn or spring; most of them prefer a sunny position. The alpine pink, *D. alpinus*, 2–5 in (5–12 cm) high, flowering in July/August, large, flesh-pink flowers, is something of an exception in being rather tender, and thus best suited for growing in an alpine garden. *Dianthus plumarius* and the Cheddar pink, *D. gratianopolitanus* (pink-flowered) have produced so many charming garden varieties that confusions are bound to arise. Its low-growing, grey-green tufts of foliage with relatively long-stalked flowers are most attractive in a rock garden or on a dry stone wall, and are very good as cut flowers. Varieties are white, pink and dark red, some are double. For half-hardy annual and biennial pinks, see chapter ANNUALS AND BIENNIALS; for hardy perennial pinks see chapter HARDY PERENNIALS.

Draba, **Whitlow grass, draba.** Height 2–4 in (5–10 cm); forms cushions and will cover quite large areas; flowering time: March/April, also May; colours: white, yellow. Planting time, according to when you obtain the plant; with a good ball of soil it can even be planted in flower. This is one of the simplest plants of all to grow, and is a charming sight with its dense clusters of leaf rosettes, green or reddish green accordingly to variety. These spring-flowering plants are happiest in poor soil. *D. aizoides*, yellow, is the first to flower, while *D. dedeana*, white, and *D. repens*, also yellow, often bear their little flowers, each borne singly on slender stems, well into May. Later in the year, too, this child of the southern mountain ranges of Europe is attractive with its many seed-heads; it seeds itself freely. It will also, of course, grow in crevices or in joints between paving stones.

Erigeron speciosus, **Fleabane, erigeron.** Height 4–16 in; spread: 4–5 in (10–15 cm); flowering time: July/September; colours: orange, red, blue, pinkish mauve; planting time: March/April; situation: sunny. The aster-like, ray-petalled flowers are generally borne in the form of a branched cluster on hairy stems. Erigeron used to be a rather tender little plant, but growers have developed varieties, from the violet-blue 'Darkest of All' to the semi-double deep pink 'Dimity', which are most attractive either in the rock garden or a flower bed, have a long flowering season, and are easy to grow; a particularly rewarding plant.

Euphorbia, **Euphorbia.** Height, between 2 and 16 in (5 and 40 cm), according to variety; usually forms broad, bushy plants; flowering time: April/May and May/June; colour: yellow; planting time: whenever you like; situation: sunny. Most rock gardens contain *E. myrsinites* spreading its curious gothic-looking stemmed rosettes wherever you look. *E. polychroma,* up to 16 in (40 cm) high, can also be planted in very dry and sunny positions; its yellow bracts, borne above dense, rounded bushes, give the impression that it is flowering over a long period.

Gentiana, **Gentian.** Height 4–12 in (10–30 cm); spread: 4–6 in (10–15 cm); flowering time: May–August/September; colour: blue; planting time: early spring; situation: not too sunny. All species of gentian should be planted out from pots with a good ball of soil. Some species, among them the large-flowering, stemless *G. acaulis,* as well as the erect *G. septemfida,* up to 12 in (30 cm) high, like light, stony soil, with some humus in it. Autumn flowering forms, such as *G. sino-ornata,* dislike lime. If you plant these and similar species together, you can have gentians in flower from May to September. They often seem to be doing rather poorly their first summer, but in their second year they begin to perform better. There are also yellow and white flowering species.

Geranium, **Crane's bill.** Height 4–6 in (10–15 cm); flowering time: June/September; colour of flowers: white, pink, red, blue; planting time: autumn or spring; situation: sun or partial shade. There are a number of species, such as *G. cinereum, G. dalmaticum,* and *G. wallichianum,* also hybrids and varieties, of this easily grown plant to give plenty of summer colour in the rock garden.

Gypsophila, **Gypsophila.** Height 2–4 in (5–10 cm); spreads very vigorously; flowering time: June/August; colour: pink; planting time: whenever you like; situation: sunny. The dwarf forms, which make cushions or mats of foliage, are very easy to grow, do well in full sun on dry, sandy soil, can be used as an edging plant and in crevices or joints of walls, but may spread so much as to become a nuisance. Along with the pale pink *G. repens* 'Dubia', *G. r.* 'Dorothy Teacher' also has bluish leaves.

Helianthemum, **Rock rose, helianthemum.** Height 4–8 in (10–20 cm); forms bushy plants ; flowering time: June/August; colours: from white and pale yellow to pink, salmon and orange to red; planting time: autumn or spring; situation: sunny. There are single and double varieties of this sub-shrub, which is low-growing and spreads along the ground; it is a rock garden plant found everywhere. Very free-flowering, easy to grow, and so vigorous that its long shoots often have to be cut back hard.

Helianthemum, Rock rose

Heuchera, **Coral flower.** See chapter HARDY PERENNIALS. The beautiful Bressingham hybrids and other new varieties, with their delicate bell-shaped flowers borne above graceful rosettes of leaves, are really rather large for the rock garden; but they do so well in poor soil and sunny positions on its little terraces, slopes and dry stone walls that one may legitimately make room for them here.

Heuchera, Coral flower

Iberis, **Candytuft.** Height 4–8 in (10–20 cm); spread, 8–12 in (20–30 cm); flowering time: April/June; colour: white, planting time: autumn or spring; situation: sunny. Among the stock inhabitants of all sunny rock gardens. An evergreen, completely hardy sub-shrub. The broad, prostrate *I. saxatilis* grows 4–6 in (10–15 cm) high, and is also very suitable for dry stone walls. Best-known species: *I. sempervirens* in many cultivated forms. Pretty mingled

Cushion-forming flowering plants for the rock garden. *Left to right:* dwarf phlox *(Phlox subulata)*, pink — not yet in flower — *(Dianthus)*, forget- me-not *(Myosotis)*, alyssum *(Alyssum saxatile)*. *In the background:* candytuft *(Iberis sempervirens)* and dwarf iris.

Top left: double kingcups *(Caltha palustris). Top right:* water lily *(Nymphaea). Bottom left: Primula rosea. Bottom right:* spiderwort *(Tradescantia virginiana).*

with the blue, red and purple of aubrietas, the sulphur-yellow of *Alyssum saxatile* or the soft blue of dwarf phlox. For annual form, see chapter ANNUALS AND BIENNIALS.

Iris, **Dwarf irises.** Height up to 8 in (20 cm); spreading their rhizomatous roots gradually to form groups of flowers; flowering time: May/July; colour of flowers: white, golden yellow, violet. The wild form and the many garden hybrids of the *I. barbata nana* group like as dry and sunny a place as possible, which does not, of course, mean they cannot be grown near other, larger irises in a rock garden site close to water. The whole tribe does very well on a dry stone wall. There are many other so-called botanical species of these small irises, as well as the dwarf bearded iris, and they are suitable for the rock garden, being only 16–24 in (40–60 cm) high at most. *I. graminea* has fragrant, light violet flowers and grassy foliage. *I. setosa*, the dwarf form, has bluish mauve flowers. A charming dwarf iris, *I. lacustris*, is only about 4 in (10 cm) high. Taller are *I. pumila* and its varieties. Plant in autumn, or immediately after flowering, and move as seldom as possible.

Leontopodium, **Edelweiss.** Height 4–6 in (10–15 cm); spread, about 8 in (20 cm); flowering time: July; colour of flowers: white; planting time: autumn or spring, best planted from pots, with ball of soil intact; situation: very sunny. The garden forms of the true alpine edelweiss, *L. alpinum*, have slightly grey foliage. Also to be recommended: *L. palibiniana* and *L. aloysiodorum*. The edelweiss, of course, should go in the sunniest, driest, stoniest part of the rock garden. If you can add limestone grit to the planting site you will raise particularly fine, downy white specimens. Even in very dry periods and after flowering, edelweiss should not be watered. Annual division and replanting, especially of older plants, is good for it.

Myosotis, **Forget-me-not.** Height 4 in (10 cm); flowering time: May; colour: blue with white at the base of the calyx. The alpine forget-me-not, *Myosotis alpestris*, is really only a form of the ordinary woodland forget-me-not. It has shorter, denser clusters of flowers, and is fragrant. Its calyx bears individual hairs. Transplanted to a lowland garden, its alpine characteristics soon disappear and it reverts to its original form. One more proof that growing alpines in rock gardens at lower levels is not an easy task. A choice alpine species is *M. rupicola*, with deep blue flowers.

Oenothera missouriensis, **Evening primrose.** Height 8–12 in (20–30 cm); flowering time: July/October; colour of flowers: yellow; planting time: spring rather than autumn; situation: sunny. This perennial, with prostrate, red-tinged stems lying along the ground, narrow, leathery

Oenothera missouriensis, Evening primrose

green leaves and large flowers, profusely borne, is an essential plant for the rock garden. But it does take up a lot of room and can be ruthless in looking after its own interests. However, the mysterious effect of the large, bright yellow flowers opening in the evening is all the more beautiful for that. They do indeed shrivel very quickly into an ugly brown mess, but regular, daily dead heading stimulates further flowering enormously. Do not just remove the remains of the flower; the fan-shaped seed capsules form at the base of the long calyx, close to the stem itself, and the important point is to remove them. As well as the lovely *O. missouriensis*, I recommend *O. tetragona*, erect, with brownish leaves, and *O. pumila*, a genuine dwarf form growing only 5 in (13 cm) high. The newer hybrid varieties are worth noting, too.

Oxalis, **Oxalis.** Height up to 10 in (25 cm); spread about 2 ft (60 cm); flowering time: May/August; colour of flowers: pink, white. Pretty plants with deeply cut clover-like leaves, easy to grow in any position. Most useful for rock gardens include *O. acetosella*, *O. adenophylla*, and *O. magellanica*, with its bronzy green leaves. Beware – oxalis can become invasive!

Papaver alpinum, **Alpine poppy.** Height 4 in (10 cm); flowering time: May/July and July/August; colour of flowers: white, yellow, orange. Once it has settled in the alpine poppy asks for almost no attention, while its graceful bearing, striking, slightly hairy leaves and pretty flowers make it one of the most delightful of the smaller species of poppy. It does well in light soil, with sun or half-shade – conditions which are easy to find in a rock garden. The Iceland poppy, *P. nudicaule*,, height 12–16 in (30–40 cm), is worth a mention; there are many beautiful varieties, and colours include bright red and deep pink.

Phlox, **Dwarf phlox, moss phlox.** Height 4–8 in (10–20 cm); spread, 8–10 in (20–25 cm); flowering time: April/June; colours: white, pink, blue; many varieties; planting time: March or September; situation: sunny. These alpine phloxes, which form mats or cushions in rock gardens, on dry stone walls, in the joints between paving stones, or are used as edging plants, are cultivated in general like their big sisters in the herbaceous border. Plant them with a good ball of soil intact, or propagate by cuttings in May. *P. douglasii,* 2–4 in (5–10 cm) high, white and bright blue flowers borne in May/August, is very pretty; so is *P. amoena* 'Variegata', with coloured foliage and lilac-pink flowers, of the same height.

Potentilla, **Potentilla.** Height 4–8 in (10–20 cm); spread, 4–6 in (10–15 cm); flowering time: May/August; colour of flowers: yellow, yellowish red; planting time and root division: autumn; situation: sunny. All the small potentillas, among them *P. aurea* 'Plena', double golden yellow, flowering time July/September, and *P. verna,* flowering in spring, like good nourishing soil which should not be too dry. *P.* × 'Tonguei', prostrate, with apricot, crimson-blotched flowers, is good for green ground cover.

Primula, **Primula, auricula.** Height mainly up to 12 in (30 cm); forms large, rather fleshy rosettes of leaves; flowering time: April/July; colour of flowers: white, yellow, red, mauve, purple, in pastel tones; fragrant. Will grow in half-shade in any reasonably good garden soil containing humus. The alpine auricula, *P. auricula,* which likes lime, is particularly suitable for an alpine garden. Flowering time April/June. It likes stony soil and does well in crevices in a dry stone wall. Situation: sun to half-shade. *Primula auricula* 'Blue Velvet' has blue flowers with a distinct white eye and leaves dusted with white.

Pulsatilla, **Pulsatilla, Pasque flower.** Height 6–8 in (15–20 cm); spread, 4–6 in (10–15 cm); flowering time: April/May; colour of flowers: white, pink, red, bright violet-blue; planting time, autumn or early spring; situation: sunny, dry. There are various forms of the species *P. vulgaris.* All pulsatillas like lime and dislike damp.

Sagina glabra 'Aurea', **Pearlwort.** Height 1 in (3 cm); forms golden mossy cushions; flowering time: June/August; colour: white; planting time: April and August; situation: sun to half-shade, not too dry. The charming sagina is indispensable anywhere you want a soft, thick, mossy cushion. It will grow in the joints between paving stones. If it is neatly cut back from time to time it makes a good narrow edging plant. It will fill gaps between other small plants in the rock garden, and is good as a ground cover plant. Divide in April or August; plant in clumps and give it a good watering, and you will find that the separate

groups of sagina very soon grow to form an unbroken surface again.

Saponaria ocymoides, **Saponaria, soapwort.** Height 6 in (15 cm); spread 4–6 in (10–15 cm); flowering time: June/August; colours: pink, red. This charming dwarf form, which makes dense cushions, is cultivated like its larger version among the perennials of medium height. Dwarf saponaria will do well even in very dry places, grows and flowers diligently, and has a sweet fragrance. Single and double flowers.

Saxifraga, **Saxifrage.** Height between 2 and 10 in (5 and 25 cm), according to variety; flowering time: March/April, May/June, going on into autumn, according to species or variety; colour of flowers: white, yellow, pink to deep carmine; planting time: autumn or spring; situation: sunny, dry. There are also shade-loving species. The name 'Saxifrage' covers a large group of plants, all of which, as the Latin origin of the word tells us, are 'Stone-breakers' – i.e. they overcome the inhospitable nature of stone, and will grow in very stony places. We can distinguish between cushion-forming, moss-like, lime-encrusted and rosette-forming species; they all belong to the stock plants of rock and alpine gardens. To pick out some of the prettiest and most interesting: *S. granulata* differs from the rest in forming fleshy roots like tubers, which can be divided for purposes of propagation. Plant in March/April. *S. moschata* is only 2–4 in (5–10 cm) high, forms dense cushions, and produces a wealth of white or yellow flowers in May. *S. umbrosa* belongs to the rosette-forming group, grows up to 12 in (30 cm) high, has white or pink flowers, and needs shade for its mat-forming, freely produced and extensive runners. *S. aizoon* is one of those saxifrages which have silver, lime-encrusted, rosettes; it has many cultivated

Saxifraga, Saxifrage

forms, white flowers are borne in May/June, 10 in (25 cm) tall. As I said before, there are as many different saxifrages as there are weeks in the year. They are all undemanding plants, do not like too much sun, but can tolerate moisture.

Sedum, **Stonecrop, sedum.** Height 4–8 in (10–20 cm); mostly cushion or mat-forming; flowering time: June/September; colour of flowers: white, yellow, pink to dark red; planting time: any time; situation: very sunny, very dry. The various species of sedum too are old stalwarts of the rock garden. They will easily take root in joints of walls, in crevices of paved paths, on slopes or as edging plants, are simple to grow, and spread very easily. To name some of the best known favourites: *S. obtusatum,* 2–2½ in (5–6 cm) high; flowering time: July/August; colour of flowers: yellow; forms large red cushions. *S. floriferum* 'Weihen-stephaner Gold', favourite ground cover plant, yellow flowers borne in July/August. *S. ewersii,* also known as the Himalayan sedum, height 8–12 in (20–30 cm); flowering time August/September; colour: pink, purple, notable for its rambling stems with their bluish green foliage. *S. spectabile,* height 8–12 in (20–30 cm); flowering time: August/October; colour: pink; this is the latest sedum to flower.

Sempervivum, **House leek, sempervivum.** Height 4–6 in (10–15 cm); flowering time: July/August; colour of flowers: yellow, pink, red; planting time: whenever you like, other than during flowering; situation: very sunny, very dry. The decorative, succulent green rosettes edged with brown crowd each other close, and here and there you see stems shooting up from the mass of foliage, bearing charming, star-shaped flowers in clusters. The flower stalk rises from the middle of the leaf rosette; once it has faded the mother plant dies, but runners will already be forming at the neck of the plant or in the leaf axils, bearing pretty little baby rosettes, which will grow and bear flowers in subsequent years. Sempervivums are an adornment to the rock garden, and have so many different forms that it is difficult to choose. Among them are *S. arachnoideum,* the cobweb house leek, with coral-red flowers rising from a web of small, silver-haired rosettes; *S. kosaninii,* flowering in July, particularly large rosettes, 2–3 in (6–8 cm) across, with dark green leaves tipped with purple and bearing glandular hairs; a whole range of beautiful, larger hybrid forms, of which I will mention only two: 'Alpha', with brownish green rosettes, silvery in the middle, and 'Rubin', leaves deep tipped with green, dark pink flowers. The most commonly found is *S. tectorum* in many variations. All sempervivums make what might be called negative demands: no fertilizer, no water, really poor soil, very sandy, if possible mixed with some builders' rubble (but not containing cement). Propagation is easy; the plants do it spontaneously.

Silene (Heliosperma), **Silene, campion.** Height 2–6 in (5–15 cm); flowering time: May/June, July/September; colour of flowers: pink; planting time: directly after flowering; situation: very sunny. The main species are *S. alpestris, S. acaulis,* and *S. schafta.* Apart from spreading by putting out suckers, these are charming rock garden plants.

Solidago brachystachys, **Dwarf golden rod.** Height 6 in (15 cm); flowering time: August/September; colour of flowers: yellow; planting time: spring; situation: sunny. Golden rod has been a distinguished member of the autumn-flowering perennial group for some years, since growers have managed to breed out its tendency to be invasive and other undesirable qualities. The small forms are particularly charming, and you can create some very good effects with them in late summer in the rock garden.

Stachys lanata, **Stachys.** Height up to 12 in (30 cm); flowering time June/July; colour of flowers: purple; planting time: spring; situation: sunny. The silvery white, velvety foliage of this prostrate species will last until well into winter. The non-flowering 'Silver Carpet' is the finest form.

Stachys lanata, Stachys

Teucrium, **Germander.** Height 4–8 in (10–20 cm); spread 4–8 in (10–20 cm); flowering time July/September; colour: yellow, rose-pink; planting time and division in spring; situation: sunny to very sunny. Rewarding and easy to grow. *T. chamaedrys* and *T. polium* are charming plants, sub-shrubs, though forming loose mats, with glossy evergreen greyish leaves; they flower profusely for many months. Not nearly so well known as they deserve to be. Can be clipped like box.

Thymus, **Thyme.** Height 4–8 in (10–15 cm); flowering time June/August; colour of flowers white, pinkish mauve, red; planting time spring or autumn; situation: sunny. Some of the pretty garden forms of this familiar shrub, which forms large cushions or mats, are distinguished by their interesting foliage. *T. citriodorus* has variegated leaves and fragrant pale mauve flowers. *T. serpyllum* varieties include the woolly grey mats of 'Lanuginosus', the green mats and red flowers of 'Coccineus' – the only red-flowering form. They all spread vigorously, but you can put bulbs in among them; bulbous plants seem to like the shelter of clumps of thyme and will do well.

Veronica, **Speedwell, veronica.** Height 2–8 in (5–20 cm); flowering time April/May, May/June and August/September; colour of flowers: white, pink, many blues; planting time autumn or spring; situation: sun to half-shade. The dwarf forms of veronica, much more modest than *V. longifolia*, mentioned in the chapter HARDY PERENNIALS, will grow in any garden soil. *V. prostrata*, mat-forming, china-blue flower, needs some time to get going, so do not be impatient if it seems to be doing poorly for one or two years. *V. incana* is rather taller. Its silvery leaves make a very pretty background for the profusely borne, bright blue flowers. *V. selleri* is the latest flowering of all, forming compact clumps with spikes of dark blue blooms.

Deciduous and evergreen dwarf shrubs

Along with small perennials and mat- or cushion-forming plants, dwarf deciduous shrubs have always been stock plants in the rock garden – indeed, they give it much of its particular character. First and foremost these are small, deciduous shrubs suitable for sunny and more or less dry positions, and generally happy with the usual environment of the rock garden. But there can be rock gardens of a different kind, according to the potentialities of a garden, or the special interests of its owner: modified rock gardens beside water, layouts chiefly meant to grow heathers, or planned to keep company with groups of larger shrubs, which will mean shade and humus in the soil. In any case, along with small deciduous shrubs there are some interesting dwarf evergreens; their only trouble is that in some circumstances one must bear in mind their dislike of any lime content in the soil. The same rules of planting and upkeep apply to both groups as for their relatives; see the chapters HEDGES AND FLOWERING DECIDUOUS SHRUBS, and EVERGREEN SHRUBS, TREES AND CONIFERS. **LH** at the end of a plant description indicates that it is a lime-hating plant.

Acer palmatum, **Japanese maple, red Japanese maple.** Most valuable in the rock garden on account of its magnificently shaped and coloured foliage. The two varieties *A.p.* 'Dissectum' and *A. japonicum* 'Aconitifolium' have deeply divided, bright green leaves with wonderful autumn colouring ranging from yellowish red to carmine or golden yellow to red.

Berberis, **Barberry, berberis.** There is a whole range of evergreen dwarf forms of this genus. To name just a few: *B. buxifolia* 'Nana' is 12–16 in (30–40 cm) high, bears golden yellow flowers in April/May and large berries with a blue bloom in autumn, has reddish brown foliage. *B. candidula* is a small shrub with pendulous, spiny branches and leathery leaves; bears golden yellow flowers in May. Most of the deciduous barberries grow too large. A charming exception is *B. thunbergii* 'Atropurpurea Nana', with red foliage, no more than 20 in (50 cm) high.

Calluna, **Ling, heather.** Height 16 in (30 cm); colour of flowers: white to purple. **LH**

Cotoneaster, **Dwarf cotoneaster.** About half a dozen of the many species and varieties of cotoneaster are dwarf forms that are great favourites with rock gardeners. The most important of the very small, prostrate cotoneasters, evergreen and only 8 in (20 cm) high, are *C. dammeri* and *C. dammeri radicans*, with white flowers amidst dark foliage; very useful for ground cover and bright red fruits in autumn. *C. horizontalis*, which has spreading, fan shaped branches, pretty little white flowers in May and plentiful red berries, as well as foliage which stays on the shrub well into the autumn, although it is really deciduous, is so familiar that it has been nicknamed 'the herring-bone shrub'. Another deciduous species is *C. adpressus praecox*, up to 20 in (50 cm) in height, with arching branches, attractive wavy leaves, a mass of pink flowers in May, and red fruits which unfortunately fall in September. Finally, another particularly attractive evergreen: *C.* 'Skogholm', whose low, spreading branches almost disappear in May under their burden of white flowers. The orange berries above gleaming green foliage are a charming sight in winter, and a treat for blackbirds.

Cytisus, **Broom.** Cytisus is the genus to which *C.* × *praecox*, flowering in April/May, belongs; like many people, we have it on our terrace wall in the rock garden as a background plant. The dwarf brooms flower in May/June, weaving a golden yellow carpet with their prostrate twigs. They include species such as *C. decumbens*, only 8–12 in (20–30 cm) high, which can also be planted in the joints of a dry stone wall, and the slightly taller *C. hirsutus*. *C. purpureus* 'Incarnatus' is interesting because of its mass of purple-red flowers; the dwarf *C.* × *kewensis* flowers very profusely and grows to only 12 in (30 cm).

Daphne cneorum, **Daphne, garland flower.** One of the little natural wonders of the plant world: evergreen, only 4–12 in (10–30 cm) high, with aromatically fragrant, rose-pink umbels of flowers borne in April/May; prefers strong sun, dry, stony soil or a dry stone wall – and tolerates lime.

Cytisus, Broom

Erica tetralix, **Heather, cross-leaved heath.** Height 10 in (25 cm); flowers white or carmine. **LH**

Gaultheria, **Gaultheria.** Height 8 in (20 cm); white flowers, pretty; white, sometimes pink berries. Also *G. procumbens*, creeping carpet of dark green leaves, bright red berries.

Genista, **Broom.** *G. lydia* is small, spreading, yellow-flowered. *G. sagittalis* is a mat-forming sub-shrub for very poor, dry, but lime-deficient soils and valuable as a mid-summer shrub; *G. tinctoria* 'Plena', the familiar old dyer's greenweed, has thin shoots trailing along the ground and produces a surprising mass of double orange-yellow flowers in June/July; a gift for the very sunny rock garden with poor soil, and for terraces, slopes and inclines.

Hebe, **Hebe, New Zealand veronica.** Hebes are strange evergreen plants, often looking like conifers. Many are completely hardy and grow well in coastal or industrial areas. The flowers are white or purple, and produced from spring to autumn. Of the dwarf forms suitable for rock gardens, growing less than 24 in (60 cm) high, are: *H. armstrongii*, 'Carl Teschner' and *H. pinguifolia* 'Pagei'. All like well-drained soil and plenty of sun.

Hypericum, **St John's wort.** Height 8 in (20 cm); invasive, forming bushy plants; flowering time: June/August; colour: golden yellow; planting time: autumn or spring; situation: sunny. The best dwarf forms: *H. coris*, *H. fragile*, *H. hyssopifolium* and *H. polyphyllum*. All these robust, shrubby plants work hard at putting out runners, are almost evergreen, flower freely, and present the beginner with no problems – the problems come later, when you want to get rid of them.

Jasminum nudiflorum, **Winter jasmine.** Has its limitations as a plant for the rock garden, since it always needs some form of support and drastic pruning to keep it dwarf. But its primrose-yellow flowers are such a feast for the eye in winter that one ought really to try and find a place for it. It is very easy to grow, and will also trail over terrace steps. There is also *J. parkeri*, up to 12 in (30 cm) high, a dainty, twiggy shrublet for a warm corner, covered with yellow flowers in June.

Moltkia petraea, **Moltkia.** Hardy and very easy to grow, with a preference for narrow crevices in walls and full sun; a beautiful little blue-flowering sub-shrub from the mountains of northern Albania. Height 6–12 in (15–30 cm). Sometimes listed among perennials as *Lithospermum* – it is worth seeking out.

Pernettya prostrata, **Pernettya.** Height up to 12 in (30 cm). *P.p. pentlandii* is a vigorous prostrate form with glossy green leaves and black berries. **LH**

Potentilla, **Potentilla.** The dwarf forms such as *Potentilla fruticosa* 'Arbuscula', 12 in (30 cm) tall, bearing golden yellow flowers for weeks on end in summer, or the prostrate, white-flowering *P. fruticosa mandshurica*. These are only two of the several small potentillas available.

Rhododendron, **Rhododendron.** In many small species and varieties. Here are a few examples: 1) Evergreens such as *Rhododendron calostrotum*, height 8–12 in (20–30 cm), bright purple flowers in May; *R. forrestii* hybrids, height 6–16 in (20–40 cm), deep red flowers in May – among them the delightful prostrate form *R.f. repens*, height 6–8 in (15–20 cm); *R. williamsianum* hybrids, small varieties (about 12 in (30 cm) high, mostly pink. 2) Deciduous 'azaleas'; with a few exceptions these are too tall for the rock garden. However, the evergreen Kurume hybrids in many colours remain small enough. **LH**

Roses in the rock garden. There are several varieties of the miniature group which grow only 8–12 in (20–30 cm) high. They are interesting plants on dry walls or in trough gardens too. 'Snow Carpet' is a delightful, almost evergreen, prostrate variety.

Spiraea, **Spiraea.** Dwarf spiraeas such as *Spiraea japonica* 'Bullata' 16 in (40 cm) high, dark red, and the beautiful *S.j.* 'Alpina' (height 8–12 in (20–30 cm)), pink flowers borne in June/August, are a valuable contribution to the dwarf shrubs.

Vinca minor, **Lesser periwinkle.** The versatility and adaptability of this plant to sun or shade are so well known that I need only mention the fact that the range of colours has been extended to include white and reddish violet varieties.

Some delightful dwarf conifers

Dwarf conifers, like dwarf deciduous shrubs and evergreen hardwoods, are very much part of the whole picture of the rock garden; they round off the planting of a dry stone wall very nicely, and will live happily in troughs for years. Cultivate according to the rules for the large forms; container growing has made it much easier to plant them and extended the planting season. Many new varieties are being introduced in a range of different shapes and colours. Here are some attractive small forms:

Chamaecyparis obtusa, **Cypress.** Among other dwarf forms there are *C.o.* 'Nana Gracilis', with deep green, fan-shaped branches, and 'Nana Lutea', with golden yellow needles. *C.o.* 'Pygmaea' is even smaller than these two forms. All three are very slow growers.

Juniperus, **Juniper.** There are at least half a dozen delightful small forms. *J.* × *media* 'Pfitzerana' is very well known; it has spreading branches and delicate, slightly pendulous twigs bearing grey-green needles; the form 'Aurea' has golden yellow foliage. It takes both of them years to reach a height of up to 60 in (150 cm). The prostrate blue *J. horizontalis* 'Glauca' is very beautiful; its branches, lying flat along the ground, form dense mats of only 8 in (20 cm) in height; it grows very slowly and will tolerate shade. The scaly-leaved juniper, *J. squamata* 'Meyeri', can be recognized by the silvery shimmer of its bluish needles;

height, up to 50 in (130 cm); shorten the tips of the young shoots.

Picea, **Spruce.** Even if one took only the species *P. abies* (*P. excelsa*) and its cultivated varieties, the spruce would provide a considerable range of dwarf conifers of great richness of shape and diversity of colour, some of them bearing very decorative cones. *P.a.* 'Pygmaea' forms round little bushes, with bright green foliage; *P.a.* 'Nidiformis' grows very slowly, up to an eventual height of 24–32 in (60–80 cm); and *P. glauca* 'Albertiana Conica', will only reach 4 ft (120 cm) at maturity. *P. procumbens*, with apple-green foliage, is a prostrate form for clothing walls and there is also a dwarf spreading Colorado spruce, *P. pungens* 'Procumbens'.

Pinus, **Pine.** The pine, too, has long been at home in the world of the rock garden. The mountain pine, *P. mugo*, grows broad rather than tall; the even more graceful prostrate dwarf pine, *P.mugo pumilio*, is suitable for very small rock gardens, as is *P.m.* 'Humpy'.

Taxus baccata, **Yew.** The prostrate yew, *T.b.* 'Repandens' can also be used as a ground cover plant.

Tsuga canadensis, **Hemlock.** Recommended: its beautiful dwarf form T.c. 'Prostrata', which likes shade, grows to 40 in (100 cm), at the most, and bears attractive cones.

18
Ornamental grasses and ferns

Ornamental grasses and ferns belong to a group of plants which unfortunately tend to receive too little attention. Nonetheless, they can be extremely decorative, and will last all the year round.

All the ornamental grasses like full sun to half-shade, and are easy to grow and to propagate by division. It must be admitted that even the best of the cultivated forms can develop an invasive tendency. But they will grow as happily beside water as they do set in a lawn as single specimens, or as dwarf forms in the rock garden. The group comprises some most interesting plants, from the 13 ft (400 cm) bamboo (*Arundinaria japonica*) and its hardy relatives such as *Sasa tessellata* or *Sinarundinaria murielae* to the graceful purple moor grass (*Molinia caerulea* 'Variegata'), only 12 in (30 cm) high. They are also very useful in dried flower arrangements for the winter months. First of all one should mention the pampas grass, 8 ft (250 cm) high (*Cortaderia selloana*), whose tall, spiraea-like, silvery plumes are as decorative indoors as out. Special characteristics of the Chinese reed (*Miscanthus sinensis*) are the golden yellow autumn colouring of its foliage and its tall, silvery flowerheads. It is a close relative of the equally interesting variety *M. sinensis* 'Zebrinus'; both are among our best and most vigorous ornamental grasses. As with some other plants, their tendency to spread has to be checked; a useful trick is to plant the roots in an old bucket without a bottom, as described in the previous chapter HARDY PERENNIALS, and let the edge of the bucket project very slightly above ground level.

The very beautiful *Molinia altissima* can be found in any large catalogue of perennials: its tall blades will last for months, it has golden autumn colouring, is easy to grow, and is up to nearly 6 ft (180 cm) tall. The charming *Molinia caerulea*, already mentioned above, has inflorescences up to 4 ft (120 cm) high. Another tall grass is the bottle-brush grass, *Pennisetum alopecuroides*, with graceful hanging foliage and red flower panicles up to 3 ft (90 cm) tall. Feather grass (*Stipa gigantea*) grows to about 40 in (100 cm).

Smaller grasses I can recommend are the picturesque *Avena candida* (*Helictotrichon sempervirens*), with blue-grey, narrow, upright blades only 3 in (8 cm) tall, and the familiar little *Festuca glauca*, 4–8 in (10–20 cm) high, both suitable for the rock garden. Finally, another particularly attractive species of *Festuca*, *F. scoparia*, whose tufts of long bright green hair-like leaves form dense clusters.

Most of these ornamental grasses are completely hardy; only the tall bamboo and pampas grasses may need some slight protection. The best planting time for most grasses is early spring – late March early April – just as growth begins – but many can be bought from garden centres in pots or containers and planted out at almost any time. They should always be well watered after planting.

Outdoor ferns need a shady position among shrubs or under trees. The most handsome of all is the royal fern, *Osmunda regalis*. Other decorative tall ferns are the *Polystichum* group, especially the soft shield fern, *P. setiferum*, also the male fern, *Dryopteris filix-mas*, the lady fern, *Athyrium felix-femina*, and ostrich fern, *Matteuccia struthiopteris*; they all grow to 24–40 in (60–100 cm). Smaller species, like the evergreen *Blechnum spicant*, the sensitive fern *Onoclea sensibilis*, maidenhair spleenwort *Asplenium trichomanes*, the evergreen hart's tongue *Asplenium scolopendrium*, and the polypody (*Polypodium vulgare*), growing only to 8–16 in (20–40 cm), are also suitable for shady parts of the rock garden. Their descriptive names in themselves indicate that the shape of the plants is often very odd. In fact this group of spore-bearing plants, despite the absence of flowers, has many beautiful types of foliage to offer the gardener. The evergreen forms in particular mingle with other plants to make interesting groups, and create a picturesque effect, even in the snow.

Very attractive and easy to care for: a bed of pebbles or gravel, with ornamental grasses, set in a paved area.
Background: Miscanthus sinensis.
Foreground: Festuca scoparia.

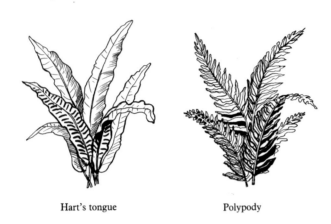

Hart's tongue   Polypody

Outdoor ferns are best planted in earliest spring. Planting sites must be well prepared, with plenty of sharp sand, peat, leaf-mould and compost worked in when the ground has been deeply dug; the topsoil should have good humus content. Like most woodland plants and evergreens most ferns dislike lime. Apart from planting new acquisitions, existing mature groups can be divided at the same time. Clumps of ferns are easy to divide. The rhizomatous, spreading species, like the polypody mentioned above, can even be divided into several pieces, each of which will produce an individual plant the following year.

Small evergreen species should be placed nearer to the front of a bed; large species should not be planted too close together, as this will limit their growth and diminish the fine effect that can be produced by these proud woodland plants. Of course the surrounding plants should be kinds that go well with ferns. Perennials which like shade, such as foxglove and astilbe, and hardy cyclamens, and ground cover plants, along with lily of the valley and pachysandra, are only a few possible examples.

19
Water gardens

Even in a small garden, water is a beautiful and ever-changing feature, breaking up the view and enlivening the whole place. There is always something to look at – morning, mid-day, evening and night. Water lilies open in the morning, and the higher the sun rises the more birds visit the pool. In early spring bees will come to drink there; later in the year dragonflies whirr above its glittering surface; one can be regularly visited by swallows, blackbirds, starlings, not to mention cheeky sparrows, who splash and bathe at the edge of the water. Finally, you can sit by its side at night and watch the reflection of the full moon, like a shower of golden coins in the dark water.

After this introduction, I need hardly explain any further the attraction of a water garden. Nowadays there are as many designs made for such installations as for swimming pools, and a great deal has been written about putting them in and running them. However, the ecological function of such pools means there are some other questions to be answered.

1) The question of position: an ecological garden pool must be in the sunniest part of your garden; the community of plant and animal life will be able to develop properly only in bright light and water that is not too cold. Sunlight and warmth stimulate water plants to flower; in shady places most of them will only make vegetation. Plants grown on the edge of a pool can, however, be shade plants, if necessary.

2) The question of space: it is easier to manage and maintain a large pool, deep enough not to freeze right through even in very cold weather, than a small, shallow one, where the fish will suffer from lack of oxygen even in stormy summer weather. As a rule of thumb, we may say that a surface area of 12 sq yard (10 sq m) should have water 30 in (76 cm) deep. In small gardens it may well be necessary to have a smaller and shallower pool. The drawings on these pages show that the effects of various different kinds of shape can be taken into account.

3) The question of water is a good deal more important for a garden pool than a swimming pool, or sprinklers, sprayers, and so on, but it can be solved independently of the orginal hardness of tap water used to fill a pool in the first place. It is quite possible to avoid accumulations of algae and muddy water. There are three things to remember: let the water run in slowly, do not change it if possible, and (at the start, anyway) add no fertilizer.

4) The question of the actual soil at the bottom of the pool is not as important as is commonly thought, since aquatic plants get their nourishment from the water as well as the soil. Also, the plants can be grown in containers. However, loam is better than sandy soil. It is essential for all organic components of the soil to be thoroughly decomposed, so that they cannot give rise to any process of rotting. Good garden soil or well-matured compost is best.

5) The population problem, i.e the number of fishes and amount of plants in relation to the water content of the pool: the beginner in particular should note that too few are better than too many. Overcrowded pools with too many fishes and too many plants usually suffer, in addition, from their owners' insistence on feeding the fish; people are always throwing in something, commercial fish food or white breadcrumbs which lie about decomposing and infecting the water. The correct thing to do is to give the fish almost no food after an initial period in spring; they should feed themselves partly on insect life in the pool, and partly on the plants. The fresher and thus harder the water, the fewer fish you should have. Again as a rough rule of thumb, one 5–6 in (12–15 cm) fish to a square yard (square metre) of water is enough in March/April, when the water-gardening season begins. Fish in garden pools grow fast, and they tend to increase and multiply during the summer months.

One can make pools with cement walls, but it is much easier to line the excavated area with either rigid plastic pools, of formal or informal shape, or with flexible plastic or butyl rubber liners. Any firm specializing in pools and their contents can advise on the modern methods and materials used for pool making.

How to plant

Whether your pool is of geometric design or built to look like part of the natural landscape, there are various different ways of planting it.

1) Pockets in which the plants can be put directly are built into it. Only for those plants which can spend the winter out of doors, with or without water.

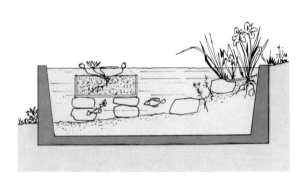

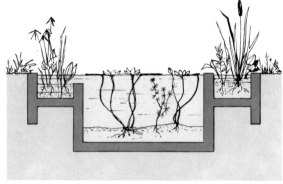

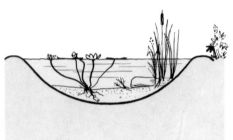

Upper left: garden pool with vertical sides on a sloping site; soil and stones arranged inside to create different levels.
Upper right: garden pool with two areas of shallow water; one high and one low wall between them and the main pool.
Right: a pool in a rounded shape, with gently sloping sides, is more natural in many ways than pools with almost vertical sides.

2) Pockets are again built in, but of the right size to take plant containers flush with the tops of the holes. The visual effect is pleasing, and you can take tender plants out for the winter if you have a heated greenhouse.

3) No pockets: hardy plants are set in mounds of soil with a few stones to hold them in place. The danger here is that the plants may spread and it will be difficult to keep the pool tidy. I would not advise this method.

4) Plant containers are set on the flat bottom of the pool, and can simply be lifted out in autumn or on bricks to raise them to the correct height if necessary. You can, of course, cover the bottom of the pool with a shallow layer of gravel and press the containers into this.

5) Aquatic plants, like land plants, have their correct planting distances, which should be observed. Large, vigorous water lilies need up to 1¾ sq yd (1½ sq m) of pool surface; arrowhead or cyperus should be planted with a space of 16–20 in (40–50 cm) all round them; you can plant five to eight of those smaller plants which will take root in the shallows near the banks per square yard (square metre). These smaller plants will need 4–8 in (10–20 cm) depth of water. Once again, too few are better than too many, since the rooted plants will nearly always be joined by floating plants laying claim to their share of space, and they are all inclined to produce a lot of foliage in summer.

Planting depth, planting sites, planting time

The well-being of aquatic plants depends very much on their having the correct depth of water, so we have to adjust our wishes to the facilities available. A pool only 24 in (60 cm) deep is unsuitable for those large water lilies which need at least 4 ft (1·20 m) depth of water; flowering plants like frogbit, flowering rush and arrowhead, on the other hand, like flags, bulrushes and reeds need shallow water, only about 4–6 in (10–15 cm) deep, while a whole range of our prettiest hardy water lilies and water lily hybrids are happiest planted out in about 20 in (50 cm) of water. Any further details are given in the following survey of aquatic plants. If your pool has sloping sides you can build in ledges as underwater planting sites at any level. If it is a pool with straight sides you can have projecting bays or little platforms on which to place plant containers, though the planting of such pools, especially by the banks, can never be so natural as when you have a natural transition between water and land.

Small groups of pools like this are first and foremost for aquatic plants; they are usually too small for fish.

Water lilies, all hardy

Name	Flowering time, colour	Depth	Remarks
Nymphaea alba	June onwards, white	40–80 in (100–200 cm)	European, many fine hybrids. Clear, cold water
Nymphaea × marliacea 'Albida'	June onwards, white	up to 48 in (120 cm)	Many and large flowers
Nymphaea × marliacea 'Rosea'	June onwards, flesh-pink, pale pink	up to 48 in (120 cm)	Many and large flowers
Nymphaea tuberosa 'Rosea'	June onwards, double, pink	24–40 in (60–100 cm)	Fragrant
Nymphaea tuberosa 'Richardsonii'	June onwards, white	24–40 in (60–100 cm)	Many and large flowers
Nymphaea 'Attraction'	June onwards, red	24–40 in (60–100 cm)	Large-flowering
Nymphaea × marliacea 'Chromatella' (golden cup)	June onwards, sulphur-yellow, 6–7 in (15–18 cm) across; also for cut flowers	24–40 in (60–100 cm)	Brown-patterned leaves
Nymphaea 'Lucida', 'James Brydon', 'Indiana', 'Sunrise'	June onwards, yellow to copper, pink, red	16–40 in (40–100 cm)	Many other varieties, all colours but blue; free-flowering
Nymphaea 'Gonnere' ('Snowball')	June onwards, pure white	16–40 in (40–100 cm)	Very rewarding
Nymphaea 'Odorata Alba'	June onwards, white	12–20 in (30–50 cm)	Fragrant
Nymphaea 'Froebelii'	June onwards, reddish purple	12–20 in (30–50 cm)	Good for small pools
Nymphaea × laydekeri 'Purpurata'	June onwards, deep carmine	12–20 in (30–50 cm)	Also other varieties
Nymphaea 'Pygmaea Helvola'	June onwards, canary-yellow, fringed petals	4–6 in (10–15 cm)	Leaves marked with brown
N. 'Pygmaea Alba'	June onwards, white	4–6 in (10–15 cm)	Also other varieties
Nuphar lutea (yellow water lily)	June/Aug., bright yellow	24–80 in (60–200 cm)	Usually very vigorous. Underwater leaves are evergreen
Nuphar pumila	June onwards, bright yellow	4–20 in (10–50 cm)	Underwater leaves evergreen; will tolerate full shade

When you are planting deep pools with pockets in the bottom you must keep the water level low at first after putting in new plants, and gradually raise it as the plants grow. If you are planting water lilies in containers, you go about it the other way around: place stones under the containers, and remove them gradually to lower the plants. In all cases there should not be more than 4–6 in (10–15 cm) of water above the leaves as they develop; this will help keep them at the right temperature. Ordinary mineral fertilizers, even in tiny amounts, should never be added. The earliest planting time for water lilies and other aquatic plants is the end of April, and it is better to wait until the middle of May; even hardy European plants need the water to be warm enough for them to take root successfully. Beginners should beware of being tempted to experiment by misleading descriptions in catalogues. My survey of

Perennial plants for shallow water (2–8 in (5–20 cm))

Botanical name	English name	Appearance of plant, height above water	Flowers, other comments
Acorus calamus	Sweet flag	Height about 24 in (60 cm), leaves bright green, swordshaped. *A.c. variegatus* has decorative variegated leaves	June/July; yellowish brown
Butomus umbellatus	Flowering rush	Reed-like, three-edged leaves. Height about 24 in (60 cm)	June/July; clusters small pink flowers
Calla palustris	Bog arum	Height about 8 in (20 cm), broad heart-shaped leaves, shiny; trailer	June/July; greenish white, typical arum flower shape
Caltha palustris	Marsh marigold	Height 1–1½ ft (30–45 cm); dark green leaves	April/May; yellow flowers
Cyperus longus	Sweet galingale	Tall, grass-like leaves; height about 3 ft (1 m)	Aug/Sept; red-brown plumes
Glyceria maxima (spectabilis) 'Variegata'	–	Height up to 3 ft (1 m); variegated leaves	Summer; useful for disguising pool edges
Hottonia palustris	Water violet	Height up to 24 in (60 cm). Fine pinnate foliage, brittle stems and leaves. Depth of water up to 12 in (30 cm)	May/July; pink flowers on long stems
Menyanthes trifoliata	Bog bean	Height up to 12 in (30 cm), leaves trifoliate, borne on stems and leathery	May/June; pinkish white flower clusters
Mimulus ringens	Lavender musk	Height 1½ ft (45 cm)	July; bluish mauve; growth upright
Pontederia cordata	Pickerel weed	Height 1½–2 ft (45–60 cm); glossy, heart-shaped leaves	July/Sept; delphinium-like blue flowers
Ranunculus lingua 'Grandiflora'	Spearwort	Narrow lance-shaped leaves. Depth of water 2–12 in (5–30 cm)	June/Aug; large yellow flowers. Easy to grow
Sagittaria sagittifolia	Arrowhead	Height of the European species about 20 in (50 cm), tolerates up to 20 in (50 cm) depth of water	June/July; easy to grow. Pure white.
Typha angustifolia, *T. latifolia*	Small reed mace, cat tail	Height up to 4 ft (125 cm), grass-like leaves	Summer; club-shaped flower heads; large vigorous species
Typha minima	Dwarf reed mace	Height up to 12 in (30 cm), narrow, grassy leaves	Summer; roundish club-shaped flower heads
Veronica beccabunga	Brooklime	Height up to 9 in (23 cm), dark green leaves	Summer; small blue flowers

suitable plants for a pool is divided into three parts: water lilies and their many varieties obviously deserve a special table of their own; then come other perennial aquatic plants (often called marginal plants), and then floating plants. Among these there are some plants whose submerged leaves increase the oxygen content of the water and thus help to purify it. They are referred to as oxygenating plants. In this context, waterweed deserves special mention. All plants with filigree-like submerged leaves, which affect a large area of the surface, are good for purifying and clearing the pool too. They include the water violet (*Hottonia palustris*).

Bog gardens and banks

Do not plant the banks of the pool until the pool itself is finished. I should explain that by 'bog gardens' I do not mean just the extreme edges of the pool, where those plants grow which have their roots in the water, about 2–8 in (10–20 cm) deep, but bear their foliage and flowers above water level. The bog garden I envisage is a transitional area with loamy soil containing some humus, which can be kept moist all the time and if necessary irrigated from the pool, but does not have even a shallow water level of its own. This is quite easy to manage; we created such a bed by sinking large metal sheets 24 in (60 cm) into the ground to keep the marshy area and the lawn next to it apart. This strip of bank can be in light shade, since there are plenty of plants which do well in such conditions.

I have already mentioned those flowering plants, ferns and ornamental grasses suitable for marshy areas and banks by water in the plant lists found earlier in the book, but I would just like to remind you of the irises which like moist conditions, such as *Iris kaempferi*, *I. laevigata* and *I. sibirica*, creeping jenny (*Lysimachia nummularia*) and many primulas, such as *Primula rosea*.

In addition, here are some typical plants found in such areas: the familiar marsh marigold, *Caltha palustris*, only 12 in (30 cm) high; marsh spurge, *Euphorbia palustris*, 24–40 in (60–100 cm) high, with reddish yellow foliage; skunk cabbage, *Lysichiton americanum*, sulphur-yellow, flowering in April/May, and *Lysichiton camtschatcense*, very pretty, white flowers appearing a little later; a strange-looking plant is *Podophyllum emodi*, up to 20 in (50 cm) high; and finally the Trinity flower or spiderwort, *Tradescantia virginiana*, which has white or violet flowers, not just a plant for a marshy area but also in other places like any normal perennial: the exception that proves the rule.

Muddy water and clear water

When you are filling an artificial pool with water from the tap it is a good idea, if you can, to add a proportion of clean rainwater uncontaminated by industrial pollution. Once the pool is going properly the water should be changed as little as possible – ideally, you want to leave it as it is. Fish and aquatic plants hate hard tapwater. And if some supposed animal-lovers had to go through what fish endure from constant changes in the water, they would not saddle them with a splashing fountain. Quite apart from that, any constant overflow of hard water into a pool is enough to stir it up into a muddy-looking brew. The harder the water and the more lime it contains, the faster brown algae will form under the influence of sunlight, making the water look muddy.

Floating plants

Botanical name	English name	Appearance of plant	Flowers, other comments
Azolla caroliniana	Fairy moss	Resembles duckweed; also for pools in half shade	Reddish in autumn; favourite food for goldfish
Eichhornia crassipes	Water hyacinth	Floating stems and leaves, stems up to 3 ft (1 m) long. Careful – it spreads fast, ideal for spawning fish	Pale lavender; not hardy so overwinter under glass
Hydrocharis morsus ranae	Frogbit	Kidney-shaped leaves	July/Aug; pure white. Buds spend winter at the bottom
Stratiodes aloides	Water soldier	Sword-shaped leaves	July/Aug; white. Plant spends winter at the bottom
Trapa natans	Water chestnut	Quadrangular, long-stemmed floating leaves	Insignificant flowers; preferably soft water, plenty of sun, rather tender

Those who make the mistake of replacing this apparently 'dirty' water with fresh, clear tap-water find themselves back with the same problem; the alkaline reaction of hard water stimulates the appearance of algae. On the other hand, the algae disappear once the water is in that slightly acid state which is most suitable for fish and plants. This is best obtained by ensuring the correct proportion of oxygenating plants and large-leaved water plants – about two-thirds of the water surface area should be covered. Once this happens there are no algae, and the old water in the pool takes on that clear, golden shade which allows you to see every pebble at the bottom.

Goldfish are best

I would advise you not to experiment with fish in garden pools, but make straight for goldfish, which are not at all boring; there is considerable variation within the type. They are still the standard fish for a pool, they always look decorative in good clear water and, in the way of the carp family they are well behaved, and soon become so tame that their owner's footsteps become the signal for a pathetic begging performance. But don't give them too much; remember that vegetable food is good for them. Fairy moss (in fact a fern), *Azolla*, is a great delicacy for goldfish, and they like waterweed, *Elodea*, so much that they should always have some in their winter quarters; they like to nibble the tender roots of floating plants, which should therefore be lightly anchored to the ground in the shallows near the bank, to be on the safe side. It is also advisable not to introduce fish to a new pond until a month after planting, so that the plants can become established.

Care of fish is not really the concern of a gardening book but I will just remind you that if they are to spend all winter in the pool they need 20–25% of the surface kept free of ice if they are to have enough oxygen. The most reliable way to do this is by using a thermostatically controlled immersion water heater which is floated on the water, since hacking holes in the ice and putting in wisps of straw is not a pleasant job in severely cold weather.

PART IV:
VEGETABLES AND FRUITS

20 Growing vegetables for pleasure

After years when no one showed much interest in the kitchen garden, many people have now gone back to growing their own vegetables. There is not much point in going into the various different causes underlying this; let us look at things as they are now, and we shall see that a good deal has changed even in the traditional field of the vegetable garden. The systematic layout of our grandparents' gardens, with their rotation of crops and strict division into beds for gross feeders and beds for moderate feeders is only of marginal interest; we have found in modern times that it is quite possible to incorporate edible plants into the picture of the garden seen as a whole. And this is what makes growing vegetables so enjoyable.

In fact, we are dealing with something emotional rather than rational: in some way or other man is the master. You can cultivate your garden as you wish, grow the things you like to eat, and will never be able to buy as fresh, with so many health-bringing qualities. And this very personal relationship we have to the growing of vegetables in our leisure-time gardens has already found its expression in garden design, as you can see in the plans in the chapter DESIGNING YOUR GARDEN, which show what emphasis the garden planner now has to place on the growing of fruit and vegetables. The plans will also give you an insight into the basic structure of the layout, upon which the success of your crop depends to a certain extent.

Our vegetables do not, of course, have to hide. I am not advocating growing them as a kind of 'extra' in the flower garden, hidden away among more decorative plants. Indeed, edible plants – or some of them, anyway – have a beauty of their own. For instance, if you are planting a large single specimen somewhere, you might as well have an edible rhubarb as an ornamental one, and get beauty and utility at the same time. But apart from such possibilities as this, Chinese cabbage makes an interesting edging plant, or blue-flowered borage is quite in place in a border, while ordinary vegetable beds of lettuce and radishes, dwarf beans, cucumbers and celery can be attractive in themselves. Then again, you have all the pleasures of anticipation as you watch them grow and look forward to eating them – a little psychological twist which leads quite naturally to our modern feeling that the whole garden is a single unit, and a very pleasing one. And that is the whole fun of the thing.

If we are trying to find a golden mean between the decorative and the useful, it can only be done by disregarding quite a number of notions that used to be accepted. The old basic principles of vegetable growing have had to be either partly or entirely revised; seed produced by modern plant breeders gets better and more versatile all the time; and, thanks to scientific theories which have been put into practice, feeding, pest and disease control, and cultivation in general, have all been made much simpler. However, some basic facts are as valid as ever. Among them is the realization that we cannot do away entirely with the principle of rotation of crops. If you grew tomatoes, celery or brassicas on the same patch of ground year in, year out, you would not only get a smaller crop within quite a short time, but it would be much more vulnerable to pests and diseases. Hence we really do need to plan a rotation of crops carefully, with an eye to the future, and taking into account the different nourishment required by different kinds of plant.

However, it is not necessary to go in for 'mono-culture', with only one kind of vegetable to a bed. Clever dovetailing

Vegetable beds are usually 4 ft (1.20 m) wide; 12 in (30 cm) is enough for the narrow paths between them. Beds should not be raised; if they are their edges will dry out.

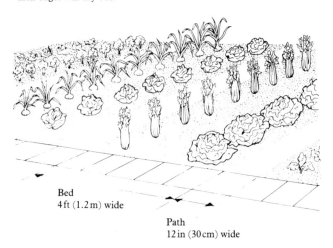

Bed
4 ft (1.2 m) wide

Path
12 in (30 cm) wide

There are plenty of tomatoes now available that can be grown from plants in the garden. Regular feeding and removal of the side shoots will help to produce fruits like those shown here.

Four tasty vegetables which are quite easy to grow in the garden. *Top left:* capsicums. *Top right:* peas. *Bottom left:* cabbage. *Bottom right:* carrots.

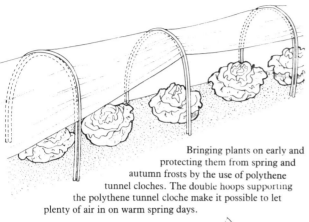

Bringing plants on early and protecting them from spring and autumn frosts by the use of polythene tunnel cloches. The double hoops supporting the polythene tunnel cloche make it possible to let plenty of air in on warm spring days.

Mulching vegetables with plastic; small sheets of black polythene held in place with stones or bricks round individual plants. Also suitable for bushes or small trees.

of different vegetables, sown and harvested at different times, can enable every area of the vegetable garden to be in continuous use. This is the 'catch cropping' method, whereby you can grow vegetables that ripen early or late, grow fast or slow, in such a relationship to each other that the main crop shares the space in which it is growing with an early crop of some fast-growing plant, and then can be followed by a late crop of something else. It is possible to make the different crops follow on so smoothly that in practice the ground is never without a protective layer of covering plants throughout the vegetative season. There are many tried and true examples of catch-cropping; you will find them mentioned in the individual descriptions of the vegetables. And there is something else that ought to be mentioned: 'bolting', the tendency of plants to flower prematurely and form seeds; we are familiar with bolting in lettuce and cabbages which fail to form good hearts, in spinach which grows branches like a miniature fir tree, in carrots, celery, leeks and onions. It may be the result of the wrong choice of varieties, or sowing early varieties too late in season, or by certain weather conditions or changes of temperature. Seed may have been sown in soil that is still too cold, or raised in a warm frame kept at too cool a temperature – this has been shown to be a cause of bolting, particularly in celery. And there is no doubt that the quality of the seed itself has something to do with it; I will just repeat the warning against using up old seed and keeping your own which was discussed in the chapter on SOWING AND PLANTING OUT.

If you have enough space and enthusiasm to devote to serious vegetable growing, I again suggest you refer to a specialist book.

Crisp and fresh salad vegetables

Even the gods of ancient Greece ate salads, along with their nectar and ambrosia. Lettuce, the basic salad plant, was sacred to no less a goddess than Aphrodite, who was said to have laid young Adonis on its leaves. No wonder we still consider salad in all its forms the source of health and youthfulness.

Lettuce Seed takes 8 days to germinate. You can buy the first seedlings of the year, raised in boxes or peat pots in February, and plant them out after hardening off from the middle of March – only in very sheltered places. Make the first sowing in a nursery bed in the open from the middle to the end of March, then make successive sowings at intervals of two to three weeks. Sow summer varieties until the beginning of July. Sow winter varieties in September. Plant out in rows four weeks after sowing: planting distance 8–10 in (20–25 cm) and the same between the rows for early varieties, 9–12 in (23–30 cm) or more for later and giant varieties. Prepare the planting site with plenty of fertilizer; give top dressing of liquid feed later. Lettuce is also a good catch crop to grow among cucumbers, tomatoes, kohl rabi, celery and other vegetables. Do not transplant lettuces after mid-April as this may cause them to bolt.

Seed should be sown very thinly so that it is possible to lift out the seedlings later with their own little balls of soil. Planting out should never be done on hot days or in bright sunlight, and great care should be taken that the seedlings are not planted too deep and no soil touches the heart of the plant. Plant as high as possible, in fact, to avoid fungus infections. Do not wet the lettuce leaves when watering. After planting, hoe between the rows and water at frequent intervals, daily in hot weather.

Especially in the hot summer months, when cabbage lettuce is often inclined to bolt without forming a heart, crisp or curly lettuce is a welcome addition to the range of lettuces. It is more than a filler of gaps; its large heads are both crisp and tender, and it has a fine, refreshing flavour. When preparing it, remove the outer fringed or curly leaves as well as the hard stalk. Planting distance is much the same as for cabbage lettuce. It does better than cabbage lettuce in very wet or very hot weather, and almost never bolts. Similar in flavour and cultivation is the long-leaved cos lettuce; there are now varieties which need no tying.

Cabbage lettuce: early varieties: 'Valdor', 'Arctic King', 'May King'.
  early summer varieties: 'Fortune', 'Suzan', 'Tom Thumb'.
  summer varieties: 'Avondefiance' (especially good in dry summers), 'Buttercrunch'.
  autumn varieties: 'Imperial Winter', 'All The Year Round'.
Crisp lettuce: 'Great Lakes', 'Windermere', 'Webb's Wonderful'.
Loose-leaved lettuce: 'Salad Bowl'.
Cos lettuce: 'Paris', 'Little Gem', 'Winter Density'.

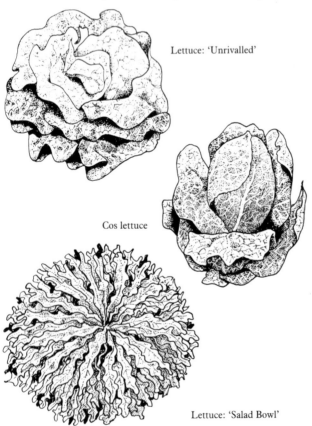

Lettuce: 'Unrivalled'

Cos lettuce

Lettuce: 'Salad Bowl'

Endive Germination time 6–8 days. Sow successively from the end of April to the beginning of September, plant out in rows at a distance of 12 in (30 cm), and the same between the rows. As soon as the outer leaves begin to droop outwards, taking on a rosette shape and showing the well-developed heart of the plant, tie the plants up with raffia or rubber bands for blanching. Do this only in dry weather. If they are to be self-blanching, plant rather closer together. Blanching time 8–12 days in summer, up to three weeks in autumn, and winter. Pick from autumn through to winter. The slightly bitter but pleasant flavour is explained by its relationship with chicory.

Sow in succession: 'Batavian Broad Leaved', good for immediate use, 'Moss Curled' as a good standard variety, and 'Batavian Green' as a late variety (not self-blanching, but can be used over a long period).

Endive

Chicory This salad vegetable is like the closely related endive in flavour but more like Chinese cabbage or cos lettuce in appearance. Germination time 3–6 days. It can only be sown in the open where it is to grow, from the end of June to the middle of July. Thin out to a distance of 12 in

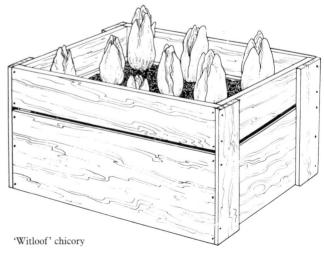

'Witloof' chicory

(30 cm) after 14 days. Before sowing apply fertilizer at a rate of 3 oz (80 g) per 10 sq ft (1 sq m). One or two weak applications of liquid manure will stimulate growth and the formation of good hearts. Varieties such as 'Red Verona', 'Sugar Loaf' and 'Winter Fare' are harvested and eaten like lettuce in autumn and winter.

To produce blanched 'chicons', you will need to sow a variety such as the Brussels 'Witloof' chicory. Lift the roots and cut off the foliage in October. Then plant the roots close together in pots or boxes of soil and store in a warm completely dark place. When the 'chicons' are large enough, cut and eat raw in salads or cooked as a vegetable.

Chinese cabbage

Chinese cabbage A very tasty and healthy salad vegetable for the first half of winter; stands up to cold temperatures as low as 22°F (−5°C). Sow very thinly in rows from mid-May to the beginning of August, or better still, make holes with a dibber and plant three seeds in each at a distance of 9 × 9 in (25 × 25 cm), the same between the rows, thin out the two weaker seedlings later. Seedlings do not transplant successfully. Germination time 8–10 days. Protect the seed you have sown from flea beetles. A very welcome late crop; the longish heads, rather like cos lettuce, will be ready for cutting within ten weeks, but can stay out in the open until November. Prepare for salad like endive, or cook as for spinach. In addition, these are very decorative plants in the garden.

'Nagaoka F$_1$ Hybrid' and 'Sampan F$_1$ Hybrid' have a good flavour.

Corn salad, lamb's lettuce Germinating time 8 days. Sow outside April through to September in rows at a distance of 5–6 in (12–15 cm). Cover the seeds very thinly and press down slightly; they find it difficult to germinate in crumbly soil. A good late crop on weed-free land. Pick as you need it from summer onwards. Use it like lettuce. Freezes in sharp frost.

'Large Leaved Italian' and 'Large Leaved English' give good yields but need protection from frost.

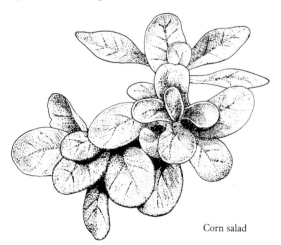

Corn salad

Radish Germination time 8–10 days. Make a first sowing at the beginning of April, or earlier in favourable conditions. Follow up with successive sowings every fortnight till the beginning of September; in summer sow in half-shade and keep the soil very moist. Sow very thinly, if possible singly or in pairs, with a planting distance of 1–2 in (3–5 cm), about ½ in (1 cm) deep, and press gently in. Radishes take about 30 days from sowing to harvest. Sow early varieties in sun, successive summer varieties in half-shade, use early varieties again for autumn sowings and sow in sun. Large winter radishes should be sown in July and August and thinned to 6 in (15 cm) apart.

If you sow radishes in beds on their own you do not understand the real point of catch cropping. Radishes are useful little plants which are happy in any odd space or corner among other vegetables so long as the soil is friable and contains humus. They should have one or two weak top dressings of liquid feed, since the aim is to produce a root which grows fast and easily; if this root growth is hindered the plant may 'bolt' prematurely, and the radish itself become tough and hairy. Radishes both large and small are thirsty plants. They should be watered daily in summer, even in half-shade during dry spells. Their worst enemies are flea beetles and cabbage root flies. See chapter PLANTS NEED PEST AND DISEASE PROTECTION.

'Cherry Belle', 'Saxerre', 'French Breakfast', 'Sparkler', 'Scarlet Globe' and 'Long White Icicle' for early and late sowings, and 'China Rose', 'Black Spanish Round' and 'Mino Early' for winter radishes.

Celery Very useful for salads, with its good crunchy texture, also for cooking. It is available in two forms: one type needs blanching, the other is self-blanching. Prepare the soil thoroughly in winter, adding plenty of compost, peat or shredded bark. Sow in gentle heat late March to early April, or buy seedlings in May/June. Germinating time 20–30 days. Plant out 9 in (25 cm) apart May/June. Self-blanching varieties can be planted on flat ground, but those that require blanching should be set in trenches 18 in (45 cm) deep and 12 in (30 cm) wide. For the latter varieties, prepare the soil at the bottom of the trench thoroughly, adding plenty of humus matter. It is important to make sure celery plants never go short of water, and giving them a liquid feed at regular intervals is very beneficial. Varieties to be blanched should have their stems tied together with raffia, when they are dry and when they have reached a height of about 12 in (30 cm). Gradually earth up the stems at intervals as growth continues.

Celery should be ready for harvesting from late summer through to winter, according to sowing time and variety.

'Giant White' and 'Giant Pink' are good varieties that do need blanching. 'American Green' and 'Golden Self Blanching' need no earthing up but are not generally completely frost-hardy.

Root vegetables: nourishing and tasty

Root vegetables, though they belong to more than one plant family, have certain similarities of function – which is to form aromatic, well-shaped, tasty 'roots'. They do not always do this as well as they might because of insufficient care in the preparation of the soil. If you sow carrots in, say, rough soil full of stones and clods of earth in a new garden plot, there is nothing they can do in the circumstances but twist and turn until they produce forked, misshapen roots, as the drawing shows. As a general principle for all roots, then: the soil should be deeply worked, rich in humus, and contain some sand – that is, it should correspond to the ideal soil of traditional gardening lore. Potatoes are often said to be useful for clearing weedy ground. This is true in a way because the amount of cultivation they require gives a good opportunity to get rid of the weeds!

Potato A basic vegetable to every household. Although not raised from seed from flowers they are grown from small tubers from a previous crop which are called 'seed tubers'. It is not a good idea to use your own 'seed tubers', as these may be affected by disease, but to buy in new ones each year which are certified disease free.

For cropping purposes potatoes are usually grouped into three categories: first early (planted late March), second early and main crop (planted late April). They all like a rather acid, humus rich soil to which 4 oz (120 g) per square yard (square metre) of a general purpose fertilizer has been added beforehand.

To plant the 'seed tubers' make drills 6 in (15 cm) deep and 24 in (60 cm) apart, set each 'seed', which should be about the size of a hen's egg (cut them into pieces, each piece with a bud (eye) if they are larger), 12–16 in (30–40 cm) apart. Plant them 'rose' or 'eye' end upwards. Cover with soil, and then, with a draw hoe, pull soil up over each row until the ridge is 4–6 in (10–15 cm) high. This will protect the young shoots from frost. Cultivate regularly between the rows so that you will have loose soil for further earthing up at two to three week intervals, so that only 6 in (15 cm) of foliage is above soil level. Water regularly and thoroughly during dry weather to encourage large tubers.

Early potatoes are ready for digging up with a fork in June or July, and second earlies and main crop varieties should be harvested from August onwards. The delicious first earlies should be dug and eaten fresh, as should be the second earlies, but the main crop potatoes can be lifted and stored in a dry, frost-proof place. Only store completely healthy tubers or they will become disease ridden.

Potato blight fungus can be a devastating disease and it should be sprayed against regularly from the end of June onwards.

Useful varieties of potatoes are:
First earlies: 'Irish Peace', 'Epicure', 'Dunluce', 'Maris Bard'.
Second earlies: 'Craig's Royal', 'Maris Peer', 'Pentland Dell', 'Wilja'.
Main crop: 'King Edward', 'Croft', 'Desiree', 'Maris Piper', 'Drayton', 'Pink Fir Apple'.

Carrot Germination time 18–21 days. First sowing, in favourable climates: whenever the ground is open, usually not before early to mid-March. Sow in shallow drills at a distance of 10 in (25 cm). Mix the seed with sand to ensure thin sowing. An indicator crop of radish or lettuce, one seed to 4–6 in (10–15 cm), is a good idea. Sow summer varieties in March/April; winter carrots from the beginning of May onwards; autumn carrots in June; carrots are ready for use on average 12–18 weeks after the seedlings come up. Start harvesting at the beginning of July. Late cropping carrots can be lifted in October and stored in dry sand or soil in a dark, frost-free place.

Growing carrots is easy and gives you a high yield so long as you avoid certain basic errors. Error no. 1 is sowing on incorrectly fertilized land. Carrots dislike too much nitrogen, but need plenty of potash and enough phosphates. Work fertilizer containing humus into the soil the autumn before sowing, and give two or three top dressings during the main growing season. Error no. 2 is sowing too thickly. Carrots do not transplant well, and the seedlings you have to thin out are merely wasted, unless they can be used in salads. Thin out the seedlings of early and mid-season varieties to a distance of about 1 in (2 cm) when they are 1½–2 in (4–5 cm) high. The larger, longer winter varieties need a distance of 12 in (30 cm) between rows, and at least 2 in (5 cm) between one plant and another. Error no. 3 is to keep carrots short of water. If you want an early crop you must water the plants from time to time. Do not give too much water at once, and do not give a thorough soaking after a long dry period, or the roots may crack. Watering every three or four days is enough; keep hoeing in between times. To a certain extent you do need green

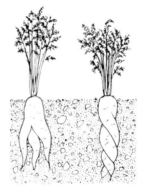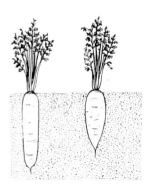

Carrots need good, friable soil, free of stones, to produce straight roots.

fingers for growing carrots – that delicacy of touch or finger-tip control that helps you to draw out the shallow drills correctly, cover with a thin layer of compost after sowing, and judge the moment for lifting the carrots with the aid of a fork. Go carefully at this point: broken roots left in the earth are the gardener's loss but the voles' gain. The carrot fly dislikes wind, so choose open positions for planting.

Early varieties: 'Tiana'F_1 hybrid (smooth skin and little core, very early) and 'Amsterdam Forcing' (stump-rooted and delicate in flavour, but does not give a very high yield). Medium early: 'Early Horn' (medium long, not given to cracking, also suitable for sowing in July to give a late crop), also 'Chantenay Red Cored' and 'Early Nantes'. Late varieties: 'James' Scarlet' (long, tapering roots), 'Autumn King' (long red-cored roots), and 'St. Valery' (sweet, with little core).

Beetroot Germination time 10–14 days. Do not make the first sowing for summer use before mid-April. The next sowing, for autumn and winter use, can be made from the middle of May onwards. Make successive sowings until the end of June, or, for 'baby beets' the end of July. Distance between rows 8 in (20 cm); put in 2–3 seeds at a time at a distance of 6–8 in (15–20 cm); or distance between rows 12 in (30 cm), 2–3 seeds placed at 4–6 in (10–15 cm) intervals. Press the soil down. The seedlings should be thinned out later to leave the strongest. Thinnings with roots intact can be planted elsewhere and will take root easily. The soil should be manured with 1½–2 oz (40–60 g) of compound fertilizer per sq yd (sq m). One application of fertilizer is enough.

Cultivation in general is much the same as for carrots. The soil should be nourishing and deeply dug. Give a frequent light hoeing during the growing season, and keep at constant level of moisture to prevent hindrance of the root development and bolting. Beetroot for winter use is a good crop to grow after early peas. 'Baby beets' can be obtained if you sow the 'Globe' varieties in July. Thin out the young plants to only 2½–3 in (6–8 cm), and lift them when the roots are 1½–2 in (4–5 cm) in diameter. In all cases the crop must be lifted before severe frosts begin. Damage done as the roots are being dug will cause the juice to leak out sooner or later, and they will not keep so well. After lifting the roots, free them from any clinging soil and twist off the foliage just above the crowns (do not cut it). Store in dry sand, in a frost-free place.

Recommended: 'Boltardy', a handsome dark red 'Globe' beet, without the usual formation of rings, fast-growing, resistant to bolting and very suitable for catch cropping or a late crop; 'Cheltenham Green Top', a long, cylindrical root of good quality and high yield.

Kohl rabi Germination time 6–12 days. Sow in an outdoor nursery bed at the beginning of April, with successional sowings every fortnight till the beginning of June.

Thin out to 9 in (23 cm) in rows at a distance of 12 × 12 in (30 × 30 cm). Seedlings may be transplanted at these distances. Harvesting time is about three months after sowing.

Kohl rabi is suitable for growing as a catch crop among lettuces, cucumbers, carrots, onions, or in gaps among tomato plants and young soft fruit bushes. The edible portion is the swollen stem just above soil level and its taste is halfway between that of cabbage and turnip.

Kohl rabi is adaptable and, like lettuce, relatively easy to grow. It has a short lifespan, which makes it a good catch crop. There is only one thing it really has to have: plenty of water! Without water it will easily become hard and hairy in hot weather. Kohl rabi does best in warm, well-drained soil. One more thing: one must take care that kohl rabi is not planted too deep. Its swollen root, the beginnings of which can be seen in the young plants, must be at just the right height: not too far above the surface nor right down in the soil, or they will not form properly. Keeping the young plants warm as they grow helps prevent bolting in cool, spring weather.

Good varieties: 'Lanro', 'Purple Vienna' and 'White Vienna'.

Kohl rabi

Parsnip Germination time 20–60 days. Like carrots, parsnips need a deep soil with plenty of humus in it, and the ground should be well-prepared during the winter. The seed should be sown thinly and shallowly during March and April in rows about 12 in (30 cm) apart. Thin the seedlings, when large enough to handle, to 6–8 in (15–20 cm). In dry weather water them regularly and cultivate them as you would carrots.

The fleshy roots will be ready for harvesting in late autumn, but exposure to frost does give them an extra sweet flavour. Although they can be left in the ground during the winter, to prevent having to try and dig them out of iron-hard frozen soil, some roots can be lifted and stored in dry sand or soil.

Useful varieties with resistance to parsnip canker disease: 'Avonresister' (rather smaller than usual roots and can be grown only 3 in (8 cm) apart); 'Tender and True' and 'White Gem'.

Turnip Germination time 7–14 days. Grows best in well cultivated, fairly rich soil. Sowings can be made from the end of March to the end of July to give a succession of roots. The rows should be about 15 in (40 cm) apart, the seed sown shallowly and the seedlings thinned to 6–8 in (15–20 cm) in the rows. The earlier sowings will provide roots suitable for eating in 8–10 weeks. The roots from later sowings can be harvested in November and stored in dry soil or sand for use during the winter. Cultivate like carrots.

Recommended: 'Purple Top Milan', 'Golden Ball' and 'Snowball'.

Swede Another useful root vegetable, particularly for winter cooking. Some people consider it has a better flavour than the turnip, being milder and sweeter. It is grown and harvested in exactly the same way as the turnip, but is best sown in early May in the North and late May in the South to avoid mildew.

Good varieties: 'Marian' (resistant to club root and cracking) and 'Mancunian'.

A few fruits eaten as vegetables

Vegetable fruits grown in the open are something of a speciality, not always for the beginner. They are generally from warmer climates than our own, and need a bit of coaxing to do well outdoors. Even those claimed to be well acclimatized will usually fail in a cool, rainy summer without much sun; tomatoes and cucumbers will do poorly, and the more distinguished members of the family, such as melons and aubergines, will never form fruits at all. Their perpetual problem is getting their feet cold. A good precaution is to add some well-moistened peat and humus-based fertilizer to the planting site; this may not promote warmth quite as much as the traditional use of horse manure, a favourite method in the good old days when people could go out and collect it off the streets to sell to growers of cucumbers and tomatoes, but we do have other ways to increase the supply of warmth too. Mulching is one, or small squares of black polythene placed round each individual plant so that the ground keeps warmer and is free of weeds over an area of 12 × 12 in (30 × 30 cm) all round it. This method has proved particularly useful in growing tomatoes.

Artichoke (Globe) Decorative thistle-like plants that can take their place in the flower border as well as providing delicious fleshy scaled flower heads for eating. Germination time 14–21 days. As globe artichokes are perennial plants, living three or more years, prepare a humus-rich well drained position in a sunny situation for them. Sow the seed outdoors in March or April. Draw shallow drills about 12 in (30 cm) apart, then thin the seedlings to 6 in (15 cm). When large enough, move the young plants to their permanent positions, spacing them 24 in (60 cm) apart each way. They will not flower the first year.

Plants are best discarded after their third year's crop has been gathered. Reduce shoots to three per plant and plant a new row each spring. The heads must be cut in late June while the inner 'leaves' are still tight together, otherwise the succulent basal parts will become tough and stringy to eat.

Once you have a stock of plants, new ones can be raised by detaching rooted suckers in the spring. Globe artichokes are not completely hardy in exposed positions, so some form of winter protection is advisable.

Recommended varieties: 'Gros Vert de Laon', 'Gros Camus de Bretagne' as young plants and 'Green Globe' for raising from seed.

Globe artichoke

Tomato As a sun-loving plant from tropical climates, the tomato needs a much longer time for its growth and maturing than the relatively short European summer can offer. They need to have a good start when you plant them out and should be sturdy, compact plants with a good ball of soil, well hardened off, in plastic or peat pots, and 10–12 in (25–30 cm) high.

Tomato beds should be in a sunny, sheltered position. Dig the bed deeply in autumn, if possible, and work in plenty of nourishing humus matter. In spring, apply compound fertilizer at the rate of 1½–2 oz (50–60 g) per

Young tomato plants. *Left:* Bad. *Right:* Good.

sq yd (sq m). Tomatoes need plenty of feeding, as they put their roots down a long way. Dig the planting holes in late May, 24–28 in (60–70 cm) apart and with 32 in (80 cm) between the rows, putting in stakes in such a way that the tomatoes will be facing south when tied to them. Put a small quantity of damp peat and planting compost in the hole, then plant the tomatoes with their balls of soil intact and almost up to the lower pair of leaves; the stem will then put out additional roots. Fill the holes with the same mixture of peat and planting compost, press down well, and make a depression in the soil round the plant for watering. If all is as it should be, and you water thoroughly, the young plant should stop drooping in a day or so. It can then be tied lightly with raffia or soft string. Tomatoes can also be grown in pots of compost or special growing bags of peat, placed in a sunny position.

Cover the young plants with plastic covers, or at least with paper bags, on cool May nights, to protect them from any danger of late frosts. Once they are growing well and beginning to put out shoots from the leaf axils, these side shoots must be removed; leave only the top shoot (in exceptional cases, two shoots) to grow taller. To remove side shoots, simply take them by the stem and break off

Removing side shoots from tomato plants; break them off with your fingers as close as possible to the main stem.

with a sideways movement. Do not touch the wound; it will heal over quickly without danger of infection.

Tomatoes will keep growing steadily if they get a top dressing of tomato fertilizer regularly and are watered frequently in dry periods. If in bags of peat, watering and applying liquid feeds, as per the manufacturer's instructions, is vital, because it can be death to the plants if they have too little or too much of either. Break off side shoots at least every fortnight, and keep tying the tomato plants back to their stakes. They will soon be covered with large leaves and tempting trusses of fruit. Water only at the base of the plant, and avoid wetting the leaves. If the trusses of fruit develop leaf shoots these, too, are broken off. However, do not remove healthy leaves either during the period of growth or in autumn; they are essential for the nourishment of the fruits even in the later stages of ripening, and even tomatoes growing in the shade will turn red and will, moreover, be nicely thin-skinned. An exception: as soon as

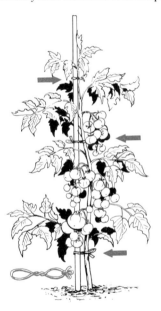

The right way to tie up tomatoes.

you see any leaf mould infection the leaves nearest the ground should be removed. Pinch out the growing tops of the plants at the beginning of September; or when four flower trusses have appeared. The crop must be gathered before the first frosts and kept somewhere dark and moderately warm to finish ripening.

Bush tomatoes, which are becoming popular, are not tied up, and their side shoots are allowed to grow, but it is a good idea to protect the fruits in wet weather by covering the ground immediately under the plant with boards, wood shavings or polythene. Otherwise, grow exactly as described above.

Recommended: 'Ailsa Craig' (thin-skinned, well-flavoured fruit, good for eating raw), 'Outdoor Girl' (robust, high yield, but not such an intense flavour), 'Sioux', 'Golden Sunrise' (a yellow variety), 'Gardener's Delight' (small fruits, but a very heavy crop of red 'cherry tomatoes', very sweet; suitable for freezing), and 'Marmande' (large, irregular, fleshy fruits with few seeds).

Bush tomatoes: 'Sigmabush F_1 Hybrid' (early to medium early), 'Roma' (resistant to fusarium disease), 'Minibel' (small plants but prolific croppers).

Cucumbers Germination time 10–12 days. Sow in the open in early May. It is best to make successional sowings at intervals of eight days. Plant seeds in a single row, two or three at a time, at a distance of 4–8 in (10–20 cm), thin out the weaker seedlings later. The first of the crop will be ready to pick 9–10 weeks after sowing.

Special care should be taken over the preparation of a cucumber bed. Plenty of humus matter is worked into the soil during autumn digging. In spring, draw out a furrow about 8 in (20 cm) deep in the middle of each bed and add more well moistened humus matter. Put back the soil dug out of the trench; the result should be a little mound all along its length. Flatten out planting sites with your hand and put in the seeds or young plants. Distance from one planting site to another should be 8–12 in (20–30 cm). While the cucumbers are still small the ground on either side of the mound can be used for catch crops; large varieties of radish, early kohl rabi and lettuce are particularly suitable, because they give the still tender cucumber plants some protection from wind. They will be ready to pick before the cucumbers begin to spread.

Cucumbers and marrows bear both male and female flowers. *Left:* female cucumber flower, clearly showing the ovary which will develop into a cucumber. *Right:* male flower without ovary; it will fall off the plant along with its stalk when it fades. Most varieties bear flowers of both sexes on the same plant. It is not necessary to cross pollinate outdoor cucumbers; this will happen naturally.

Once the fourth or fifth leaf has formed, around the middle of June or a few days earlier, earth up the plants lightly. The newer varieties can be successfully trained up pea netting tripods, or a length of wire netting 24–32 (60–80 cm) high. Cucumbers must be kept very moist in fine weather; spray the young plants with soft water as well

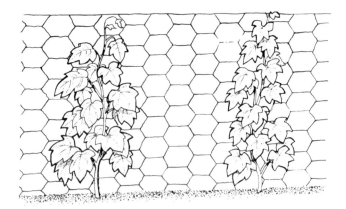

Ridge cucumbers trained up wire netting. A tripod of poles can also be used.

as watering around the roots. Give plenty of fertilizer! Apply a couple of cans of liquid feed in the correct solution every fortnight, keep on hoeing and earthing up: cucumbers take kindly to this treatment and will repay you with fine, sweet-tasting fruits.

Cucumbers suffer less from pests than from certain typical diseases, such as cucumber wilt, cucumber mildew and cucumber mosaic virus; these can also affect pumpkins and marrows.

For pickling: 'Hokus', 'Venlo Pickling', both suitable for training up wire netting. For salads: 'Burpless Tasty Green', 'Nadir F_1 Hybrid', 'Kyoto', 'Burpee F_1 Hybrid'.

Pumpkin and marrow Sow *in situ* in late May, putting in two seeds at a time, rather deep; germination time 6–8 days. Or raise in pots under glass from the middle of April onwards and plant out after mid-May. The plants will need at least 5 ft (1½ m) space all round them. Harvest marrows in July/August, pumpkins in September/October, before the first frosts.

Even if marrows and pumpkins were not so good to eat one would still want to grow them just for pleasure. Everyone enjoys watching the golden globes of pumpkins or the big green cylindrical marrows growing in the shade of their huge leaves. They do not demand nearly so much attention as cucumbers; there are only three things they cannot stand – one is cold, the second is ordinary garden soil and the third is drought. Dig holes or build mounds (according to whether the planting site is dry or moist) and prepare them specially for marrows or pumpkins, in much the same way as the trench in a cucumber bed. Plant 2–3 seeds in each hill in late May, or transplant your young plants carefully after the middle of May, when they have rooted well. In the early stages the seedlings will be as tender as cucumbers, and will need the same amount of protection. But given plenty of nourishment and water, and frequent applications of fertilizer after rain, they will generally grow to a considerable size. If you want to raise giant marrows or pumpkins, leave only three or four fruits on the plants and nip off the others as they begin to form. Put a slate, board or tile under them if they are lying on the ground.

Recommended: 'Long Green', 'Long White' and 'Long Green Striped' marrows, and 'Mammoth' and 'Hundred-weight' pumpkins.

Baby marrow, courgette, zucchini These delicately flavoured vegetables from Italy are baby marrows, picked when they are 4–8 in (10–20 cm) long and cooked by stewing or baking. Cultivate like marrow or cucumber.

Recommended: 'Zucchini F_1 Hybrid', 'Golden Zucchini', 'All Green Bush F_1 Hybrid'.

Capsicum (red pepper, green pepper, chilli) The green, yellow or red fruits are useful for salads or cooking. Most varieties need to be grown in a heated or cold greenhouse, but some can be grown in pots or peat bags in a sunny sheltered position in the garden, especially in the southern parts of the country. Seed should be sown in heat eight weeks before planting out time, which should not be before June. The seedlings are best transplanted into peat pots and are ready to go outdoors when fully hardened off and 6–8 in (15–20 cm) high. Tall varieties will need the support of a cane. Water regularly and spray the plants when in flower to help pollination and the formation of fruits. Regular feeding at fortnightly intervals with a liquid fertilizer is beneficial.

The hardiest variety is 'Canape', and 'Gypsy' and 'Twiggy' both grow well in the south.

Peas and beans

When you stop to think of it, peas and beans are among the tastiest and most useful of all vegetables. One important reason is that these leguminous plants have a special quality of their own: they improve the soil with the help of the little bacterial nodules which develop like small round growths among the root fibres of the plants, and produce nitrogen.

However, as experienced gardeners will know, these nodules are not at work during germination, or until after the plants have reached a certain stage of growth. Thus it is a good idea to give your peas and beans something by way of a snack when you plant: compost, shredded bark or damp peat and 1¾ oz (50 g) of compound fertilizer to the square yard (square metre). This is enough to bridge the gap in the early period of growth. Later on, when you want to take down the pea and bean plants to make room for another crop, do not uproot the haulm but cut it close to the ground, leaving the roots to continue production of nitrogen for some time longer, and provide nourishment for the next crop.

Pea Germination time 6–15 days. Successional *in situ* sowings of first early peas, second earlies and main crop varieties from early March until the end of June (with the first sowings given cloche protection), will provide the crops from mid-June until late September. To extend the season further, a sowing of first earlies at the beginning of July will be ready for picking in October. Make successional sowings every three weeks in drills 2 in (5 cm) deep, with a distance of 20 in (50 cm) between rows and 1–1½ in (3–4 cm) between seeds. Alternate beds of peas with other vegetables instead of keeping them all together.

There is a distinction to be drawn between dwarf peas and tall peas. Dwarf peas are low-growing, do not need pea sticks, and can be sown in three rows in a bed 4 ft (120 cm) broad. Tall peas grow to 3–5 ft (1–1·50 m), and must have some kind of support, either pea sticks or pea netting, up which they can climb. Varieties of medium height, up to about 32 in (80 cm), will need some support too. Arrange peasticks along the inside of each row of plants. When sticks or netting supports are to be used only 2 rows can be planted to a bed, with 20–24 in (50–60 cm) distance between them, so that the peas will get enough light and air. The only peas not requiring support are the leafless varieties which are self-supporting by their tendrils.

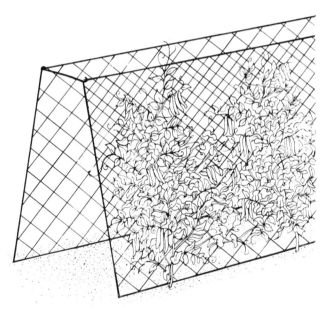

Netting support for tall peas.

The chief enemies of the germinating seed are, of course, sparrows and blackbirds. Protect them with twigs, or with pea guards of narrow-meshed wire netting 4–5 in (10–12 cm) high over the seedbeds. They should stay in place until the little plants have reached a reasonable height; then hoe between the rows and earth up slightly.

Good varieties of peas are:

First earlies: 'Feltham First', 'Hurst Beagle', 'Little Marvel', 'Kelvedon Wonder'.
Second earlies: 'Hurst Green Shaft', 'Onward', 'Victory Freezer', 'Bikini' (self-supporting).
Main crop: 'Gloriosa', 'Sleaford Three Kings', 'Alderman', 'Bellatrix British Bred'; also the petit pois varieties 'Recette', 'Waverex', 'Cobri'.

French bean and runner bean Germination time 8–14 days.

Dwarf or climbing French beans: a preliminary soaking in water aids germination. Very tender to frost, so do not sow in the open before May. Sow them in groups, or in hollowed planting sites, 6 to 8 seeds in a group with a distance of 16–20 in (40–50 cm) all round each seed, or in rows 24 in (60 cm) apart, placing 2 beans at a time at intervals of 6 in (15 cm). Make successional sowings until July. According to variety, you can pick the first beans 55–60 days after the seedlings come up.

Runner beans: sow in a circle round the bean poles, 6 to 8 beans to a pole or sow 6 in (15 cm) apart in double rows 12 in (30 cm) apart. Quantity of seed, germination time and so on as for French beans. Successional sowings until the end of June. They grow rather more slowly than French beans.

There is an old country saying that 'Beans in the ground should hear the church bells ring', meaning that they should not be planted too deep if they are to germinate fast and strongly. As with most other seeds, beans should be covered, at most, by twice their own thickness of soil. If they do not have warm enough soil, the beans will freeze and rot before they germinate, or be infected with a fungus disease or eaten by pests in the ground. Apart from soil temperature, dressing the seed is important.

I always plant both French and runner beans in a bed of good, moist, peaty compost, which will not pan over, and will keep the beans warm and help them to swell. Earthing up is not essential, but does make it easier to keep weeds down. Otherwise beans are very little trouble to grow; you have only to keep them free of weeds and see they get enough water. Frequent hoeing is recommended.

Bean poles are always put in the ground before the climbing beans are planted. (Dwarf French beans need no support.) There are various different methods. Some people make tripods or pyramids, others put in rows of poles crossing each other with a horizontal pole tied along the top to hold them in place. Then there are frameworks consisting of poles driven vertically into the ground and curved, crossed or tied together in various artistic ways. I have had very good crops of beans for several summers without going to any of this trouble; I simply use poles, each stuck 20 in (50 cm) deep in the ground like a flagstaff. I grow two rows of beans to a 4 ft (1·20 m) bed, 24 in (60 cm) apart, with 24 in (60 cm) between one pole and the next, and 6–8 beans round each pole – in a semi-circle, to make cultivation easier. If only four come up that is quite enough

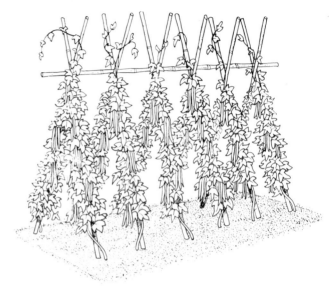

Wooden bean poles arranged in the traditional way.

to ensure a good crop. Wire netting, string, nets or canes can also be used as supports for climbing beans. It is better not to keep your own seed, which may pass on disease. Beans are 'left-hand twiners', something to be remembered if you have to give them a little help in starting to climb.

The bean harvest can be extended over a considerable period. If individual beans stay on the plant too long they will take undue toll of its vigour and hinder the further formation of flowers. Hence those beans ready to pick should be cropped thoroughly every third day, at least during the main harvest season. Picking itself is another story; so many beans are torn off in a hurry, much to the detriment of the plant. If you cannot pick them off cleanly by hand, use a pair of scissors.

Dwarf French beans, green, stringless: 'Tendercrop', 'Admires', 'Oland'.

Dwarf French beans, yellow-podded, stringless: 'Pencil Pod Black Wax', 'Kinghorn Wax'.

Climbing French beans: 'Largo', 'Selka'.

Runner beans, green-podded: 'Sunset' and 'Enorma' (flat pods), 'Scarlet Emperor', 'Kelvedon Marvel' (grow to medium height); 'Butler', 'Mergoles New' and 'Red Knight' (stringless).

Runner beans as decorative plants are mentioned in the chapter CLIMBING PLANTS.

Broad bean Germination time 10 to 12 days. Sow out of doors *in situ*, as early as possible, about the beginning of March, in rows with 20–24 in (50–60 cm) between them, and a distance of 8–12 in (20–30 cm) between beans, putting the beans in 2½ in (6 cm) deep. Alternatively, sow in groups of 4 beans with a distance of 16 in (40 cm) all round them – preferably not in beds of their own, but as single or double rows, or in among other crops. Taller varieties will need some supporting. This is best done with strong poles at the end of the rows, canes at intervals between, and lengths of string tied round at 12 in (30 cm) intervals.

Blackfly are especially prone to attack beans which have been planted late and have thus not developed very far by the end of May, the main breeding season for aphids. Broad beans are not sensitive to cold. However, though otherwise undemanding, with a preference for heavy, loamy soils, they do like to have the benefit of a general purpose fertilizer three weeks before planting.

When the first thick, green pods are setting, pinch out the growing tip to help avoid blackfly.

Sturdy, high-yielding varieties are 'Aquadulce' (which can be sown in the autumn for early cropping), 'Meteor', 'Imperial White Windsor', and 'The Sutton' (dwarf).

Leafy brassicas and spinach

We are always being told that brassicas, with the exception of cauliflower, are a purely agricultural crop today, and no longer have any place in the garden; first, because they are a coarse vegetable, and second because they take up a relatively large amount of room. In fact when one goes into it, this is not so at all.

Gardening experts have found that cabbage, in particular, is grown a great deal in gardens and allotments, not so much the later and more difficult varieties as the early or mid-season kinds, which are delicately flavoured and good for salads. Red cabbage and savoy are also widely grown. Kale is more of a regional dish, and Brussels sprouts are likely to make up a good deal of leeway with the new and very promising hybrids which have become established. This was exactly what happened with kohl rabi, which has found its way back into private gardens since new strains were developed in which the root was not inclined to be woody.

However, it is not just a matter of the quality of seeds or young plants; the gardener has to do quite a lot himself, beginning with good hoeing, since constant aeration of deeply dug, rich soil is important. Care should be taken to rotate your crops and not grow cabbage and other brassicas in the same beds as before – leave an interval of some years, if possible, since brassicas are very prone to diseases and pests whose spores or larvae may live on in the ground for quite a long time, and will attack immediately if you are unwise enough to plant in the same place two years running. It is equally important to destroy all remains of leaves, stalks and roots once the crop is gathered. They should not be left in the ground or even put on the compost heap, but burnt at once. Along with other common pests, the brassica family is at risk from club root, gall weevil,

cabbage fly and cabbage white butterfly, and increasingly from weevils attacking the shoots; see the chapter PLANTS NEED PEST AND DISEASE PROTECTION.

Cauliflower and winter cauliflower (heading broccoli) Germination time 6–12 days. Sow early varieties under glass in rows in January/February; a first sowing of later varieties can be made in a nursery bed in the open at the beginning of April, and a second such sowing from the middle of May to the beginning of June for winter cauliflower. It is often more convenient to buy good young plants. Plant out in staggered rows with a distance of 20 × 20–24 in (50 × 50–60 cm) – early varieties from the beginning to the end of April, late varieties June/July. Harvest early varieties in June/August. Harvest late varieties in September/November, and winter cauliflowers from January to May. You can grow an early crop of winter spinach or corn salad before the early varieties and follow them up with a late crop of endive. Cos lettuce and small radishes can precede the later varieties in their bed, and so long as no curds (flowerheads) have formed you can grow radishes or lettuce as a catch crop. Work compound fertilizer into the soil at the rate of 1½–1¾ oz (40–50 g) per sq yd (sq m). Give three to four top dressings of ¾–1 oz (20–30 g) per sq yd (sq m) at intervals of two weeks.

Getting well-developed cauliflowers depends on growing them carefully quite as much as on your luck with quality of seed, situation and weather. Early varieties are more difficult than late ones, but cauliflowers in general demand good, deep-dug, well manured soil, plenty of room, and so much moisture and feeding that you have to keep on watering them and must give three or four applications of fertilizer. When the flowers or 'curds' are the size of a fist, one or two of the taller leaves should be bent across them to protect them from the heat of the sun or winter weather; this is necessary if you want heads that are white and tender.

For summer and autumn cropping: 'Dok', 'Alpha', 'Snowball', 'Autumn Giant'. For winter and spring use: 'English Winter' and 'Walcheren' varieties.

Broccoli, sprouting, and calabrese Sprouting broccoli, a close relative of the cauliflower, produces white or purple 'flowering spears' from January to May. Calabrese is available in several varieties, and these produce green 'heads' from August to November. Germination time 7–12 days.

The centre head should be cut first and side shoots then develop. Sow in March under glass, or in the open in a seed bed in April. Plant out from the middle of May onwards at a distance of 24 × 24 in (60 × 60 cm). Manuring: work compound fertilizer into the soil at a rate of 1¾–2 oz (50–60 g) per sq yd (sq m). Water now and then. Top dressings of fertilizer are desirable but not absolutely essential for good results.

Broccoli

Sprouting broccoli: varieties of 'Purple Sprouting' and 'White Sprouting'.
Calabrese: 'Green Duke', 'Romanesco', 'Corvet'.

Cabbage It is only really worth growing varieties for summer and autumn cabbage; those for winter storage can be left to commercial growers. Raising cabbages from seed is easy and is better than buying young plants. Germination period 7–12 days. Prepare the soil in autumn, working in plenty of humus. Work in compound fertilizer in spring at a rate of 1½oz (40g) per sq yd (sq m). A slight top dressing and water in dry periods is desirable. Avoid any pauses in growth. Sow the seed in specially prepared beds March/April. Plant out in rows in mid-April to May, at a distance of 20 × 20 in (50 × 50 cm). Cabbage takes 100 days to grow; harvest in July to October. Catch crops for growing among the mid-season and later varieties: lettuce, radish.

Red cabbage is cultivated in very much the same way, but it takes more out of the soil and needs longer to mature before harvesting.

Good varieties: 'Hispi', 'Minicole', 'Histanda', 'Primo', 'Aquila', 'Marner Allfruh', and the red varieties 'Niggy' and 'Langedijk Red'.

Savoy cabbage Similar in cultivation to ordinary cabbage, but it is easy to raise yourself, in successional sowings made from spring to autumn. Sow thinly in rows in a nursery bed every fortnight from the end of April onwards, prick out to a distance of 2 in (5 cm) on all sides as soon as the first leaf develops, plant out as usual after the appearance of the fourth leaf. Savoys like heavy soil; feeding and care as for cabbage.

Early savoy: 'January King', 'Best of All', 'Aquarius'.

Brussels sprouts Germination time 7–12 days. Sow in an outdoor nursery bed from March to April. Plant out in May/June, in rows at least 20 in (50 cm) apart. Put out the plants as far apart as possible, up to 32 in (80 cm) planting distance. The ground must be well firmed. Start picking in October; the crop can go on all winter.

It is necessary to pinch out the tip only if the formation of the sprouts does not seem to be going very well in October.

Varieties for cropping from ealy to late winter: 'Peer Gynt', 'Goldmine', 'Mallard', 'Roodnerf Seven Hills', 'Fortress' and 'Sigmund'.

Kale, borecole Germination time 6–12 days. Sow from mid-April to the beginning of June or later in a nursery bed. Plant out in rows from the beginning of July to the beginning of August, at a distance of 16 × 16 in (40 × 40 cm) or more, according to whether you are growing dwarf, medium-height or tall varieties. It is possible to sow *in situ* in rows relatively close together at the end of July. Harvest: November to March. Kale can stand severe winter conditions. Lettuce, spinach, peas and French beans can be grown as an early crop before kale.

Recommended varieties: 'Dwarf Green Curled', 'Tall Green Curled', 'Fribor' and 'Pentland Brig'.

Spinach Germination time 6-14 days; the seed must be fresh. Work in 1 oz (30g) of compound fertilizer per sq yd (sq m). Sow summer spinach at intervals of two weeks from March to July, sowing thinly in rows with 8–10 in (20–25 cm) between them. The leaves will be ready in 21–28 days. Sow for use in autumn in the last part of July and in August. Winter spinach: sow twice at intervals in September, thinly, in rows 8 in (20 cm) apart.

To make germination easier, soak the seeds in water at room temperature for 24 hours before sowing. Keep them thoroughly moist immediately after sowing too; later on, however, spinach does not tolerate wetness. It is not usual to transplant seedlings, so sowing thinly is important. Enough room between the plants, 9–12 in (23–30 cm), will ensure particularly good leaf development.

New Zealand spinach, which forms a larger, bushier plant than other spinaches, is sown after frost danger is over. It needs watering well and is harvested for a long period in summer by taking a few leaves from each plant. (There are no named varieties.)

For spring, autumn and winter use: 'Sigmaleaf' (bolt resistant) and 'Broad Leaved Prickly', sowings made from March onwards. For summer use: 'Perpetual Spinach' (leaf beet) and 'Jovita'.

Various kinds of onion

Onions, and their cousin garlic, have been at the forefront of international cookery over the centuries, and are at least as important to European *cuisine* as the various spices brought home from the East by the Crusaders. They can claim a place in literature dating back to classical antiquity, like lettuce, already mentioned as the food of the Greek gods. And if Goethe paid tribute to the delicacy of Sicilian lettuce, Shakespeare, in *A Midsummer Night's Dream*, comments on the fondness for onions displayed by southerners and by his own countrymen, in Bottom's warning to the Athenian workmen putting on their play: 'And most dear actors, eat no onions nor garlick, for we are to utter sweet breath.'

Are onions difficult to grow? Many people say they are because they have had crops fail, owing to repeated mistakes in cultivation. Preparation of the soil is most important. Owners of garden plots on new sites would be well advised not to try growing onions straight away, but to wait until other plants have grown in the new garden soil for two or three years, and then start with onion sets. It is difficult to grow onions, too, in soil that is heavy, cold, damp, over-shadowed, or dug too keep; you will get stalk-like roots instead of bulbs that keep well.

Onion 1) If you are sowing onions from seed: germination time, 7–14 days in ground that has warmed up a bit. Sow in the open in March, very thinly, in rows 8 in (20 cm) apart, a bare ½ in (1 cm) deep. Firm the soil, and keep it moist and free of weeds during germination. Thin out to 2–3 in (6–8 cm) about 4 weeks after the seedlings come up; the thinnings can be transplanted. Plant them carefully, not too deep, and water well. Thin a second time to 6 in (15 cm) for large bulbed varieties. Harvest: usually not until August/September.

When there is a short growing season, in the North for example, plant onion 'sets' (partly developed bulbs) 3–4 in (8–10 cm) apart instead of sowing seed.

2) Spring onions: these are sown thinly at the beginning of August in rows and can be 4 in (10 cm) apart, covered with a little peat during the winter. Germination time 7–14 days. They are hardy, and even if conditions are not ideal will produce silvery white little onions in May; the plants should be only 1 in (2·5 cm) apart in the rows to prevent bulbs forming. Spring onions like good soil with plenty of humus, but do not work in any peat. Continuity of this type of salad onion may be obtained by using the thinnings of main crop onions.

Onions prefer rich, friable, previously manured soil. Before they are planted, the soil should be given an application of fertilizer at the rate of 1½ oz (40 g) per sq yd (sq m), and subsequently they should have one or two top dressings. Onions are shallow-rooting plants, so you need only break up the surface of the bed with a cultivator or small rotary hoe when preparing it in spring. Do not hoe too deep later on, or you may damage the bulbs just under the surface of the ground. They should be so close together that they seem to be pushing each other up above ground. Hoeing and weeding are essential in growing onions; weedy beds mean a poorer crop.

There is a good deal of controversy over whether leaves should be bent over before the onions are lifted or not. In general, wait for the leaves to topple over and wither of themselves in the natural course of the plant's maturing. However, if the bulbs have not matured at the right time – say because of a cool summer – then bending over the leaves is a permissible emergency measure. Any seed-bearing stems that shoot up in the course of the summer should be broken off.

To bridge the gap between spring sown onions maturing August/September, there are the Japanese onions which are sown in August and are ready for lifting in June. They last well in store until the autumn.

'Stuttgart Giant' is the best known variety for onions raised from seed or 'sets'; in addition, there is 'Sturon' which produces round bulbs from 'sets'; 'Ailsa Craig' 'Hygro', 'Rijnsburger Wijbo', and 'Bedfordshire Champion' produce large onions from seed. Spring onions: 'White Lisbon' and 'White Lisbon Winter Hardy'. Autumn sown Japanese onions: 'Express Yellow', 'Senshyn Semi-Globe Yellow', 'Imai Early Yellow'.

Shallot Next to cooking-onions, shallots look like elegant ladies beside a farmer's wife. They are raised and propagated by 'sets' only; the little offsets form as a dense cluster around the parent bulb in summer. They are divided and planted out in rows in April, at a distance of 6 in (15 cm) around each 'set', in good soil, just deep enough for the tip of the little bulb to peep out. Cultivate as for onions. After harvesting, which usually takes place in July, the clusters of bulbs are divided, dried off well; pick out the smallest as 'sets'. In mild areas they can go back into the ground in September/October; elsewhere plant them in spring. Shallots are very useful in the kitchen; they keep well, do not shoot, and have a delicious flavour, both mild and sharp.

Grow the virus-free varieties 'Dutch Red', 'Dutch Yellow', and 'Long Keeping Yellow'.

Leek Germination time 10–14 days. Sow in a frame from March onwards, or in an outdoor nursery bed from April. Plant out summer leeks at the end of April to the beginning of May, winter leeks at the end of May to the end of June or beginning of July, in furrows with 12 in (30 cm) between them, 6–8 in (15–20 cm) deep. Distance between plants, 8 in (20 cm). Harvest summer leeks from September onwards, winter leeks from October onwards.

Most gardeners will buy young plants. If you want to grow leeks successfully you should prepare a particularly good bed for them; leeks are gross feeders, and need well-manured soil to form their plump white columns. Give plenty of nourishment later on too. Both roots and leaves should be slightly trimmed before planting; cut back the outer leaves only to half. Leeks should be planted deep, up to their green leaves. The main jobs you have to do for them in summer are hoeing, weeding, and earthing up, and giving strong solutions of liquid fertilizer now and then after rain. As the leeks grow taller earthing up should proceed gradually until the soil almost reaches the point where the leaves and stem part company. This is particularly important for winter leeks left out in the open, and earthing up should go on until mid-September. Summer leeks are often ready for use by July. The stems will be up to 10 in (25 cm) long, and 1–1½ in (3–4 cm) in diameter. Winter leeks, planted out from their seedbed in June or even the beginning of July, grow to the same length but are rather thicker, with a diameter of up to 2½ in (6 cm), or more. They can be harvested any time there is no frost. Store some in an empty frame or cool cellar, with sand round them, as a reserve for frosty periods.

Early autumn leeks: 'Autumn Giant'; autumn and winter leeks: 'Catalina' and 'Musselburgh' (both mainly autumn); 'Giant Winter'; (especially hardy).

Perennial rhubarb

Bearing in mind the rotation of crops, and so on, we have to change the beds where annual vegetables are grown regularly – but a rhubarb bed will remain a rhubarb bed for a long time to come.

Rhubarb is usually grown as a single specimen, and if necessary it can be transplanted once, though the next crop after transplantation may be rather scanty. Just to set the record straight: rhubarb, a hardy perennial of the *Polygonaceae* or knotweed family, is not really a fruit, but a 'sweet vegetable' – or at least, one that is always cooked with sugar, not salt.

Rhubarb Being a gross feeder and thirsty drinker, rhubarb needs plenty of room (1 sq yd) (1 sq m) per plant), deeply dug, very rich soil and plenty of moisture. It tolerates half-shade. Planting time autumn or spring. Planting holes should be deep enough to give the roots plenty of room; they should not be bent or twisted. Fill up the holes with compost or damp peat, just covering the crowns of the plants. Firm the surface and water thoroughly. No stems are pulled during the first year. Later, harvest from April to June once a week. Stems are pulled off by hand, just above the crown. When flowers form it is necessary to remove the entire flower stem with all its leaves, as early as possible. Give several top dressings of liquid fertiliser during the cropping period.

Rhubarb can be raised easily from seed. Sow 1 in (2·5 cm) deep in spring, thin to 6 in (15 cm) apart and set the plants in their permanent position in autumn or the following spring.

'Holstein Blood Red', 'Champagne Early' and 'Victoria' are good red-stemmed garden varieties.

21
Fruit trees

Fruit trees all belong to the *Rosaceae* family, and fall into two categories. One, containing apples and pears, has fruits with a core of five compartments, each containing two brown seeds, developed from the ovary, while the fleshy part of the fruit is a pseudocarp formed from the base of the flower. The other group, represented chiefly by cherries, plums, peaches and apricots, gets its name of 'stone fruit' from the hard protective shell around the actual kernel or seed.

Many fruit trees can be pollinated only from other trees if they are to be fertile. However, pollen carried by insects, or less commonly by the wind, will give rise to seeds and fruits only if it comes from another variety which is compatible with the tree on the receiving end. Moreover, we can distinguish between good and poor pollinators. These days we know exactly which varieties are good for each others' fertility. In the case of apples and pears it is possible to buy what are called 'family trees'. These have rootstocks which have been grafted with usually three varieties which are carefully selected to ensure that they cross-pollinate each other. Such trees are ideal where space is limited in the garden.

A very high proportion of the pollination of blossom is carried out by bees. Growing fruit without the aid of bees is almost as impossible as growing fruit without preparing the soil properly and giving water and fertilizer. It is a good idea to take a look over your garden fence at your neighbours' plots – and not just to see if they have trees which will fertilize yours. You can get a much better idea of what to plant yourself by seeing which varieties do well and which do not in your own neighbourhood than you would from any theoretical consideration. There are, of course, certain basic rules, such as the fact that if peaches and apricots are to do really well they need a mild climate with an average annual temperature of not below 46–50°F (8–10°C), and an altitude not above 820 ft (250 m), while a slightly cooler climate and an altitude up to 1,970 ft (600 m) is quite all right for all the less tender types of fruit. Apples and all plums need more rainfall than pears and cherries. The ground-water level should be taken into consideration too.

The ideal is well cultivated, moderately heavy, loamy soil containing humus, which is slightly acid. If the soil is very sandy, fruit trees which looked very promising in their youth may do badly later on, if they are long-lived kinds. Shorter-lived forms will not become exhausted in this way if they get plenty of fertilizers. Even in fruit growing we should bear rotation of crops in mind, and avoid exhausting the soil, with consequent failures. Do not plant a fruit tree of the same species where one has stood for some time before.

However, over-eagerness on the part of the gardener himself constitutes the greatest danger to fruit trees, even if conditions for growing them are good. People will insist on cramming too many young trees into a small area. They have to wait several years before the trees bear fruit, and by that time none of them have enough light, air and space to develop properly. Removing the worst offenders is annoying for the gardener who planted them, and does not create the same effect as would have been achieved by planting fewer trees in the first place.

If, then, you are going to plant fruit trees you must give the matter a lot of thought. Every species of fruit tree has some forms which take up only a limited amount of space throughout their whole lives, so that you are not sacrificing half your garden for the sake of one large tree. You should consider pest control, too, when making your choice. A small pyramid tree of dessert apples, an espalier or bush tree of 'Morello' cherries are all much easier to keep under control than the head of a standard or half-standard grown on a vigorous wild rootstock.

Cultivated fruit trees: the result of horticultural breeding

Fruit trees do not grow from seed 'naturally' in the usual sense of the word; they are nearly always raised by non-sexual means. This 'vegetative propagation', when the eye or slip of one plant is grafted on to the rootstock of another plant of a similar or closely related species, makes it possible for the hereditary characteristics of a particular variety to be passed on unchanged from one generation of young trees to another. It is possible to grow trees on their own roots; you may plant the pip of an apple or pear, or a

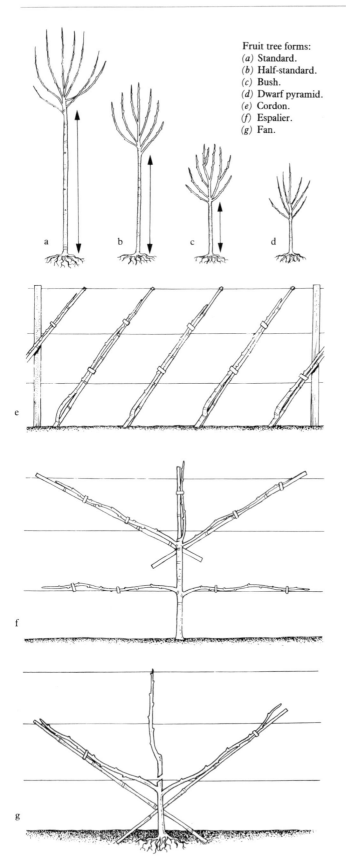

Fruit tree forms:
(a) Standard.
(b) Half-standard.
(c) Bush.
(d) Dwarf pyramid.
(e) Cordon.
(f) Espalier.
(g) Fan.

cherry, peach or plum stone and get a seedling to come up. However, if it is allowed to carry on growing it may revert to the wild, or at least differ considerably from its parents.

It does very occasionally happen that a chance seedling of this kind will be lucky, and produce good fruit without grafting. A lucky accident like that produced the Danish apple variety 'Ingrid Marie'; the parent tree bore its first fruit in 1915, in a teacher's garden on the Danish island of Fünen, and the quality was subsequently preserved by repeated vegetative propagation.

Grafting is a curious phenomenon. Two individual plants are artificially joined together by the gardener, and continue their lives on a single root, with the same sap running through them. But although they grow to form a single unit, each keeps its hereditary characteristics, although their mutual influence on each other helps the grower to achieve the size of tree and yield of fruit desired.

Old and new use of rootstocks

Almost all fruit trees are grafted on specially graded rootstocks. The process involved is most easily illustrated by the apple, and I shall be taking that as the prime example in the following description. Rootstocks of other fruits which are of importance to your garden will be mentioned in the individual descriptions.

There used to be just three large groups of rootstocks for grafting: standards and half-standards were grafted on wild rootstocks of very vigorous growth, then there were the less vigorous rootstocks and the dwarfing stocks. Professor Hatton of the East Malling research station in England created a new and more exact system, in which the letters EM(= East Malling) and roman numerals were used.

In fact, these days the rootstock types are designated only by the letter M followed by a number. For general purposes, I will simply point out that M9 is a dwarfing stock, M7, M26 and M106 are stocks of medium vigour, M2 and M111 are vigorous and M104, M16 and M25 are very vigorous.

The basic principle is the fact that the growth of the scion depends on the capacity of its stock to form roots. Over and beyond this, every variety of apple has its own habit of growth. If the root formation is weak, the whole rootstock will be of weak growth, and will pass on this quality to the grafted part of the tree, whose own growth will then be restrained even if it was originally from a stronger-growing variety. However, if the scion itself was from a less vigorous variety in the first place, then growth of the entire tree will be very restricted. A suitable combination of variety and stock is used for whatever form of tree you wish to plant. Pre-trained espaliers are not often available from tree nurseries, but it is easy to train them yourself from one- or two-year-old trees. There is no difficulty in getting young shoots to grow the way you want them.

Apple 'Newton Wonder'.

'Count Althan's Gage', excellent both as a dessert gage and a cooker.

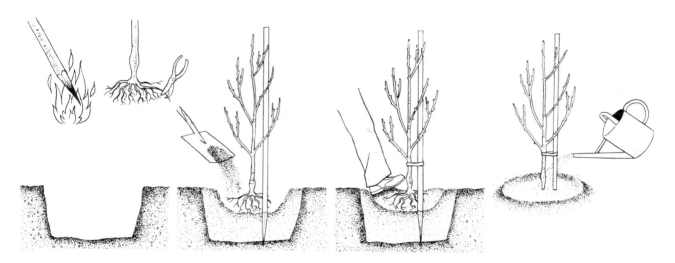

Planting fruit trees

Once you have settled the question of rootstock, the form of tree you want and the space it will need, taking into consideration climate and soil as well as your own choice of variety, there is not much left to go wrong with the actual planting. There is much to be said in favour of autumn rather than spring planting in light to medium soils and situations that are not too exposed. The soil will still contain some warmth, the young tree's foliage will have dropped and its wood ripened, and it will thus be better able to heal the wounds created by root pruning and take root in its new place before winter sets in. The shorter the time between lifting it from its old place and putting it in its new one the better. Spring planting is more usual in heavy soils and cold situations.

If a tree has to be transplanted early, before it has lost its leaves, they should all be cut off, leaving only a small part of the leaf stem on the tree. However, this means the loss of nourishment contained in the leaves, and the normal growing period will not have come to an end yet, so it should only be done as an emergency measure.

In theory, one is supposed to dig an enormous planting hole of 1 sq yd (1 sq m) in area and over 28 in (70 cm) deep in properly prepared garden soil, but it is not really necessary to go about things so elaborately. As a rule of thumb a hole wide enough to accommodate the roots and 20 in (50 cm) deep (for all forms) is enough. For small bush trees, cordons and pyramids to be planted in borders, holes dug big enough for the roots are quite adequate. The composition of the soil should correspond to the variety of fruit. A mixture of good soil peat-based compost and, on sandy soils, some loam is generally best as topsoil.

All trees on weak-growing stocks must be tied to good, weather-proofed stakes, and stronger-growing trees will also need them for a few years. Put up wires and so on for espaliers before you plant. Distance between plants and the framework to which they are trained should be 4–6 in (10–15 cm).

Planting fruit trees. Dig a hole, leave the topsoil on top. Weather-proof or singe the stake and put it in before planting. After pruning the roots put the tree in the hole on the south side of the stake and a hand's breadth away from it. Put back the soil, shake the roots and tread the soil down. The point of union with the rootstock should be 2 in/5 cm above the ground. Tie loosely and water. Fruit trees need good firm planting – air pockets and loose soil make it difficult for them to take root.

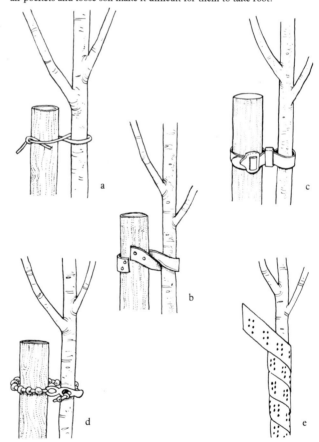

Four examples of the right way to tie a tree to a stake: (a) With a withy, (b) a piece of old bicycle tyre, (c) & (d) two proprietary ties, (e) a useful way to protect young trees from being nibbled by game – wrap synthetic material round them.

When pruning roots trim the ends with a sharp knife, making a slightly sloping downwards cut, remove broken or bent parts, and cut the broken places smooth. A good sound root system should consist of the main roots and enough fibrous roots to stimulate rooting and growth. If your tree has been out of the ground for some time it should have the roots soaked in water overnight, or at least for some hours, before you prune them.

Planting is much easier with two people: one to hold the tree at the right height in the middle of the planting hole and spread the roots correctly, while the other shovels soil from round the edge back into the hole. Shake the stem of the tree slightly to make sure the crumbly soil gets right under the roots. All trees will settle slightly after planting, so the soil around the stem should be mounded up about 3–4 in (8–10 cm) at first. If you are planting a fairly large tree you can tread down the soil in the hole lightly when it is half full. There is no need to do this with small trees, but plenty of water should be given to the whole area around the tree, in several applications (form a depression in the soil so that the water will collect there). Finally, the area round the tree is covered with well-moistened peat compost. Later on you should water only once a week, but do it thoroughly using water that is not too cold if possible. Before the tree has settled tie it lightly to its stake with twine; do not replace the twine with a proper tree tie until spring, after autumn planting, or until the following autumn after spring planting. Tree ties used to be of hemp or coconut fibre tied in a figure-of-eight around stem and stake; these days we have weather-proofed, elastic tree ties made of synthetic materials. The ties should not be loose, or the tree may rub open places on its bark, but they should not constrict the outward growth of the stem.

Whether or not to prune the tree itself at planting time is a debatable point. One proposition put forward is that pruning the parts of the tree above ground is a natural complement to root pruning and so is absolutely necessary. If possible, root pruning, planting, and pruning the tree itself should all be done at the same time, to consolidate the inner equilibrium of the tree, though it is usual to leave the pruning of trees planted in autumn until the next March, just before new growth begins, to avoid the danger of frost damage to the branches that have been cut back. Trees planted in spring, however, can be pruned along with the root pruning before they are put in the ground, or it can be left until the following autumn.

When pruning, do not crush or tear the bark, and always make your cut just above an outward-facing bud, or one in an angle; such buds are technically known as 'eyes'. The surface of the cuts should be as small as possible, but should slope slightly. Apples and pears are not pruned as hard as stone fruits. The peach needs the hardest pruning of all stone fruits, and should be cut back to five or six good strong eyes. When you are pruning espaliers at planting time you want to take account of the growth of branches along a flat surface, as opposed to the three-dimensional formation of the heads of free-standing trees, and so the lower shoots are not cut back so hard in relation to the upper branches or pair of branches. The eye lying just below the pruning cut should always face away from the espalier.

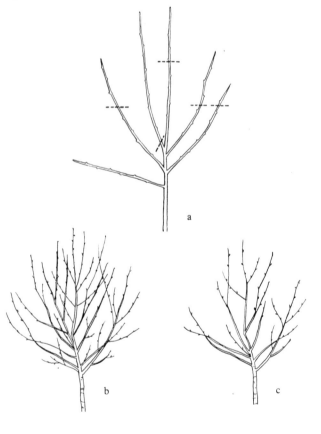

Left: Synthetic tree tie, weather-proof, elastic, adjustable and thus able to 'grow with the tree'. *Below:* Labels tied with wire are dangerous, and must be removed in good time. The modern type of label is made of synthetic material.

Above: (*a*) Correct pruning at planting time: dotted lines indicate where cuts should be made. The lowest shoot could be left to form fruiting wood. (*b*) & (*c*) Pruning a three-year-old apple tree to the right shape; before and after.

Cultivation of the soil, feeding, quality of the fruit

Once you have grasped the connection between soil, feeding, and the growth of cultivated plants you will of course see that all a fruit tree wants is to be kept in a state of good physiological balance in a suitable position with the right kind of feeding. Regular and correct pruning also contribute to its well-being. Plenty of light, well aerated soil and proper provision of water are basic to the health and fertility of fruit trees. As we found in the chapter THE SOIL, good cultivation leads to the best and most economical use of water. Thus an area of topsoil which is always kept in a good, loosely broken-up condition for a considerable distance around the spread of a fruit tree will help it absorb nourishment in the form of liquid fertilizer, especially in the case of apple trees, which need plenty of moisture. This is most important for all varieties of dwarfing rootstocks, which are particularly shallow-rooting. However, the more vigorous rootstocks do not root deeply either, so do not keep the soil worked too deeply.

Orchards of trees with nothing growing under them are seldom found in modern gardens, and most gardeners dislike the old idea that a tree should have a circular bed left round it, mulched with moist material such as peat or grass clippings. We prefer to see an unbroken stretch of grass, and people are always looking for ways out of the dilemma which will be fair to both fruit trees and the lawn in which they stand. It is quite true that a stretch of dense turf right up to the trunks makes it impossible for the soil to 'breathe' properly, means you cannot work the soil in the area covered by the head of the tree, and makes watering and feeding difficult, at least during the growing season. However, I have been growing fruit trees in a lawn for over ten years now, and have proved to my own satisfaction that it is not necessary to leave a circular bed free so long as you cut the lawn twice a week, if possible, from about the middle of May to the end of August.

If there is no need to take a lawn into consideration, feeding of fruit trees follows the rhythm of the year's growth. The trees need most feeding early in spring, when new growth begins, and when the new shoots are growing from the middle to the end of June, so they should get their main applications of fertilizer at these times. This means feeding at the beginning of March, and then again after the blossom is over and when the flower buds for next year are beginning to form (the end of June to the beginning of July) with a compound fertilizer, always applied moist at these times of year. Or you can use one of the artificial fertilizers specially developed for fruit trees for spring and summer manuring; if the ground is moist enough it can be scattered dry and lightly hoed in in spring, but it should always be applied in liquid form in summer. Potash free of chloride but with a high magnesium content is recommended. Use these fertilizers according to the instructions.

If you are not giving fertilizer salts in the form of a compound, but mixing them yourself, use 1 oz (30 g) each of sulphate of ammonia and sulphate of potash per sq yd (sq m) every February, plus the same amount of superphosphate every third year. If you find leaf spots or bitter pits appearing, stop giving potash fertilizer for a couple of years.

If artificial fertilizers are used in spring and summer, it is essential to supply humus by working an organic compound fertilizer into the soil in autumn, or applying it at the end of winter, when you can crumble it and scatter it on the ground dry, and dig or hoe it lightly in. Use according to the instructions, but remember that the amounts recommended will be right only for the trees themselves, not necessarily for anything growing under them. Dwarf fruit trees need relatively more feeding than standards – trees planted close together will need more than single specimens. Finally, the roots which absorb nourishment best are not those close to the trunk or immediately below the spread of the tree, but the outer ones, lying well away from the parts of the tree above ground. One researcher found that a tree whose head had a diameter of only 5 ft (1·50 m) had a rooting area with a diameter of almost 30 ft (9 m). This was an extreme and perhaps exceptional example, but it does show that we ought to apply fertilizers to the ground around free-standing trees for at least 3 ft (1 m) beyond the spread of the branches, and the whole area around dwarf forms or in enclosed orchards should be fed.

Apply lime every three years on soils that are short of it. Remembering that some materials are not compatible with others, we should apply lime on its own, preferably 3–4 weeks before the application of fertilizer in March. Apply it when the ground is fairly dry and hoe it in at once. Correct quantities: on light to medium heavy soils give 4½–5½ lb (2–2.5 kg) carbonate of lime per 12 sq yd (10 sq m); on heavy soils, 2–3 lb (1–1.5 kg) hydrated lime over the same area.

Fruit trees can easily suffer from lack of water in hot, dry summers, even the large ones, with their thousands of leaves all evaporating water. A medium-sized fruit tree loses about 15 gallons (70 litres) of water a day by evaporation and transpiration in hot summer weather. Watering fruit trees is not a matter of giving them a refreshing shower-bath with a sprinkler in the evening, after the heat of the day; it means carrying large cans or getting out the hose and soaking the ground so thoroughly, at least in the area under the spread of the branches, that each square yard (square metre) gets 2½–4 gallons (10–15 litres) of water. Espaliers on sunny walls are often in particularly urgent need of watering, but other fruit trees will be glad of it too.

Finally, there are two things one should remember about the management of fruit trees in summer: from the biological point of view, harvesting prospects for the current year are decided in June, but at about the same time, and until the beginning of September, all European fruit trees are also forming their flower-buds for next spring. We should respect this wonderful natural harmony between the crop now maturing and the flowers to come. Do not be disappointed if you find small fruits lying under the trees every morning in the early weeks of summer, even when there is no sign of pests or disease; this process of 'June drop', whereby the tree disposes of any excess of blossom that has successfully begun to form fruit, is a natural load shedding, and should be completed by the human hand. The tree will ripen as much fruit as it can, shedding the surplus – hence 'June drop'.

This is a particularly important consideration for newly planted trees, and those in their second year of growth, even if it goes to your heart to break off the first fruits of your labours. A young tree needs all its strength first and foremost to put down good roots in its new position. This is why no fruit should be allowed to form for the first year after planting. In the second and third years, apples and pears which are growing very strongly may keep some of their fruit. You can leave more on cherry and plum trees, while peach trees are usually so well developed by this time that they need no thinning of the fruit.

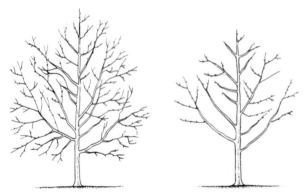

Diagrams showing the thinning out and routine pruning of an apple tree with too dense a head.

The thinning process is not done just for the sake of young, growing trees. It is often necessary to thin fruit on mature trees, so that they will bear large, handsome fruit instead of a great many poorer specimens: something we should always aim for. The number of fruits borne should stand in a healthy relationship to the area from which the tree draws nourishment, the amount of foliage, and the fruiting capacity of the plant in general. To give you a very rough guide: there should be about twenty to forty leaves close to each fruit. If you thin out according to this rule of thumb you will be sure of making enough space for fruit of good quality to ripen; remove those fruits which are too close together, look rather poor, or show any signs of infestation by pests. Thinning should be done when the

fruits are no larger than walnuts. The tree may look a little bare when you have done with it, but it is better to pick two large apples or pears at harvest time than five little ones weighing much the same as your two fine specimens.

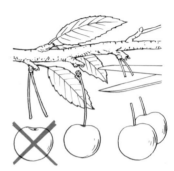

Never pick cherries without their stalks. Either remove them where the stalk joins the branch, or – with specially juicy varieties – use scissors to cut the stalk.

The art of tree pruning

We come here to a matter containing the essence of all horticultural experience: in general because the natural laws governing the growth of plants must unite with precise principles of breeding developed over many years in order to achieve the forms of trees and kinds of fruit we want and, in particular, because the different species, types and varieties of fruit need different handling. An apple tree needs different treatment from a pear or a plum; a standard needs different treatment from a pyramid or an espalier; the vigorous variety should not be treated in the same way as a weaker-growing one, and finally, the needs of a young tree are different from those of a mature or elderly one. In addition, we have to consider the influence of soil and climate, the effects of other aspects of horticulture, in particular feeding. Pruning calls for understanding of the entire nature of a fruit tree, and we have to take a long-term view. The following remarks apply primarily to apple trees, but hold good for most other fruit trees too; deviations from this norm mainly affect cherries, plums and peaches.

First, the formation of the head of the tree: this covers the distribution of the main branches, their relationship to the length of the trunk in the case of a pyramid form, or the creation of what is called an 'open head' with no central axis, as is found in many espalier formations, and some standards and bushes too. There is a time limit to the formation of the head; it can only be done in the early years of the tree's life, and is generally started at the nursery and then carried on by systematic pruning until the correct shape is developed. The three or four leading shoots should stand in a healthy relationship to each other, and not cross or be in one another's way; there should be no lop-sided effect caused by the direction of the prevailing wind, or the presence of a house wall close by, which can influence the shoot formation, and the inner part of the head should not look bare, but present a harmonious picture of its general growth. This form of pruning the tree to shape will be completed as the years go by, and replaced by pruning to maintain that shape; which means keeping a constant watch on the form that has been developed and removing any deficiencies in its structure.

There are certain rules for the early formative pruning to shape a tree. Cutting back hard will generally produce vigorous new growth, cutting back less severely will produce new growth in the form of more but less vigorous shoots. This makes it possible to even out branches growing upwards at different rates, while those tending to put out horizontal shoots are always left longer than shoots higher up the tree and growing vertically. The result is that hard pruning means cutting back to the old wood, which, especially with stone fruit, means no formation of flowers; light pruning means cutting back the growing tips to cause the formation of short shoots and blossom.

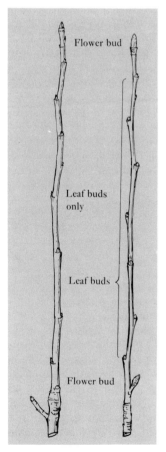

Left: One-year-old woody shoot of an apple tree with leaf buds only. *Right:* One-year-old fruiting shoot of an apple tree with flower buds.

Flower bud

Leaf buds only

Leaf buds

Flower bud

Initial pruning to shape the tree, entailing relatively hard cutting back of the leading shoots, should generally be completed in the third year. The laterals on the main

branches of stone fruit trees need not be cut back so hard, since doing so may put too much of a strain on the ability of the wood to put out shoots. Pruning both in the initial stages and for subsequent maintenance is usually done during the winter period of dormancy between mid-January and the middle to the end of March. Removing suckers coming up from the roots is part of the general care of fruit trees; they are particularly prone to spring up as a result of deep planting. Do not cut them off above ground; remove them carefully from their underground point of junction with the root. Shoots put out from the trunk, found particularly often on stone fruit trees, should also be removed. We treat them like weeds and break them off at such an early stage that they have no chance to become woody. Another problem is presented by sudden long shoots developing at the top of a tree, not quite so easy to deal with, as we shall see in a moment.

As for the actual technique of pruning: remember the rules for pruning at planting time – do not break, tear or split the wood, or harm the bark; use a pruning knife or really sharp secateurs or pruning shears which will not crush the shoots, leave the cut surface as small as possible and slanting slightly outwards, remove superfluous wood immediately above an outward-pointing eye. When large branches and twigs need to be removed to thin the tree, use a proper pruning saw and work close to the trunk to avoid leaving ugly stumps vulnerable to dampness or bacterial infection. With a really large branch one can saw off half its length in the first place, and then get to work on the stump without the hindrance of a heavy piece of wood which could even be dangerous as it breaks off. This also prevents tearing the bark or splitting the wood, and you are left with a smooth wound which can finally be trimmed with your pruning knife. All large cut surfaces should be sealed with grafting wax or a special preparation to help them heal up faster.

Another important point in shaping the head of your tree is training shoots the right way without pruning them. A crooked leading shoot can gradually be made to grow the right way if you tie it to a stake fastened into the tree rather lower down. Obstinate branches which are essential to the formation of the head can also be trained by tying or, if they are growing at too narrow an angle, pieces of wood can be wedged into the tree to act as struts and create an angle of about 60° between trunk and laterals. You have to be careful over this operation; it is a good idea to wrap the ends of your strut in a piece of cloth or old bicycle tyre, to avoid damaging the bark. Pieces of forked branches can be used in the same way. Training of this nature is done in summer, while the shoots are still pliable and have not become woody. Pruning to create and maintain the shape of the tree is, of course, bound up with the need to persuade the head to form fruiting spurs.

What do we actually mean by 'fruiting spurs'? You only have to look at an apple tree to see. Along with the strong, slender woody shoots you will see shorter growths which

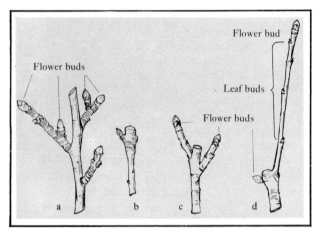

Short fruiting spurs on an apple tree: (a) gnarled spur, (b) one-year-old stump of a fruiting spur, (c) two-year-old stump of fruiting spur with short shoots, and (d) fruiting tip grown from stump of previous fruiting spur.

are almost knobbly, often branched, and bear flower buds covered with brown scales instead of the pointed wood buds smoothly embedded in the sides of the woody shoots, which will develop into new shoots and leaves. These fruiting spurs are often branched at the end of the shoots, and if the buds develop they will produce (in apples and pears) a large cluster of blossoms, three, four or more of which will become fruits if all goes well. Such thick flower clusters are less common in stone fruits, which usually produce separate flowers close to the wood buds, with the exception of the cherry, which often produces flower clusters too.

These important flower buds develop on wood that is a year old or more. They are not usually pruned out. However, desirable as the formation of many flower buds and fruiting spurs may seem, it must not be allowed to harm the development of long woody shoots. Excessive formation of fruiting spurs to the detriment of woody shoots is almost as bad a sign for the growth of the tree as a whole as its opposite, the excessive formation of exclusively woody shoots (which admittedly occurs more often). When the tree is mature and the shape of its head has been developed, this excess formation of woody shoots may be due to incorrect pruning, but it is also the result of wrong feeding, and especially giving too much nitrogen. Woody shoots and fruiting spurs should stand in a healthy relationship to each other, a phenomenon we describe as 'physiological equilibrium'.

In this connection I should mention the familiar appearance of long slender shoots like arrows rising from the tops of old, bent branches, and rapidly growing upwards. It is obvious that they should not occur on healthy, well developed trees, and where they do suddenly appear, in considerable numbers, they are always a danger signal indicating that there is something wrong in the nourishment of the tree. It could be too much feeding and watering

after a long period of neglect; it could be the removal of too many shoots during pruning, which has stimulated the growth of these sudden new shoots. They can also occur as the result of frost damage, drought, disease in the upper part of the tree, or simply as a sign of ageing, and in the latter case they should not all be removed. A few should be retained, as replacements for branches that are becoming exhausted, to form a basis on which to construct a new head; the process, however, is usually too long-drawn-out to be employed for small trees.

Apples and pears

Apple The apple has meant more to the human race from very ancient times than almost any other cultivated plant. It is hard to imagine a garden without an apple tree, though we can no longer pass them on from one generation to another; few people have room for really large, spreading standard apple trees. As you will have seen from the preceding section, the apple serves as a model for all other fruits and fruit trees. The rules for growing fruit trees in general, right down to the latest technical refinements, are derived from the qualities and cultivation of the apple.

There are only a few thoughts to be added about the nature of the apple and its inclusion in the limited space of small modern gardens. The table on pp.214–15 gives information on general methods of cultivation and choice of varieties. By now, moreover, the reader will have realized that the smaller forms which bear fruit earlier are probably the best choice these days, and so I shall turn to the one generally recognized as the best: the dwarf pyramid, which can now look back on several successful decades of growth. Its great advantages are: 1) it needs only 10–13 ft (3–4 m) of space, and so you can grow several varieties, from early apples to good keepers, even in narrow borders or beside garden paths (see the chapter DESIGNING YOUR GARDEN); 2) it starts to bear fruit as early as its third year, and stays so small that you can pick it and prune it without needing a ladder; 3) if you ever want to make drastic changes in your garden, a pyramid apple bush can be transplanted without much risk, even at the age of 8 or 10 years.

A small tree of this sort is, of course, grown on a dwarfing rootstock, and accordingly needs as mild a climate as possible, good soil, and proper care. It will not live for more than 20 years, but that does not decrease its general usefulness in the garden. When it comes from the nursery it will usually still have the basic shape of a tree with branches growing upwards. Prune the roots well, and plant according to the directions given previously, driving a stake about 6 ft (2.5 m) tall into the ground first. Be careful to tie the tree to the stake loosely; tie firmly with a tree tie or a figure-of-eight knot some six months later, after the earth has settled.

Dwarf apple before and after routine pruning.

As usual, the young tree is pruned next spring if planted in the autumn, but at the same time as planting if it is put in in the spring. The leading shoot, which will form the middle axis, is cut back to 7–10 eyes, about a third of its original length. Leave only 3–5 side shoots, cutting back the stronger ones to eight eyes and the weaker ones to five. Very weak shoots which are already growing horizontally may be left alone; they may bear the first fruits next year, though any fruit forming during the first summer must be removed. After this you can leave the young tree to start growing.

In July of the first summer, however, you should start tying down the young side shoots to their horizontal formation. The pliable young twigs must not be bent down any *further* than to the horizontal, in which position they are tied to the stem with raffia, or better still with soft string. Another way is to let the strings drop to the ground and hold them down individually with stones or bricks.

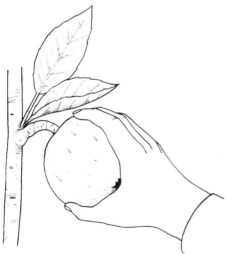

Picking fruit. Ripe apples, pears and other large fruit should be taken gently in the whole hand and turned upwards, exercising slight pressure only. That way the stem parts from the tree quite easily. Apples and other large fruit, once picked, should not be dropped or thrown into a receptacle, but placed there individually by hand.

We have always found this is a better method than tying the shoots to the stem, since the strings cannot slip and it is easy to make adjustments. The shoots should not be tied so tightly or so close to the tip that they are bent over and retain a downward curve when they become woody. All strings, and so on, are left in place for only one winter.

Training the head of the tree in subsequent years follows the same principle. The older your pyramid grows, the fewer branches there are to be tied down, and you will get plenty of fruit from the lower laterals. Occasional pruning to rejuvenate the tree will make sure that it does not stop putting out new shoots entirely, and normal, regular summer and winter pruning will ensure that its elegant and delicate shape does not degenerate into a dense bush.

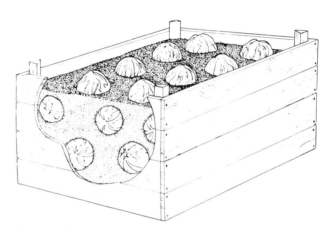

Storing apples. A good old custom: wrap dessert apples in tissue paper, place them in dry peat, not touching each other. Cover with more peat. Keep in a cool, dark, frost-free place.

Pear There are many similarities between apples and pears from the point of view of their cultivation, which makes it easier for us to understand the growing of pears. However, there are also some important differences.

Apple trees like humidity in the air, but dislike bright sun and constant hot weather; the pear, however, can hardly be warm and dry enough above ground. It wants very deep, warm, moist and rich soil for its roots, though. It is particularly fond of lime, but will tolerate sandy soil if grown on a quince stock. The best quality dessert pears will grow really successfully only in mild climates which are also suitable for grapes and peaches. It is better to grow more robust varieties in exposed areas, though they may not be good keepers. Here again pears are different from apples, which will often stay fresh and sound for months, right into the next year, while pears can only be stored for relatively short periods and are often best kept by bottling them and as dried pears cut into slices.

The question of the rootstock is easy. Wild rootstocks are

chosen for all standards with large heads and a long expectation of life; general conditions of growth resemble those of apples on wild rootstocks. According to variety, these trees may not bear fruit until between their sixth and tenth years of life. All small forms of pear are grafted on the much weaker-growing quince stocks; namely Malling Quince A and Malling Quince C. These produce reasonably small trees which fruit early. Not all pear scions take well on quince stocks. Some seem to be doing well at first, but later show poor growth and lack of vigour. This is known as 'incompatibility'. Those varieties incompatible with quince stock have to be grafted on an intermediate scion which is compatible with quince. For instance, the nurseryman will start by grafting a compatible variety of pear such as 'Beurré Hardy' on the quince stock and, once this scion is a year old, will graft on to it the scion of a variety such as 'William's Bon Chrétien', which will form the head of the tree. It is not surprising that double-grafted young

trees, bought under guarantee from a nursery, are rather more expensive.

With the exception of the variety 'Conference', pears are not self-fertile and two or more varieties of the right group will be required to ensure fruit production. When you buy your pear trees, seek advice as to which varieties to buy.

Preparation of the planting site, planting itself, along with pruning and root pruning, further care of the soil and feeding, as well as the control of pests all follow the basic rules mentioned previously. Bushes grown on quince stock are preferable to the more vigorous varieties grown on pear stock in private gardens these days, for reasons of space. A bush pear with a trunk about 20 in (50 cm) high is preferable because it will begin to bear fruit earlier too. Since almost all varieties of pear tend to make a lot of narrow, vertical growth with few side shoots, you should try to prune so as to mitigate this tendency and produce a more spreading, well-branched head.

Recommended varieties of apple

Variety	Ready to eat	Fruit	Habit of growth, yield	Cultivation
'George Cave'	August	Pale yellow, red flushed, medium size, pleasant sharp flavour	Medium vigorous; high but not regular yield	Good to average soil; not for very exposed situations
'James Grieve'	Sept.–Oct.	Waxy yellow with red; broad cone shape, large; fragrant, juicy	Medium vigorous, very high yield, regular	Good soil, not too harsh a climate; good pollen producer; blossom tender to late frosts
'Arthur Turner'	Aug.–Oct.	Greenish yellow; medium size, moderately fragrant. Good cooker	Medium vigorous, very high yield, regular	All right on average soils; sensitive to frost; good pollen producer; prone to canker on damp soils
'Fortune'	Oct.–Nov.	Yellow with red flush; crisp with juicy flavour	Medium vigorous regular cropper	Not demanding; frost resistant
'Grenadier'	Oct.–Jan.	Green cooking variety; medium size	Medium vigorous; good regular yield	Grows well in most situations, but prefers deep, well drained soil
'Cox's Orange Pippin'	Nov.–Feb.	Greenish yellow tinged with red; medium size; superb aroma, very good flavour, sweet, mellow and juicy	Medium vigorous; early, medium high yield	Not particular about soil and climate; prone to scab, canker and aphids
'Egremont Russet'	Oct.–Nov.	Medium sized, brownish yellow fruit, white, aromatic flesh	Medium vigorous, late cropper, high yield	Especially for northern areas, good pollinator; very resistant to disease

Variety	Ready to eat	Fruit	Habit of growth, yield	Cultivation
'Newton Wonder'	Nov.–Mar.	Yellow, flushed and striped scarlet, culinary and dessert	Vigorous, inclined to biennial bearing	Good for northern conditions
'Spartan'	Nov.–Apr.	Dark crimson; medium size; firm flesh, good flavour; excellent dessert apple	Medium vigorous; bears well if not pruned too hard	Rather demanding; good pollen producer
'Ellison's Orange'	Oct.	Greenish yellow flushed crimson; medium size; firm flesh, good flavour	Not vigorous; moderate yield; sometimes biennial bearing	Good soil, warmth and sun; reasonably self-fertile
'Charles Ross'	Oct.–Dec.	Pale yellow or green with reddish russetting; very large, fragrant; good keeper	Very vigorous; high but not regular yield	Does well on chalk soils in all parts of the country
'Sunset'	Nov.–Dec.	Yellow with red flush and some russeting; excellent flavour	Vigorous; regular cropper	Grows well, often where 'Cox's Orange Pippin' fruits poorly

Recommended varieties of pear

Variety	Ready to eat	Fruit	Habit of growth, yield	Cultivation
'Doyenné du Comice'	Nov.–Dec.	Bright yellow, red-cheeked, spotted; medium size, juicy, fragrant	Medium vigorous; high yield	Warm position, otherwise undemanding; not prone to disease
'Conference'	Oct.–Nov.	Dark green with russeting; sweet and juicy	Medium vigorous, rather pendulous; high yield	Undemanding; does well on light, dry soils; self-fertile
'William's Bon Chrétien'	Aug.–Sept.	Yellowish green; large, with juicy white flesh, spicy; best variety for preserving	Medium vigorous, good yield	Not for exposed situations; self-fertile
'Onward'	From mid-Sept.	Yellowish green, stippled with red; large, fragrant	Medium vigorous erect, moderate yield	For warm situations, otherwise undemanding
Improved 'Fertility'	Mid-Sept.–Oct.	Small yellow pears, roundish and of good flavour	Medium vigorous, good yield	Warm situations, otherwise hardy
'Glou Morceau'	Nov.–Dec.	Yellowish with some russetting, large, oval, fine flavour	Vigorous, pyramid shaped; late but high-yielding	Undemanding
'Beurré Hardy'	End of Sept.–Oct.	Greenish yellow, some russetting, medium-sized; white flesh, juicy; will keep till November	Medium vigorous, slender, high yield	Undemanding; scab resistant

Stone fruits

Quince Growing quinces is very easy, though the downy-skinned fruits will do better on good deep soil, with enough warmth and moisture, than on poor ground. They like plenty of mild fertilizer too. The finely branched roots do not go deep, so one must be careful in working the soil around them. The natural form of the quince is a bushy tree which reaches a height of 10–13 ft (3–4 m), and needs growing space of 13–16½ ft (4–5 m). It begins to bear fruit in its third to fourth year, and if cared for properly will go on fruiting regularly for many years. Quinces are usually grown on their own roots. Pruning is limited to occasional thinning and the shortening of shoots that have grown too long. 'Pear' quinces are preferred to 'apple' quinces because of their larger fruits, but there is very little difference in flavour. All quinces are self-fertile. See p. 218 for varieties.

Cherries, sweet and sour The wild sweet cherry, *Prunus avium*, and the sour cherry, *Prunus cerasus*, ancestors of our many garden varieties of sweet and sour cherry, are native to Europe: the sweet cherry as a wild form grows to a considerable height, while the sour cherry was cultivated as a garden plant by the ancient Greeks.

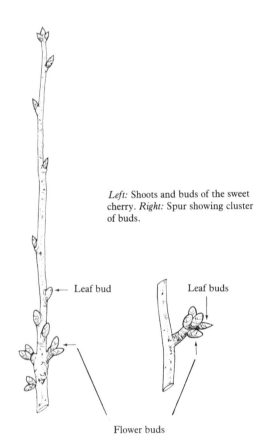

Left: Shoots and buds of the sweet cherry. *Right:* Spur showing cluster of buds.

— Leaf bud

Leaf buds

Flower buds

Sweet cherries are predominantly grown as standards and half-standards; however, standards of lower growth can be found, and are naturally much more convenient for carrying out routine care, as are fan-shaped forms. The rootstock most generally used for all cherries is Malling F12/1 which produces large trees but some varieties are available on the semi-dwarfing 'Colt' rootstock. If you find you have acquired a large tree along with your garden you are well off, since sweet cherry trees can live to a great age in suitable situations. A high-yielding cherry tree in your own or a neighbour's garden is a delightful thing for children; cherries are more fun for nibbling at than any other fruit. Cherries vary in character; some have smooth, soft skins, soft flesh and dark juice, others have a firmer skin and firmer flesh, and juice which is almost colourless. All sweet cherries, except 'Stella', are self-sterile, and some varieties are incompatible, so one must be careful, when growing them, to take their relative fertility and different flowering times into consideration. Seeds seldom breed true, but produce trees which revert to the wild and bear small fruits. Being a genuine child of nature the sweet cherry needs no regular pruning. All it asks is to have its roots and head trimmed at planting time, and a little occasional thinning. The worst pest to attack it is the cherry blackfly, which can cause a lot of damage. Birds may take your whole crop too. Damp situations with a high ground-water level and still, moist air are as bad for sweet cherries as too much nitrogenous fertilizer. They do best in an open position where the topsoil contains plenty of lime.

Sour cherries are the least demanding of all fruit trees. Give them a little extra lime and they will be happy on any kind of soil, bearing fruit year in, year out, with very little attention. Their main representative, the 'Morello' cherry, will even flourish in half-shade and situations which get only occasional sun, and also does well on west and east-facing walls; it is one of the best fruits for jam-making. Cut back the thin twigs regularly, or they will soon become whippy, and it will do even better. 'Morello' cherries are self-fertile, and so there is no need to plant more than one variety.

Pruning at planting time must be drastic, so that all remaining eyes develop and you avoid ugly bare patches in the middle of the head, which hinder healthy growth. The main leading shoot should be cut back far enough for a bush tree to develop a stem height of 20–24 in (50–60 cm). The main point to remember in the pruning of older trees is to open out the head at the top; old trees can sometimes be rejuvenated to stimulate growth. For varieties see p. 219.

Plums, damsons and gages Questions of pollination are not so important when you are choosing varieties of plum, since they are mainly self-fertile, and even with those that are not the problem of incompatibility hardly ever arises. The usual rootstock is the St Julien A, a plum,

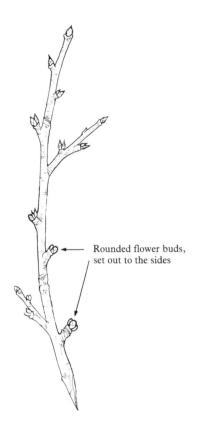

Rounded flower buds, set out to the sides

Fruiting spurs and buds of plums and gages.

than older trees. Before planting drive a weather-proofed stake into the ground to reach up just below the head of the tree. The tree tie must not rub the bark because of the danger of gummosis.

When you plant a peach tree the middle shoot must be pruned to ⅓ of its original length if the plant is to do well. Weak side shoots are removed altogether, and the 4–6 strongest shoots around the main stem are cut back to no more than 2–3 eyes. Later on it is better to thin out the fruits too much rather than too little every year; you will get better individual peaches. Peach trees need cutting back regularly even when they are mature, but they are pruned during or just after flowering instead of during the dormant period. Some people put off pruning till as late as the beginning or middle of July. The same reasons apply in both cases: to avoid the danger of frost damage to the cut surfaces and to have a better view of the arrangement of fruits and shoots.

For survey of varieties, see p. 220.

I have pruned my own peach trees for years now during or just after flowering; I can use the flowering twigs as cut

which prefers a damp situation and gives a rather earlier yield; the more vigorous Myrobalan B plum is suitable for dry situations. See p. 219 for varieties.

Peach The peach has been known as the most luscious of tree fruits produced in mild climates for hundreds of years. It grows best in a climate where grapes can be grown. It does well against sunny walls, and in wheat-growing districts. It is better not to try growing it in exposed areas with a harsher climate. Its soil requirements are much like those of the grape: warm, deep soil, well-drained and rich, but containing little lime. Heavy, cold, clayey and wet soils are unsuitable; so are those which are dry or have only a shallow layer of good topsoil. The early blossom may suffer from sharp winds and cool, rainy spring weather accompanied by late frosts, while a generally unfavourable position will increase the natural tendency of the peach to gummosis (oozing of gum) and curtail its normal life expectancy of 15 to 20 years.

The peach is self-fertile, and some varieties will breed fairly true from seed. These varieties are perhaps more robust but less luscious than the usual varieties, which yield very successfully.

Peach trees take root with relative ease, but one has to beware of frosts even in climatically favoured places. Early spring has always been considered the best planting time. One-year-old plants from a good tree nursery are better

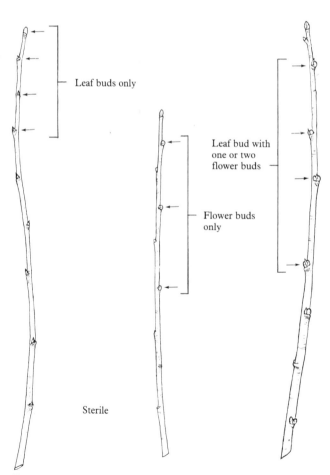

Leaf buds only

Leaf bud with one or two flower buds

Flower buds only

Sterile

Shoots and buds of the peach: left to right, one-year-old woody shoot ('rogue'), false fruiting shoot (too weak), true fruiting shoot (good mixture of flower and leaf buds).

217

flowers, and spare myself the work of thinning them out later at the same time.

An understanding of the formation of peach shoots and buds is necessary for correct pruning:

1) Woody shoots which bear only longish, pointed wood buds all along their length are shortened as the occasion demands.

2) False fruiting shoots bear flower buds only. These shoots are usually weak, will soon look bare, and seldom produce good fruit. Remove them.

3) True fruiting shoots have wood buds at their base and stem, but predominantly 'combined' flower buds, as they are called, in the middle of the shoots. These can be recognized by their usual combination of two flower buds and one wood bud. They are the most valuable shoots; cut them back to no more than 8 combined buds.

4) Twigs bearing clusters consist of short shoots 1½–3 in (4–8 cm) long, ending in a cluster of many flower buds. Leave them alone; they will usually produce some very fine fruit in their first year only, and then die down of themselves.

5) Premature shoots, usually bearing flower and wood buds are made on one-year-old wood during the mid-summer growth period, and are mostly removed down to the basal eye. If you decide to leave one or two for the sake of forming the head of the tree, cut them down to 2–3 eyes.

The peach, then, should be pruned rather too severely than too lightly. If the fruits are still growing too close together, thin them out in June, as for stone fruit. Usually allow about 30 leaves per fruit – only on the branches immediately surrounding the fruit, of course; I don't mean that one should count up the entire foliage of the tree and divide it by the number of peaches.

Diverging from the general rules of feeding and watering fruit trees, peaches should not be given too much nourishment in spring. If they do get too much they will use it primarily to produce woody shoots and leaves. Wait until the little peaches are about the size of walnuts, and then you can give plenty of water and frequent applications of fertilizer, which will also help to stimulate the formation of next year's flower buds. Feeding should go on until mid-summer, to ensure that the peach tree, which is slightly tender to frost, has well-ripened wood before the onset of winter. In soil deficient in lime it is important to make up for the deficiency at the correct time of year.

Nectarines Nectarines are a form of peach and require exactly the same treatment, except that care should be taken to ensure they are adequately watered when the fruits are swelling to prevent the skins splitting. See p. 220 for varieties.

Apricot Apricots are valued for their suitability for winter preserves, unlike the peach, which is best eaten raw. Their basic requirements are much more like those of the peach, but they are a little more demanding to grow. However, though the apricot is more frost tender than the peach because it blossoms so early, the tree itself is hardier.

Success in growing apricots depends on having a sheltered situation, protected from sharp winds, but not in glaring sunlight. Owners of gardens adjoining their houses will find it surprisingly easy to fulfil these conditions, in most cases. Like the peach, the apricot prefers well-drained, easily warmed soil; water-logging and too much rainfall encourage gummosis.

Feeding and watering are the same as for the peach. It is necessary to thin fruit which is too densely borne. Pruning is more like the pruning of plum trees.

'Moor Park', with its large juicy fruits produced about mid-July, is the only variety generally available.

Two good quince varieties

Variety	Ripening time	Fruit	Habit of growth	Soil and climate
'Vranja'	Oct.–Nov.	Large fruit of excellent flavour	Shrubby round-headed tree; large dark green leaves	Warm situation, not too dry; resistant to frost
'Pear Shaped'	Oct.–Nov.	Large to very large, true pear quince, bright golden yellow flesh	Shrubby tree; high yield	Warm situation, good soil

Recommended varieties of sweet and sour cherries

Variety	Ripening time (= week of cherry season)	Fruit	Habit of growth	Soil, climate
Sweet cherries				
'Frogmore Early'	Early-late July	Large, red on yellow; very sweet	Light, spreading head	Rich light soil in sheltered position
'Napoleon Bigarreau'	Late July	Red, tinged yellow; firm fleshed, very juicy	Vigorous, early, high yield	Likes light soils but not too particular
'Stella'	Late July	Dark red, juicy, very large, thin skinned; self-fertile	Handsome, spreading, open growth	For light soils
Sour cherry				
'Morello'	July–Aug.	Shiny dark red, large, best variety	Self-fertile, medium vigorous; best as bush or espalier	Will grow in light shade

Recommended varieties of plums, damsons and gages

Variety	Harvesting time	Fruit and yield	Cultivation
Plums and Gages			
'Czar'	End of July–mid-Aug.	Dark blue, large, very sweet and juicy; frees itself from stone; very high yield, drops easily	Easy to grow; resistant to disease; for any situation; self-fertile
'Oullin's Golden Gage'	Mid-Aug.	Yellow, medium sized; soft and sweet, modest yield	Vigorous; needs regular pruning; also thinning; self-fertile
'Victoria'	Mid to end of Aug.	Red, yellow speckled, large fruit, golden yellow flesh, very juicy and fragrant; high yield	Strong, broad growth; very resistant to disease; self-fertile
'Count Althan's Gage'	Mid-Sept.	Dark red	Vigorous, good cropper
'Marjorie's Seedling'	Sept.–Oct.	Deep purple, medium sized fruit; cooks well	Vigorous, easy to grow, self-fertile
'Rivers' Early Prolific'	Late July	Dark blue with bloom; medium sized, oval, spicy, early, high yield	Hardy and undemanding
'Early Transparent Gage'	August	Yellow fruits speckled with red; medium size; flesh comes off stone easily; very fragrant; high yield; good for dessert or cooking	Fairly compact habit; self-fertile

Variety	Harvesting time	Fruit and yield	Cultivation
Damsons			
'Merryweather'	Mid-Sept.	Black fruits, like a small plum but with strong damson flavour	Vigorous spreading tree; self-fertile
'Prune Damson'	Mid-Sept.	Large blue-black fruits; good flavour; heavy cropper	Vigorous; self-fertile
Gages			
'Greengage'	Sept.	Sometimes tinged with red; medium size, roundish, excellent aroma. Best for cooking	Grows well; tender to frost; prone to pests; self-sterile

Recommended varieties of peach and nectarines

Variety	Harvesting time	Fruit	Cultivation
Peaches			
'Amsden June'	Mid- to end of July	Dark red skin, fine down; white, sweet flesh; clings to stone; best early variety	Warm climate, light to medium soil; given these conditions, not prone to peach leaf curl
'Duke of York'	Mid-July/Aug.	Greenish yellow tinged dark red; flesh white and juicy, good flavour, partly free from stone	Vigorous, quite hardy
'Peregrine'	Mid-Aug.	Greenish yellow, slight red tinge, tender yellow flesh, very large fruit, good aroma	Light to medium soil
'Bellegarde'	Early Sept.	Yellow tinged with red; very large fruit, juicy, fragrant, free from stone	Very vigorous and high yielding in warm areas
Nectarines			
'Early Rivers'	End of July	Large, green-yellow, scarlet-flushed fruits; tender, good flavour, white flesh	Warm climate and not exposed to cold winds; slightly frost tender
'Lord Napier'	Early Aug.	Large pale yellow fruits, brown flushed; white flesh of good flavour	Light, free-draining soil, warm climate; slightly frost tender

22
Soft fruits

Only too often soft fruit bushes and cane fruits are the 'poor relations' of the garden, grown in any old corner and treated incorrectly or not tended at all. And yet proper planting and regular care is so easy, and could be so rewarding. Always buy disease-free plants to get you off to a good start.

While you cannot lump all soft fruits together, the following individual descriptions will show that they do have many similarities, and this makes routine care easier. One of these similarities is in feeding. In fact, feeding as for flowering shrubs would be enough to ensure that soft fruits did quite well, but if you are keen to get even better and regular harvests, you can also scatter 1¾–2 oz (50–60 g) of superphosphate per sq yd (sq m) round the shallow-rooting bushes and canes in early autumn, hoe in lightly, and water thoroughly to make sure it sinks into the ground. Before the first frosts, so long as the ground is still open, or alternatively very early in spring, you can apply sulphate of potash fertilizer and nitrogen (in the form of sulphate of ammonia), both at the rate of 1½–1¾ oz (40–50 g) per sq yd (sq m).

I must admit, however, that the use of individual mineral fertilizer salts by amateurs is not always advisable; it can easily lead to mistakes and wrong feeding. For instance, one often sees the leaves of currant and gooseberry bushes curling and developing a brown edge, and later falling: a sign of lack of potash, or damage done by wrong fertilizer applications. It is necessary to keep an eye open for these things. Moreover, winter feeding can be provided instead by the use of a slow-working compound fertilizer, or one of the various organic fertilizers, which helps to improve the soil texture at the same time.

Raspberries Sub-shrubs with perennial roots, bearing woody, non-branching canes which come up one year and bear fruit the next summer before dying down, thus leaving room for the new canes which have come up that year. Each plant, therefore, always shows two kinds of wood. Growing summer fruiting raspberries is child's play; cut the fruiting canes, which often reach a height of 6½ ft (2 m), right down to the ground soon after harvesting is over in August, and remove weak shoots, leaving only four to six equally strong young canes. Keep an eye open

for any further suckers that may develop and remove them. Autumn fruiting varieties must not be pruned until February, when all canes are cut to the ground. This is because the fruits are borne on canes that develop during the summer. If any canes are left unpruned they will fruit in July, but this is not generally advisable. It is better to plant both summer and autumn fruiting raspberries.

The best way to grow raspberries in the garden is on a simple framework of poles driven into the ground and strong wires stretched horizontally between them, so that the canes can be neatly tied up. If you are putting in new canes, the site should be dug to a depth of 20–24 in (50–60 cm). Apply fertilizer according to the state of the soil. Preparations should be completed in time for planting not too late in autumn. Spring planting is possible, but not such a good idea because of the risk of drying out. It is essential to cover the planting site with some form of moisture-retaining material. Once the framework is erected and your canes have been delivered, dig the planting holes at a distance of 16–20 in (40–50 cm) from each other along the row, with 5 ft (1·50 m) between rows. Trim the strong, fibrous roots slightly, cut broken parts cleanly, and shorten the parts of the canes above ground to 20–24 in (50–60 cm), according to their probable vigour of growth. Fill in the planting holes, tread down lightly, and water well. Covering the planting sites with a damp peat or shredded bark mulch will encourage the plants to take root.

Let the canes grow during their first summer; some may even bear a few berries. A well-tended raspberry bed can bear good crops on the same site for at least ten years. Apply lime every three years if necessary. For feeding see previously, also the chapter HOW PLANTS FEED.

Blackberries, loganberries and hybrid berries The foregoing remarks about summer raspberries can equally well be applied to blackberries. The blackberry, too, is a sub-shrub with a perennial root, and its two-year-old canes grow and trail even more vigorously. The canes, which may be 5½–6½ yd (5–6 m) long, can be used to trail over arches and arbours in festoons, as well as tied up to wires, walls, and free-standing trellises. But if the usually thorny branches are not trained and tied, and thinned at the right

Recommended varieties of raspberry

Variety	Fruit and yield	Other comments
'Malling Jewel', early-mid season	Medium-large, firm, good flavour, heavy yield	Suffers little from fruit rotting in wet season
'Glen Clova', early-late	Medium size fruit at start of season, but smaller later, good quality, heavy yield	Establishes quickly
'Malling Admiral', late	Excellent flavour, suitable for all purposes, heavy yield	Resistant to many diseases
'Delight', early-mid season	Very large, excellent flavour, heavy yield	Resistant to many diseases
'Zeva', Sept.-Nov.	Very large, excellent flavour, heavy yield, for all purposes	Will also fruit in July on 2-year-old canes
'Fall Gold', Sept.-Nov.	Round yellow fruits, sweet flavour, heavy yield	Popular change from red fruiting varieties

time, plants soon get completely out of hand. Pruning is particularly important directly after harvest. All canes which have finished fruiting are removed right down to the ground. Then one must get to work on the side shoots which have grown from the 'eyes' of the main long shoots during the summer; these side shoots may be very long themselves, especially in rambling varieties, and they themselves will not bear any fruit, but simply deprive the plant of vigour to no purpose. When they are just beginning to get woody at their lower ends they should be cut down to the lowest or basal eye, which will usually then develop into a fruiting cane the following year. If the side shoots begin to grow again as a result of damp weather or pruning too early they must be cut back again in autumn.

As with summer raspberries, all weaker shoots growing from the rootstock are removed close to the ground during this summer pruning operation, leaving the plant with only three to six strong canes (decide how many according to its age and general condition). Give them correct care, and you will be rewarded with a good crop next year. Feeding is as for other soft fruit bushes.

Planting blackberries is a job better done in autumn than spring, and follows the same basic rules as for raspberries. Spring planting is advisable only in areas with a harsh climate and where the soil is heavy, and thus has difficulty in warming up. Canes are cut back to three eyes, earth up the young plants slightly, and give winter protection by covering the soil around them.

A well-trained hedge; blackberries should not form a wild tangle.

These hollyhocks give a garden the 'cottage garden' look. Annual, biennial and perennial forms are available.

Lily *(Lilium speciosum rubrum)*.

The very vigorous 'Himalaya Giant' has everything you could wish for: it is easy to grow, making no great demands on the soil, and is resistant to late frosts. It is good for growing over fences, or as a hedge or protective screen. Planting distance for fences and hedges, about 13 ft (4 m). Harvest time from September till October.

Other good varieties: 'Bedford Giant', puts out shoots less vigorously and ripens from the beginning of July onwards. Planting distance 3–5 ft (1–1·50 m). 'Oregon Thornless' is a smooth stemmed variety, vigorous and bearing good crops of superb flavour; the later fruiting varieties 'Smoothstem' and 'Thornfree' are similar.

The 'Thornless Loganberry', (thought to be a cross between a raspberry and blackberry) produces very large, deep red fruits, up to 2 in (5 cm) long, in July/August. This free-cropping plant is cultivated like summer fruiting raspberries, as is another hybrid, the 'Thornless Boysenberry', which is supposed to be a raspberry/blackberry/loganberry cross. The purplish black fruits in July and August are excellent for cooking.

Currants The general rules of root pruning, thorough preparation of the soil and feeding before planting all apply, though the planting holes should be rather larger than those dug for raspberries. Plants should have a space of 5–6½ ft (1·50–2 m) all round them; if planted as a hedge against wires, 3 ft (1 m) is enough. Buy only plants guaranteed free of disease from a reliable nursery. Best planting time: mid-October to the end of November. Spring planting should not be done too late, and you have to be more careful to avoid the soil drying out, and not harming the plants. Cover the ground around the plant with damp peat or shredded bark and water thoroughly at once. Even bushes which have been in place a long time will need frequent, thorough watering in summer, because of their very dense and extensive roots.

The basic rules of pruning black currants are simple: old wood must be removed at its base to let light and air into the middle of the bushes, which tend to be overcrowded with branches and leaves. The old wood can be recognized by its dark bark. Hardly any pruning is done for the first two years after planting, but the bushes should be regularly thinned from their third year onwards, so that they never have more than a quarter each of one-year-old, two-year-old, three-year-old and four-year-old shoots. If you treat them properly they can live for many years without becoming exhausted. Other refinements of pruning depend partly on variety. The end of February is the best time to prune.

Red currants and white currants are not pruned in the same way as black currants; cut back lateral shoots close to their base and shorten leading shoots by half in the dormant season. Also cut out a certain amount of old wood.

You should not confine yourself to one variety only, because of their different harvesting seasons. This applies to black currants in particular, where the presence of several varieties will even improve the fertility of your plants. All soft fruit bushes are in fact self-fertile, but pollination from other varieties increases the productivity of black currants to a quite remarkable degree.

Recommended varieties of red, white and black currants

Variety	Fruit and yield	Other comments
Red and white currants		
'Jonkheer van Tets', earliest variety	Large red berries in long clusters, very sour, bright red juice, high yield	Flowers early, not very frost-tender; easy to grow, erect habit
'Laxton's No 1', early–mid-season	Dark red berries, thick clusters, very sweet; heavy yield	Makes a large and sturdy bush
'Stanza', mid-season	Long clusters of dark red berries, very sweet, high yield	Needs good soil, plenty of manure; late flowering so misses frosts
'Red Lake', mid-season	Long clusters of red berries; high yield	Rather sensitive to frost; likes a rich soil; medium strong growth
'Raby Castle', late	Medium length clusters of medium sized red berries, bright red juice, very high yield	Easy to grow, vigorous, erect shoots. A little irregular in cropping
'White Versailles', early	Loose clusters of large white berries, very fragrant	Rather sensitive to frost; no special problems; medium strong growth

Variety	Fruit and yield	Other comments
Black currants		
'Tenah', early	Good heavy clusters of fruit; remain on bush for a long time	Useful for all purposes
'Tsema', early	Very vigorous, heavy cropper	Fairly vigorous bush
'Blackdown', mid-season	Large, well-flavoured	Makes a large bush
'Boskoop Giant', early	Ripens before all others, huge bunches of large berries	Grows wide and spreading. Needs a position protected from cold icy winds
'Jet', late	Firm fruits on long stalks until September	Flowers late, so avoids frosts and irregular cropping

Gooseberries Since I have described currants in some detail, there is not much left to say about gooseberries and their cultivation, as they resemble red currants in many ways. Employ the same methods of cultivation, though planting distance can be about a quarter less than for currant bushes. When you are pruning, the tips of all shoots should be removed by at least half a finger's length and burnt, to control gooseberry mildew disease. This is a very effective measure, and should be adopted even when you are also going to spray the bushes, beginning at the end of April (see section on principal diseases and pests of most plants in the chapter IDENTIFYING PESTS AND DISEASES). The gooseberry is generally easy to grow, but though it likes warmth its berries do not care for too much bright sunlight as they ripen. A very well-drained, dry soil is not ideal either; gooseberries should really have loamy, mois-ture-retaining soil with a good humus content. Correctly treated and given the right kind of weather, a good mature gooseberry bush should provide plenty of fruit. Almost all varieties benefit from the removal of about a third of the berries while they are still green; bushes of varieties grown especially for their unripe green berries can be completely stripped. Bad weather, especially late frosts in May, which are dangerous to all fruit, and heat and drought in mid-summer, can reduce the yield considerably, and lay the plants open to pests and diseases. The worst offender is gooseberry mildew, along with aphids, and gooseberry sawfly.

Available varieties of gooseberry include long and oval kinds, hairy and smooth, small-fruited and large-fruited, yellow, green and red berries. See the following survey for varieties.

Recommended varieties of gooseberries

Variety	Fruit and yield	Other comments
'Whinham's Industry', late	Dark red, large, short hairs; can be picked green; very good yield	Will not tolerate dryness or bright sun; vigorous upright habit, not very compact, good for hedges; rather prone to mildew
'Whitesmith', early	Yellowish white, large, hairy berries, very thin-skinned, good for picking when green; very high yield	All situations; likes some shade; very vigorous, erect habit; resists mildew well, not always responsive to spraying
'Careless', mid-season	Pale green; large; thin, smooth skin; good flavour; very high yield	Not sensitive to sun or dryness; broad, compact growth; prone to mildew
'Leveller', mid-season	Yellowish; smooth, oval, large; firm-skinned; pleasant flavour, medium yield; most widely grown dessert variety	No risk of frost damage; vigorous spreading growth, proof against mildew; damaged by lime sulphur sprays

23
Strawberries

In the Middle Ages *Fragaria*, the 'fragrant fruit', was known only as a wild berry. However, from the 17th and 18th centuries onwards breeders put a lot of effort into improving it, until the small but delicious and aromatic berries became one of the finest of all cultivated fruits. Thanks to the versatility of its many cultivated forms, the strawberry can be grown anywhere: in enormous strawberry fields where the fruit is raised commercially on a large scale, in hothouses which produce expensive early crops, in strawberry beds laid out in the traditional style, as welcome companions to annuals and small perennials in flower beds or, in the form of Alpine strawberries, which make no runners, as an edging along the side of paths.

For years the best strawberries for eating and preserving were the very well-flavoured and well-shaped, but only medium-sized varieties. These days one of the many new trends in strawberry growing is towards giant fruits; very large berries used to be less well-flavoured, but this tendency seems to have been largely bred out of them. There are even varieties which bear really enormous berries weighing 1¾–2¾ oz (50–80 g) each, and fruiting not just once, but twice – in June and in August/September.

Some important details of cultivation

Strawberry beds should be sunny; an easterly aspect and a bit of shade in the middle of the day are particularly favourable. Soil: strawberries like sandy loam, rich in humus and kept at a constant level of moisture. The soil should be given as much well-matured compost as possible, along with well-moistened peat. The simplest way to prepare a strawberry bed is to dig it deeply the year before planting, in late autumn, let the earth lie in large clods during the winter, and apply a good fertilizer early in spring according to the general rules of feeding, working it into the topsoil. Follow this up by planting a crop of dwarf peas or beans, which will create nitrogen and can further improve the soil structure, acting as green manure, making it ready for planting from August onwards.

Additional watering is especially necessary in dry weather from the time strawberry plants put out their first shoots until the flowering season, and again from the end of harvest to October, since very dry soil means a poorer crop. New strawberry beds in particular need to have a careful eye kept on them; the ground must be really damp.

There used to be no problem about what method of cultivation to use, since all strawberries were grown in a three-year cycle. These days, however, strawberries are also grown as annuals, biennials, and a mixture of the two. Once you get the hang of it, these new methods of strawberry growing may give you a bigger crop, though they do mean more work.

The trick of getting a better yield in spite of the strawberry's short fruiting season lies in planting closer. In the three-year method, an average of 8–10 strawberry plants is put in per sq yd (sq m); for two-year cultivation the average is 12–14 plants, but if you are growing strawberries as an annual you can put in 20 or more plants. If they get a good start in the best possible soil, planted early enough to develop well the first autumn, you can expect to get a considerably larger crop next summer per sq yd (sq m) than you would from the wider-spaced plants of the three- and two-year cultivation methods. But it is absolutely essential to refresh the ground by rotation of crops; if you keep growing strawberries in the same place, however much fertilizer you apply you will be disappointed, since using the ground for the same purpose is bound to diminish the crop and encourage disease. So if you are going in for annual cultivation of strawberries, you need more space for crop rotation and you will have to put more work into it than if you adopt the two- and three-year methods.

The three-year method: plant two rows in the normal 4 ft (1·10 m) bed, with a space down the middle 28–32 in (70–80 cm) wide. Distance between plants in the rows: 10–12 in (25–30 cm). This corresponds to the figure I mentioned above of 8–10 plants per sq yd (sq m).

The usual 4 ft (1·20 m) bed is planted in much the same way for two-year cultivation, except that the plants are closer together, 8 in (20 cm) apart in their rows. As with the three-year method, you can tend the plants and pick the berries comfortably, working from the empty space between the rows, which makes the removal of runners in particular an easier job.

It is really worthwhile going in for annual cultivation of strawberries if you can get hold of especially strong young plants, preferably raised in pots, very early in the planting season – if possible the beginning to the middle of August. Four rows are planted in the usual 4 ft (1·20 m) bed, the rows being only 12 in (30 cm) apart, and the distance between plants 3–4 in (8–10 cm). You will have to allow for a little more trouble when it comes to picking. However, you will not have to do any work between the rows in late summer and autumn, since the whole bed is cleared immediately the harvest is over.

If you can't make up your mind, you might try a combination of annual and two-year cultivation. In its simplest form it goes like this: plant as for annual cultivation, but immediately the crop is over remove just one row, leaving the two remaining rows 24 in (60 cm) apart. Apply plenty of compost or well-moistened peat and peat-based compound fertilizer to the space now laid bare. Thin out alternate plants from the rows, so that those remaining have space to grow and produce a second crop next year. There is not much point in hoping for a third crop. Another suggestion, suitable for vigorous varieties, is to plant three rows 16 in (40 cm) apart in the 4 ft (1·20 m) bed, and put in the plants 6 in (15 cm) apart. Treat in the same way as above.

Strawberries which produce two or three crops of berries a year, and the so-called perpetual fruiting varieties, have become increasingly popular, especially for small gardens where space is limited, because even if the weather brings disaster in the shape of a night frost to the first flowers, you still have the prospect of a crop later on. They are especially suitable for planting in groups in the leisure garden, where they can look very effective. Some new varieties in this group have been recognized as high-grade developments. However, a lot of unreliable claims are made by advertisers, so it is as well to be cautious.

Plants and their runners

Gardeners will probably buy the plants for a new strawberry bed from a reliable source, extending the cropping season and suiting it to the needs of their families by putting in groups of early, mid-season and late varieties at the same time.

Once your strawberry bed has really got going, you will probably feel you want to propagate your own new plants. Use only runners from absolutely healthy parent plants which have borne well in their first and second years, and which you have marked with a stick or label for the purpose. Never use runners from plants which have produced an excessive amount of leaves or which show any signs of disease. Take only the well-rooted, strong young plant which is nearest to the parent from no more than five runners. See chapter INCREASING PLANTS.

When and how to plant

The usual time for planting strawberries is late summer or early autumn. We are always being urged to plant as early as possible – but no young plant raised normally will be mature enough for planting before early or mid-August. If the weather is very dry it is better to wait until it becomes damp and cool, or at least until there is plenty of dew at night to create better conditions for planting. Strawberries to be grown as annuals, however, should be planted in July if possible, or during the first third of August at the latest, and efficient suppliers will stock plants which have been specially treated for this purpose; they are, of course, correspondingly more expensive.

Planting: a description is given in the first section of this chapter on details of cultivation, and see also the drawings in the chapter SOWING AND PLANTING OUT. I must repeat my warning: do not plant strawberries too deep. Thorough watering is usually necessary. Putting a handful of well moistened granulated peat into each planting hole is especially beneficial in warm, later summer weather. Don't

Use only the strongest strawberry runners, closest to the parent plants when increasing stock.

forget to make a little depression where water can seep in around each plant.

Many amateur gardeners have followed commercial growers in using polythene film as a mulch. The usual procedure is to provide the soil with enough fertilizer for two years, work it to a fine tilth, and cover it with black polythene sheeting. Either bury the edges of the polythene or anchor it with bricks or stones and then plant the young strawberry plants in slits or holes previously made for them, at the correct planting distance. The job demands a certain amount of dexterity and care. The polythene film, held in place by soil or stones, keeps the soil friable, moist and free of weeds, keeps the fruit clean, and rainwater will get in through the planting holes.

Routine care, harvesting, removing runners, feeding, winter protection

The soil of a strawberry bed should always be kept crumbly and free of weeds. Shallow hoeing and weeding has to begin immediately after planting, and must be resumed as soon as winter is over. During flowering, however, the soil should be kept wet and compacted, not hoed so that warmth stored up in the soil during the day can be given up at night to warm the air round the flowers on cold nights.

Keep hoeing, weeding and watering to a minimum during the period between flowering and gathering the crop. The ripening fruit can be protected by putting suitable material underneath it – thin polythene sheeting or straw – to keep it from rotting and getting dirty.

Pick only completely ripe berries. The berries themselves should not be touched; nip them off, or even better cut them off by the stalk, never pulling them away from the calyx, and put them in small, shallow containers so that they do not press against one another. Be careful not to shake or jolt them; any pressure or damage to the outer skin means loss of flavour and keeping quality. There is no point in picking unripe berries, since if they are ripened off the plant they will not develop their proper flavour and scent. The best time to pick is early in the morning, when the berries are still cool from the night. A little dew on them does no harm; berries picked when they are wet from rain should be dried off in a cool place. If dirty fruits have to be washed they should be used immediately or carefully spread out on a cloth to dry. But they will generally have lost their shiny red bloom. Remove any misshapen, mouldy or damaged fruits when you are picking; do not put them on the compost heap, but bury them in the ground, if possible along with some lime, because they are nearly always capable of carrying infection. The plants should be picked every 2–3 days in fine weather.

Strawberries should never be picked without the green calyx. Nip them off, or better still, use garden scissors.

Strawberry plants begin to form runners while the fruits are ripening. Simply pull them off as they form.

In the following weeks, the plants will form their buds for next year, at the same time nourishing those runners left on purpose for future use. This means that the provision of nourishment is important, and it should go hand in hand with plenty of watering. Short-strawed horse manure used to be the traditional fertilizer – another reason for making use nowadays of fertilizers rich in humus or based on organic materials.

Enemies of the strawberry

A plant which produces such tempting fruit so close to the ground is naturally prone to attack from pests and diseases. Among the most important fungoid infections is grey mould, which can cause heavy losses, especially in wet summers. Strawberry mildew attacks the early varieties in particular; if there is a lot of rain in warm spring weather the undersides of their leaves can easily become infected by the powdery mould, and the fruits too may be affected. Leaf spots attack the foliage during or after harvest: the remedy is to remove and destroy the diseased leaves. Plants affected by virus disease should be burnt. For descriptions and the control of such typical strawberry pests as strawberry mites, red spider mites, eelworms and strawberry beetles, see the chapter PLANTS NEED PEST AND DISEASE PROTECTION.

For recommended varieties of strawberry please see following page.

Recommended varieties of strawberry

Variety and harvesting time	Fruit	Other comments
'Pantagruella', very early	Medium-sized, crops in quick succession, medium red, sweetish, mildly fragrant, firm	Compact plants, can be set 9 in (23 cm) apart; very early flowers, beware of frosts
'Tamella', early in first year, mid-season in second	Very heavy crop. Large, very firm, dark red all through, sharp refreshing flavour	Flowers level with the leaves; many runners, fairly resistant to drought and mildew
'Grandee', early	Very large cone-shaped fruits, firm, brick-red, fine flavour	Does well even on dry soil, robust, long-lived; rather prone to mildew and red spider mite; good yield
'Talisman', early	Large, longish fruits, bright red, fragrant, firm	For average soils; medium-strong growth, many runners; may crop again at the end of September; healthy, high-yielding
'Gento' (perpetual), June–Oct.	Very large, dark, rather soft	For average soils; strong, large-leaved, healthy
'Cambridge Favourite', mid-season	Large, longish blunt or pointed fruit, dark shiny red, excellent flavour	Prefers light soil rich in humus; thick bright green leaves protect flowers and fruit; quite a high yield in situations not too sunny, but often suffers from red spider
'Rabunda' (perpetual), June–Oct.	Wedge-shaped, shiny, carmine-red, firm, lasts well, mildly fragrant, good for freezing	Very popular variety; small flowers hidden among the leaves, little risk of frost damage, robust, high-yielding
'Domanil', late mid-season	Large firm fruits; heavy yields	Average to light soils; healthy; good for freezing
'Ostara' (perpetual), June–Oct.	Small to medium, firm, shiny dark red, sweet, fragrant	Produces a good crop; berries well displayed
'Litessa', mid to late	Round to longish fruits, bright red, fine fragrance, firm-fleshed	Strong growth; can be planted in spring; heavy cropper
'Bordurella' (perpetual)	Medium, shiny, good quality, fragrant	Almost no runners so can be grown in flower borders; heavy cropper
'Baron Solemacher' (perpetual), alpine strawberry	Small, twice the size of wild strawberries	The best alpine strawberry, easy to grow, soil not too dry, half-shade, vigorous growth with no runners; propagation only from seed

PART V:

PROTECTING PLANTS

24
Weeding made easier

The fight against weeds used to be a trial that accompanied the gardener through from spring to autumn. Despite all your efforts, weeds will still grow faster than the plants you are trying to raise, taking all the best nourishment from the soil and so harming the health and vigour of your plants. It has been claimed, statistically, that hand weeding used to account for about a quarter of all time spent working in the garden. No wonder we used to describe weeds as our most expensive plants – while generations of children, forced to help with the weeding, grew up to dislike gardening.

For the last twenty years or so, however, the chemical industry has made the battle against weeds one of its chief concerns, developing new and better weedkillers, or herbicides, all the time. These days professional gardeners, agriculturists and forestry workers can save themselves vast sums of money by using such weedkillers, and we amateurs find them useful too. Adherents of the ecological school of thought do oppose a full-scale chemical war on weeds: however, the use of chemicals in the garden has its limits anyway. But these ecologically minded people do have a point when they describe weeds as a necessary part of the community of plant life on a particular piece of ground, with their own special tasks to perform – and this, in fact, raises a whole new question.

What is a weed?

The traditional and rather ambiguous answer is: 'A weed is a plant growing in the wrong place.' That is to say, all kinds of wild and cultivated plants are lumped together with genuine garden weeds if they appear in a certain place where the gardener does not want them. There is an old saying that 'Where weeds grow, nothing else can', but that does not give the complete picture: a watchful and industrious gardener can find another old saying to set against it – 'All weeds will give way to proper cultivation.' Which, again, is true only if you do not weaken the fight, and if your neighbours are of the same way of thinking.

Many genuine garden weeds really are dangers, because they act as host plants to pests and diseases. For instance, shepherd's purse harbours the fungus *Plasmodiophora brassicae* which causes club root, and in spring it may well become a breeding colony for the first generation of cabbage white butterflies. Pea rust disease over-winters in the rootstock of the weed cypress spurge; annual meadow-grass is a favourite retreat of snails. Looking at it this way, it is good advice to deal with all weeds at the seedling stage; wait until they come into flower, and you are wasting your time. When weeds are to go on the compost heap, let them dry in the sun first. Diseased or seed-bearing parts of plants, as well as pieces of root still capable of growth, should be carefully collected and burnt.

However, not all the qualities of weeds are harmful; some may have medicinal properties, or be useful for making herbal teas, they may provide nectar for bees or be eaten as a substitute for vegetables. Finally, thanks to the fact that they originate from a great diversity of plant families, they are 'pointers' to show you the composition of your soil and what you can do to improve it. Here are some such indicators:

Lack of lime: knotgrass, stinking chamomile, sorrel, wild heartsease.

Poor nourishment and sandy soil: field scabious, whitlow grass, corn spurrey, hieraciums, golden rod, blackeyed Susan.

Good soil, rich in nourishment: bishop weed or ground elder, stinging nettle, charlock, coltsfoot, fathen (chenopodium), groundsel.

Extremely alkaline soil: field madder, fumitory, Venus's looking glass, hoary plantain.

Too much nitrogen content (over-manuring): annual stinging nettle, chickweed, groundsel.

Wet, marshy land: reeds, rushes, kingcups.

Need we know every weed by name?

Many gardeners think that this, like a detailed knowledge of pests and diseases, is unnecessary since they must all be more or less wiped out anyway. However, this is only partly true; a certain knowledge of the biological basis upon which modern weedkillers work helps us to use them properly. For instance, lawn weeds such as dandelion, buttercup, ribwort plantain, knotgrass and daisy belong to the 'broad-leaved' dicotyledonous plants, those with two seed leaves, destroyed by means of hormone weedkillers to promote growth which cause them literally to grow themselves to death. Monocotyledonous plants, which have only one seed leaf and grass-like leaves, on the other hand do not respond to this hormone treatment, and so the correct use of it will not harm them.

On the other hand, there are chemicals used only to kill monocotyledonous weeds – so-called weed grasses. Most important for our purposes, however, is that group of chemicals which affects both dicotyledonous plants and monocotyledonous grasses. With the aid of these total weedkillers, we can keep paved areas, paths and terraces weed-free over a long period. There are also treatments that work only on the surface and do not penetrate the soil, so that plants sheltered from a spray, or those that come up shortly after the weedkiller has been applied, will not be affected.

Of course none of these weedkillers should be used for any but its own specific purpose – thoughtless or incorrect application could have devastating results, and destroy exactly those plants you wanted to protect from weeds.

Annual and perennial weeds

This division of weeds according to their life span is important in getting rid of them: annuals reproduce mainly by dispersal of seeds, while perennials tend to form extensive root systems; getting rid of these used to be one of the least pleasant of garden jobs, though it is much easier these days.

Yet again, however, one should be careful not to value the chemical miracle-workers of today too highly. In the small garden, especially in vegetable beds, hoeing and weeding are still the best way to keep the weeds down, because you are breaking up the soil at the same time. Moreover, you can curtail the growth of weeds among your cultivated plants to a considerable extent by mulching with damp peat, shredded bark or grass clippings. Black garden plastic sheeting is useful in its place. Like peat and grass cuttings, it promotes friability, though of course it doesn't look quite as nice as many nature-loving gardeners could wish among their rows of strawberry plants. Incidentally, grass clippings have the same drawback as soon as they begin to turn yellow, so it is best to use them under shrubs rather than on open flower beds.

Biennial and perennial weeds will survive any attack unless you know precisely what to do with them. Here are a few examples.

Ground elder flourishes underneath bushes, but will also spread in lawns. It sends roots down into the ground as far as 20 in (50 cm). If the ground elder comes from your neighbour's weed-ridden garden, all you can do is sink strips of roofing felt or some such material, at least 24 in (60 cm) wide and tarred on both sides, into the ground along the garden boundary, or else dig a deep, narrow ditch.

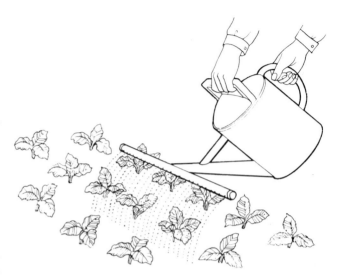

A spray-bar instead of a rose on a watering can makes it easier and safer for applying weedkillers among rows of plants.

Buttercup, a familiar meadow flower, will take a firm hold anywhere in the garden, seeds itself lavishly, and forms an extensive and strong root system.

You can easily get rid of dandelions by picking off all flowers and digging up the deep tap-roots; or by adding a pinch of salt to the heart of the rosette of leaves.

Couch grass and bindweed are among the worst weeds of all. They send out runners and roots yards (metres) long and going as far as 24 in (60 cm) down into the ground. Any part broken off that is not picked out and destroyed will form a new plant. With these weeds the appropriate chemical control is the answer.

Some useful weedkillers

Total weedkillers These will kill all plants with which they come in contact. Examples are: simazine and sodium chlorate, which will have a residual effect and keep the treated area free of weeds for up to a year or more; needless to say plants should not be sown in the treated area for 12 months or so after treatment. Paraquat, diquat and glyphosate, which again kill all plants treated, are not residual in the soil, so sowing or planting can take place once the weeds have had a chance to die.

Selective weedkillers These are mainly used on lawns as they do not kill grasses and are of the hormone type. Examples are mecoprop, dicamba, 2,4-D, MCPA and ioxynil. Proprietary products may contain a mixture of these chemicals. Some, used at the recommended dosage rate, may be used to kill broad-leaved weeds among crop plants. Some of these lawn weedkillers also contain fertilizer to encourage grass growth to fill the patches left by dead weeds.

Moss, lichen and other algae chemical killers
Among these are tar oil, dichlorphen, chloroxuron and ferric sulphate, or combinations of them. Great care must be taken to ensure that the correct products are selected for use on paths, drives or lawns.

Take care when spraying weedkillers

By their very nature, chemical weedkillers are lethal to plants and some also affect human beings, pets and wildlife. Always follow the manufacturers' instructions very carefully; also, only spray on a windless day so there is no danger of chemical drifting onto the wrong plants in your garden or, worse still, those in your neighbours' gardens. If, for any reason, you think there will be any drift of weedkiller spray, even if the day appears windless, it is a wise precaution to cover cultivated plants in the vicinity with newspapers or polythene sheets before spraying. This only takes a few moments to do and the covering can be removed as soon as the sprayed area is dry. For further care when handling chemicals, see chapter PLANTS NEED PEST AND DISEASE PROTECTION.

25
Pest and disease protection

The question of plant protection is a constant subject of argument among gardeners. Controversy centres on the use of chemical sprays, and we must not overlook their possible dangers. The conclusion drawn from those dangers by opponents of chemical means of protection is that we should leave nature to deal with pests in her own way, and biological equilibrium will prevent any major disasters. Unfortunately, this often-quoted 'biological equilibrium', which pre-supposes a state of nature untouched by human hand, simply does not exist in our gardens any more. Every time you put a spade into the soil you are changing its nature to achieve your own ends, creating a cultivated area of land. Growing a number of plants of the same kind increases the danger of pests and diseases spreading. We can no longer look to nature to keep them down and preserve the balance. It is surely permissible to use chemical methods here – indeed, we all need to make use of carefully controlled modern methods of plant protection to ensure that enough nutrition is provided.

For a start, we have indirect, preventive measures of controlling pests and diseases: the various forms of soil cultivation, addition of humus, application of fertilizers, can all have preventive qualities. Many fungoid parasites, the cause of many diseased seedlings, live in the ground and attack their host plants there. After the host plant has gone they are in conflict with the other micro-organisms living in the soil; the richer the soil in micro-organisms the better able it will be to keep down those organisms that carry disease. Well-planned rotation of crops, such as used to be generally practised in vegetable gardens, will help the soil to disinfect itself biologically.

Experience also shows that strong-growing plants are well able to overcome individual weak parasites of themselves. We should also pay attention to the varying tendencies of different plant varieties to be prone to disease. Resistance to disease, in fact, is one of the main concerns of modern horticultural science. However, not all parasitic damage done to plants can be controlled by preventive measures. Many parasites will make their way to host plants through the air – either actively flying, or borne on the wind – and increase and multiply there more or less freely according to weather conditions. The only way to

deal with situations like these is to control them directly, usually by chemical means. These days it is very seldom that biological measures are sure to be really effective.

However, so far as the use of chemicals in private gardens is concerned there are certain basic differences from their use in commercial nursery gardening. The nursery gardener usually has large areas of land growing the same kind of plant, and has to aim for the best possible product – on economic grounds of competition with other growers. The amateur gardener, on the other hand, has a great many different edible and ornamental plants all growing in a limited space, and as they grow so close together their needs will be different from those of commercially cultivated plants. Then again, gardeners do not generally expect quite as much as nursery gardeners from their crops. We are happy to put up with a spot or two of rust or some other small flaw if it means we can avoid using a spray which may be very effective, but is highly poisonous and means we must wait a long time before eating any crops on which it is used. The demand for sprays containing as little poison as possible, entailing the shortest possible lapse of time between their last use and the gathering of a crop, is perfectly justifiable, and my remarks on the right preparations to choose are based on it. I shall also recommend,

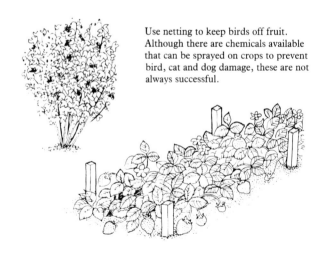

Use netting to keep birds off fruit. Although there are chemicals available that can be sprayed on crops to prevent bird, cat and dog damage, these are not always successful.

where possible, substances which have more than one use – of course, there is no single spray which will protect all plants from all harm, and probably there never will be.

All the chemical pesticides referred to in this book have been cleared by the Government's Pesticides Safety Precaution Scheme and they, and many others, are listed in the *Directory of Garden Chemicals* produced by the British Agrochemical Association each year. Gardeners who wish to know more about their armoury of chemicals, or who have any doubts, can always consult this Association, or pesticide manufacturers direct.

Choosing the right insecticides and fungicides

There are so many different substances, grouped together under the general heading of pesticides, available for protecting our garden plants that choice is quite difficult. The following description of the most important different groups should make things easier. First we must distinguish between the various causes of harm. There are two main groups: plant parasites, which cause and carry disease, are mostly fungi, while animal pests are mostly insects. Hence we have fungicides and insecticides. Insecticides will have no effect on fungoid parasites, nor on bacterial and virus diseases. Conversely, fungicides will have no effect on insect pests. Both fungi and insect pests have several stages of development, and insects, especially, cannot always be controlled by the same substances at all stages of their lives.

We distinguish between insect eggs, larvae, pupae, and the adult form. Larvae may also be called maggots, mites, grubs and caterpillars, and can sometimes do more harm than the adult insects, e.g. maggots which attack fruit, or the caterpillars of the cabbage white butterfly.

When it comes to fungi, we have the actual fungus tissue, or mycelium, and various forms of spores which serve for reproduction and dispersal. Most fungicides combat infection, and are designed to kill the spores during their incubation period. They are, thus, only preventive; there are few substances which have any kind of curative effect, and some are not available to amateurs. The idea of a 'cure', taken over from human medicine, does not apply in quite the same way to the plant kingdom; harm that has already been done cannot actually be put right, only prevented from spreading.

Apart from the two main groups of fungicides and insecticides, there is a range of pesticide sub-groups:

Acaricides, for use against mites and spiders, e.g. red spider; also partly effective as a fungicide.

Algicides, for controlling algae, moss and lichen.

Larvicides, for use against insect larvae, e.g. the cockchafer bug.

Molluscicides, for use against slugs and snails.

Nematicides, for controlling nematodes; partly effective as a disinfecting agent for the soil, and against germinating weed seeds.

Ovicides, for use against insect eggs, e.g. the eggs of red spider mites.

Rodenticides, for keeping down rodents, e.g. voles, moles, field mice and harvest mice.

Herbicides, for killing weeds (see chapter WEEDING MADE EASIER).

Obviously these substances, like the general insecticides and fungicides, cannot be used to replace each other, and you must always follow the instructions carefully.

A considerable part of all pesticides consists of the active agent they contain. Since many firms manufacture preparations using the same active agent, or combination of agents, they choose different trade names for them.

Virus and bacterial diseases: what are they?

Virus diseases occur in humans, animals and plants. Smallpox, poliomyelitis, rabies, foot and mouth disease and fowlpest all come into this category. Viruses are mysterious organisms, on the borderline between the organic and the inorganic. Their destructive forces can develop and increase only in living tissue, and they cannot be controlled by chemical means. In the plant kingdom, virus diseases are passed on partly by simple contact, partly by insects which suck up enough of the diseased sap of one plant to pass on the infection to another. One of the worst offenders in this area is the green peach aphid. It passes from peach trees to potato plants in summer, and causes serious virus disease in them. Altogether, the peach aphid can pass on no less than some 70 virus diseases to different kinds of cultivated plants. Some viruses are even 'inherited' from generation to generation, in seeds and fruits.

The best known virus diseases are the mosaic diseases, and those that cause discoloration and distortion of leaves, met with in many important edible and flowering plants. Cucumber, lettuce, marrow, spinach, tomato, chrysanthemum, dahlia, geranium, lily, sweet pea and tulip are all prone to virus infections. Soft fruits, too, are attacked by a range of dangerous virus diseases. More and more virus diseases are being discovered, a painful fact disclosed at every large plant protection congress so far held. Almost no form of plant is immune.

Private gardens can be protected from virus disease only by strict observation of the general rules of plant protection and hygiene. Among these is thorough spraying against aphids and their eggs early in the year, and the use of seeds and plants which you know come from reliable sources. Diseased plants should not be used for vegetative propagation, and plants showing severe symptoms should be destroyed.

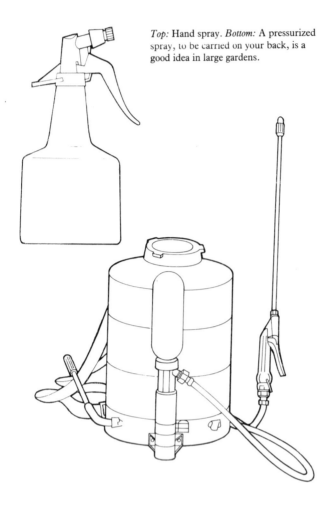

Top: Hand spray. *Bottom:* A pressurized spray, to be carried on your back, is a good idea in large gardens.

Fungicides

Fungi are reproduced in general by various kinds of spores, dispersed by wind and rain, or clinging to seeds. Infections can also arise from soil-borne fungi which may adhere to tools, stakes, or from dormant spores in the remains of harvested crops. Temperature and moisture are important in the spread of these parasites. A rainy summer will encourage many fungus diseases; but plants are more susceptible to infection by powdery mildews when affected by drought.

Most fungi grow in the inner parts of plants, where they escape our efforts to destroy them. Many fungicides can only prevent the development of spores on the surface of plants, though systemic fungicides are now available which help to prevent diseases by their activity in the plant sap; so they not only kill fungi but also protect against further attacks for about two weeks.

Two systemic fungicidal chemicals are propiconazole and carbendazim, both for use against a wide range of diseases on ornamental plants; the former is particularly effective against rust diseases.

Other fungicides which only protect plants against attacks of disease include copper formulations (particularly useful against damping-off disease of seedlings and peach leaf curl), sulphur (but beware spraying varieties of fruit which are not tolerant to sulphur), benomyl, dinocap, mancozeb and calomel (mercurous chloride); this latter chemical, in accordance with EEC regulations, must only be used against club root of brassicas and treatment for onion white rot.

Insecticides

We distinguish between those insects that eat or nibble, and those that suck. However, the way in which they get their nourishment makes little difference to our means of controlling them these days, since many insecticides are poisonous whether the plant sprayed is eaten or simply touched by insects.

Insecticides are applied directly to the plants or the soil around them, either in liquid or dust form. They act in three main ways: (1) by killing on contact; (2) by leaving the chemical agent on the plant which the insect eats and then dies; and (3) by being absorbed into the sap (the systemic insecticides), so that sap-sucking pests are killed. The systemic insecticides are particularly useful as they are not washed off by rain and can last effectively for 2–3 weeks.

Again, I will mention only a few of the very many insecticides on the market: those which are best suited to the needs of amateur gardeners.

Two of the most useful systemic insecticides are dimethoate and pirimiphos-methyl which both kill a large range of insects, as well as being effective against red spider mite (which means you don't have to use a special acaricide).

The situation is much the same with certain bacterial infections, though we do not meet with them quite so frequently in our gardens. For instance, there is bacterial canker and crown rot in fruit trees and leafy gall of ornamentals. There is no means of curing the latter disease and affected plants should be removed and burnt.

Seed dressings and seedling protection

All seeds and seedlings can be attacked by infections at an early stage, and result in considerable loss; the only way to control these infections is to take long-term preventive measures and prompt remedial action. Treatment should not wait until the plants are beginning to grow; it should start, if possible, even before sowing, since many dangerous plant parasites live in the soil or cling to the seeds. A naphthalene soil sterilant applied before sowing will kill most active soil pests. Seed dressing applied to the seed, and applications of the correct chemical insecticides and fungicides to the seedlings, are both important protective measures, which can apply to the growing of flowers as well as vegetables.

The right time to spray most fruits in early spring is at the 'green bud' or 'mouse-ear' stage when a systemic fungicide and a systemic insecticide can be used.

Of the kill-by-contact type of chemicals, I would suggest gamma HCH (BHC), fenitrothion and malathion, all of which are also persistent and last on the plant for 2–3 weeks. Derris (rotenone) is an old favourite and very safe to use.

Another insecticide which kills a wide range of pests is permethrin, which becomes harmless quickly so that sprayed vegetables can be eaten quite safely within several hours of spraying.

There is a school of thought that with all the modern chemicals available, it is unnecessary to apply winter sprays to fruit trees and ornamental trees and shrubs. However, there is no doubt that tar oil still does a first rate job at clearing these plants of overwintering pests (aphids, apple sucker, scale insect, mealy bug), lichens and the like and I would suggest it is well worth doing. It is advisable to apply it really thoroughly, and include all wooden stakes and supports. Follow-up sprays of systemic insecticides and fungicides at the various bud and fruitlet stages of fruit trees will then go a long way towards healthy pest-free plants.

Take care when handling chemical substances!

Many, but not by any means all, of the chemicals used for spraying plants are poisonous, to a greater or lesser degree, to humans and household pets, especially in their undiluted form.

Use chemicals only when they are really necessary and look at the labels to make sure you have the product you require.

Always keep packets, tins and bottles locked up or in well-labelled containers, well out of the way of children and pets.

Never store plant sprays close to any foodstuff.

Never turn them out of their original packaging into another container.

Read the instructions carefully, and follow them.

Do not exceed the recommended concentration (too strong a concentration may not be effective).

Mix only as much spray as you need; do not keep any that is left over, and if possible use it up by spraying it on plants. If you do have any surplus spray left over pour it away into the main drainage system, such as an outside drain or w.c.

Do not spray or dust in windy weather.

Try not to spray open blossoms when bees are about, even if the substance you are using is labelled as safe for bees. The best times are morning and late afternoon, when the sun is not strong enough to cause scorch.

Wear protective clothing while spraying.

Wash thoroughly after the job – have a bath or shower.

Clean all equipment used thoroughly. Do not apply pesticides with apparatus which has been used for weedkillers.

Observe the correct time lapse between the last application of spray and picking your crop; take note of any spray or dusting powder that drifts on to the plants growing under those you are treating, so that you can observe the correct time lapse for them too. Sticking to the correct concentration is as important as keeping to the correct waiting period, since they have a mutual influence on each other.

Do not keep diluted chemicals; they deteriorate quickly and may damage plants.

Never put chemicals into containers that might mislead people, especially children, into thinking they are safe to eat or drink.

26
Identifying pests and diseases

People often ask whether it is really *necessary* to be able to recognize the different pests and diseases which attack plants as all you have to do is carry out the correct spraying instructions. Personally I feel that you *will* want to know exactly what you are trying to control, and why.

General pests and diseases

Common on many kinds of trees, shrubs, flowers, fruit and vegetables:

Ants seldom attack plants, but their workings are unsightly on lawns and paths, and may smother seedlings or upset their roots. Ants also 'nurse' aphids and often carry them from one plant to another. Destroy the nests with boiling water, paraffin, liquid derris or a proprietary ant-killer. If you cannot find the nest, sprinkle a little sugar and watch the ants carry it away.

Aphids, among the notorious greenfly and blackfly, there may also be white, reddish or blue-tinted ones. Sometimes found on roots as well as the leaves and stems from which they suck the sap. Aphids usually exude a sticky substance over the foliage on which black moulds grow.

Spray or dust with malathion, derris or a systemic insecticide.

Capsid bugs, green or reddish brown, 1/3 in (1 cm) long, cause rusty-looking pin-prick holes in the leaves and damage the growing point, often making it fork.

Spray with a systemic insecticide.

Centipedes, unlike millipedes (q.v.), are beneficial, have one pair of legs to each body segment, which is generally flat, not round, and run away when disturbed.

Chafer beetles The grubs are fleshy, curved, white with brown heads, and feed on plant roots, often causing a sudden wilting. Dig up and destroy, or water or dust the soil with bromophos or diazinon.

Cuckoo spit is the white froth surrounding a small, pale greenish yellow insect, called a leaf hopper, usually found on stems.

Spray forcefully with malathion or a systemic insecticide.

Cutworms (surface caterpillars) are greyish black caterpillars feeding at or just below ground level at night. Plants wilt or may be cut right through.

Collect and destroy or dust or spray around plants with gamma HCH (BHC), bromophos, diazinon, or chlorpyrifos.

Damping off is generally confined to seedlings growing in frames or under glass and is due to several fungi which make the stems collapse at soil level.

Use sterilized soil composts; avoid excessive moisture; ventilate. Water with captan or copper compounds.

Earwigs feed at night particularly on greenhouse plants and dahlias. They usually hide during the daytime.

Keep the borders tidy; dust with gamma HCH (BHC) or trap in pieces of sacking, crumpled paper or straw and burn.

Eelworms are minute – only the largest are visible. They live in soil and in many plants, cause stunted, malformed growth and premature leaf drop.

No cure: destroy infested plants; grow a non-related group on the infected site.

Flea beetles (turnip fly) attack seedlings which then look 'blue'; small holes appear in the leaves.

Spray or dust with derris or gamma HCH (BHC); clear up rubbish. Treat seeds with seed dressing before sowing.

Leaf miners The larvae of several species live in the tissue of leaves and make characteristic tunnels.

Spray with systemic insecticide or squash the miners with finger and thumb.

Leaf spots, generally round and brownish, are caused by several different fungi.

Use proprietary copper spray.

Leaf spot

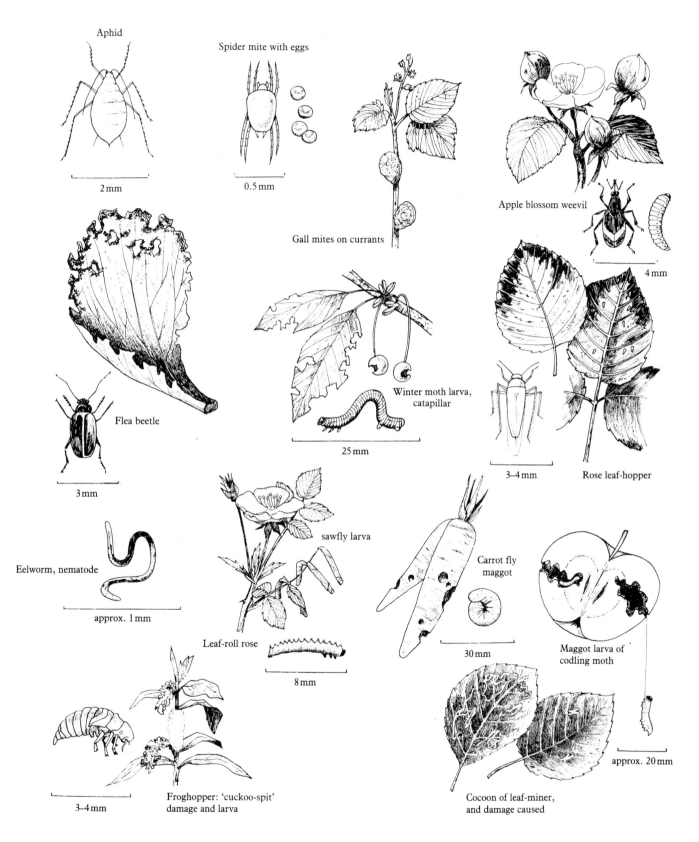

Aphid

2 mm

Spider mite with eggs

0.5 mm

Gall mites on currants

Apple blossom weevil

4 mm

Flea beetle

3 mm

Winter moth larva, catapillar

25 mm

3–4 mm

Rose leaf-hopper

Eelworm, nematode

approx. 1 mm

sawfly larva

Leaf-roll rose

8 mm

Carrot fly maggot

30 mm

Maggot larva of codling moth

approx. 20 mm

Froghopper: 'cuckoo-spit' damage and larva

3–4 mm

Cocoon of leaf-miner, and damage caused

Insect pests on edible and flowering plants

Leatherjackets, the dirty, greyish legless grubs of the daddy-long-legs, up to 1½ in (4 cm) long, feed on plant roots and may cause sudden wilting. Generally only serious in neglected gardens or after breaking up old turf.

Dust or spray with diazinon or chloropyrifos.

Mildew may be the surface powdery mildew causing a whitish or greyish bloom, or the deeper downy mildew which generally forms yellowish patches on the leaves, a greyish or purplish downy growth on the underside. Tree shoots may wither.

To control both forms of mildew use a systemic fungicide.

Millepedes differ from centipedes in being cylindrical with two pairs of legs to each body segment. They usually curl up when disturbed. Most millipedes do not attack plants but extend the damage of wounds made by other insects.

Dust seedlings with gamma-HCH (BHC) (not on potatoes or carrots), chlorpyrifos or trap in pieces of carrot or potato.

Red spider occurs as grey or red mites in webs on the undersides of leaves, making them look dry, rusty or silvery.

Spray with malathion, derris or systemic insecticide.

Rots due to fungi or bacteria which often enter through wounds or bruises, especially on crops in store. They may be wet or dry. Stem-rots also occur, causing a sudden wilting, or a dry canker.

Remove and burn infected plants.

Pear rust

Rusts cause small brown, reddish or orange spots on leaves.

Remove infected leaves at once; if bad, burn plants. Spray with propiconazole.

Sawflies or **Slugworms** The larvae of some sawflies resemble caterpillars while others look like small slugs. They feed on shoots and leaves, often eating away the surface or rolling the leaves up.

Dust or spray with a systemic insecticide or malathion.

Slugs and **Snails** do enormous damage, much of it invisible below soil level. Slugs feed all the year, snails hibernate in rubbish, behind rocks, etc.

Use a bait containing metaldehyde, or sprinkle methiocarb.

Thrips are small black 'midges' which do little damage out of doors, but often spoil the look of plants by scraping the surface tissue.

Spray with malathion.

Virus diseases are carried in the sap and spread by sucking insects or even the gardener's hands and tool. Attacked plants look 'unhappy' or stunted, often with an unusual 'spiky' appearance or a rolling, crinkling or mottling of the leaves.

No cure. Burn badly-infected plants; keep control of aphids and other sucking insects; buy only healthy plants from reliable sources.

Wasps do not harm plants but can spoil fruits and be a nuisance in both house and garden.

If possible, trace nest and destroy with carbaryl powder.

Weevils Small beetles with snout-like heads. Adults feed on leaves, their legless grubs on roots.

Trap in crumpled pieces of sacking or corrugated paper and burn; dust with gamma HCH (BHC).

Wireworms are shiny yellowish brown grubs seen particularly when old turf is broken up. They take five years to mature and reach ¾ in (2 cm) in length, feed on plant roots or cause seedlings to wilt and die.

Trap in pieces of potato or carrot, dust with gamma HCH (BHC) or treat soil before sowing and planting with chlorpyrifos.

Woodlice Grey, scaly pests which like damp places and organic matter; they do little damage to plants.

Dust with carbaryl.

Other pests and diseases

Several other diseases are confined to certain groups of plants. The more important are:

Apple blossom weevil grubs feed on the flower; the dead petals form a brown cap.

Use proprietary spray or dust, such as fenitrothion, just before the flower buds open.

Apple and pear scab causes dark patches on young leaves, which quickly become brownish black. Later, fruits show black spots and cracks.

Spray with lime-sulphur, proprietary captan spray, or systemic fungicide at regular intervals.

Scab

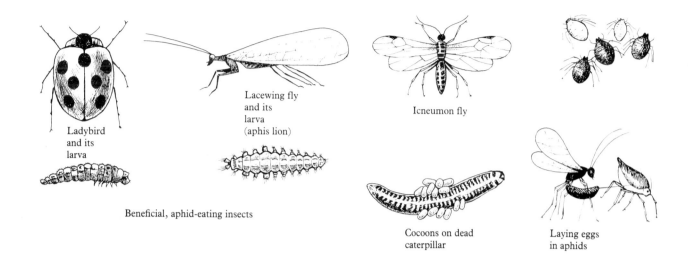

Ladybird
and its
larva

Lacewing fly
and its
larva
(aphis lion)

Icneumon fly

Beneficial, aphid-eating insects

Cocoons on dead
caterpillar

Laying eggs
in aphids

Apple suckers are small, flat, yellowish to green sticky insects found in young leaves and blossoms. Buds die or fail to set fruit.

Apply tar oil winter wash and spray with malathion later in the season.

Big bud of currants. Minute mites live in the buds which swell and fail to open and fruit.

Pick off and burn infected buds and spray with lime-sulphur when leaves are the size of a five pence piece and before the flowers open. Do not use on sulphur-shy varieties.

Black spot of roses causes black spots or blotches on the leaves which fall. It may end in complete defoliation.

Remove and burn infected leaves, use a proprietary captan or systemic fungicide spray. Drench bushes and soil around them with a copper compound in winter.

Brown rot causes many kinds of fruit to rot and drop off. Collect and burn infected fruit.

Cabbage caterpillars occur on all brassicas and must be controlled while young before they enter the developing hearts, by spraying with derris, permethrin or, in the early stages, with a systemic insecticide.

Cabbage root fly attacks all brassicas, the grubs eat the roots, causing wilting or a blue, stunted appearance.

Treat seed bed with diazinon, dip roots in calomel dust paste before planting or apply chlorpyrifos after planting.

Cabbage white fly A small fly which usually does little harm unless it gets into the hearts.

Pick off and burn any lower leaves with eggs or larvae on undersides; burn old stumps from an infected crop; spray with malathion.

Canker Several fungi cause a dry decay of many tree branches usually in form of a depressed or ragged area; whole shoots may die.

Cut out and burn infected parts; destroy badly-attacked trees; always prune carefully and cover cuts and wounds with a pruning cut compound.

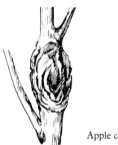

Apple canker

Carrot fly makes foliage wilt and turn reddish. Roots are attacked by small colourless maggots.

Sow thinly to avoid singling; in bad areas defer sowing till June; use a seed dressing when sowing and diazinon when seedlings emerge.

Club root, common on brassicas and some flowers, causes rough swellings on the roots. Plants look blue and stunted.

Lime regularly; avoid growing on infected soil, or dip plants in a paste of moistened calomel dust before planting.

Codling moth larvae (principally on apples and pears) eat out the centre of the fruit in late summer.

Spray with fenitrothion in mid-June and repeat twice at 14-day intervals.

Fire blight occurs on certain shrubs and trees. The pear 'Laxton's Superb' is particularly susceptible. Leaves wilt and turn brown but hang on the tree as though damaged by fire. The disease must be notified to the Ministry of Agriculture who will advise on control.

Moths of many kinds cause harm through their caterpillars which eat and sometimes strip the foliage of trees and shrubs. Some form tents or webs as protection.

Spray with malathion; break up tents.

Narcissus fly (bulb fly) The grubs live inside the bulb, which gives only a weak or distorted growth.

Avoid planting soft bulbs; in bad attacks, dust with gamma HCH (BHC) every fourteen days during May and June, getting the dust well into the neck of the bulbs. Soak lifted bulbs for 2–3 hours in liquid gamma HCH.

Onion fly Whitish grubs tunnel in the bulbs in early spring.

Apply diazinon to soil before sowing or planting. Dip seedlings in paste of calomel dust.

Pea moth Its larvae are the cause of maggoty peas.

Spray with fenitrothion when the flowers open and repeat 14 days later.

Peach leaf curl The leaves of peaches, nectarines and apricots affected by this disease curl, thicken and develop red areas.

Spray with a copper compound or mancozeb in mid-February and again in autumn.

Potato and Tomato blight causes the leaves of potatoes and outdoor tomatoes to become blotchy and, in severe cases, the stems to wilt so that the plants die and the tubers and fruits rot.

Spray regularly with a copper compound or mancozeb from July until harvest.

Raspberry beetle The small pale coloured larvae feed on the berries of all cane fruits.

Spray or dust with fenitrothion or derris as recommended by manufacturers of these products.

Strawberry grey mould (botrytis) This fungus causes strawberry fruits to rot and get covered with a grey mould.

Use a systemic fungicide when the flowers first open and repeat as recommended.

Grey mould on strawberries

Index